The Genius of their Age

The Genius of their Age

Ibn Sina, Biruni, and the Lost Enlightenment

S. FREDERICK STARR

OXFORD
UNIVERSITY PRESS

OXFORD
UNIVERSITY PRESS

Oxford University Press is a department of the University of Oxford. It furthers the University's objective of excellence in research, scholarship, and education by publishing worldwide. Oxford is a registered trade mark of Oxford University Press in the UK and certain other countries.

Published in the United States of America by Oxford University Press
198 Madison Avenue, New York, NY 10016, United States of America.

CIP data is on file at the Library of Congress
ISBN 978-0-19-767555-7

DOI: 10.1093/oso/9780197675557.001.0001

Printed by Sheridan Books, Inc., United States of America

Felix, qui potuit rerum cognoscere causas
"Happy is he who has come to know the causes of things."
Virgil (70–19 BC), *Georgics*, II, p. 490.

Contents

Introduction

This is a book about two of the most outstanding thinkers to have lived between ancient Greece and the European Renaissance: Ibn Sina and Biruni. Both are known to specialists who have explored and analyzed their writings (what remains of them) for 150 years. But the general public has yet to discover these men and to appreciate their achievements. I hope this will help in that effort.

The relative obscurity of Ibn Sina and Biruni may be partly because they did not spring from the seats of ancient culture that are traditionally studied—the Mediterranean Basin, Middle East, India, or China. Rather, they were born in the tenth century in Central Asia. Most saw this vast and loosely configured part of the world as remote and troubled, the scene of endless clashes between nomadic peoples and cultures. This perception has now begun to change, as a new generation of scholars, writers, and filmmakers has drawn attention to the glories of the so-called Silk Road. Central Asia was a crossroads in the trade routes that existed for millennia linking economic and cultural centers in Europe and the Middle East with their counterparts in India and China.

Our subjects are two giants of a lost era of enlightenment. There are, nonetheless, many reasons that neither has become a household name. Not the least of these are their own names, which, transcribed from the Arabic, are bewilderingly complex: Abū-'Alī al-Ḥusayn ibn-'Abdallāh Ibn-Sīna, and Abū al-Rayḥān Muḥammad ibn Aḥmad al-Bīrūnī. Medieval Western translators Latinized Ibn Sina, as "Avicenna." Those Europeans in the Middle Ages who had even heard of Biruni conjured up several Latinized versions of his name, the most common of which was "Alberonius."

In spite of their names, neither was an Arab. Both were Central Asians of Persianate stock. This meant that their native languages were part of the diverse group of languages that dominated Central Asia, Afghanistan, and what is now Iran, much the way several distinctive Germanic languages—Dutch and Danish, for example—are spoken in central and northern Europe today. Both became known by their Arabic names because they wrote mainly in Arabic, the language of learning in the Muslim world, just as Latin was in the West. Ibn Sina and Biruni were both born within the borders of what is now Uzbekistan. Neither ever set foot in Greece, Rome, or even Baghdad. They spent their lives in what is now Uzbekistan, Turkmenistan, Afghanistan, Iran, and Pakistan.

Notwithstanding their obscurity to the general public, the scholarly literature is bulging with encomia of these two men. Biruni has been hailed as "an eleventh-century da Vinci," "one of the greatest scholars of all times,"[1] "forerunner of the Renaissance," a "phenomenon in the history of Eastern learning," "a universal genius," and simply, "The Master." In 1927, George Sarton, the Belgian-born chemist who pioneered the systematic study of the history of science, pronounced him "the finest monument to Islamic learning." Ibn Sina has similarly been praised as "The Preeminent Master," "the Prince of Physicians," "by far the most influential of the Islamic philosophers,"[2] and "arguably the most influential philosopher of the pre-modern era." More than one European historian praised him as "the Father of Modern Medicine," while counterparts in the Eastern world have named him "The Leader among Wise Men," and even "The Proof of God."[3]

I encountered Ibn Sina and Biruni while writing my previous book, *Lost Enlightenment: Central Asia's Golden Age from the Arab Conquest to Tamerlane.* I was intrigued to discover that these two giants of their age were roughly contemporaries, that they knew each other, and that they engaged in one of the most vitriolic disputes of the era while still in their twenties. Neither was what in Yiddish would be termed a *nebbische*, inconsequential and weak. Indeed, they both were larger-than-life figures who embodied the highest achievements of a moment when Central Asia and the Middle East were the global epicenter of intellectual achievement—what some have called the Muslim Renaissance. I vowed to delve deeper into the vast literature on them both, separately and in tandem.

I discovered that scholars had long been plowing this field. Most, if not all, were champions of one or the other, Biruni or Ibn Sina, but few were of both. In the process of defending their hero, they advanced a heady list of claims regarding his preeminence. Biruni, for example, is said to have founded both astronomy and trigonometry as independent fields of enquiry and advanced the field of spherical trigonometry. None surpassed him in asserting that mathematics can faithfully represent reality. Using a formula that did not re-appear again until the seventeenth century, he devised the first example of a calculus of finite differences.[4] His scholarly champions claim that, aided by simple but highly sophisticated instruments of his own design as well as new methodologies in geometry and calculus, he measured the diameters of the earth and moon more accurately than anyone else until the seventeenth century. They further claim that he employed the same innovative method to expand the parameters of the known world and even hypothesized the existence of North and South America as inhabited continents. Beyond this, they argue, he advanced the thesis that all motion is relative, a concept later developed further by Galileo, Newton, Descartes, Leibniz, and, finally, Einstein in his theories of relativity.

These champions also credit Biruni with having invented the concept of specific gravity and weighing minerals to a degree of accuracy not surpassed until modern times. Further, he pioneered the fields of cultural anthropology and sociology and vastly expanded the study of the history of science, hydrostatics, and the comparative study of religion. One scholar has argued that he was the first to introduce Indian yoga philosophy to the Middle East and Western worlds. Several specialists maintain that he invented the concept of integrated world time and world history, and that he preceded Europeans of the Renaissance in building a globe of the world and in propounding a theory of oceanography. His innovations in all these fields combined sophisticated mathematics with an appreciation of the impact of language, religion, and culture on human life. Biruni is also credited with dozens of discoveries in chemistry. Many consider him to be the father of modern pharmacology and plant biology.

As to Ibn Sina, his champions argue that he did nothing less than create a single, integrated, and comprehensive intellectual framework that encompassed philosophy, science, medicine, and religion. By means of his revisionist logic, he reconfigured Aristotle's grand synthesis of all knowledge and in a manner that confirmed a place for religious faith, whether his own, which was Islam, or the other religions of the Book. He has also been credited with being a founder of scholastic philosophy.[5] Experts on medieval thought argue that in his attempt to explain the nature of creation itself, St. Thomas Aquinas's *Summa* drew directly on Ibn Sina. Many tout Ibn Sina's contributions to geology, mathematics, and, perhaps above all, medicine.

Historians of science have advanced the claim that Ibn Sina summarized all known medical knowledge and ordered it under a single, logical, and accessible structure. Comprehensive in scope, his *Canon of Medicine* focused attention on neurological questions, the functioning of the brain, and the environmental and psychiatric conditions essential for the restoration and maintenance of health. Among his many innovations were the precise rules he laid down for the conduct of clinical trials of new medicines. Many argue that the *Canon of Medicine* served as the basis of medical education and practice throughout the Middle East, Europe, and parts of India for six centuries and was widely seen among experts as the single most enduring work in the history of medicine.

The validity of some of these claims has been the subject of scholarly debate for over a century. In some quarters the mere mention of one or another of these assertions gives rise to vitriolic responses from those whose studies have led them to different conclusions. It is not my intention in this book to adjudicate all these claims, counterclaims, and counter-counter claims. To do so would require more than a lifetime of further study, which I have neither the time nor the inclination to carry out. Nor, I might add, do any of those who pursue these studies today. Nearly all are specialists in one or another of the many disciplines and fields involved and not in the whole of the work of either Biruni or Ibn Sina, let alone both. This is no criticism, given the amazing productivity of our two subjects. Ibn Sina's main medical text alone fills more than 5,000 pages in modern editions.

Moreover, much of the scholarly literature, especially in the field of philosophy, is written in a language known mainly if not exclusively to academics. This lends precision but at the cost of going beyond the reach of most educated readers.

Related to this is linguistic provincialism. During the century and a half when Russia ruled Central Asia, a distinguished school of oriental studies grew up in Moscow, St. Petersburg/Leningrad, and Central Asia itself. As of 2021, Tajik scholars at the Center for Avicenna Studies in Dushanbe have turned out nine volumes of the translated works of Ibn Sina, with more to come.[6] Not only have Russian, Tajik, and Uzbek scholars undertaken a massive program of translation and editing, but they have also produced sophisticated studies of Ibn Sina and on Biruni's research on mathematics, astronomy, minerology, and geodesy. P. G. Bulgakov of the Academy of Sciences of Uzbekistan, for example, wrote *The Life and Works of Biruni* (*Zhizni i trudy Beruni*), by far the most exhaustive biography of either figure. Though it was published in Tashkent over fifty years ago, it is scarcely ever cited abroad. And whereas Eastern scholars avail themselves of studies written in English, French, German, and Arabic, the same cannot be said of most of their Western colleagues' use of Russian sources.

Nonetheless, we owe profound thanks to the work of that intrepid group of specialists. No doubt I have failed to cite all of their vast (and constantly expanding) corpus, for which I apologize in advance. The writer of a book on the New York literary scene in the 1950s and 1960s once failed to cover the works of novelist Norman Mailer. When Mailer opened the book he turned at once to the index. Where "Mailer" should have appeared alphabetically, the author had penned in the margin, "Sorry, Norman."

This book will not lay out in detail everything our two subjects wrote about in mathematics, philosophy, astronomy, metaphysics, medicine, anthropology, geodesy, or religion. Anyone interested in the ongoing research in any one of these (and other) fields would be best advised to turn to the specialized monographs. My main purpose is to explore the lives of these two gifted thinkers and to place their writings in the context of the times in which they lived. With the notable exception of Bulgakov's work on Biruni, even the best of the existing biographies are cursory. Authors of the more specialized studies tend to employ biographical information as a garnish rather than the main course.

My intention is to rescue from oblivion whatever can be known of their lives, not only as intellectual giants but as people. I will seek the human realities of their worlds, where they differ and where they overlap: their backgrounds, temperaments, and personalities; their educations; their patrons and supporters as well as their critics and enemies; the religious and civil strife, bloody wars, and massive dislocations of their times, and how they dealt with them; and, finally, their relations with each other.

In the main section of the book I present the careers of these two figures as parallel lives, identifying differences and similarities. This approach to biography is by no means original. Two thousand years ago the Greek-born Roman citizen Lucius Mestrius Plutarchus, known as Plutarch, invented the idea of paired biographies and developed it in *Parallel Lives*. Plutarch demonstrated the virtues and failings of carefully selected pairs of Roman and Greek leaders. Many great writers have turned to Plutarch's *Lives* for its insights into human character.

Biruni and Ibn Sina were both products of the same culture of Central Asia and lifelong members of the small elite of highly educated persons who had the means and inclination to pursue knowledge for its own sake. Yet they could not have been more fundamentally dissimilar. The next section will show how they both realized this from an early age, turning them into lifelong competitors and rivals. In their twenties they sparred ferociously, and in their thirties they began avoiding each other. Their temperaments could scarcely have differed more radically. Ibn Sina was a courtier and bon vivant, while Biruni spent much of his life toiling alone, benefiting from official patronage but remaining on the margins of public life. Ibn Sina was a larger-than-life personality who aspired to create a single umbrella under which all knowledge could be organized. Biruni, by contrast, reveled in every discrete phenomenon, and proceeded to generalize only on the basis of what he had observed at the level of specifics.

Ibn Sina epitomized the kind of logical and metaphysical thinking that held sway in both the Middle East and the West for centuries. Applying them to topics as diverse as theology and medicine, he demonstrated the tools of logic that would help us to establish truth. Biruni, by contrast, was critical of proofs reached by logic alone and instead championed mathematics as the premier tool for establishing truth. At the same time, he believed that both nature and human affairs can be understood by closely examining them over time. Ibn Sina, with his focus on ultimate causes, had little use for such an approach, which he considered a diversion. It is no wonder that they emerged early as competitors.

Though vast differences in temperament, lifestyle, interests, modes of analysis, and styles of expression separated these two innovators, there are striking similarities. In geology, for example, they both held that the earth and human life itself, rather than remaining as they were at the moment of Creation, had undergone profound changes, both evolutionary and cataclysmic, over the course of millennia. They agreed that vast deserts had been formed by the retreat of seas, leaving alluvial deposits that dried out over time. That they explored these issues at all—both viewed geology and paleontology as secondary concerns—testifies to the fact that Ibn Sina and Biruni were intellectual omnivores. Their written output spans as many fields and subjects as those offered at a modern university. Biruni once declared that an educated person should learn the essentials of every field of knowledge.[7] Ibn Sina bragged about having actually done so, and then linking them by means of a single philosophical construct.

Both Biruni's and Ibn Sina's lasting contributions to world civilization lay not just in *what* they did but in *how* they did it. Both believed passionately that the most fundamental mark of humanity is its ability to reason. This, they held, reflects mankind's essence and highest manifestation. In an age of profound upheaval, wars, and religious strife, both committed their lives to the exercise of reason, and both suffered for having done so. At differing times each of them was sentenced to be beheaded. Theirs is a story of breakthroughs and insights, but also of endurance and tenacity.

Both Biruni and Ibn Sina were graphomanes who committed their every thought to writing. An army of copyists then "published" the resulting manuscripts, leading to other copies, which were then edited (and distorted) by each successive copyist. For more than a century, scholars and writers from Britain, Egypt, France, Germany, India, Iran, Pakistan, Russia, Uzbekistan, and the United States have prowled through archives worldwide in search of manuscripts. Surviving works by Biruni and/or Ibn Sina are housed in the Bodleian Library at Oxford, the Topkapi Palace and Ottoman State Archives in Istanbul, the National Archive in Tehran, the University Archive in Leiden, and the National Archives in Cairo. The total number of works attributed to Ibn Sina is over 400. This includes books (which were actually long scrolls), short texts, brief notes, and letters. More than a dozen of these titles would each comprise a large modern volume. Some 250 survive in whole or in part.[8] Biruni once drew up a list of 140 books and studies from his own pen (ignoring many shorter pieces and letters), and he did this fourteen years before he stopped writing.[9] In the end, Biruni's output was comparable to Ibn Sina's. One scholar has estimated that Biruni's works would fill at least forty large modern volumes.[10]

It is a tragedy that so many works by these two great minds have simply vanished over the centuries. Biruni, for example, listed three major books on astronomy that are now lost. Neglect, deliberate destruction, and wars (including the Mongol invasion) all took their toll on both writers' legacies. So did beetles, moths, silverfish, booklice, and mold—all the enemies of parchment and vellum. This means that our conclusions about the achievements of these great thinkers are inevitably based on fragments of what they actually wrote. Nonetheless, the quest for lost manuscripts continues. In 1959 an Indian researcher, prowling through ancient papers at the shrine of a seventeenth-century Sufi mystic at Ahmadabad, India, discovered a previously unrecorded treatise by Biruni.[11] One source of other recent finds is quotations from now-lost works by Ibn Sina or Biruni, found in the compositions of later writers.

Discovery is only the first step in reclaiming lost works. Each new text must then be authenticated. Disputes over the views of both figures led some to compose what bibliographers call "pseudoepigraphia" and what the rest of us call forgeries. Such texts present what the forger *wanted* Ibn Sina or Biruni to have written. And because a lavishly ornamented forgery could satisfy a collector's demand more than most workaday copies of authentic texts, it often survived through the centuries. Moreover, the surviving authenticated texts are themselves not yet ready for scholars to pore over them. For one thing, medieval copyists were notoriously sloppy, often misreading the original document and just as often leaving out words, lines, and even whole sections of the original. Some original texts are illegible, or inaccurate, or marred when the copyist blithely has introduced his own revisions. In spite of all these challenges, translators have focused on the works of Biruni and Ibn Sina for a millennium. Thomas Aquinas, Dante, and Chaucer all read Ibn Sina in Latin translations. Neither Copernicus nor Tycho Brahe nor Galileo knew of Biruni's existence, but they studied the translated works of his later followers. No language has a monopoly. Authoritative translations of specific works by both writers are scattered among English, German, Russian, and French. The book you are holding is based on all of these translated texts.

Where written evidence lags, modern archaeological research has come to the rescue. Thus, an excavation at the ancient town of Paykent in Uzbekistan turned up an apothecary shop of the period immediately preceding the appearance of Ibn Sina's treatise on medicine. Among the Paykent finds were examples of nearly every type of chemical and medical equipment mentioned in his *Canon of Medicine*. Another example is the 1908 discovery in Samarkand of the remains of the great astronomical observatory built by Tamerlaine's grandson, Ulugbeg. Although constructed three centuries after Biruni's death, Ulugbeg's observatory was a lineal descendant of Biruni's and sheds light on the Central Asian tradition of astronomy.

A problem in studying polymaths is that the expertise of most modern specialists—including myself—rarely extends beyond one or two of the many relevant disciplines. This is understandable, given the number of points at issue in every one of the relevant fields. Yale scholar Dimitri Gutas devoted a 600-page study solely to Ibn Sina's relationship to Aristotle. Moreover, the present state of our knowledge of their lives prevents us from providing definitive portraits. To cite but one example, both Biruni and Ibn Sina, at certain phases of their lives, worked as senior statesmen, policymakers, and strategic thinkers. Yet all the official papers that documented their activities were destroyed many centuries ago or lost to neglect.

What we do know, however, is that the lives of these two thinkers were packed with drama, crises, and stunning achievements. Separated from their world by a millennium, we have much to gain from reflecting upon their lives and works today. The story of Ibn Sina and Biruni transcends the centuries, offering insights into their tireless efforts to expand the realm of human knowledge, and occurred in a part of the world that today sometimes invites concerns over the role of advanced learning and science. That these two larger-than-life figures should inform such discussions a full millennium after their deaths is appropriate, for in the end, though they were the geniuses of their age, they rise above time and place, religion, and politics, to stand as citizens of the global world of ideas and giants of human achievement.

1

Together and Apart

Our story begins at the one place where Ibn Sina and Biruni appeared at the same time. The ancient Central Asian region of Khwarazm (variously known as Khorezm, Choresm, and Choresmia) is located 100 kilometers (60 miles) south of the Aral Sea, along what is today the border between Turkmenistan and Uzbekistan. It is remote from just about anywhere of note: some 3,000 kilometers (1,800 miles) east of the Muslims' old capital, Damascus, Syria; 2,500 kilometers (1,550 miles) east of the Christians' capital, Constantinople; 2,000 kilometers (1,200 miles) northeast of the seat of the Muslim Caliphate, Baghdad; and 2,200 kilometers (1,400 miles) northwest of the ancient Indian centers of Lahore and Delhi. Beijing is 4,600 kilometers (2,800 miles) to the east.

Yet Khwarazm was midway along one of Eurasia's most heavily traveled trade routes. Land routes linked it directly with the Middle East, North Africa, Europe, India, and China. Also, the great Amu Darya River, known to the ancient Greeks as the Oxys, flows directly through Khwarazm. This navigable waterway gave the region access to Afghanistan and the Indus Valley and, indirectly, to China. Today the entire region of Khwarazm is a desert, while the desiccated Aral Sea has become an ecological disaster. But 1,000 years ago the territory flowered, thanks to sophisticated underground hydraulic systems that supplied its cities with fresh water and irrigated the countryside surrounding them. Along with the trade routes, this plentiful water enabled the region's economy to boom, beginning in the days when Rome flourished.

Khwarazm developed its own language, religion, arts, and sciences.[1] Kath, the ancient capital of this Persianate people, was a bustling international entrepot. Along its narrow passages were shops where merchants from the Mediterranean and the Bay of Bengal rubbed shoulders. In the suburbs were factories that turned out cotton cloth, ironware, pottery, and finished goods, all for export. The populace freely practiced a variety of religions, which included both Syrian and Greek Christianity as well as Judaism, Zoroastrianism, Manichaeism, and Buddhism. In the seventh century a tide of Muslim warriors poured out of the Arabian deserts, bent on capturing this wealthy land. In hard-fought battles they seized Khwarazm's riches, forced most of its inhabitants to convert to Islam, and destroyed all vestiges of its indigenous culture, including whole libraries. The loss was incalculable. Fortunately, a few fragments and memories of the past survived, and by the tenth century, Khwarazm once more came alive. Kath revived and trade again flourished, giving rise to new public and private wealth. Muslims now controlled the government, but they allowed adherents of other religions to continue to practice their faiths. Travelers from East and West noted the presence of a lively intellectual life. By the time Ibn Sina and Biruni arrived there as young men in 1004, Khwarazm had become a land-based version of today's Dubai, with people coming from far and wide to make money and partake of its cosmopolitan culture.

In 993, a new dynasty seized power in Khwarazm. The Mamun family[2] promptly moved the capital from flood-prone Kath to Gurganj, located on the west bank of the Amu Darya. The site, now called Kunya Urgench, lies near the northern border of Turkmenistan. The new rulers fortified the place and built a sophisticated new hydraulic system to provide water for the town and its gardens. The Arab Caliphate in Baghdad was on its last legs, a situation that easily allowed the founder of this new dynasty, Abu Ali Mamun, to convince the caliph to grant him the title of "Shah of Khwarazm." In keeping with the tradition of eastern potentates, his son, Abu al-Abbas Mamun, and his *vizier*[3] or minister, an erudite man named Abu'l Husain as-Suhayli, set about attracting to their court the most creative minds available.[4]

Suhayli did his job well. The renowned medical expert and polymath Abu Sahl al-Masihi had come to Gurganj during the previous reign and Suhayli persuaded him to stay. A Christian from the Caspian region, Masihi was a contemporary of both Biruni and Ibn Sina. He had already written important works on medicine, including *Fundamentals of Medicine, One Hundred Medical Problems*, and a monograph on smallpox. He also penned a book exploring the question of whether the earth was stationary (as was assumed at the time) or rotated on its axis—an issue Biruni would later address. Masihi was to become a close friend of both Biruni and Ibn Sina. His example helped inspire the latter to undertake his *Canon of Medicine*. Masihi dedicated a dozen works to each of his friends. Nonetheless, though he is the only person known to have maintained close links with both Biruni and Ibn Sina, there is no evidence that he ever brought the two together. Masihi was to spend his last days in the company of Ibn Sina.

Hasan bin Suwar bin al-Khammar was another distinguished scholar whom Suhayli attracted to Gurganj. His name in Arabic indicates that he was the son of a wine merchant. A Syrian Christian from Baghdad, and thirty years older than either Ibn Sina or Biruni, Khammar had already written a large volume on medicine that earned him the sobriquet of "the second Hippocrates."[5] Through Khammar, Ibn Sina gained access to key documents and to his colleague's vast clinical experience. That Ibn Sina respected him so highly is no small matter, for Ibn Sina tended to be most critical of those from whose works he borrowed most heavily. Khammar's relationship with Biruni extended beyond Gurganj, for eventually they were forcibly exiled to Ghazni in Afghanistan, where they both spent the rest of their lives, Biruni as court astrologer and Khammar as court physician.

Still another member of this intellectual elite was Abu-Abdallah al-Natili, a medical expert and also a philosopher. Natili was respected for having edited the Arabic translation of an ancient text on pharmacology by the Greco-Roman physician Dioscorides, who died in 90 AD. Dioscorides's five volumes had been the bible of pharmacology for ten centuries, and Natili was its premier living expert. Ibn Sina knew him well, as his father had brought Natili into his household to tutor his young sons. But unlike Masihi and Khammar, Natali was rewarded with his students' lasting contempt. This nonetheless did not prevent Ibn Sina from drawing heavily on Natili's work when writing his own volumes on pharmacology. Biruni was also to rely on Natali's work, albeit with greater respect for his source.

Displaying a commendable ability to forget the past, the Mamun shahs also attracted to their court in Gurganj the immensely talented brother of the deposed ruler at Kath, Abu Nasr Mansur ibn Ali ibn Iraq. The princely Ibn Iraq had served as stepfather to the orphaned Biruni and had tutored him since childhood. Ibn Iraq was himself a distinguished mathematician and astronomer, the first to come up with a proof of the theory of sines, those equations that relate the lengths of the sides of a triangle to its angles. He also wrote a treatise on astrolabes, the instrument invented by ancient Greeks for measuring the altitude of stars and planets above the horizon and for determining both latitude and local time. All of these were issues that were to claim Biruni's attention.

These, then, are some of the intellectuals whom the shah of Khwarazm and his minister assembled at the court at Gurganj. There were surely others whose names did not come down to us, for regional rulers in that era strove to outdo one another in their ability to attract talent, measuring their success by both the quantity and quality of their catches. What is most striking about Mamun's court is that scientists rather than poets dominated its cultural life. Doubtless, there were also poets whose job was to turn out panegyrics glorifying Mamun. Regional potentates typically maintained many such versifying publicists on their payrolls. But the surviving record suggests that mathematicians, philosophers, medical doctors, and astronomers reigned supreme in Gurganj.

What, besides generous patronage, enabled these scholars to interact so productively with one another? In the Muslim East, the "dark ages" had ended in the eighth century, in Baghdad, the seat of the caliphate. In an astonishingly brief period of time linguists in Syria, Iran, Iraq, and Central Asia translated a significant part of the written legacy of ancient Greece into Arabic, the lingua franca of the Muslim world. Greek Christians from Syria figured centrally in this effort for the simple reason that they knew both languages. Thanks to the patronage of the Abbasid caliphs and also to the work of Syrian Christian bishops in Syria, Iran, and Central Asia, an enormous body of classical Greek learning became available in translation. In Gurganj two centuries later, this renaissance blossomed a second time, with the rise of the Mamun family. These treasures of ancient wisdom were available in Khwarazm, where Biruni was born, as well as in Ibn Sina's birthplace, Bukhara.

In its extent and intensity, this early renaissance at the far eastern periphery of the Muslim world equaled, and in some respects surpassed, what took place half a millennium later during the European Renaissance. Of course, this rediscovered trove of ancient knowledge was accessible only to those who could read Arabic. Indeed, a knowledge of Arabic was the key factor in enabling the ethnically and linguistically diverse band of thinkers and poets assembled in Gurganj to work together. Though Khwarazm had a Persianate language of its own, trade had made it a linguistic hodgepodge. But within the Mamuns' court, Arabic prevailed, even though it was a second or third language for most of those assembled there.

Mamun, shah of Khwarazm, had personally recruited Biruni—the talented young native son of Khwarazm—to join his stable of intellectuals. Biruni's other chief patron was Mamun's vizier, Suhayli. It was also Suhayli who had heard of Ibn Sina's achievements in his native Bukhara and who learned that the young doctor and scholar was in need of a job. Knowing that Ibn Sina had studied Islamic jurisprudence and had also worked in the finance office of Bukhara's ruler, Suhayli invited him to Gurganj and offered him a job managing the government's legal affairs. Ibn Sina gratefully accepted the offer, grateful also for the excellent salary that went with it. In 1004 he traveled to Gurganj and presented himself to Suhayli. It was understood from the outset that Ibn Sina was there also in the capacity of medical doctor, and that, in addition, he would continue to pursue his work as a philosopher and metaphysician.

This illustrious band of thinkers all lived and worked under the same patronage, interacting daily with one another. Later miniature paintings invariably depict the sages of Mamun's court seated together, in a group. For roughly two decades, down to its destruction in 1017, Gurganj thrived, a global beacon of intellectual excellence in Central Asia.

For both Biruni and Ibn Sina, their time in Gurganj proved immensely useful. For now, I'll focus on the mere fact that they were there at the same time. Biruni spent the years 997 through 1017 in Gurganj and Ibn Sina the years 1004 to 1011. Thus, the two of them were together in the same place for a total of seven years. They would both have been called upon constantly to participate in all the rites of a small but ambitious court. Besides formal presentations and disputations, these gatherings would have included diplomatic receptions, religious and secular celebrations, even wine-drinking rituals,[6] in addition to informal gatherings in pleasure gardens. Under such conditions, Biruni and Ibn Sina would most certainly have interacted almost daily. And yet, neither at the time nor in all their voluminous later writings did either Biruni or Ibn Sina so much as mention the other.

This cries out for an explanation. One possibility is that they were both too busy with official events and their own work to have acknowledged the other in writing. This seems unlikely. In later writings they both managed not only to note others who were present in Gurganj but to salute them as colleagues and friends. Yet when Ibn Sina dictated his autobiography, he did not even mention Biruni. And while Biruni had no interest in autobiographical writing, in his later technical works he frequently dropped friendly asides about people he had known in Gurganj. In none of these notes did the name of Ibn Sina appear.

Another point of observation is the difference in their status. Biruni, as a royal appointee, outranked Ibn Sina, who owed his position to the minister, Suhayli. But Ibn Sina, though a newcomer with a job in the government, was already renowned for his medical expertise and his writings on philosophy.

Gurganj was surely a hierarchy-conscious society, but at the exalted level at which both men operated, the difference in their rank would have been reflected mainly in the seating arrangement at court *levees*, not in their daily schedules. A third is that they were both loners. No evidence supports this hypothesis. Both of them knew and interacted with the other intellectuals who graced the Gurganj court. Three of them—Ibn Iraq, Khammar, and Masihi—were to depart from Gurganj together, as a group, along with one or the other of our two subjects.

According to nearly all the sources, Biruni was seven years older than Ibn Sina. It has been suggested that this difference in age accounts for their mutual estrangement. This argument fades upon closer inspection. Two highly respected scholars have recently presented evidence that Ibn Sina was in fact born not in 980, as was long asserted, but around the year 973, if not slightly earlier.[7] The 973 birthdate would have made Ibn Sina and Biruni exact contemporaries. This could have become the basis for a lasting friendship. Just as likely, though, it could have made them both prone to all the competitive urges natural to aspiring and supremely self-confident young males of the same age.

I would favor the last hypothesis. In Sir Arthur Conan Doyle's 1892 story, *Silver Blaze*, Sherlock Holmes solves the mystery of the disappearance of a famous racehorse by noticing that at a crucial moment the dog at the stable where the horse was kept did not bark. The total absence of evidence of direct interactions between Ibn Sina and Biruni seems comparable to the dog that didn't bark. Their mutual silence stands as mute testimony. Both Biruni and Ibn Sina had basked for years in praise of their talents. Each had his own areas of expertise, though their general interests overlapped significantly. Comparisons between them, both by others and by themselves, would have seemed inevitable. As contemporaries, each had come to view the other as a competitor, rival, or even an enemy.

The silence between Ibn Sina and Biruni cannot be explained by looking only at their interaction, or lack thereof, in Gurganj. Both men had lived active lives prior to their joint presence at Ali Ibn Mamun's court during the years 1004–1011. Each brought to Gurganj his own well-developed interests and points of view. To understand the coldness between these rising stars we need to look at their respective biographies prior to their arrival in Gurganj.

2

Privileged Prodigies

Most biographies take note of their subjects' childhood and then move quickly to their lives as adults. To do this in the case of either Ibn Sina or Biruni would be a serious mistake, for their early lives were intense and extraordinary. Their boyhood experiences set them on paths they were to follow to their dying days. Today we would term them both "early starters."

Biruni was an orphan. In a later poem he reveals that he had no idea who his father was, let alone his grandfather.[1] His name, which in the Persianate language of Khwarazm meant "someone from the suburbs," suggests that he hailed not from Kath but from one of the outlying towns or villages. How he ended up as the ward of the brother-in-law of the last ruler of Khwarazm remains an utter mystery. But it happened, and it was to define Biruni's entire life and career. Biruni's stepfather, teacher, and patron, the former prince Ibn Iraq, enjoyed every possible privilege, which he shared with his young charge. Biruni had not been born with a silver spoon in his mouth but he acquired one at a very early age. Ibn Iraq spent his days indulging his own passion for learning, a passion that he passed on to his young ward. Biruni was to follow in his footsteps, sharing especially Ibn Iraq's passion for mathematics and astronomy.

Ibn Sina, by contrast, was born to wealth. His father came from the cosmopolitan and, in former times, deeply Buddhist province of Balkh in what is now Afghanistan. His name "Sina" was also to be found in the ancient Zoroastrian holy book, the *Avesta*; it meant "a learned one." When the ruling Samani family in Bukhara gave the aspiring official a senior promotion, the elder Sina crossed the Amu Darya (Oxus) River to take up an appointment as senior administrator in the town of Afshona, northwest of the capital. There he married a woman from an old Buddhist town in the Bukhara region. Except for sharing this fact, Ibn Sina never mentioned his mother. After the birth of a second son, the father moved the family to Bukhara itself. He made the move to assure that his sons would receive a good education. But he may also have done so in hopes of a further promotion in the Samani bureaucracy.

Thus, Ibn Sina grew up in the family of an ambitious, upwardly mobile, and cultivated senior civil servant.

Over their careers, Biruni and Ibn Sina followed in the footsteps of the men who raised them. Like his mentor, Biruni was drawn into public life only briefly, and with disastrous results. By contrast, several regional potentates would later judge Ibn Sina to be an effective administrator and policymaker. For his part, Ibn Sina considered it natural to serve in official roles, which he did, twice, as vizier, or prime minister.

As a matter of course, both boys received the religious training expected of all young Muslims. This meant studying the *Quran*. Ibn Sina would later boast that as a youth he had "mastered"—read, "memorized"—Islam's holy text in its entirety. Biruni was also exposed early to holy writ (though he made no claim to having memorized it). Both would also have studied one or more of the several recently issued collections of the *Sayings* (*hadiths*) of the prophet Muhammad. The relative authenticity of these competing compendia was the subject of heated polemics at the time, not only among religious scholars but also the educated public. To the extent that they followed such debates, both Ibn Sina and Biruni gained their first exposure to the world of textual criticism. In any case, neither ever turned his back on this early religious training. Their later works frequently open with formulaic invocations of the Deity. Both assigned to God the central role in the drama of creation. And they both explored the question of God's role in human affairs. But where Ibn Sina's focus was consistently on God's immanence and on the intellectual processes by which the human mind can know of it, Biruni, a born comparativist, tended to ask how people of different religions and cultures viewed the divine presence in earthly matters. Both were adept at citing holy writ though Biruni, unlike Ibn Sina, often used the *Quran* instrumentally, invoking it to defend his own positions against critics. There is no evidence that his early education went on to include an exposure to the "science of religious discourse," or *kalam*, the systematic study of Muslim writings.

Ibn Sina, too, seems to have passed over *kalam*. In contrast to Biruni, however, he was exposed from early childhood to religious debate. His father was an enthusiastic convert to the esoteric, controversial, and by this time, strictly banned doctrines of the Ismailis, the branch of Shiite Islam that had become the most potent religious and political competitor to the Sunnis. Boasting a strong and often contrarian intellectual tradition in religious affairs, the Ismaili Shiites had long concentrated on converting the Sunni lands. By the middle of the ninth century their missionaries flooded capitals in Central

Asia and Persia. These proselytizers crowned their mounting successes with their conversion of the Emir of Bukhara to their cause. Soon thereafter they established their own caliphate in Cairo, which the Fatimids had conquered in 969.

However, in gaining these triumphs the Ismailis had overplayed their hand, by alienating the orthodox clergy. In Bukhara, these guardians of the faith had them summarily tossed out and banned from all the Samanis' lands. But Ismailism was not so easily crushed. By the time Ibn Sina was born, Ismaili missionaries were once more crisscrossing Central Asia. Ibn Sina's father responded to their call and became an Ismaili and a Shiite. Notwithstanding the fact that the Sunni government he served had strictly outlawed Ismailism, he even invited a pair of Ismaili missionaries to live with his family at their home in Bukhara and to use it as a base for their proselytizing. This move, as bold as it was illegal, occurred during Ibn Sina's boyhood. He later recalled hearing his father and his guests discussing Ismaili doctrines in whispered conversations in his family's home. In his autobiography Ibn Sina solemnly recorded that he had been "unconvinced" by the Ismaili's arguments. But this was almost certainly mere boilerplate, for to have admitted otherwise would have led to his being banned from any post in the Sunni world.

In spite of this obligatory denial, Ibn Sina's early contacts with the Ismailis were to have two important long-term consequences. First, they convinced him that the great questions of faith and of God's role in human affairs were of the utmost importance. And second, they aroused his curiosity over why we deem one assertion to be valid and another not. This led him to inquire into the austere logical processes that enable us to establish the truth or falsity of any given statement.

During the next phase of their educations, young Ibn Sina and Biruni veered off in opposite directions. Biruni, firmly under the tutelage of Ibn Iraq, focused entirely on those subjects that were of interest to his mentor, namely, mathematics, geometry, geography, and astronomy. He was, in short, Ibn Iraq's apprentice. Ibn Sina, by contrast, studied philosophy with a tutor whom his father had brought into the household. This was Abdu Abdallah Natili, the same man who later showed up in Gurganj. In his dictated autobiography, Ibn Sina bragged that he had astonished Natali with his ability to conceptualize categorical statements, and he ridiculed his tutor for "claiming to be a philosopher." Whatever his shortcomings in the eyes of his young student, Natali introduced Ibn Sina to the translated works of Aristotle. Ibn Iraq did the same with Biruni. As a result, both were to emerge from their early education deeply engaged with the writings of the ancient Greek whom the medieval Muslim world called simply "*The* Philosopher."

In the twenty-first century it is not easy to appreciate the importance of Aristotle in both the East and West over a thousand years go. We have first to reject the idea that "philosophy" is limited to the specialized field that modern undergraduates study (or seek to avoid studying). Rather, "philosophy" embraced all knowledge, including subjects as diverse as physics, ethics, astronomy, botany, psychology, geography, politics, astronomy, poetics, rhetoric, logic, meteorology, and the analysis of dreams, as well as what we now consider philosophy itself. It was Aristotle who was the first to seek to integrate all of these subjects, and many others as well, into a single system of thought. Reading Aristotle challenged both young men to explore all fields, as The Philosopher himself had done. It was Aristotle who inspired them to take a comprehensive approach to knowledge and to identify the underlying processes of analysis appropriate to each subject. And if Aristotle was an inspiration, he was even more a challenge, a giant whose works had to be mastered, revised, rejected, or transcended.

Beyond his comprehensive grasp of all that was known, however, Aristotle focused on *how* we should think about all those subjects—in other words, on knowing as such. It was on this issue that Ibn Sina and Biruni came to occupy sharply different positions. Aristotle and his voluminous writings were their common starting point. Yet for all his centrality in their lives, the great thinker of the fourth century BC was not the sole inspiration for our two rising intellects. Both also took inspiration from other early Greek thinkers and especially from the scholars and scientists who had congregated in the great city of Alexandria in Egypt. Founded in about 325 BC by Aristotle's pupil, Alexander the Great, Alexandria was the intellectual center of the world for the next seven centuries. Here scientists and thinkers in many fields carried on the traditions of Aristotle and of his teacher, Plato, merging them in some fields and advancing them separately in others. Throughout their lives, a main focus of both Ibn Sina and Biruni were writings by those who had once lived and worked in Alexandria.

Nonetheless, it was becoming clear that Ibn Sina and Biruni drew quite different waters from the same well. Biruni studied Aristotle diligently, but he devoted serious attention also to other ancient Greek thinkers, notably the mathematician Pythagoras, who argued that numbers and quantity offer the keys to all understanding, and Ptolemy, whose second-century AD *Almagest* was the greatest ancient treatise on mathematics, and whose *Geography* remained for a millennium the classic exposition of the physical features and human settlement of the known world. At some point in his early education, Biruni also encountered the works of Euclid, who died in 270 BC and whose *Elements* systematized geometry as it then existed.

While Biruni gravitated toward mathematics, geography, and geometry, Ibn Sina found himself continually reverting to the question that had been raised in his mind from his contact with the Ismailis and his confrontation with Natili—namely, how can we gain access to firm truths? Beginning in his teenage years and extending throughout his life, he was convinced that the great tool for establishing all truths is logic. As propounded by Aristotle, logic not only gave Ibn Sina the opportunity to lay bare the intellectual underpinnings of any specific field but to discern the intellectual bridges between seemingly separate branches of knowledge.

This view of logic as a kind of universal solvent lay behind the young Ibn Sina's tendency to emphasize certain of Aristotle's works over others and also to seize on ideas from later Greek thinkers like Plotinus, whose works from the third century AD were known to him only through paraphrases or fragments cited in the works of others. In most cases, what attracted Ibn Sina was the author's zeal to uncover the sources and unity of all knowledge.

Reviewing the curricula followed by these two young scholars in the late tenth century, what stands out is the utter dominance of works by writers from classical Greece. Yet the span of time between them and the eras of Aristotle and Ptolemy was greater than the interval between them and our own time. And the physical distance between Bukhara or Khwarazm and Alexandria was nearly four times greater than it was to Baghdad, the capital of the Muslim Caliphate.

Besides being immersed in philosophical works of the ancient Greek masters, both Biruni and Ibn Sina were exposed to more practical studies. Once again, this led them down different paths. In the case of Ibn Sina, we detect again the hand of his worldly and ambitious father, who sent him to study law with Ismail az-Zahid, a distinguished local savant. Jurisprudence in tenth-century Bukhara meant Islamic law, specifically of the Hanafi school, the more moderate and intellectually open of the four systems of jurisprudence that had by then taken hold in the Muslim world. Ibn Sina's father wanted his son to master a field that offered good jobs and the prospect of professional advancement. Ibn Sina did not disappoint these hopes. He later boasted that he was able to serve as a court lawyer by age sixteen. That said, Ibn Sina's interest in the law was less in the details of evidence and judgment than in its method of posing questions and raising objections. As scholar Dimitri Gutas has pointed out, Ibn Sina's real interest was in what we now call dialectics, the rigorous back-and-forth process by which two parties can arrive at truth.[2] In his autobiography, Ibn Sina boasted about his having been "one of az-Zahid's most skillful questioners." He was like the law student who passes over his mastery of torts and brags instead about the smart questions he posed in class.

There was a deeper significance to this braggadocio, for by the time he dictated his autobiography to an assistant some twenty years later the mature Ibn Sina wanted to indicate that even at a young age he had mastered the use of dialectics and syllogisms that were to become the keys to many of his later achievements. Thanks to his earliest training, Ibn Sina understood dialectics as the process by which one can discover truth by considering the opposite proposition. This is what Socrates practiced throughout his dialogues and which we still refer to as the "Socratic method." And it is what Ibn Sina was bragging about having mastered when he spoke of his ability to pose sharp questions to his law tutor, az-Zahid.

When Ibn Sina studied law—or any other subject—his goal was to discern the specific process by which the author reached his conclusions. He specified three of these: through analogy, by which an unknown is true because it is *analogous* to a known truth; by induction, which seeks the common element uniting several observed phenomena; and by syllogism. Of these, he considered syllogism to be the one reasoning process that leads to certainty. Aristotle codified syllogism as a branch of logic and offered a bewilderingly opaque definition of it, calling it "discourse in which, certain things being stated, something other than what is stated follows of necessity from their being so."[3] A rudimentary example, known to every first-year philosophy student, would start with the premise, "All men are mortal," then proceed to the second premise, that "Socrates is a man," and finally to the conclusion, that "Socrates is therefore mortal." Leaving aside the many other types of syllogisms, Ibn Sina early discovered that a simple method for verifying any given statement began by pinpointing the premise on which it is based. With this in hand, one could figure out the crucially important second premise or "middle term" and thus the syllogism as a whole. This, he discovered, was possible even if the assertion in question was not stated in the form of a syllogism.

Ibn Sina's process of identifying that middle term has variously been described as "figuring out," "intuiting," "hitting on," and even "guessing."

Ibn Sina himself grandiosely termed the process a "divine effluence."[4] No wonder he believed that sanctified prophets and "messengers of God" have no need for syllogisms, since they unerringly grasp all matters intuitively.[5] As he was later to explain at length, true prophets, who possess all the human faculties in their perfection, are illuminated by what he termed the Active Intelligence, who is identified with Gabriel, the angel of revelation. Acknowledging that he himself was not a prophet or messenger of God, Ibn Sina concentrated on identifying the syllogisms underlying all kinds of assertions and then to intuiting their middle term. This process, not mathematics or the understanding of history, provided the key that enabled him, as he firmly believed, to get quickly to the heart of any field whatsoever.[6]

Except for metaphysics. Both the purpose and processes of metaphysics and its associated areas of logic stumped young Ibn Sina. In his autobiography he claimed to have read Aristotle's *Metaphysics* forty times but without comprehending either the questions it addressed or the answers it offered. But then, he added, a chance encounter on the streets of Bukhara changed all this. As Ibn Sina strolled by a book stall, an over-eager peddler thrust into his hands a secondhand work he was selling on commission. But even its cheap price did not entice him. However, the salesman persisted, and Ibn Sina walked away with a study entitled *On the Objects of Metaphysics*. Its author was Abu Nasr Muhammad ibn Muhammad al-Farabi, a fellow Central Asian from what is now southern Kazakhstan, who had lived three generations earlier. Few if any have surpassed Farabi in the range and depth of his understanding of Aristotle, and no one surpassed him for the calm and rational manner in which he explained it all. From Farabi's slim treatise Ibn Sina grasped that cosmology and the logical processes it required constituted the master science, one that explains the core realities which all the other fields embody in their separate spheres. Because cosmology addresses the First Cause and the relationship to it of human consciousness, or the Soul, Ibn Sina concluded that serious advancement in all areas of learning would be impossible until he had grasped it.

Even before his encounter with Farabi, Ibn Sina had begun compiling a kind of card catalogue of syllogisms, which he arranged according to their premises. He worked meticulously, like an explorer laying precise paths into a forbidding forest. Now, with the help of Farabi, he had at hand a rough map of the forest as a whole. He suddenly felt free to wander anywhere and to appreciate the flora of each sector of the intellectual woodland. Better yet, he was convinced that he had hit upon a method for grasping the Forester who had first planted the woods, and the key to appreciating His work.

Meanwhile, Ibn Sina's father's eagerness to equip his teen-aged son with practical skills led him next to apprentice the young man to a merchant. That the merchant in question was no mere bazaar trader is shown by the fact that he based his accounting not on the prevalent local method of counting but on "Indian numbers"—in other words, the Indian system of numbers that we (incorrectly) call "Arabic" numerals. This in turn introduced Ibn Sina to the mysteries of Indian mathematics.

Yet another practical sphere in which Ibn Sina acquired competence as a young man was medicine. We do not know whether he turned to this field because his father saw it as yet another career possibility or out of personal curiosity. Once engaged, though, Ibn Sina pursued it with a passion, poring over whatever books on the subject he could find. By the 990s, a reader of Arabic could have access to a formidable range of ancient and modern treatises on medicine. Hippocrates, known today for the "Hippocratic oath," was acknowledged as the fountainhead of medicine but remained largely unknown, for only fragments of his writings survived in any form and even these had yet to be translated into Arabic. By contrast, many other ancient medical treatises were available. Some of these had been translated directly from the Greek, and others came via the Syriac language, rendered into Arabic by Syrian Christians. Thanks to this multicultural effort, works by Galen, the great second-century physician and philosopher, were readily available to Ibn Sina in Bukhara. Galen's output was stupendous: when nineteenth-century German scholars issued an edition comprising only his medical works it came to 20,000 pages. In the Muslim East, as well as in Renaissance Europe, Galen was the starting point for all medical studies and continued to dominate medical thought down to modern times.

Access to Greek learning had sparked a boom in medical research and writing across the Middle East and especially in Baghdad and Central Asia. Among the pioneers had been a Central Asian native named Ali bin Sahl Tabari, a ninth-century scholar who wrote one of the Muslim world's earliest treatments of medicine. Bukhara had more recently been home to a number of prolific medical writers in both Arabic and Persian, and in Biruni's home region, several writers had issued their own compendia of medical knowledge.

If Farabi opened Ibn Sina's mind to formal channels of enquiry, Farabi's older contemporary, Abu Bakr al-Razi, stimulated, challenged, and even threatened the aspiring doctor in both his medical and philosophical interests. Known in the West as Rhazes or Rhasis, this late ninth-century giant of fields as diverse as philosophy, astronomy, theology, and astrology had founded the premier hospital in Baghdad before returning to his native Rayy (now Tehran), where he became the most prolific and prominent authority on medicine in the Muslim world. He also became one of its most controversial thinkers. Razi's bold questioning of religious verities, no less than his medical expertise, defined his legacy.

Razi was to loom over the lives and thought of both Ibn Sina and Biruni. He pioneered the use of controlled experiments to test treatments and drugs. He produced treatises on subjects as diverse as kidney stones, diabetes, colic, and hemorrhoids. His legacy was his *Comprehensive Book of Medicine*, a twenty-three-volume collection of his research and musings that students compiled after his death in 925 on the basis of his clinical notes. Razi pioneered the distinction between smallpox and measles and was the first to identify alcohol and sulfuric acid as distinct substances. Immediately reproduced in scores of copies, Razi's vast compendium became the standard source for all medical experts who read Arabic, and eventually for Europeans as well, thanks to early translations into Latin. Razi's *Comprehensive Book of Medicine* was on Ibn Sina's reading list throughout his training years and beyond.

Ibn Sina apprenticed under two prominent Bukhara practitioners, Abu Mansur al-Qumri and Abu Sahl al-Masihi. His old tutor, Natili, was likely a third.[7] Masihi was the expert on medicine who was to appear at the court of the Mamuns in Gurganj a few years later. Besides his mastery of the practical sides of medicine, Masihi brought a keen interest in the structure of knowledge as a whole and the place of the medical sciences in it. His treatise *On the Categories of the Philosophical Sciences* laid out a complete curriculum covering all fields of philosophy and science. While he included a large section on those fields of study that were based on mathematics, pride of place went to logic in all its dimensions and to Aristotle as its master. Masihi tucked medicine into the end of his curriculum as one of the non-mathematical "applied sciences,"[8] along with agriculture and mechanics. Notwithstanding his later eminence as a doctor, Ibn Sina was to perpetuate Masihi's somewhat disparaging attitude toward the entire field of medicine.

Ibn Sina plunged into his medical studies with such ardor that, as he proudly reported in his *Autobiography*, he was treating patients in his sixteenth year—the same year in which he boasted that he began practicing law. He proved so expert that when the ruler of Bukhara came down with an unknown illness, the royal physicians sought his advice. The treatment Ibn Sina proposed proved successful, so much so that the grateful emir rewarded him by giving him access to the royal library. This meticulously catalogued institution—called "The Storehouse of Wisdom" (Siwan al-Hikma)—was for Ibn Sina a kind of university. Whether by taking notes or by using his prodigious memory, the young doctor left the place with materials that would serve as the foundation for all his later medical studies.

During the same years, Biruni, too, was pursuing practical studies. Unlike Ibn Sina, he was uninterested in recording the details of his early years. But we have at least the outline of his activities, thanks to side comments that he sprinkled throughout his later writings. They reveal a young man deeply engaged with the concrete realities of the world around him and fascinated by everything.

As noted, Kath, where Biruni was born and where he lived until the capital of Khwarazm was moved from there to Gurganj, presented a heady environment of multiculturalism. Even if Biruni's stepfather, the princely mathematician Ibn Iraq, did not send him to learn the commercial arts, as did Ibn Sina's father, his charge had no lack of contact with traders and businessmen from many lands. What he learned from them went far beyond the realm of commerce. From a Byzantine trader in Kath, Biruni learned the Greek names of scores of plants, which he was to use in his last work, and also about Christianity and its holidays.[9] Others regaled him with stories of their homelands and their religions. Biruni's contacts with merchants and traders opened for him a window on the customs and beliefs of peoples throughout the known world. A quick study, the young man also picked up the rudiments of several foreign languages.

Ibn Iraq introduced his pupil to several skills that were deemed essential in Khwarazm. As a parched land rendered fertile and habitable only by irrigation, Khwarazm prioritized anything connected with water management. Biruni had to learn how to measure large tracts of land, calculate the volume of water covering entire fields, and gauge precisely the small differences in altitude that make irrigation possible. Coincidentally, the master of these arts and of the mathematics behind them had been born and raised in Khwarazm a century and a half before Biruni and was still revered there. Muḥammad al-Khwārazmī's, The Compendious Book on Calculation by Completion and Balancing, or simply Algebra, written about 830 AD, summarized and expanded the knowledge amassed by ancient Greeks on that field of mathematics. No armchair academic, Khwarazmi explained algebra in basic terms, using words rather than numerical equations. Moreover, he presented these techniques in terms of the problems of everyday life, including the division of real property among competing heirs and, significantly, irrigation. These and many other questions, as Khwarazmi showed, were best resolved by the use of simple algebra.

In light of Biruni's frequent later citations of Khwarazmi's work, it is worth pausing to appreciate Khwarazmi's achievement. The Scottish mathematicians J. J. O'Conner and E. F. Robertson wrote of his concise little volume that it represented a "revolutionary move away" from the Greek notion of mathematics, which was "essentially geometry." By offering a unifying theory that "allowed rational numbers, irrational numbers, geometrical magnitudes, etc., to all be treated as 'algebraic subjects,'" Khwarazmi's algebra "gave mathematics a whole new development path much broader in concept than that which had existed before, and provided a vehicle for future development of the subject."[10] This branch of mathematics took its name from the title of Khwarazmi's book, *Algebra*. Moreover, a Latinized version of al-Khwarazmi's own name gave us the term "algorithm," which figures so prominently in today's digital world. Beyond all this, Khwarazmi did pioneering work in trigonometry, astronomy, and geography—all subjects that were to remain at the center of Biruni's interests.

As with Ibn Sina, the final stages of Biruni's education, while grounded in practicality, in no way diminished his interest in the Great Questions. The same inquisitiveness that had led him to pore over Aristotle's writings now led him to the second-century thinker Claudius Ptolemy, who was the first to combine a systematic knowledge of astronomy and mathematics with the study of geography. Ptolemy's *Almagest* provided the starting point for Biruni's research on the heavens, just as Ptolemy's *Geography* was to provide the background against which Biruni did all his own innovative work in that field. No other scholar, ancient or contemporary, was to figure more prominently in Biruni's later life than Ptolemy.

Recognizing Biruni's interest, Ibn Iraq invited his young protégé to assist him in addressing an astronomical problem drawn directly from Ptolemy, namely, to determine what astronomers call "the obliquity of the ecliptic." The ecliptic is the path the sun follows through the sky, and its "obliquity" is the angle of that path in relation to the axis of the earth's rotation. Ibn Iraq followed many earlier researchers in trying to measure this. Biruni joined him in this enquiry, which was rendered ever more complicated when it was discovered that over the course of each century the angle was decreasing by

.013 degrees. The cause of this phenomenon had perplexed researchers for centuries.

Biruni's infatuation with mathematics and astronomy was no accident, for both disciplines had long been subjects of inquiry in Khwarazm and Central Asia. Centuries before Khwarizmi and Ibn Iraq, a pagan ruler had ornamented the halls of his palace at Toprak with a gracefully flowing design that a Russian archaeologist, M. A. Orlov, identified as precisely rendered logarithmic spirals. Closer in time to Biruni, the great city of Merv, in what is now Turkmenistan, boasted what was at the time the most renowned observatory in the world.[11] Another city near Merv, Mavrud, gave rise to a whole family of innovative astronomers. Ibn Iraq and Biruni were thus heirs to a living tradition. Ibn Iraq was one of the co-discoverers of the law that defines the relationship between the sides of a spherical triangle and the sines of the opposite angles. Even as a very young man Biruni was intensely engaged with this problem and prompted his teacher to write a treatise on it, now lost.

Both the request and the teacher's response prove how early Ibn Iraq came to recognize his student as his intellectual equal and, eventually, his collaborator in research. Biruni's research agenda over the next forty years was shaped significantly by problems to which his teacher first introduced him. I've noted Ibn Iraq's treatise on astrolabes, the brass instrument invented by the Greeks to measure the altitude above the horizon of stars and planets, solving a number of thorny problems in astronomy and navigation. Arabic scientists had already made it the most precise scientific instrument of the Middle Ages. Decades later, Biruni followed suit with his own treatise on astrolabes, in which he offered yet more improvements that enabled one to calculate both latitudes and time more precisely. Columbus navigated his way to the West Indies with the aid of an astrolabe that had been improved by Arab astronomers, as well as by Ibn Iraq, Biruni, and their successors.

Ibn Iraq was also responsible for nourishing Biruni's passion for geography. Ibn Iraq had been among the several Eastern scholars who followed Ptolemy in seeking to pinpoint the latitude and longitude of cities. The key to solving this challenge was to combine precise measures of time and distance. Ibn Iraq's research, which he shared with Biruni, focused on correcting what he politely termed "difficulties" in Ptolemy's *Geography*. What began as a kind of student project for Biruni became a fixation and remained among the main foci of his lifelong research. No single problem occupied him more consistently or more productively than the relationship of geographical space and time.

In this and other works Biruni followed his teacher in seeking to test propositions advanced by the ancient Greeks and, when necessary, to correct or even reject them. Ibn Sina did the same with Aristotle's writings on logic and other subjects. Indeed, this process of testing the ancients became for both a ruling and common passion to which they dedicated their otherwise very different careers. Both launched into this practice not to overthrow the ancient authorities, whom they both revered, but to refine the masters' work by offering more precise and accurate answers to the same questions. In the end, they succeeded in fundamentally recasting, if not replacing, the achievements of their ancient mentors and, by so doing, advancing new approaches to knowledge.

3

Promise and Disruption

Biruni and Ibn Sina completed their basic training and apprenticeships by the age of seventeen. They had shown exceptional talents but also benefited from a privileged upbringing amid conditions of utter security. Neither had had any need to find regular employment, and they were free to plunge into creative work, taking advantage of whatever possibilities were offered them. For both, this meant being open to wealthy individuals who would approach them with a question and offer generous rewards for the answer. They came to depend on individual patronage, though such commissions were invariably of short duration. When a patron's request meshed with their own interests, this was an ideal arrangement. However, both Biruni and Ibn Sina were soon to discover that a patron's interests rarely coincided with their own.

Ibn Sina undertook his first major project—a short treatise entitled *A Compendium of the Soul*—at his own initiative. But on the first page he placed a fulsome dedication to the emir of Bukhara, who had rewarded Ibn Sina by giving him access to the court library and from whom he evidently hoped to receive further support. The subject was to remain one of the thinker's major concerns.[1] His last work, written almost four decades later and entitled *On the Rational Soul*, focused on the same issue.

To modern ears, mention of the "soul" immediately suggests that the author's main concern must be narrowly theological. In the case of Ibn Sina, though, it would be more accurate to say that his early study dealt equally with the concerns of psychology and epistemology. Psychology, as philosopher Peter Adamson reminds us, derives from the Greek term for the soul—*psych*—and focuses on human consciousness at its most fundamental level. As to epistemology, that is the study that asks how and with what degree of certainty we know what we know, whether about the soul or anything else. Aristotle, Ibn Sina's ultimate master, had discussed them in his treatise *On the Soul*. Following his own teacher, Plato, Aristotle had distinguished between our physical bodies and our consciousness. He then considered this non-corporeal consciousness in animals as well as human beings and asked what specific role it performs for each species, including humans. The human intellect, Aristotle argued, arises from the nature of the soul. The soul is non-corporeal, yet it can act upon the physical self. This insight intrigued Ibn Sina, who switched the focus to two very different questions: first, if the soul is non-corporeal, where does it come from, and, second, can it survive the body's death?

Ibn Sina was among the first Muslim intellectuals to raise these fundamental questions. The answer he developed in this work and later studies plunged him deep into the question of defining God as the First Cause. This was to be one of several issues that Ibn Sina was to examine in great depth in later writings and which, through him, were to have a profound impact not only on later Muslim thinkers but also on Jewish and Christian savants.[2]

Ibn Sina's second effort was *The Compilation*, a comprehensive overview of philosophy commissioned by a Bukhara neighbor and literary scholar by the name of Arudi.[3] Only parts of this multi-volume text survive, but its headings included logic, physics, metaphysics, and theology, each of which Ibn Sina broke down into sub-fields. Curiously, the section on physics included a section on meteorology, but astronomy, mathematics, biology, geology, mineralogy, for example, found no place in the work. Perhaps this was because Arudi was uninterested in them. Ibn Sina himself declared that he wrote the piece "in the manner which Arudi requested." At the same time, the fact that he deviated so far from the complete Aristotelian program offers a foretaste of his own later intellectual priorities. Ibn Sina provided an overview of large parts of "philosophy" as it was understood at the time. Dimitri Gutas, evaluating *The Compilation* in the context of the later writings of Albertus Magnus, Thomas Aquinas, and their followers, concludes that it was "the first medieval philosophical summa, which can be said to have signaled the beginning of scholastic philosophy."[4] He might have added that this was the work of a teenager.

Ibn Sina's third and fourth projects were again commissioned by a neighbor, this time one Abu Bakr al-Baraki. Of this patron we know nothing, except that he sought the young man's comments on the main issues in philosophy and Quranic exegesis, and that he was also interested in practical ethics.[5] The result was a lengthy study of Aristotle's logic, in which Ibn Sina further plumbed issues of consciousness and the soul. He also turned out a separate essay entitled *Piety and Sin*. Both works are lost, but Ibn Sina himself wrote that they offered what he considered to be deep analysis "about divine punishments descending upon corrupt cities and tyrants and . . . how truth emerges victorious." Using what had by now become his customary logic, he demonstrated how such judgments "arose from the first principles which necessitated them, [and] which descend from God."[6]

Biruni meanwhile continued to explore astronomy, mathematics, and geography, to which Ibn Iraq had introduced him. None of Biruni's writing from this early period survive, if indeed he even set down his findings in complete form. In fact, it was not until the nineteenth century that anything was known about the start of Biruni's independent work as a scientist beyond his own passing reference to having damaged his eyesight while observing a solar eclipse. This note, written when Biruni was in his forties, enabled a Russian scholar to demonstrate that the young man had used a simple instrument of his own design that consisted of a ring and an alidade or pointer. Data from this instrument, along with the astronomical tables of the ninth-century astronomer Habash from the city of Merv, enabled Biruni to gauge the height of the sun at both the vernal and autumnal equinoxes.[7] Biruni was sixteen at the time. Using the same equipment, he employed an unusual method for estimating the obliquity of the ecliptic at the equator and arrived at results that closely approximate those achieved by the Canadian-American astronomer Simon Newcomb in the nineteenth century.[8]

By his early twenties Biruni was devising more complex and innovative astronomical instruments. One of these consisted of a large semi-circular structure with a diameter of 7.5 meters (25 feet), a gnomon, and a linear gauge for shadows. Another was inspired by Ptolemy, who wrote of having built a globe on which he placed all known locations according to their latitude and longitude. Biruni constructed his own globe,[9] with a diameter of 5 meters (16 and a half feet), the first of several he built, and began what became a lifelong effort to add new locations as he found them or learned of them from others. He was to receive little credit for this, however. Even today most histories give credit for the first globes not to Ptolemy or Biruni but to the fifteenth-century Nuremberg textile merchant and cartographer, Martin Behaim.[10]

In these early projects Biruni was trying to sort out the discrepancies he found between the geographical data collected by Ptolemy and those included in recent books by Central Asian mapmakers and geographers. Among the latter was the prodigiously talented Abu Zayd al-Balkhi from the Afghan city of Balkh, who issued the era's best maps. Biruni also examined the geographical findings of Balkhi's student, Abu Abdallah Jayhani, who, while serving as the Samanis' prime minister in Bukhara, managed also to write *A Book of Routes and Kingdoms*. Biruni came to the conclusion that all measurements taken on the ground were bound to be flawed and that the only way to achieve accuracy was by applying the techniques of astronomy and trigonometry, which are of course the foundations of today's Global Positioning Systems (GPS).

Biruni and Ibn Sina launched their careers under near-perfect conditions. They lived in wealthy and relatively peaceful cities that were open to the world. They enjoyed comfort, security, and the support of patrons, neighbors, and friends. Above all, they had access to translations of the most sophisticated body of philosophical and scientific writing ever produced, and to mentors who challenged them to grapple with that corpus. As a result, it was natural for them to seize upon whatever issues most challenged them intellectually and to pursue them in an atmosphere in which they were undistracted by extraneous concerns or dangers. They quickly assimilated what masters of their field had achieved in the past and began to push that legacy further, modifying and even challenging their preceptors as they did so. It was an idyllic moment for them both.

Yet it was clear by their early twenties that they had evolved in quite different directions. Two factors divided them from the outset. While Ibn Sina claimed later to have rejected the rationalistic and mystical teachings of the Ismaili missionaries whom his father brought into their home, he was nonetheless attracted to the questions they raised. His first two patrons shared his concern with the "eternal questions" of faith and reason, and his lesser interest also in mathematics and astronomy. Biruni had grown up under the intense influence of his guardian and mentor, Ibn Iraq. Of course, Ibn Iraq prescribed the customary training in religion and Aristotelian metaphysics and logic. However, he also initiated his young charge into his own specific passions, bringing him into the theoretical and practical work of his teacher, and in time making him his partner and co-researcher. This was to influence all Biruni's later development. It is no exaggeration to say that Biruni's later career was a continuation of Ibn Iraq's labors.

The comfort, security, and intellectual freedom that Ibn Sina and Biruni enjoyed during the first two decades of their lives soon ended abruptly. Except for brief periods of respite thereafter, they were to pass the next half century amid unceasing turmoil and strife, and this would have profound consequences.

4

Caught in the Whirlwind

For both Ibn Sina and Biruni, the turning point in their lives can be dated to the years 992–995, when they were in their early twenties. Radical change engulfed both their worlds. Chief among them was the collapse of the Samani family dynasty. They had been born under Samani rule—Ibn Sina at the Samanis' dynastic seat at Bukhara and Biruni at Kath, the capital of the semi-autonomous Samani province of Khwarazm—and shaped by Samani values.

Originally a Buddhist family from Afghanistan, the leaders of the Samani clan had crossed the Amudarya River into what is now Uzbekistan and formed a state at Bukhara in 819. By setting up an efficient tax system, one that could sustain an army and bureaucracy, the early Samani emirs created an umbrella of stability that they eventually extended over nearly all of Central Asia. This gave rise to a burgeoning economy based on mining, agriculture, manufacturing (mainly cotton cloth and metal goods), and international trade. To support such trade the Samanis erected large and comfortable caravanserais or hotels along all the main routes linking their lands to the larger world.

Meanwhile, the Muslim Caliphate in Baghdad had entered a long period of decline, opening space for Bukhara, which for a century became the preeminent center of culture at the heart of Eurasia. The Samani court attracted poets like Rudaki, who wrote in Persian and accompanied his sung recitals on the lute. Also in evidence were writers like Abu Nasr Narshakhi, a native of Bukhara who became its chief historian, and a whole cadre of astronomers from Merv and Mavrud. In the same years, diligent religious researchers from the Samani lands assembled five of the six most authoritative collections of Muhammad's hadith.

The Samani state's bulwark against its enemies, both foreign and domestic, was the army. Comprised mainly of battle-toughened Turkic slaves who were recruited from the nomads in the countryside, the army was also the Samanis' chief point of vulnerability. These enslaved soldiers had little in common with their overlords in Bukhara, not in ethnicity, language, culture, or, in the early years, religion. To assure the loyalty of so large and alien a force, the viziers in Bukhara made a point of promoting the most reliable of their Turkic slaves to the rank of general. However, this alone did not assure their loyalty. Bukhara was therefore forced to make huge payments to the Turkic generals. This practice swelled the cost of the military to the point that it exceeded every other item in the Samani budget. When even money did not suffice, the Samanis adopted the risky practice of granting their Turkic generals extensive territories as fiefdoms. This system worked surprisingly well for several generations, but by the late tenth century it came under withering attack from three separate but interrelated forces.

The first was entirely predictable. The Samanis' initial successes owed much to their style of governing: they centralized only the collection of taxes and otherwise had left local lords in charge of their territories. But the same centrifugal forces that had caused the Samanis to distance themselves from Baghdad now caused leaders of the local landowning classes (*dihqans*) to assert their independence from Bukhara. This decentralizing trend arose especially in Khwarazm and in Khorasan, the large regions on the borderland between what is now Afghanistan, Iran, and Turkmenistan.

The second force was a newly emerging grouping of Turkic tribes in what is now Kyrgyzstan and western Xinjiang in China. A dynamic leader, Ilek Khan, forged these disparate tribes into an effective confederation. Quite separate from the nomads who staffed the Samanis' army, the Karakhanids, as they are called, adopted Islam and came to admire what they considered the Samanis' worldly and modern lifestyle. But they were also intent on conquering Bukhara and other Samani-ruled regions, including Khwarazm and Khorasan. To resist the Karakhanid army, the Samani emirs greatly expanded their own Turkic forces and imposed onerous new taxes to pay these added hirelings. This in turn stiffened the resistance of Samani landowners everywhere, including those in Biruni's homeland of Khwarazm and its capital, Kath.

Keenly aware of these developments, the Samanis' neighbors to the west, in what is now Iran, set out to attract the leaders of Bukhara's wayward territories to their own camp, creating the third force. The Buyids, as they are known, patronized a rich cultural life in their main cities and up to this point had maintained cordial relations with Bukhara. This arrangement had thrived even though the Buyids were Shiia Muslims and the Samanis were Sunni. However, when the Buyids began exerting pressure on Bukhara, Samani landowners in Khwarazm and Khorasan began flirting with them in order to exert leverage against Bukhara's high tax policies. Either lower our taxes, they warned, or we will shift our loyalties to the Buyids.

Together, the confluence of these three forces created a spirit of secessionism across the Samanis' lands. Strong leadership might have enabled them to weather these centrifugal forces, but the last three Samani rulers in Bukhara (including Ibn Sina's patron, the emir Abu Muhammad Nuh) vacillated between inaction and risky adventurism. In a panic, they granted near-unlimited power to one of their youngest Turkic generals, the ambitious but only marginally loyal Sebuktegin. To sweeten the deal, they also made him overlord of the province of Ghazni in Afghanistan. The rise of the Karakhanids, the secessionist movements in Khwarazm and Khorosan, and pressure from the Buyids led directly to the collapse of the Samani state. It also wrought crises in the lives of Biruni and Ibn Sina. For Biruni, who until now had largely ignored geopolitics, the crisis was unexpected, sudden, and crushing. As he later recalled, "Disaster took me by surprise, erasing all that I had known and all the fruits of my endeavors."[1]

The immediate cause of this downturn in his life were two ill-advised acts by the rulers of Khwarazm. First, the reigning shah of Khwarazm in Kath, Ibn Iraq's brother, took advantage of the confusion in Bukhara to declare his independence from Samani control. Immediately thereafter, Mamun ibn Muhammad, the local emir in the nearby city of Gurganj and a Samani loyalist, mounted a counterattack against the rebellious dynasty in Kath. In 994 the combined force of Sebuktegin's nominally loyal Turks and Mamun ibn Muhammad's troops from Gurganj destroyed the Iraq dynasty's army at Kath. The rebels were marched off to the Samani emir Nuh II, who blinded and then executed them. Other members of the Ibn Iraq dynasty and those who supported them, including Biruni's mentor and colleague, Abu Nasr Mansur ibn Iraq, and Biruni himself, were branded as rebels and outcasts. The capital of Khwarazm now moved officially from Kath to Gurganj.

With nothing but the clothes on his back, Biruni fled into the desert south of Kath and then westward all the way to the city of Rayy, the seat of the Shiite Buyids. Arriving penniless and without friends, he was fortunate to be given lodging by a kindly merchant. Biruni's only known contacts in Rayy were two brothers who traded in rare jewels and metals at the local market, a far cry from the privileged circles in which Biruni had moved in Kath. At one point Biruni even had to endure the insults of "a well-to-do ignoramus," whose sole claim to authority was that he was rich. With no alternative, Biruni was to spend the next two years in Rayy. He had left behind his globe, his astronomical and geodesic instruments, and all of his books, which were destroyed during the rebellion.

What remains of medieval Rayy has today been absorbed into the burgeoning Twentieth District of the capital of modern Iran, Tehran. By the time of Biruni's arrival, Rayy, a 6,000-year-old trading center, had become a leading entrepot on the routes from the Middle East to Central Asia and India. Ruled by a wealthy branch of the Shiite Buyids, Rayy boasted rich libraries, was the seat of a major Syrian Christian bishopric, and was the headquarters of what remained of the Zoroastrians. It had also been the birthplace of the renowned if controversial Persian medical pioneer, Abu Bakr al-Razi. The memory of Razi's achievements and also of his subversive philosophical ideas was very much alive in Rayy when Biruni arrived there in 994. More recently, the ruler at Rayy, Fahr ad-Daula, had attracted to his court the great Central Asian mathematician and astronomer Abu Mahmud Khujandi from Khojent, in what today is Tajikistan. Khujandi had achieved distinction in trigonometry by demonstrating how the law of sines could be applied to spherical triangles. He was also a pioneer in trying to explain the impossibility of solving certain equations in rational numbers. This problem, identified first by Pythagoras and known since the seventeenth century as "Fermat's Theorem," was definitively solved only in 1994 by the English mathematician Andrew Wiles. When Biruni arrived in Rayy, Khujandi was applying his expertise in mathematics and trigonometry to astronomy.

It was a coup for the emir to have attracted Khujandi to Rayy. To honor his renowned guest, Fahr ad-Daula funded the construction of an observatory, where Khujandi carried out the studies that were to be the capstone of his career. Prior to Khujandi, astronomical calculations had been based on direct observations—a dangerous practice when they involved the sun. Khujandi's observatory consisted of an enormous and fixed mural sextant covered by a cupola. Light penetrated through a small hole, or diopter, to a darkened chamber, where there was an equally large but movable alidade or pointer. Used carefully, this system made possible precise measurements of the angles of heavenly bodies, including the sun.

Khujandi's goal was to pin down the earth's axial tilt, in other words, to solve the problem of determining the same "obliquity of the ecliptic" that had interested Biruni. Khujandi knew that Ptolemy had concluded that it was 23 degrees and 52 seconds and that Indian astronomers had found it to be 24 degrees. Khujandi bested Ptolemy by calculating the tilt to be 23 degrees, 32 minutes, and 19 seconds. Another of his innovations was his discovery that the obliquity of the ecliptic was changing through time. Khujandi also realized that his own measurement of this shift was off by two seconds. Given that he had proudly drafted a treatise on his grand new observatory, proclaiming, "I invented it!" this was more than embarrassing.[2] The question was what to do. How had this error occurred and how could it be corrected?

Biruni, who had arrived in Rayy penniless and lacking letters of introduction, had somehow managed to win Khujandi's confidence. Some early writers claimed that Biruni did this by pointing out to Khujandi that the error in his measurement of the obliquity of the ecliptic had been caused by the settling of one of the massive walls of his instrument. Biruni himself denied having made this discovery.[3] He did, however, compose a meticulous study of this innovative instrument, a work that gained wide repute and eventually became the basis for the design of the three greatest observatories of the Muslim world: his own in Ghazni, Tusi's in Maragha, and Ulugbeg's in Samarkand.[4] In the end, Khujandi, the world's leading astronomer and mathematician, treated Biruni as an equal. His influence on the young scientist was to equal that of Biruni's first mentor, Ibn Iraq.

Biruni's interests in Rayy were not limited to mathematics and astronomy. He was befriended by some jewelers, and this inspired him to begin studying minerals, an interest that would eventually result in his inventing the concept of specific gravity. He also found time to begin compiling a catalogue of Razi's writings on mathematics, philosophy, astronomy, and religion, as well as medicine. Many years later Biruni would return to the study of this immensely talented but controversial figure.

Biruni's productive days in Rayy were not to last. Even at the time of his arrival the situation there was descending into chaos. The ruler, whose Persian name was Abulhasan Ali ibn Hasan but who had early been awarded the pompous Arabic title "Pride of the Dynasty" (Fahr al-Dawla), spent most of his adult life fighting his brothers over their inheritance. When two of his brothers died in 983–984, he had claimed their lands and granted to himself the further honorific title "King of Kings" (Shahanshah). A decade later, just as Biruni was fleeing Kath, Fahr al-Dawla foolishly tried to seize one of the Samanis' richest regions for himself. When his forces were decisively repulsed, unrest broke out back in Rayy. Then Fahr al-Dawla's highly competent vizier died, as did Fahr himself, in 997. At this point Mamun Ibn Muhammad destroyed the Ibn Iraq dynasty and prepared to move the capital from Kath to Khwarazm, his own city. As noted, he brought glory to himself by forgiving Ibn Iraq for the sin of being related to the fallen shah and invited him to his court. By 997 Biruni had moved back to his hometown.

Ibn Sina had for a time managed to avoid poverty and the loss of his books and equipment. But then fate turned against him, too. This upheaval began in the spring of 992, when the army of the Karakhanid leader Bughra Khan was poised to attack Bukhara. The Samani emir tried desperately to mount a defense by cutting a deal with one of his Turkic generals, Faikh, an enslaved man who had himself been in rebellion only months before. But Faikh failed and was captured. The emir himself barely escaped from Bukhara before Bughra Khan's army took the city.

Within months, the leader of the Karakhanid army of occupation fell gravely ill. Before abandoning Bukhara, he named an undistinguished uncle of the last Samani emir as his puppet ruler. At this, the Turkic general Faikh again mounted a rebellion. But the old emir managed to return to his capital and promptly turned over the defense of his failed realm to his seemingly more loyal Turkic general, Sebuktegin, and his son, Mahmud. With no money to pay them, the emir gave Sebuktegin a fancy title and handed control over Bukhara's richest province, Khorasan, to Mahmud. With these moves, this Turkic clan of the former enslaved now had the weakened Samani government by the throat. Meanwhile, Faikh managed to free himself and raise yet another army. Mahmud beat him back in Khorosan, but Faikh quickly recovered, scored a victory against Mahmud's army, and then moved north to stir up the trouble that ended with the fall of the Ibn Iraq dynasty in Khwarazm.

These are the chaotic developments that shaped Ibn Sina's world between the time he first emerged as a medical practitioner and his departure from Bukhara in 1004. Amid this constant turmoil he somehow managed to practice medicine, teach a few students, and even write his first philosophical works.

Further complicating Ibn Sina's life at this time was the death of his father. Though his father doubtless left an inheritance, Ibn Sina did not have enough to live on, especially during the economic collapse caused by the travails of the Samani state. Nor was his medical practice at all lucrative. Although he took on a few advanced students who paid him for his instruction, that activity, too, failed to meet his needs. He therefore took a bureaucratic post in what was left of the Samanis' financial administration and continued in that capacity until the dynasty's final collapse.

The impact of this first period of turmoil on the lives of Ibn Sina and Biruni was to confirm rather than undermine their commitment to the studies they had developed in their earlier youth. For Biruni this meant a focus above all on mathematics and astronomy and their practical application. For Ibn Sina it meant medicine and "thinking about thinking," that is, the rational processes by which we can gain certain knowledge of everything from nature to God. In short, neither abandoned those interests in the face of adversity. Ibn Sina's office job did not prevent him from continuing his medical studies and even allowed time for him to write his first philosophical treatises. Biruni resigned himself to living as a pauper in order to work under the tutelage of the great mathematician and astronomer Khujandi. Thanks to their persistence, both gained recognition and admiration among an ever-widening circle of the intellectual cognoscenti of Central Asia and the Muslim East.

5

Arguing Aristotle

It was inevitable that Biruni and Ibn Sina would eventually come to each other's attention. As I noted earlier, we don't know precisely how this happened. Copies of some of Ibn Sina's four treatises and compendia may have found their way to Biruni in Rayy or Kath, while word of Biruni's work with Ibn Iraq and Khujandi may also have reached the cultural elite of Bukhara and hence Ibn Sina. Under any circumstances, they would surely have met before long. But rather than wait for that moment, Biruni took it upon himself to write a long letter directly to Ibn Sina.

Specialists have long argued over the year in which Biruni initiated the ensuing correspondence, with claims extending from 997 to 1010.[1] But thanks to the diligence of the Soviet historian of science, P. G. Bulgakov, we can be certain that Biruni sent off his first letter from his home in Kath in the winter of 997–998. This led to a correspondence that extended over half a year. Such an exchange of letters was possible because the Samanis' mail system, renowned in its day, managed to continue functioning during this final period of dynastic decline. The Biruni–Ibn Sina correspondence originally consisted of at least three long letters from each side. Unfortunately, the only surviving text of the exchange is an incomplete manuscript copy of a copy, comprising thirty-five pages of modern print and probably less than half of the original text. It was compiled by students of Ibn Sina, who quote Ibn Sina's words verbatim but present Biruni's questions and responses only in their own paraphrased form. The potential for distortion is obvious.

Biruni launched the exchange with a barrage of ten pointed questions. All concerned the interpretation of Aristotle's most significant astronomical work, *On the Heavens*. Biruni's opening gambit was to ask Ibn Sina why Aristotle denied the existence of gravity and of vacuums in space. Where Aristotle claimed that every heavenly body and force has its natural place, Biruni asserted his own view that gravity works everywhere, pulling everything toward the center of the earth unless a countervailing force prevented it from doing so. Biruni framed the question in terms of Aristotle's own distinction between heavy and light bodies, which the Greek philosopher had drawn in order to deny the existence of absolute weight. Either way, Biruni argued, there had to be gravity and also an extraterrestrial vacuum. If there was no gravity, why did the heavens appear to be moving westward and in a circular motion?[2]

In his response, Ibn Sina employed his fundamental tool for establishing truth: the syllogism. Every astronomical body has a natural position, he asserted, following Aristotle.[3] The fixed stars are such bodies. Ergo the fixed stars have a natural position. Further, they cannot be either light or heavy, for if they were light, they would be drawn upward and if they were heavy they would be drawn downward. Ibn Sina then sought to reinforce his argument by distinguishing between "actuality" and "potentiality" and then applying that distinction to astronomy. He drew this arcane distinction from Aristotle but strained to apply it to the issue at hand. Biruni curtly dismissed Ibn Sina's response as "arguing for the sake of arguing." Ibn Sina was also bothered by Biruni's claim that the stars and planets appear to be moving in opposite directions. This clearly violated Aristotle's principle, which Ibn Sina supported, that all movement in the heavens had to be strictly circular.

On this point, as for all his other responses to Biruni, Ibn Sina followed Aristotle and relied on logic rather than observation. Along the way he also belittled Biruni for challenging the authority of "The First Teacher." By contrast, the questions raised by Biruni arose mainly from observation, as did his answers. This same juxtaposition emerged from the second question, in which Biruni asked Ibn Sina to explain Aristotle's stress on the immutability of the heavens and earth. Challenging this view, Biruni pointed to the obvious geological changes that have occurred "in increments or all at once."[4] In his response, Ibn Sina agreed on the reality of geological change through time, but strictly differentiated between the earth's mutability and the immutability of the heavens.

Having found some common ground with his inquisitor from Khwarazm, Ibn Sina then pivoted and asked Biruni if he really believed that the universe had always existed, in which case there would have been no Creation and no need for a Creator. Then, assuming on the basis of no evidence that this was indeed Biruni's view, Ibn Sina accused him of having drawn his questions from the works of the religious skeptic Razi. In a gratuitous slap at that thinker, Ibn Sina declared that Razi "meddle[d] in metaphysics, exceeded his competence," and "should have stuck with setting bones and taking urine and stool samples."[5]

Biruni's further questions reveal his doubts about both Aristotle and Aristotle's critics. Thus, he simultaneously accepted Aristotle's atomism and rejected Ibn Sina's objection to that doctrine, which was based on the idea that matter cannot be infinitely divisible. Aristotle's own argument in behalf of atomism struck Biruni as weak. Weaker yet were "the words of those who raise objections to the atomists," which Biruni judged to be "even less acceptable." By this he meant Ibn Sina's argument that atomism was impossible because "anything that occupies space can be divided by virtue of the fact that space has a beginning, middle and end and can itself be divided."[6] Surprised at finding an issue on which their positions on Aristotle were reversed, Biruni asked Ibn Sina how they could resolve the standoff between the atomists and their critics. Ibn Sina, finding himself for once on the side of Aristotle's critics, tried to save his ancient master by invoking, once again, the Aristotelian distinction between what is potentially so and what is actually so. This implied that while atomism was theoretically possible, it was impossible in reality. This struck Biruni as splitting hairs.[7]

Biruni next asked why Aristotle had opposed the possible existence of other worlds, where different laws of nature might prevail. Ibn Sina defended Aristotle but then proceeded to propose that if such other worlds were separated from ours by some kind of barrier, nature there could respond to different laws. But humans are incapable of grasping this and must therefore assume, with Aristotle, that the same laws of nature prevail everywhere. To this Biruni responded with an obvious sophistry, namely, that the forces operating in another universe might be the same as in our world but opposite. Ibn Sina ridiculed this proposition.[8]

Continuing to focus on astronomy, his specialty, Biruni next questioned Aristotle's claim that the economy of space required that the shape of the universe must be spherical and not elliptical or "lenticular," that is, shaped like a lentil bean. In his typical style of argumentation, Biruni asserted that the evidence—by which he meant mathematics—lent equal support to the hypothesis that the movement of the heavens followed an elliptical or oval pattern. In doing so he anticipated by some 600 years Johannes Kepler's revolutionary view on the elliptical shape of the orbit of Mars.

Once more Ibn Sina accepted Biruni's questioning of Aristotle but objected to his assertion that either possibility would require a vacuum in space. He challenged Biruni to produce mathematical support for his view on the existence of such a vacuum. In the same vein, he defended Aristotle's assertion that the planets moved from east to west and also Aristotle's claim that the movement of the planets should generate heat. On the latter point he invoked the authority of a phalanx of ancient thinkers whose works Ibn Sina had studied, including Heraclitus, Thales, Diogenes, and Anaximander.

By this point Ibn Sina was responding to Biruni's objections regarding Aristotle the way a professor might treat a wearisome student. His frustration and mounting anger are quite understandable. The way Biruni raised and framed the questions had thrown Ibn Sina onto the defensive. Biruni's relentless questioning of Aristotle threatened to knock the props that held up Ibn Sina's worldview. Notwithstanding their several points of agreement, Biruni remained on the attack with further questions regarding the nature of heat, how heat reaches us from the sun when we know that heat rises, and the transformation of water into air through boiling. While Biruni clearly considered these to be open questions, his challenging tone assured that Ibn Sina would reply defensively.

In every instance, Ibn Sina based his response on precise definitions and distinctions based on Aristotelian logic and natural philosophy. Thus, when Biruni asked if boiling water in fact becomes air or whether its particles simply dispersed and became invisible, Ibn Sina responded with yet another paraphrase of Aristotle: "The transformation of elements into one another does not occur the way you mentioned. . . . Rather, the water particles take off their water image and put on an airy image."[9]

However tilted he might have been toward Ibn Sina's perspective, whoever prepared the manuscript of these exchanges did posterity a service by preserving not just the initial exchange but some of Biruni's responses to Ibn Sina's explanations. They were not gentle, nor were Ibn Sina's rejoinders.[10] In responding to Biruni's second question, Ibn Sina had alluded to the fifth-century thinker John of Philoponus (also known as "John the Grammarian") as "mischievous" for having broken with several of Aristotle's doctrines. Biruni denied that Philoponus was "mischievous" and pointedly called out Ibn Sina for not having read several major works by John of Philoponus that were available in Arabic. Counterpunching, Biruni then charged that it was Aristotle himself who deserved that epithet, for he was "the embellisher of his own infidelity." Having argued that the universe was eternal, Aristotle then evaded the question of whether it had a maker, that is, God. "Surely," Biruni wrote, "if actions have no beginning, it is impossible to imagine that the universe has a creator." Biruni, in other words, responded to Ibn Sina's defense of Aristotle by hurling the charge that The Philosopher and his champion, Ibn Sina, both denied the existence of God.[11]

Biruni then asked about the "self-sufficiency" of the world once it had been created. The question anticipated Newton's famous quip about God as a clockmaker, who wound his creation and then let it run on its own. Ibn Sina's arch reply was that if color and light can exist together, so can God and the earth. To imply otherwise, he warned, was to limit the sphere of divine action. Biruni appears closer to Newton at this point. Much later he was to defend the view that God continues to be engaged with His creation.

Biruni's response to Ibn Sina's objection regarding the movement of stars and planets in different directions seems particularly significant. The issue arose from the geocentric view of the universe, though of course neither disputant realized this. Instead of addressing the issue, Biruni quickly descended to ridicule. Ibn Sina had spoken of a natural movement in nature from right to left and supported this claim by citing evidence from the world of animals. Biruni retorted that this was nonsense and asked if he himself was not an animal. In the same mean spirit he again attacked Ibn Sina's equivocation on the existence of other worlds different from our own. Whoever doubts that, he argued, "is declaring that the Creator is unable to create universes beyond this one."[12] By this point Biruni was clearly furious yet remained coldly cogent. He tossed aside Ibn Sina's claims on the east-to-west movement of stars and planets with the quip that "the east of each position is simultaneously the west of another." Much later this deceptively simple one-liner was to have profound implications when Biruni argued the case for the relativity of all motion, including the movement of the earth and the sun.

I'll pause in this review of the exchange and note its increasingly hostile tone. Since only Ibn Sina's version of events is preserved, however, this calls for caution. It appears that Biruni sent his first set of questions not as a challenge but in the sincere hope of getting solid answers from an acknowledged authority on Aristotle in Bukhara. By the same token, the tone of Ibn Sina's initial replies, while offered with unfeigned hauteur, indicates that he was responding in a similarly serious vein.

Nonetheless, an increasingly challenging tone crept into Biruni's later questions, at least in the form they were reported by Ibn Sina's scribe. Thus, at one point he charged that Ibn Sina was toying with words rather than realities, and he defended his own views by saying they would be obvious "to anyone who is not stubborn and doesn't insist on falsehood."[13] And as the correspondence progressed, Ibn Sina, too, descended from a cool and scholarly mode to condescension and then outright hostility. Ibn Sina's assistant, speaking on his master's behalf, at one point accused Biruni of being "a man of poor logic who calls quantities qualities,"[14] and castigating him for "belittling someone just because he said something that is beyond your grasp."

Biruni then sent Ibn Sina eight further questions, all of them pertaining directly or indirectly to Aristotle. The opening lines of Ibn Sina's first set of responses indicate that he had dictated them to a student or assistant, who then wrote them down and sent them to Biruni in Khwarazm. In other words, Ibn Sina had ducked out of the picture, assigning the drafting of further responses to his knowledgeable and sharp-tongued student and assistant, Abu Said Ahmad al-Masumi.[15]

The first of Biruni's further questions related to the category of physics as defined in Aristotle's book by that name. Thus, he asked why a spherical glass vessel acts as a magnifying or burning glass when filled with water but does not do so when emptied. He then asked if gravity affects air and fire the same way as it affects earth and water, or if air and fire in fact oppose gravity. Next, he asked how our eyes can see beneath the surface of water when they view it from above but that the same water becomes opaque when viewed from certain angles. Yet another question challenged Aristotle's view that vacuums do not exist in nature by pointing out that a vacuum can easily be created by placing an inverted warm glass in water, which causes the water to rise within it as it cools. In a single stroke, Biruni cast doubt on one of the keystones of Aristotle's understanding of nature. And then, in a related question, Biruni asked why, if substances contract when cooled, does a bottle break when the water inside it freezes?

Then Biruni turned to Aristotle's geography. Why, he asked, does Aristotle claim that half of the northern hemisphere and all of the southern hemisphere are uninhabited when he admits that conditions in all those quarters were similar? Should not the other half of the southern hemisphere also be inhabitable? Much later, Biruni was to pursue this line of thought to its logical conclusion and, in the process, rewrite our understanding of the globe.

In his detailed responses to these questions, Masumi, on Ibn Sina's (and Aristotle's) behalf, emphatically defended the orthodox views of Aristotle's early Greek followers, who are called the Peripatetics on account of their habit of discussing issues while strolling in the Lyceum at Athens. He also reverted to quoting Aristotle's own words as defense against Biruni's criticism. On only one question—concerning the atomists and their critics—did Biruni and Ibn Sina emerge on the same side.

What permeates this remarkable exchange is the relationship of both young scholars to Aristotle. Ibn Sina presented himself as an ardent student of the Greek thinker, someone who had not only absorbed Aristotle's research on scores of subjects but assimilated Aristotle's method. Over his lifetime Ibn Sina's views on Aristotle were to evolve considerably. Later, he would see The First Teacher as a pioneer whose work, though replete with gaps and problems, nonetheless provided the solid foundation upon which he, Ibn Sina, could erect a new and even more comprehensive structure of knowledge and thereby become the "new Aristotle." And though Biruni presented himself as a critic not only of Aristotle's conclusions but of the method by which he reached them, he would continue to acknowledge his debt to Aristotle and argue that anyone serious about inquiry should study the works of that master. But on the pages of his exchange with Ibn Sina, Biruni emerged, while still in his early twenties, as the most acute critic of Aristotle until the Scientific Revolution, a true harbinger of modernity.[16]

As to Biruni's evident animosity toward Ibn Sina, this stemmed in part from the dependence of the Ibn Sina style of argument on logical consistencies and on the assumed authority of earlier writers rather than on mathematics and his own observations. So broad was the gulf between the two men that neither bothered thereafter to comment further on the other's work. A rare exception occurred several years after the exchange of letters when, in a book on the astronomical basis of geography, Biruni castigated Ibn Sina for being "not reliable" due to his insufficient command of mathematics and his reliance on the testimony of others. In a snide aside he added, "I suppose, if objections were raised against his [own] method, he would put the blame for it on others."[17]

The Biruni–Ibn Sina correspondence did not come to light until 1920, when a single copy was discovered in an archive in Cairo. Over the succeeding decades specialists translated the text into half a dozen languages—with varying degrees of accuracy. Only gradually did it become apparent that the thousand-year-old exchange of questions, answers, and challenges between these two young Central Asians represented a landmark in the history of thought. Seyyed Hossein Nasr, a historian of the science of philosophy, praised it as "an encounter which in its rigour and the significance of the questions involved marks one of the highlights of Islamic intellectual history and, in fact, of medieval natural philosophy and science in general."[18]

At a more personal level, the duel of wits between Biruni and Ibn Sina, for all its occasionally petulant and even puerile tone, brought to light the breadth of the intellectual gulf that separated them. Both seem to have concluded that the divide was unbridgeable. This, even more than the natural competition between two talented, headstrong young male contemporaries, accounts for their mutual distancing during the seven years they spent together in Gurganj. Neither then nor at any later point in their long lives did either make the slightest further effort to find common ground with the other. The silence is resounding.

6

Inventing a World History

In the six years between their correspondence in 998 and their first face-to-face meeting in 1004 or early in 1005, Ibn Sina and Biruni were deeply affected by the geopolitical conflicts generated by the collapse of the Samanis' power across Central Asia. Yet their fates, as I've noted, were sharply different, with Biruni courted by several of the region's post-Samani autocrats and Ibn Sina still struggling in an office job and trying to continue his studies. Only at the time they came together in Gurganj did Ibn Sina attain a modicum of security, and even then only briefly.

At the time of the exchange of letters, the Samani rulers seemed briefly to have emerged from the paralysis caused by their defeat at the hands of the Karakhanid army. The indecisive emir Nuh II died in 997. He was immediately replaced by his relative, Ismail bin Nuh al Muntasir, who, against all odds, aspired to reverse a century of decay and restore the Samani state. It was thanks to him that Ibn Sina found a job in the emir's financial office. The post could not have been very taxing, for he was able also to gather around himself a coterie of advanced students of philosophy and to continue his medical research and practice.

Summarizing Ibn Sina's last years in Bukhara, it is clear that they were a time of preparation, not fulfillment. He worked to refine and sharpen the approach that he had laid out in his four earlier treatises. At the same time, he deepened his thinking about medicine by extending Aristotelian categories and processes to cover the entire field. Finally, through his combative exchange of letters with Biruni, he realized that it was not enough simply to declare what he was for and leave matters there. Instead, he had to counter criticism on specific points with a more capacious structure of knowledge that would shield him from his critics' objections by relativizing them within a broader schema of his own devising.

This was Ibn Sina's frame of mind in 1004, the year he received the news that the promising young emir of Bukhara had been killed.[1] This marked the final end of the Samani dynasty and of Bukhara as the jewel of intellectual life in Central Asia and the Muslim world. With this death, the Samani bureaucracy also collapsed, and with it the job in the finance department that had briefly sustained Ibn Sina.[2] Fortunately, two of his friends from Bukhara had already relocated to the rising center that was Gurganj. They prevailed on the vizier, Suhayli, to find a paying position for Ibn Sina in the government he had formed there. Suhayli offered Ibn Sina a post in the legal department. In light of the fact that Ibn Sina had spent a year or so studying law, this was perhaps less of a sinecure than it may appear. And so the young scholar traveled to Gurganj and presented himself to the vizier and to the new shah of Khwarazm.[3] As Ibn Sina recalled in his *Autobiography*, he showed up in "lawyer's garb, wearing the profession's *taylasan* scarf turned under the chin." With unfeigned smugness he noted also that "they fixed for me a monthly salary that was enough for someone like me."[4]

During this period Biruni was back in Gurganj and working productively. The new shah had assembled a functioning government and was in the process of moving his capital to Gurganj. However, with the shah's new palace, public buildings, and even a tall "victory minaret" all under construction simultaneously, the place had become more a building site than a habitable city. Since Ibn Iraq had not yet relocated to Gurganj, Biruni returned to Kath, where he linked up again with his old mentor, and the two of them relaunched their joint projects.

At the top of their list was a scheme to employ astronomy and trigonometry to measure precisely the distance between Kath and Baghdad. This idea had been launched by a distinguished friend of Ibn Iraq's in Baghdad who bore the resonant name Muḥammad ibn Muḥammad ibn Yaḥyā ibn Ismāʿīl ibn al-ʿAbbās Abū al-Wafāʾ al-Būzjānī. Buzjani, as he is known, had focused his career on the same problems in astronomy, mathematics, and geography that occupied Ibn Iraq, and hence Biruni himself. Now in old age, Buzjani was glad to collaborate with his old friend and his brilliant young protégé on a project that was dear to all three of them. While the calculation of latitude is relatively simple, no one had yet come up with a precise means of measuring longitude. A number of methods had been applied to this classic problem, including taking measurements on the ground and combining them with complex mathematical calculations. The Buzjani team's contribution was to transform this very terrestrial issue into an astronomical problem and then to rework the astronomical evidence with the tools of trigonometry. Specifically, this called for measuring precisely the time of a lunar eclipse as observed simultaneously in two cities, fixing that moment in terms of stellar time, and then using spherical trigonometry to determine the distance between the two points. No one had ever before produced so precise a measure of longitudinal distance.

Even as this project proceeded, all was not well in Khwarazm. The fall of the Ibn Iraq dynasty had left the region as a protectorate of the Karakhanid Turks, who alone had the power to keep at bay the avaricious young Mahmud of Ghazni. For all the glitter of new construction in Mamun's new capital, Khwarazm's sovereignty remained vulnerable and life there uncertain. Moreover, Biruni still lacked the scientific equipment he needed for his own research as it had all been destroyed during the earlier fighting in Kath. These considerations, along with a flattering offer from the sovereign of the territory of a kingdom on the Caspian Sea, caused Biruni to decamp for the city of Gorgan. The region, located along the Caspian's southeast shore, was another of those many nodes of continental transport during the caravan era.

Earlier, Gorgan had ruled much of what is now southern and eastern Iran. But in the tenth century it had the misfortune of being caught between two empires, the Sunni Samanis in Bukhara and the Shiia Buyids in Rayy. When internecine war broke out among members of the Buyids' royal family at Rayy, the emir of Gorgan, Abol-Hasan Qābūs ibn Wušmagīr, known as Qabus, unwisely provided a safe haven for one of the contending brothers, Fahr al-Daula. This was the same man who sat on the throne at Rayy when Biruni was there and who was Rayy's last great patron of learning. This untimely move turned Gorgan into a hotbed of anti-Samani activity and posed a direct challenge to the Samani general Sebuktegin and his Turkic troops. Qabus fled and was not able to fight his way back to his capital until after the death of Fahr al-Daula. He and his army finally reentered Gorgan in August 998 and would rule for the next eighteen years. Biruni was to remain there for five years, a period that was to prove extremely productive for him.

Qabus was a formidable figure in the arts and sciences. He immediately began assembling at Gorgan a coterie of talented poets, admonishing them not to turn out the mindless praise of his person that was the norm for court poets elsewhere. Qabus was himself a talented poet, and his letters were long held up as models of classical Arabic prose. And while none of his many civic buildings survive, the 61-meter (200-foot) tall tomb he built for himself is today considered a treasure of Central Asian and Persian architecture and was declared a UNESCO World Heritage Site. Qabus induced Biruni to relocate to Gorgan late in 998 or early in 999.[5]

In most respects Biruni's situation at Gorgan, where he stayed until 1004, was ideal. He turned down Qabus's proposal that he work exclusively under the emir. Yet Qabus nonetheless supported him and granted him the right to seek the assistance of anyone in his realm. A number of wealthy patrons also offered support. And all the while Biruni was corresponding with his two close friends in Gurganj: his mentor Ibn Iraq and the Christian medical expert and scientist Masihi, who was himself from Gorgan. Their closeness is shown by the fact that both Ibn Iraq and Masihi dedicated numerous treatises to their friend and sent them to Biruni at Gorgan.

Research by the Soviet historian P. G. Bulgakov turned up no fewer than fifteen works written by Biruni during his stay in Gorgan.[6] While many of these were article-length studies on diverse topics, at least two were book-length volumes. Unfortunately, only three have as yet turned up in the world's archives. One of the lost texts, entitled *Keys to Astronomy*, was apparently an exhaustive review of all astronomical knowledge to date, along with a discussion of the theory of heliocentrism.[7] It must have been an immense work, for Biruni later reported that the appendix alone stretched over the equivalent of three hundred pages. A shorter piece summarized Biruni's findings on the shifting of the ecliptic over the centuries while another dealt with the problem of contradictory evidence in astronomy.

One of the surviving texts is a kind of encyclopedia of the astrolabe—as noted, the essential instrument for astronomy, mapmaking, practical navigation, and the precise determination of both time and dates for religious festivals. Knowledge of astrolabes had passed from the ancient Greek world to Rome, and then, thanks to Byzantine Greek and Syrian Christians, to the Arab and Persian East. Both the form and functioning of astrolabes evolved over the centuries, to the point that a Persian writing a century before Biruni could enumerate a thousand uses for them.[8] By Biruni's time there were more than a dozen distinct types, their colorful names evoking everything from melons and turtles to narcissus flowers. The construction of these brass instruments was precise and elegant, but the value of each type depended entirely on the sophistication with which it employed spherical geometry to project curved lines onto the instrument's calibrated flat surface. In fact, the development of a method for projecting spherical forms onto plane surfaces was among the main challenges before mathematicians at the time.

Not only did Biruni address this theoretical problem, but he made at least two major advances on its practical application. First, he proposed changes to the astrolabe that would enable the observer to measure angles by using not only the sun but also the moon and certain stars. Second, on the basis of spherical trigonometry Biruni proposed a new method for mapping a hemisphere. Unfortunately, this breakthrough in cartography, known as "globular projection," remained unknown to the world until the Italian cartographer G. B. Nicolosi reinvented it in 1660, and the English cartographer Aaron Arrowsmith actually applied it in the early nineteenth century.[9] Biruni's work on the astrolabe has been judged the most comprehensive and innovative in the entire medieval period, East or West.[10] Over the years he was to introduce an array of further improvements on this essential scientific and navigational tool.

Another of Biruni's projects at Gorgan dealt with the number system used in Sindh and India for arithmetic and other types of calculations. This work, now unfortunately lost, followed directly on the book by al-Sufi, written a century and a half earlier. It is not known whether Biruni's book played a significant part in promoting what came (again, incorrectly) to be known as Arabic numbers. But its existence proves that his later expertise on the mathematics, science, and culture of India had its origins decades before he wrote his books on that country.

The titles of a number of Biruni's writings from Gorgan indicate that officials and patrons often looked to him to explain phenomena of daily life. How, for example, does the reality of light differ "from the rubbish [about it] spread in books"? Or what about the contradictions between the observations of different astronomers? Because of the keen public interest in astrology, Biruni also issued a book-length introduction to that field, which included a cautionary discussion of whether experiments regarding the planets could determine the borders of "ill-starred or evil places." Finally, tipping his hand on the same subject, he composed "A Warning Against the Art of Deception in Prophesies Based on the Stars." Over the following decades Biruni and Ibn Sina were both to lambaste astrologists' claims to predict the future.

Biruni's final work from Gorgan, and one of the survivors, was a large book enigmatically entitled *The Chronology of Ancient Nations*.[11] An effusive dedication to Qabus came about because the emir himself had asked Biruni to provide an explanation "regarding the eras used by different nations, and regarding the differences of their roots, i.e., of the months and years on which they are based." Wandering from culture to culture and switching constantly between astronomy, religion, mathematics, history, and sermonizing, Biruni's *Chronology* has puzzled readers since the discovery of a manuscript copy in an Istanbul archive a century and a half ago.

I would argue that a powerful logic underlies the work, and it involves calendars. Today, although Muslims, Jews, Hindus, Christians, and Chinese all maintain their own calendars and celebrate their own New Year's Day, most practical matters, including those involving the functions of government, commerce, and science, are guided by a single common calendar. This global calendar enables us to place events everywhere on a single timeline. Without it, business between continents would be impossible, as would temporal comparisons across cultures and traditions. It is no exaggeration to say that this common understanding of how time should be measured, and our common calendar system, are the keys to globalism. It was not always thus. Until Biruni's era, all countries, cultures, and religious groups lived according to their own calendars. Each designated its own starting point for historical time, be it the Creation, Adam and Eve, or some later event, such as the biblical Flood. Even when they acknowledged a common starting point in historical time, as did both Greeks and Persians with the birth of Alexander the Great, they differed about when that event actually occurred.

The ancient Greeks pioneered the systematic study of history and, even today, Herodotus stands out for his curiosity about foreign peoples and cultures. Throughout his *Histories* Herodotus regales his readers with exotica gleaned from his extensive travels and face-to-face interviews. He explains how each culture preserves and protects its own history. In a typical passage he reports admiringly on how the Egyptians maintained lists of their kings dating back 341 generations. The implication in all this was that all customs and traditions are relative. Yet the broad-minded Herodotus, whom Cicero called "the Father of History," stopped short of asking how one might coordinate or integrate the Egyptian and Greek systems of time and history, or those of any other peoples. For all his interest in diverse peoples and cultures, Herodotus wrote for a Greek audience. The structure of his *Histories* allowed ample space for digressions that would inform or amuse his readers, but differing concepts of time were not among them. Herodotus and other Greeks of the Classical age were curious about the larger world, but ultimately their subject was Greece, and they remained content to view the worldwide passage of time through their own Greek calendar. The same could be said of the other peoples of the ancient world. All were so immersed in the particularities of their own culture that it never occurred to them to enquire into how other peoples might measure historical time.

Other ancient thinkers came as far as Herodotus but no further. The Roman historian Polybius composed what he called a *Universal History*, embracing much of the Middle East, but he, too, passed over the broadly differing concepts of time and of history. Instead, he shoehorned all dates into the four-year units of the Olympiads. This rendered his dates intelligible to Romans and Greeks but unintelligible to everyone else. Similarly, the first-century Jewish historian Josephus took as his subject the interaction of Jews and Romans, two peoples with markedly different understandings of time. He employed Roman chronology throughout his *The Jewish War* and *Antiquities of the Jews* and felt no need to correlate that system with the calendar of the Jews, or anyone else.

This, then, was the situation as of the year 1000. Having grown up in Khwarazm, with its rich and tragic history, and with his own many contacts with merchants and foreign travelers, Biruni was drawn naturally to history. He located copies of the most important religious and historical texts of the ancient Egyptians, Persians, Greeks, and Romans and then gathered information on the calendar systems of Muslims, Christians, and Jews. No one before him, and certainly no Muslim, had attempted to chronicle the beliefs of such diverse sects within Judaism as the Ananites, Rabbanites, or Miliadites. His account of the Jewish calendar and festivals anticipated those of the Jewish philosopher Maimonides by more than a century. He also assembled evidence on the measurement of time and history by the Nestorian (Syrian) Christians and by lesser-known peoples and sects from Central Asia. Along the way he documented the beliefs of his fellow Khwarazmians, who maintained their own calendar system, and of the region's forgotten Christian sect, the Melchites.

For anyone whose interests lie exclusively with systems for measuring time, Biruni's many asides on obscure spiritual movements can be frustrating. For example, he digressed at length on the Manicheans, followers of the third-century Persian prophet Mani, whose radical juxtaposition of good and evil challenged Zoroastrianism, Christianity, and, later, Islam. Among other details, Biruni reported that the center of Manicheanism had recently shifted from Persia to Samarkand. He also recounted the story of "al-Muqanna, "The Veiled One," a charismatic religious leader from Central Asia who had mounted an armed insurrection of white-clad warriors against their Arab conquerors. Biruni, who hailed from another region whose culture the Arabs had obliterated, recounted the story of Muqanna's heretical "people in white" with unfeigned admiration.[12]

One element that made his book as inaccessible to the general reader as it is valuable to specialists is that Biruni included an overwhelming mass of detail on all known histories and calendar systems. The only ones excluded were those of India and China, about which he confessed that he lacked sufficient written data. So thorough was Biruni that his *Chronology of Ancient Nations* remains a valuable source of data on pre-Muslim Arabs, followers of various "false prophets" in the Muslim world, and Persians and Jews. Biruni could have made it easier for his reader had he presented everything from just one perspective: his own.

But this was not his way. Unlike Herodotus, who adhered to a purely Greek perspective, or Persian writers who applied their own cultural measure to everyone else, Biruni began with the assumption that all cultures were equal. This assertion is less astonishing when viewed in context. It is unlikely that any part of the Eurasian land mass at the time spawned more people who accepted pluralism as a fact than Central Asia in general and Khwarazm in particular. A relativist's relativist, in the breadth of his perspective Biruni surpassed all who preceded him and most who followed. He even made a point of telling readers that in the course of his research he had interviewed heretics.

Biruni is arguably the first thinker to treat all religions, including his own, as equal, and to present them all without polemics. Reporting on the unfamiliar and seemingly bizarre customs of other peoples and religions, he did so clinically, without sensationalism. In each case he sought to identify the core beliefs of a given faith and then to show how they shaped its believers' understanding of time. In this relativist approach he was a practitioner of cultural anthropology many centuries before that field emerged as a scientific discipline.

Biruni could not stop there, for Qabus had made clear to him that he wanted his court scientist to devise a *single* system of time, so that henceforth he would not have to consult multiple books to find out when a given event had occurred. He also wanted one that could be applied to business and commerce as well as national history and lore. Biruni knew full well that different peoples view time differently. But, he insisted, there exists an objective basis for evaluating each system: namely, the precise duration of a day, month, and year as measured by science. Writing as an astronomer and mathematician, Biruni presented the best scientific evidence available on the length of the main units of time as perceived by each culture. Having determined the precise length of an hour, day, month, and year, he then recalculated the most important dates recorded in every system in terms of his new, autonomous, and all-embracing measure.

As he plunged into this daunting project Biruni found himself in a bewildering mess. "Every nation has its own [system of] eras,"[13] he realized, and none coincide. He argued that the confusion began with the failure of some peoples—notably the Arabs—to understand that the only precise way to measure a day is when the sun is at the meridian, that is, at noon. Errors in measuring a day in different cultures led to the creation of months and years of differing duration. The result was a hopeless muddle. Biruni seethed at the sheer incompetence he encountered on this crucial point. He then turned to the manner in which different peoples dated the beginning of historic time, at which point his anger turned to apoplexy. "Everything," he wrote with obvious frustration, "the knowledge of which is connected with the beginning of creation and with the history of bygone generations, is mixed up with falsification and myths." How can different peoples date creation as having taken place 3,000, 8,000, or 12,000 years ago? He fumed that even the Jews and Christians were at odds, with both of them following systems of time that are "obscurity itself."[14]

Biruni suggested that some of the errors could be traced to differences among biblical texts. Toward the Jews he was quite forgiving: "It cannot be thought strange that you should find discrepancies with people who have several times suffered so much from captivity and war as the Jews."[15] But Christians, by trying to blend the Jewish and Greek systems, had created an inexcusable chaos. He based such criticism on detailed studies of differing concepts of time among the Christian denominations, devoting special attention to the Syrian Church, with its strong presence in Central Asia and what is now Xinjiang.[16]

Biruni was no kinder to Arabs and Muslims. He conceded that pre-Muslim Arabs at least based their calendar on the seasons, but that their system fell far short of what the Zoroastrian Persians had devised. And while Jews, Christians, and Muslims debated their differing dates for Adam and Eve and the biblical Flood, the Persians, deemed no less intelligent, denied that the Flood ever took place.[17] When he encountered writers who did not grasp what he considered obvious, Biruni lambasted them for making "inconceivable suppositions," and "going beyond all reasonable limits." Against one he railed, "I don't know if he was really ignorant or only pretended to be," and regarding several others he called on God to "inflict on them ignominy in this world and to show their weakness to others."[18]

Such fulminations permeate Biruni's *Chronology*. Sometimes they were direct, though they were even more scathing when indirect. In chart after chart, he lists the intervals between major world events according to the various religions and peoples. Typical is his chart dating the lives of Adam and Eve, which, he observed, no one could perceive as anything but pure foolishness. Everywhere, he concluded, history is mixed with lies, as are all the cultures of mankind. In one passage, Biruni listed what each religion and people prohibited, highlighting the capriciousness and outright foolishness of most of the laws by which the pious order their lives. Having identified the cause of such nonsense, Biruni pointed to the almost universal refusal to base decisions on reason. It is not just the unreason of the astrologer, "who is so proud of his ingenuity,"[19] but the delusions of all the peoples and cultures of the world. The only ones to escape Biruni's wrath were the Greeks, whom he described as being "clever in geometry and astronomy." He continues, "They adhere strictly to logical arguments and have no recourse to the theories of those who [claim to] derive the basis of their knowledge from divine inspiration."[20]

Biruni pushed his enquiry to its logical conclusion. The chief difference among competing calendar systems was the way they account—or fail to account—for the fact that an astronomical year is 365 days and six hours long. To assume any other length—to fail, for example, to add in that extra quarter of a day—caused the dates for all feasts and holidays to migrate gradually throughout the year. To avoid this, the pre-Muslim Arabs had fixed their month of fasting, but the Muslims' month of Ramadan moved (and continues to move) throughout the year. All such errors could be rectified, he proposed, simply by adding to the calendar of 365 days an extra day every fourth year, or "leap year." Called "intercalation," this simple process became a litmus test by which Biruni measured the intellectual seriousness of all cultures. He praised the Egyptians, Greeks, Chaldeans, and Syrians for the precision of their intercalations, which came down to seconds. He was less generous toward the Jews and Nestorian Christians, though their systems of intercalation were widely copied. He acknowledged that in order to fix their market dates and holidays, the pre-Muslim Arabs had adopted from the Jews their primitive system of intercalation. But Muhammad and his early followers had rejected this, saying that "intercalation is only an increase of infidelity, by which the infidels lead people astray."

With remarkable bluntness, Biruni then announced that it was simply a mistake for the Prophet Muhammad to have rejected the adjustment of the year to reflect astronomical reality. Biruni concluded that this decision by Muhammad, affirmed by the *Quran* itself (Sura 9.37) and imposed by the early caliphs, "did much harm to the people." Some later adjustments were made, but they failed to address the core problem. "It is astonishing," he fulminated, "that our masters, the family of the Prophet, listened to such doctrines."[21]

This was but one of Biruni's ventures onto extremely sensitive territory. In another aside, he considered the Islamic custom of addressing prayers to the location of Mecca, termed the *Qibla*. After noting that early Muslims had prayed not to Mecca but to Jerusalem, he observed that Manicheans prayed toward the North Pole and Harranians to the South Pole. Thus armed, Biruni offered his conclusion by quoting with approval a Manichean who argued that "a man who prays to God does not need any *Qibla* at all."[22]

After these controversial diversions, Biruni returned to his central task. He knew that commercial interchange requires a common system of dating events and that all interactions among peoples require a common system with which to reckon the passage of time. Moving from description to prescription, he set down steps by which the mess created by religions and national mythologies could be corrected, or at least alleviated. His solution was to create a means of converting dates from one system to another. Biruni presented his system in the form of a large circular graph or chart, which he termed a "chessboard." This schema showed the eras, dates, and intervals according to each culture. Anyone who was "more than a beginner in mathematics," as he put it, could use it to translate a given date from one system to another. His invention, he boasted, would be useful to both historians and astronomers.

Going beyond his "chessboard," Biruni invented and actually constructed a geared machine that translated dates under one calendar system into another. Aside from Biruni's description, there exists an early sketch of at least part of this machine, but no one has yet attempted to reconstruct it. What can be said is that it was far less complex than the famous Anitkythera device that the modern Greek Navy exhumed from a second-century BC Greek shipwreck. Nonetheless, like that complex geared mechanism, with its thirty bronze gears, Biruni's device should earn its designer a place of honor in the history of the analog computer.

We do not know whether Biruni kept a copy of his *Chronology* or the chessboard or chronology machine that integrated all human history. The originals doubtless remained with Qabus. Nor is there any reason to think that his book gained wide dissemination, even in the Islamic world. If a copy reached the West before the nineteenth century, it remained unknown to scholarship and untranslated until 1879, when the German scholar Edward

Sachau found a nearly complete manuscript copy of the text and translated it into English and German. Today, three slightly differing copies of the original are known, one in Istanbul, one in Leiden, and a third, lavishly illustrated, in the library of Edinburgh University. Efforts are now under way in both Britain and Uzbekistan to combine all three in a definitive modern edition.[23]

Before the appearance of Biruni's *Chronology*, the concept of universal history did not exist. Nor could a comprehensive history have been written, as there was no single matrix for measuring time that extended across religions and civilizations at that time. Biruni's was effectively the first global system for measuring the passage of time and hence the first global calendar system. It was the missing key and essential tool for the construction of an integrated world history. Biruni's work applied Pythagoras's maxim that "things are numbers." By grounding his concept of human history on the solid foundation of mathematics and astronomy, he was offering a single global calendar.

It was thanks to the emir Qabus that Biruni was able to write his *Chronology of Ancient Nations*. I've noted Qabus's hostility to all forms of mindless flattery. The twelfth-century historian and encyclopedist Yaqut recorded how a poet who lauded Qabus received only trinkets for his effort, while another poet who laced his praise with biting satire received so large an honorarium that it enabled even his offspring to live in luxury.[24] Qabus's generosity toward those he respected was boundless, and he provided Biruni with whatever was needed to carry out his research and writing. At the same time, as a ruler, Qabus was both willful and brutal. The thirteenth-century writer Yaqut accused him of carrying out his policies by "chopping off heads and silencing souls. He extended this practice even to people close to him and to his trusted soldiers and followers."[25] Qabus's own grandson reported simply that "he was an evil person."[26]

For Biruni, Qabus's refusal to fund field research to measure the degrees of the earth's meridians took him beyond the pale. This was the same problem that had challenged Buzjani, Ibn Iraq, and Biruni himself, namely, how to measure the precise distance between two degrees of longitude. For whatever reason, Qabus vetoed the project. Biruni concluded he had fallen out of the emir's favor. Faced with this rebuff and fearing the consequences, he departed once again for Khwarazm, this time, as we've seen, to the new capital of Gurganj.

7

From Peace to Chaos

Biruni returned to Gurganj in the winter of 1003 and immediately plunged back into his research, studying a lunar eclipse on February 21 of that year.[1] At some point late in 1004 or 1005, Ibn Sina presented himself to the shah of Khwarazm and his vizier, Suhayli. The world's two most prominent young intellectuals were now together in the same city, even if, as I've noted, they sometimes seemed worlds apart. For the next seven years they served the same government, attended the same court functions, adorned the same intellectual salons, and shared some of the same friends. Whatever their similarities in intellectual voraciousness and ambition, their vitriolic correspondence emphasized the differences in their upbringing, training, and intellectual style—and evidently kept them apart. They arrived in Gurganj separately and from different directions. A few years later they would depart separately as well, in different directions and under very different circumstances.

Biruni renewed his collaboration with Ibn Iraq and slipped back easily into his earlier projects, carrying out detailed astronomical studies, the data from which he would later incorporate into his monumental work, *Masud's Canon*. He also compiled a comprehensive map (*zidj*) of the stars visible to the naked eye. This project gave him the expertise needed to come to the defense of his forebear from Khwarazm, the great mathematician and astronomer, al-Khwarazmi.

The founder of algebra had recently come under attack from a critic named Abu Talhi. The title of Biruni's several, hundred-page defense of Khwarazmi could not have been more blunt: *Disproving the Lie*.[2] Though now lost, the work included his dismissal of epicycles as a means of calibrating seemingly eccentric planetary motion (called "retrograde motion"). As late as the sixteenth century Tycho Brahe and Copernicus both clung to this concept, which Biruni had rejected five centuries earlier. Yet another tract presented Biruni's method for determining the chord (a straight line drawn between two points on a circle) for one degree of circumference. In this salvo, too, he sharply attacked Abu Talhi for having "overstepped all bounds and displaying impoliteness."

Other topics also engaged Biruni's attention. While determining the latitude of Gurganj, he devised a method for determining longitudes by measuring the elevation of a star or the sun and the azimuths of those elevations. "Azimuth," a term derived from Arabic, refers to the exactly calculated position of a star relative to a fixed point on earth. In a step essential for both astronomy and navigation, Biruni first employed this method for the determination of longitudes. Yet another section of this work proposed a new type of astrolabe that employed both the North and South Poles. Earlier astrolabes were designed to use one pole or the other, but not both.[3]

In his paper on astrolabes Biruni also took note of a simple method for calculating the earth's diameter. The elderly Baghdad astronomer Buzjani had hypothesized about the possibility of using the "dip angle" between a mountaintop of known height and the horizon and then triangulating, using a hypothetical line to the center of the earth. Biruni was so taken by this speculation that he added it to his report on astrolabes and even sought to test it. But the area around Gurganj was too flat for him to evaluate the validity of Buzjani's proposal. It took another decade for him to find a suitable mountain, at which time he succeeded in carrying out the necessary measurements and calculations.

One other initiative from Biruni's days in Gurganj would also have to wait for several more decades to bear fruit. As I've noted, copious amounts of jewels, minerals, and precious metals passed through the markets of Khwarazm. Many of the jewels were of dubious value, and often the pure metals had been diluted with cheap alloys. Biruni set out to find a fool-proof method for separating the genuine from the ersatz. The usual method of heating costly metal or mineral or subjecting them to acids did not produce reliable results. Instead, he proposed to determine the precise weight of a unit of each pure stone or unalloyed metal by comparing the weight of each substance to the weight of water of a constant volume and temperature. Later this led him to advance the concept of specific gravity. Only at the end of his life did he find time to elaborate and exhaustively test this concept, which he did.

Ibn Sina worked at the same relentless level of intensity as Biruni, taking full advantage of the security he now enjoyed, thanks to support from the vizier, Suhayli. We know nothing of Ibn Sina's administrative work in Gurganj; the job, after all, was merely a sinecure and a bureaucratic means of adding him to the intellectual milieu of the new capital. What we do know is that during his six years there he worked with great intensity to advance his medical practice and studies.

The praise that had been heaped on Ibn Sina by the emir in Bukhara had echoed in Gurganj, and he was quickly sought out to treat ailments. The fact that he enjoyed what he acknowledged to be an adequate salary suggests that he advanced his medical work there for its own sake and not to supplement his income. Ibn Sina himself called medicine "one of the easier sciences." and this has caused more than a few to dismiss his achievements in medicine as an elaborate sideline, not his main work. Ibn Sina's six years in Gurganj belie the claim. Not only did he continue his diagnostic work and practice, but he also amassed a vast number of texts by other experts and a quantity of his own clinical notes. By the time he left Gurganj, Ibn Sina had mastered all he needed to begin writing his grand synthesis, the *Canon of Medicine*.

Meanwhile, for his sponsor, Suhayli, he composed several texts, all but one of them pertaining to astronomy.[4] One was a commentary on Aristotle's *On the Heavens*; another covered Aristotle's *Physics*; a third was *On the Cause of the Earth Remaining in Its Position*; while a fourth, written for an unidentified theologian, was *On Space*.[5] Even if these were commissioned studies and reflected the interests of his patrons rather than his own, they were in fact a continuation of Ibn Sina's exchange with Biruni. Only in his commentary to *On the Heavens* did Ibn Sina's own cosmological interests seem evident. The absence of other works of a more philosophical character suggests that these subjects had yet to reclaim a central place among Ibn Sina's preoccupations.

The years Biruni and Ibn Sina spent in Gurganj gave them a respite from the region's relentless turmoil. The Karkhanids now occupied Bukhara. The last Samani ruler, Ismail bin Nuh al-Muntazr, mustered enough troops to attack Bukhara but not enough to drive out the Karakhanids. Nor did he receive help from the once-loyal Turks from Afghanistan, which would have made all the difference. The leader of the Samanis' Turkic forces, Sebuktegin, had died, leaving all power in the hands of his ambitious son, Mahmud. With single-minded determination Mahmud now focused not on reclaiming Bukhara for the Samanis but on consolidating control of the Afghan territories he had just inherited and on driving the rival Karakhanids from the region of Khorosan.

The murder of the last Samani ruler left standing only the two major Turkic powers, the Karakhanids and Mahmud of Ghazni. Since their main zone of contention was Khorosan, seven hundred kilometers (four hundred and thirty-five miles) to the south of Khwarazm, Gurganj found itself at peace and able once more to glory in its status as the epicenter of intellectual life in Central Asia and the Muslim East. The young shah, Abu-l Abbas Mamun, encouraged and supported this fresh effervescence of culture. But this last of the Mamuns was also a sybarite who frittered away his days in self-indulgent activities, was indecisive in matters of state, and neglected the army. These qualities were to prove his undoing. In the new shah's most fateful action, he and his cultured and effective vizier, Suhayli, parted company in 1013. Did Mamun fire him or did Suhayli quit? What is clear is that Suhayli's departure for Baghdad left the people of Khwarazm panic-stricken. Members of the Gurganj court, however, had long since sensed that Suhayli's position was shaky and knew that serious trouble was brewing. Ibn Sina was among the nervous ones, and with good reason, since he owed his job and salary to Suhayli. Even before his patron decamped, Ibn Sina sensed that his own time in Gurganj was drawing to a close.

Ibn Sina left Gurganj in 1012, a year before Suhayli's departure. Two peculiar features of his exit offer a hint as to the cause. First, rather than joining a caravan, as would have been the normal way to travel, he was accompanied only by his medical colleague and friend, Masihi, and a relative of the shah. The latter's presence in his small band confirms that he remained in the shah's good graces to the end, in spite of Suhayli's departure. And second, instead of taking either of the main routes south, both of which skirted the Karakum desert, Ibn Sina opted instead for a dangerous and uncharted path that led straight across that bleak wasteland. Only someone who was anxious to hide would have taken so perilous a route. A chronicler of Central Asian politics who was a generation younger than Ibn Sina recorded what was widely believed to have been the reason for Ibn Sina's haste. According to this writer, Beyhaqi, Mahmud sent the new shah of Khwarazm the following brazen demand that he send "several men of learning, each peerless in his science," to his court, in order for Mahmud to "derive prestige from their knowledge and capabilities."[6]

This claim gains plausibility in light of Mahmud's recent successes. By this time, he was solidly in control of Afghanistan and in the process of driving the Karakhanid Turks out of Khorasan. Thanks to these advances, he could turn his attention to assembling an entourage of poets and thinkers who would proclaim his new status and do credit to his court. Mahmud had concluded (or had been told) that Biruni and Ibn Sina were "the two wisest men on earth, with no equals anywhere."[7] But there was one problem. The shah in Gurganj, who had been forced into a marriage with Mahmud's sister, had himself appointed Biruni and was now prepared to protect him. Ibn Sina, on the other hand, was another matter. The vizier who had appointed and supported him was fast losing influence at the court. With no protector, Ibn Sina's only recourse was flight. It is clear that the young shah respected Ibn Sina, understood that he had to flee, and therefore facilitated his departure by ordering one of his own relatives to accompany him.

Where should Ibn Sina go? The Karakhanids now controlled Bukhara and the surrounding region. However, Ibn Sina had heard that Biruni's former patron, Qabus, was restocking his court with thinkers and poets. Gorgan was therefore Ibn Sina's intended destination as he fled Gurganj. His friend, the Christian doctor Masihi, accompanied him. Conveniently, Masihi was a native of Gorgan. Further details on Ibn Sina's flight come from the same early chronicler, Abu-l Fadl Beyhaqi. According to a story that circulated widely in the region, Mahmud soon caught wind of Ibn Sina's flight[8] and sent word to his troops to capture Ibn Sina at any cost and send him to Ghazni in Afghanistan. Mahmud is then said to have commissioned Ibn Iraq, who was also a talented painter, to produce a portrait of the famous doctor and philosopher—a sort of Most Wanted Poster. He ordered the reproduction of several dozen copies of the likeness and commanded that they be posted throughout the region.

Mindful of this threat, the travelers avoided the main routes and went across the Karakum desert. The choice proved disastrous. On the fourth day of their march Masihi died in a fierce sandstorm. Ibn Sina and the shah's relative proceeded alone. But rather than go directly to Gorgan, they instead visited half a dozen other centers in Khorasan.[9] The reason for this unplanned wandering was that Ibn Sina had just learned that Qabus had been incarcerated by his own generals and died in jail. This foreclosed the possibility of a job at the Gorgan court.

In none of the other cities he visited did Ibn Sina find work. This may have been because he demanded too much money. In what is arguably the only surviving indication that Ibn Sina had a sense of humor, he penned this self-deprecating couplet:[10]

When I became great, no city was big enough for me.
When my price went up, no one could afford me.

Whatever the cause, there were no welcome mats out for the wandering scholar. A visit to Abu Said ibn Abil Khair, a renowned Sufi poet and saint, further deepened his despair. A descendant later wrote that Abu Khair told Ibn Sina that he himself had already envisioned all the knowledge that the philosopher would ever acquire.[11] Frustrated, and suffering from an unidentified disease, Ibn Sina left the Sufi saint and headed for the Caspian shore. He eventually wound up in Gorgan, with no job or prospects.

Meanwhile, a two-front crisis was brewing in Khwarazm. In their last days, the Samanis had granted Sebuktegin and his son, Mahmud, overlordship of Khwarazm. The shah hoped against hope that this concession would not reduce the high degree of autonomy and self-government that Khwarazm had enjoyed under the Samanis and even, briefly, under the Karakhanids. The shah's own generals (many of whom were Turkic) and his great landlords (*dihqans*) did not share their leader's optimism. They strongly opposed Mahmud and had convinced themselves that they had the military resources to resist him. Fearing that the inexperienced young shah would cave in under pressure from Mahmud, they quietly expanded their own forces in what can only be considered an act of rebellion. Abu-l Abbas Mamun now faced dangers from two fronts.

With Suhayli gone, the shah appointed Biruni as his vizier. The thirty-seven-year-old astronomer and mathematician had witnessed the political dramas in Kath, Rayy, Gorgan, and Gurganj but had no leadership experience. Yet there was a certain logic to the shah's decision to appoint him. Amid all his other activities in Gurganj, Biruni had managed to write a detailed history of Khwarazm.[12] This important document, now lost, is said to have recounted the rise, fall, and rise of the region from ancient times to the present. The shah therefore turned for help to the man with the deepest knowledge of the region. The relationship between the two, moreover, was cordial. Biruni was well aware of his leader's shortcomings, but he respected and liked the man, even going so far as to characterize him as "learned, valiant, full of energy, and tenacious in business affairs."[13] On a more personal level, Biruni would later recall that "I never heard a word of abuse from his mouth. When angered by someone his worst swear was to say 'That cur.'"[14]

Biruni was to spend seven years as vizier to the shah of Khwarazm. The newly minted prime minister immediately began planning a strategy for dealing with the mounting crisis. His aim was somehow to appease the self-confident generals and independence-minded grandees while at the same time preventing tensions with the shah's brother-in-law, Mahmud, from boiling over. An early step was to send an ambassador to Mahmud's capital at Ghazni in Afghanistan. But the diplomat assigned this mission succeeded only in revealing to Mahmud that the great landlords and army chiefs in Khwarazm were brewing a revolt. Mahmud therefore made a bold offer: he would pull back his army and assure peace in Khwarazm if the Friday sermon at every mosque in Khwarazm would begin with a declaration, or *khotba*, acknowledging Mahmud as the ultimate sovereign.[15] Though this merely confirmed the reality of Mahmud's ultimate control of Khwarazm, the *khotba* inflamed Mamun's rebellious generals and grandees, who threatened to take up arms against the shah if he accepted it.[16] In an attempt to quell opposition within his own ranks, Mamun, presumably at Biruni's prompting, offered his generals and landlords a huge bribe of silver.

Almost as much as Mahmud's demand itself, this only fanned the rebels' fury. By this point, Mamun's situation was desperate and his mood frantic. Faced with armed rebellion at home and fearing the possibility that Mahmud's mass army would move in to suppress the mounting rebellion, he had no one but Biruni on whom he could rely.

Biruni tried to gain time by having the sultan tell the rebels that he had raised the point of the *khotba* only to test their views on the matter. This obvious lie failed to mollify the dissidents. Biruni then proposed a further move: to enter into secret negotiations with leaders of the region's remaining independent Turkic nomads. His aim was to harness their forces against the dissidents and in support of the Mamun dynasty. The shah liked the idea and was quick to claim it as his own. He sent emissaries to the Turkic tribesmen and gave them robes of honor and large sums of money to offer as payment for the nomads' loyalty. The Turks accepted the gifts and agreed to cooperate.

No sooner did the shah's delegation depart from the Turkic camp, however, than the nomad leaders informed Mahmud about what was afoot. Mahmud correctly perceived Biruni's tactic as a sign of Mamun's utter desperation. He quickly marched his main army to the Gurganj area and again demanded, as a condition for his support against the rebels, that Mamun yield on Mahmud's request regarding the *khotba*. In a last-ditch effort at compromise, Biruni got the shah to propose reading the *khotba* at every mosque in the region *except* in the capital.

When Mamun's dissident generals caught wind of their leader's maneuvers, they launched an armed assault on Gurganj. Whether their aim was merely to put a halt to further compromises or instead to force the shah to abdicate will never be known, for in the course of the rebels' attack their troops chased

Shah Abu-l Abbas Mamun to the upper floors of his palace and murdered him. Because Mamun was Mahmud's brother-in-law, his murder gave Mahmud the perfect pretext to intervene. His tactical goals were to rescue his sister, avenge the shah's murder, and, as he put it, "teach the [next] shah how to rule."[17] His strategic goal, however, was to gain hegemony over the last Central Asian emirate not fully under his control. Thanks to the addition of forces marched up from Khorasan or sent by boat down the Amu-Darya from Balkh, Mahmud's army was now enormous. According to a contemporary account, it included 100,000 horses and 500 well-equipped war elephants. By comparison, the defenders at Gurganj were able to summon a mere 50,000 fighters.[18]

Marching his immense force into Gurganj, Mahmud rounded up all the rebels and proceeded to wreak a terrible vengeance. Ringleaders of the rebellion were herded together and trampled to death by elephants, after which their bodies were paraded on the elephants' tusks and dismembered. What was left of their corpses was then hanged on gibbets next to the hastily constructed tomb of the late shah.[19] As to the rest of the rebels, Beyhaqi noted that "things were done to them that wouldn't even be done to Muslims in the lands of unbelievers."[20] He concluded laconically that "this had a most compelling and awe-inspiring impact on the populace."[21]

The death of the pleasant but feckless thirty-three-year-old Abu al-Abbas Mamun of Khwarazm marked the end of two millennia of Persianate rule in Central Asia. Biruni was fortunate not to have died in the fighting. Before Biruni could flee, however, Mahmud's Turkic fighters rounded him up, along with other former officials of Mamun's government. Within days he found himself among the forlorn mass of hostages who began the 1,200-kilometer (720-mile) trudge to Mahmud's capital at Ghazni. Beyhaqi recorded that the column of captives stretched endlessly along the entire route to Afghanistan.[22]

8

Nemesis

Mahmud of Ghazni

Up to this point the deteriorating political conditions in Central Asia had been like a bank of dark clouds hovering over the region. With Mamun's assassination and Mahmud's subduing of Khwarazam, they exploded in a furious storm. The upheaval uprooted ancient dynasties and elevated an entirely new ruling class whose members differed ethnically and culturally from their predecessors. It also destroyed old patterns of patronage, hurling artists, musicians, poets, and scientists into a maelstrom of the unknown. Ibn Sina's sudden flight to Gorgan and, later, Biruni's forced trek across Central Asia to Afghanistan were the result of forces that seemed to have singled out these two rising young thinkers.

To the extent that the forces took human form, they were concentrated in Mahmud of Ghazni. It was this new regional hegemon, and he alone, who did most to shape the conditions under which both Biruni and Ibn Sina toiled for the rest of their lives. He closed off avenues that might otherwise have beckoned them and opened up others. Mahmud both rode and directed an all-encompassing wave of change, a geopolitical tsunami that, until his death in 1030, generated bloody clashes between huge armies, caused the rise and fall of empires, and fomented bitter religious strife.

Sultan Mahmud of Ghazni was a man of short or middle height and trim build. He wore a beard to hide a face so pockmarked by smallpox that even he considered himself ugly.[1] This unremarkable figure was to forge a great empire that spanned most of Central Asia and much of the Middle East, as well as Sindh and Punjab in India. It was above all the passions and prejudices of this Turkic tyrant that shaped the world in which Ibn Sina and Biruni did their most significant work. The seat of the dynasty that gave rise to Mahmud and to his supra-national state was the city of Ghazni, some 175 kilometers (108 miles) southwest of Kabul in Afghanistan.

Much of what we know of Mahmud's life and work comes from the writings of Beyhaqi, the same writer who wrote about Mahmud's conquest of Khwarazm. For over three decades this cultured, keenly observant, and judicious civil servant toiled at Ghazni in the government's Correspondence Department. Educated in Nishapur, a wealthy and cosmopolitan city in Khorasan, Abu-I-Fadl Beyhaqi devoted his entire working life to drafting letters and documents of state for Mahmud. A closet historian, he quietly set aside copies of the most important documents that passed across his desk. His plan was to use them to document a history of Mahmud's reign and that of his son Masud that he planned to write during his retirement. However, when Beyhaqi unexpectedly fell from grace, his superiors demanded that he turn over to them his private archive. Fearing just such a move, Beyhaqi had managed to squirrel away a second hoard of documents as well as most of the private notes he had kept over the decades. Working with this trove during his long retirement, Beyhaqi composed in his native Persian an epic thirty-volume history of the entire Ghazni dynasty. Sadly, twenty-five of those volumes were destroyed or disappeared over the following centuries. Among the lost volumes were all of those pertaining to Mahmud. Fortunately, Beyhaqi had scattered information on Mahmud throughout the volumes that survived. These passages, along with less colorful histories by other early historians, have enabled scholars to sketch the outline of Mahmud's life and times.[2]

Mahmud had clawed his way to the top. His father, Sebuktegin, the Samanis' slave-turned-general, had received Ghazni, an old Buddhist center, in payment for his loyalty to Bukhara. But while Sebuktegin was fighting in distant lands, local Hindu princes seized control of his Afghan domains. Sebuktegin rushed back and recaptured Ghazni and then expanded his control westward toward Khorasan. Though he had shown every favor to Mahmud, his elder son, the dying Sebuktegin inexplicably bequeathed rule over his capital not to Mahmud but to a younger son. Only by defeating his own brother in 998 did Mahmud take control of Ghazni.

Mahmud worked relentlessly to consolidate his power. With the formidable Karakhanids he cut a deal, ceding most of the vast territories north of the Amu Darya to the only other Turkic power in the region. This arrangement freed Mahmud to focus on two much bigger prizes: Khorasan and India. Khorasan, located along the modern borders of Afghanistan, Turkmenistan, and Iran, was important to Mahmud because it lay astride the most heavily traveled route from the west to Ghazni, and because its two greatest cities, Nishapur and Balkh, were promising sources of the gold needed to pay the army. A further consideration, and an important one, was that north and west of Khorosan lay the three main trading centers of Persia: Rayy, Hamadan, and Isfahan.

Ruled by various branches of the Buyid family, these lands were also the main centers of Shiism, the dynamic movement that had split Islam into two contending worlds. In 945 the Buyids' Shiite army had conquered Baghdad itself, leaving the Muslim Caliphate beholden to Shiite power. As such, the Buyids presented a permanent threat to the Sunni Muslim rulers of Ghazni and, no less, a tempting opportunity. Mahmud assigned even greater importance to India. This land, whose border was an eight-day march eastward from Ghazni, possessed fabled riches, tens of thousands of Hindus—to fill the ranks of the barracks and slave quarters—and awe-inspiring ranks of war elephants which, if captured, could render Mahmud's army invincible. Muslim armies had penetrated Sindh (now southern Pakistan) as early as the seventh century. Mahmud now saw the opportunity to finish the job, enrich himself, and force his Sunni faith onto the populations of vast new territories. By pursuing these goals, Mahmud made India the source of his fortune and, in the Muslim world, of his glory.

Modern concepts of economics as a tool of geopolitics were all but unknown in the Muslim East and the medieval world generally. By far the most effective instrument for expanding and maintaining control were armies. Mahmud's army was enormous, surpassing 100,000 men for major battles. This huge force called for tens of thousands of bows, swords, maces, lances, shields, and massive siege engines, not to mention banners, tents, and field kitchens. Mahmud refocused the economy of much of his realm on the manufacture of these tools of war. On maneuvers, Mahmud's army was like a movable city. Indeed, his army was not simply a tool of the state but the state itself, with the society regimented and organized to meet its needs. For more than a generation, the army of Ghazni had no equal in all Eurasia. Its rise and fall defined the life cycle of Mahmud's empire.

At the very core of Mahmud's army was a cadre of 4,000 slave officers. They were the key to the command-and-control function of the entire force and of the state itself. Cut off from their own pasts, these fighters were loyal only to Mahmud. They constituted his core force in battles and his bodyguard at all times. Elaborately uniformed and equipped with gleaming curved swords, those elite units based in Ghazni would line up in ranks through which guests of the sultan would pass before reaching the foot of the throne. Slave soldiers were nothing new in the Muslim East. The caliphate itself, unable to find sufficient numbers of willing Arabs and Persians, had begun enlisting

Turkic slaves a century and a half before Mahmud.[3] Two things were particularly distinctive about Mahmud's army: the enslaved force wielded considerable power; and Mahmud, his father, and grandfather had themselves been slaves who had served the Samani rulers down to their fall.

While slave cadres were the heart of Mahmud's army, the vast majority of both foot soldiers and cavalry comprised primarily captives and local men who had been lured to fight by promises of wealth. Other rank-and-file troops—numbering in the thousands—were refugees from lands impoverished by his depredations, desperate men who had also joined the army in hopes of sharing in the captured riches. This dependence on booty meant that Mahmud had constantly to be on the lookout for new territories to conquer. Any interruption in the march of conquest imperiled the army and hence the state itself. It is above all the search for plunder that led Mahmud to mount no fewer than twenty-six full-scale expeditions into India.[4] This bloody project resulted in one of history's greatest transfers of wealth.

After each campaign, Mahmud marched long columns of captives to Ghazni, where they were dragooned into the capital's workforce or sold as slaves. Just one of Mahmud's Indian campaigns produced no fewer than 45,000 captives from Sindh and Punjab, most of whom ended up in the army. From Delhi alone Mahmud's army is said to have dispatched to Ghazni 200,000 slave girls and other unfortunates.[5] These captive Indians were to alter the demographic makeup of Afghanistan in ways that can still be discerned today. Mahmud's Ghazni emerged as the single greatest slave market in all Central Asia and the Middle East. When Mahmud issued coins with Arabic script on one side and Sanskrit on the other, he merely acknowledged the transformation wrought by his conquests.

Contemporary observers noted the striking ethnic diversity of Mahmud's armed forces. Any given unit might include Afghans, Central Asian Turks, Indians, Kurds, Persians, and Arabs. His generals presented a similar patchwork of ethnicities. Such complex agglomerations demanded constant oversight and an immediate response to insubordination. The same challenge faced all the other offices of state, including the sultan's appointed council and his five ministries. To keep these thousands in line and also to stay abreast of his foreign enemies, Mahmud created a Department of Secret Intelligence, a vast and efficient spy agency that watched over both domestic and foreign affairs. Spies, both male and female, sent messages back to Ghazni in everything from hollow staffs, the linings of boots, saddle cloths, and the insulation on water-bottles.[6] Evaluating the effectiveness of Mahmud's eyes and ears abroad, Beyhaqi recorded that the spies of Sultan Mahmud "counted the very breaths of the Khans of Turkistan."[7]

How to pay for such a vast force of soldiers and bureaucrats? Plunder helped but did not suffice. Directly under Mahmud were his governors, many of whom were themselves slaves. The governors levied harsh taxes to pay for the army and were adept at bleeding the land for goods and services. These practices steadily eroded the economy of the entire empire, a development of which Mahmud was either unaware or, more likely, unconcerned. From the outset, Mahmud's empire consisted of a mighty army with a territorial state to serve it.

Who, then, was Mahmud? His formal studies had consisted entirely of the *Quran* and of those collections of the *Sayings* of the prophet Muhammad that were deemed acceptable by members of the local Muslim *ulema*. These deeply orthodox religious leaders held that the answers to all life's questions were to be found in these two main texts of the faith. There is no evidence that Mahmud's formal education continued beyond this point. In other words, what was simply the first step in the education of Ibn Sina and Biruni comprised the entirety of Mahmud's formal training. His education did not extend to any of the writers on philosophy, history, mathematics, astronomy, and medicine.

There is no doubt that Mahmud was, in his way, pious. He was punctilious in fulfilling his religious duties, and he read the *Quran* daily. He justified his military campaigns in terms of spreading the faith and spared no effort to rout out religious dissenters of all stripes, whether Shiites or the adherents of the many dissident currents within Islam that flourished at the time, among them Sufis, Mutazilites, and Quarmations.[8] At first his government adhered to the comparatively moderate Hanafi branch of Islamic law, which prevails to this day in all Central Asia. But, according to the scholar Muhammad Nazim, Mahmud's court then shifted its loyalties to the archly traditionalist Shafi school.[9] Shafi jurists derived all legal judgments solely from the *Quran* and *Sayings* of Muhammad and resorted to reason only when clear directives were not to be found in those texts. Even then, they limited such activity to "reasoning by analogy" to the holy scriptures and frowned on all "interpretation." Shafi jurists also refused to accept local religious customs and practices as legitimate under Islam, a stricture that carried dire implications for even the most pious Muslims of other cultures.

Modern writers from Pakistan and Muslim India have heaped praise on Mahmud for spreading the faith into heretic lands. Others have scorned him for the same reason, branding him a religious fanatic and ruthless monster. Both judgments may be true, but there is a third perspective on Mahmud's religiosity. He knew that the only power that could confer a token of legitimacy on his dynasty of usurpers and slaves was the caliphate in Baghdad. But by the eleventh century, as I've noted, this bastion of Sunni orthodoxy was living on borrowed time. The Shiite Buyids had long since captured Baghdad, and the brilliant court they established there outshone the caliph's shabby assembly across town. Aside from its fading aura of orthodox piety and its power to confer legitimacy on others, the caliph had nothing.

This created a striking opportunity for mutual gain. Mahmud, with waxing power but lacking legitimacy, could make common cause with the caliph, whose centuries-old legitimacy was no longer buttressed by either money or power. Mahmud had only to declare himself the caliph's humble servant and dispatch to Baghdad caravans laden with plundered riches. The caliph, in return, had merely to acknowledge Mahmud as the sole regional hegemon and rebrand his campaigns of plunder as wars of Islam against infidels, whether Hindus, Shiites, or Ismailis. This mutually beneficial arrangement was consummated just as Mahmud's army fell upon Gurganj. For it was in that same year, 1017, that the Muslim Caliphate condemned both Shiites and Ismailis as heretics.

Mahmud took great pride in honorific titles and shamelessly awarded himself the title of sultan. He especially valued the many other religious titles the caliph in Baghdad conferred on him. One of these, "Avenger of the Faith," freed his hands to conquer at will. Such titles transformed Mahmud's pillaging campaigns in India into holy crusades blessed by the highest religious authority.[10] He reciprocated these honors from the caliph by issuing coins proclaiming his own glory on one side and that of the caliph on the other.

Notwithstanding the caravans loaded with booty he dispatched to Baghdad, Mahmud kept the most valuable trophies for himself. When he desecrated and destroyed Somnath, one of the greatest Hindu temples in India, he hauled the holy lingam stone of Lord Krishna over the 1,600 kilometers (1,000 miles) to Ghazni. There he ordered it to be installed under the entrance to his great mosque, so that every pious Muslim, entering and existing, would trample upon it.

Mahmud was a bundle of contradictions. Each of his biographers selected those aspects of his personality that best fit his own image of the man. One acknowledged that he was "self-willed, stubborn, and impatient with disagreement." But that same biographer went on to stress that the Sultan was physically brave yet showed mercy toward some of his defeated foes, even to the point of granting offices to officials from conquered lands; that he was solicitous about the education of his seven sons; and that he was responsive even to complaints from humble women who had been cheated by officials.[11] Another stressed the atmosphere of suspicion that permeated the court and Mahmud's endless double dealings with friends and foes alike. That biographer concluded with the mordant observation that "the Ghaznavid sultans were despots who held their empire together by force of arms and fear."[12]

In his personal life Mahmud was largely free of "licentious sensuality," to quote one of his admiring Muslim biographers, and lived "*more or less* in accordance with the Muslim code of morality."[13] In practice, this meant not stocking his harem with more than the accepted number of wives and slave concubines. It also allowed Mahmud to drink wine with his cronies and to maintain through his adult years an intimate relationship with a Turkmen slave by the name of Abu-l Nazim Araz.[14] Three of Mahmud's court poets all described that long-term relationship in positive terms.

From the Samani family and earlier Persian rulers, Mahmud had picked up the custom of packing his court with paid versifiers whose main duty was to compose panegyrics to the reigning autocrat and declaim them at official events. If we are to believe an early chronicler, Mahmud maintained 400 such poets, a stable of flatterers that would have enabled him to hear words of praise from a different poet every day for more than a year, without repetition.[15] Yet his support for artists and writers was apparently so open-handed that even his harshest critics acknowledge him as a great patron of culture, a veritable Maecenas. Such patronage, of course, was normal for eleventh-century autocrats. Mahmud's claim to fame lay in his ability to afford more of it than could his rivals.

Mahmud was also a builder in the grand style. He reconstructed his capital at Ghazni, constructing several immense new palaces in which he displayed his trophies of war. Both his new madrassa and the stables for his war elephants were on a similarly outsized scale. Yet more lavish was Mahmud's grand mosque at Ghazni, which was said to have outshone even the great Umayyad mosque at Damascus. Its walls were of traditional sun-dried brick, but Mahmud ordered for them to be sheathed with multi-colored marble hauled back from India.

Ghazni being cold in winter, Mahmud built an immense imperial complex at a warmer site in Helmand, 130 kilometers (80 miles) southwest of the capital near the city of Bost. Partially excavated in 1949–1951 by the Délégation Archéologique Française en Afghanistan, the reception rooms, halls, corridors, and living quarters of the palace at Lashkar-e-Bazar stretched for more than half a mile along a high terrace above the Helmand river.[16] The walls beneath the sculptured cornices of the main chambers were adorned with painted murals and colorful woven hangings, while lush carpets covered the floors. The main rooms opened onto the terrace itself, from which Mahmud and his son Masud watched choreographed elephant fights on the plain below. Mahmud erected similarly grand residences in Balkh and Nishapur, each with extensive pleasure gardens. It is said that Mahmud himself designed the palace at Nishapur. In addition to these great palace complexes, Mahmud also ordered the construction of aqueducts, bridges, and irrigation channels, one of which, just north of Ghazni, is still in use today.

Mahmud probably retained some knowledge of his ancestral Turkic tongue but also spoke both Arabic and Persian, strongly favoring the latter. Whether from reading on his own or through contact with learned men in Ghazni, Mahmud was exposed to works of Persian prose and poetry. Beyhaqi, who was no fan of Mahmud, acknowledged that he was a keen listener at court.[17] Passing over the ranks of versifying hacks, Mahmud's stable of poets included some of the greatest masters of the Persian language. Prominent among them was Abul Hasan Farrukhi, a musician and poet who managed to turn the banal panegyric into a true art form.[18] A widely cited couplet of Farrukhi's beseeched Mahmud to become a world conqueror:

The story of Alexander the Great has aged and become a legend.
Renew the story, since the new has a sweetness of its own!

Towering over all other writers under Mahmud's patronage was Abu al-Qasem Mansur, known to posterity as Ferdowsi. His masterpiece, the *Shahnameh*, or *Book of Kings*, completed by 1010, consists of 60,000 rhymed couplets and covers the full spectrum of human emotions. It immediately became the national epic of the Persian people and remains so in today's Iran. A landowner from Tus near the modern border between Iran and Afghanistan, Ferdowsi, who was born in 935, had received support from the Samani elite until the fall of their dynasty. Mahmud immediately took Ferdowsi for himself. Ferdowsi's stay in Ghazni was unhappy and brief, however. Even when he offered praise for Mahmud, rival court poets saw to it that bureaucrats withheld from Ferdowsi payment for his work. Angered and depressed by such mistreatment, Ferdowsi seized the first opportunity to flee to Tus. On the route home a gift—bags of silver coins—from Mahmud reached the inn where Ferdowsi was spending a night. The poet is said to have been so disgusted that he gave the bags to the innkeeper.[19]

Once Ferdowsi had decamped from Ghazni, Mahmud seems to have forgotten about him, naming another of his stable of writers the "King of Poets."[20] Only when a copy of Ferdowsi's finished *Shahnameh* arrived at his palace did Mahmud again turn his attention to the poet. It was said that he now regretted having alienated Ferdowsi and by way of compensation sent him another gift, consisting this time of 60,000 gold pieces, or one per couplet. But when the caravan carrying the treasure reached Tus, it met a cortege of mourners bearing Ferdowsi's coffin to the cemetery.[21]

Ferdowsi was not the only intellectual star who came into Mahmud's orbit only to be subjected to personal and professional tribulations. Ibn Sina, as we have seen, escaped Mahmud's clutches only by fleeing across the desert from Gurganj to Gorgan. But his reprieve was only temporary, for Mahmud, and then his son, Masud, were to cast a shadow over the rest of his life. Masud twice nearly captured him and succeeded in purloining much of his library. Biruni was even less fortunate. In his role as vizier to Khwarazm's ruler, Abu al-Abbas Mamun, he had devised a series of strategies for preventing Mahmud from capturing the region. But Mahmud prevailed, Abu al-Abbas Mamun was murdered, Biruni was captured, and Mahmud treated Biruni as a hostage. Only after he had spent a period in purgatory did the tyrant relent and bring Biruni to Ghazni. There he would spend the rest of his life under the controlling direct gaze of Mahmud and his successors.

9

Ibn Sina, Encyclopedist

We left Ibn Sina when he had just arrived in Gorgan in 1012 in search of work. After the untimely death of Qabus, the small capital had no royal court to speak of. However, a few governmental offices carried on, and Ibn Sina landed a job at one of them, as an official in financial administration.[1] The local intelligentsia welcomed the famous thinker to their city. Their support enabled Ibn Sina to spend the next three years in Gorgan, working productively and, in the process, finding a new direction.

Chief among his Gorgan backers was one Abu Muhammad as-Shirazi,[2] who provided Ibn Sina with a house next to his own. In exchange for this (too-cozy) arrangement, the scholar agreed to tutor his host on a range of subjects. Shirazi also commissioned treatises and whole books on topics that had aroused his, Shirazi's, curiosity. Though Ibn Sina gave his own spin to these projects, none of them reflected his own interests at the time. With no alternative at hand, the desperate Ibn Sina became a one-man think tank, contracting with private patrons who hired him to prepare papers on topics that interested them and to discuss his findings with them. This is precisely what happened when Shirazi asked Ibn Sina to help him to come to grips with geometry and astronomy. These presented no problem for Ibn Sina, who had studied geometry by plowing through the twelve books of Euclid's *Elements*, and astronomy by working his way through Ptolemy's *Almagest*. But Shirazi was an older learner and in no mood to undertake so extensive a program of reading. Instead, he demanded abridgements or digests. With no choice in the matter, Ibn Sina obliged, producing a *Summary of the Almagest*, a *Shorter Summary of Logic*, and a collection of *Universal Observations*. Later, he worked passages from these and other abridgements into his major philosophical works.

The sole project from Gorgan that Ibn Sina himself initiated bears the puzzling title *The Origin and Return*.[3] At the time he wrote it, Ibn Sina was still depressed by all that had befallen him. After complaining of the many vicissitudes he had endured, he argued, "The age of scholarship is becoming extinct, interests are turning away from the philosophical sciences towards various [other] pursuits, and hatred is heaped upon those who concern themselves with some part of truth."[4] The only thing that endures, he wrote, is the immortal Soul, or human consciousness. This treatise traced the soul from its origin in God to its existence in the physical world and then to its survival following the body's death. In his earlier writings Ibn Sina had always been the good Aristotelian, loyally endorsing the master's views and those of his ancient followers and interpreters, the so-called Peripatetics. But here, for the first time, he was adopting a more independent stance. His goal, he declared, was to "clarify what [the Peripatetics] obscured; proclaim what they concealed and suppressed; collect what they dispersed; and expand what they summarized."[5]

Sitting in on Ibn Sina's sessions with Shirazi (and leaving us a record of their existence) was a young man from near Balkh in what is now Afghanistan. Abu Ubaid al-Juzjani had traveled the 600 kilometers (360 miles) to Gorgan for the sole purpose of meeting Ibn Sina, whom he idolized as his *ustad* or master. Ibn Sina accepted him as his student, assistant, amanuensis, archivist, and the chronicler of his life and works. Ibn Sina immediately dictated to Juzjani an autobiography covering the years from his birth down to his arrival in Gorgan. That "autobiography" remains the main extant source on Ibn Sina's life. Yet, as the German scholar Guenter Lueling has pointed out, the only fact in the account that is firmly verifiable is the date of Ibn Sina's death. Everything else, Lueling argues, Ibn Sina "deliberately veiled."[6] And with good reason, for Ibn Sina had lifted several elements from an ancient biography of Aristotle and woven them into his own life story.[7] Yet to the extent that what Juzjani left us is merely "veiled" and not deliberately distorted or invented, it offers a guide to Ibn Sina's life, albeit one to be treated with great caution.[8]

In Bukhara, Ibn Sina had surrounded himself with a circle of bright and convivial students. He had assumed that these young people would grasp his thoughts and be motivated to pass them on faithfully to the next generation. Through this oral process he had hoped that his thoughts might be preserved for posterity. Now he abandoned that hope on the grounds that students may not grasp what he had to say or might pass it on in so distorted a form as to make it unrecognizable. The only way someone interested in serious philosophical thoughts could perpetuate them, he concluded, is "to record them and put them down in black and white,"[9] not as commissioned pieces or specialized treatises but as major and comprehensive works that exhaust everything known on a given subject. By this he meant literally *everything.* Only by doing so could he be sure that his ideas would out-live him.

The idea of bringing together all that has ever been learned in a given field of knowledge dates to the Greeks. Aristotle himself declared his intention to set down and analyze all knowledge. Ptolemy, Euclid, and Galen all embraced Aristotle's aspiration as their own. In some cases, the ancient encyclopedists became mere collectors. The Roman writer Pliny the Elder bragged that for his encyclopedia *Naturalis Historia*, written over several decades in the first century AD, he had amassed 20,000 facts from 2,000 works by 200 authors. But for the most renowned writers of antiquity, to be "encyclopedic" meant not only mastering all the facts but also explaining how they related to each other.

When readers in the Middle East and Central Asia gained access to translated works of the Greek encyclopedists, they followed the same impulse. The ninth-century encyclopedist Ibn Qutaybah sought not only to collect all knowledge but also to organize it. This urge spread even to many who had not the slightest interest in what the ancient Greeks had to say. Soon there were encyclopedic collections covering everything from plants, animals, and freaks of nature to astrology and bizarre customs. A single collection of poems and songs, issued in Arabic by the scholar Abu al-Faraj from Isfahan, ran to 10,000 pages. During Ibn Sina's boyhood a fellow Bukharan put the finishing touches on his encyclopedic *Keys to the Sciences.* Its author, Muhammad bin Yusuf al-Khwarazmi (no relation to the earlier al-Khwarazmi whose works inspired Biruni), was a senior official who sought to condense the best of ancient and modern learning into one volume. Against this background, one can surmise that even the many competing compilations of the *Sayings* of the Prophet Muhammad reflected the widespread urge for encyclopedic knowledge that accompanied the penetration of ancient Greek learning into the Muslim world.

By the era of Ibn Sina, the rough format that the more thoughtful encyclopedists developed had gained wide acceptance. It consisted of three components: first, a presentation of what the ancients had to say on a given subject; second, the identifications of problems or outright errors in the ancient texts; and third, the compiler's suggestions on how to address those difficulties. Ibn Sina gravitated naturally to this format. In fact, many of his early writings can be viewed as compilations with commentaries, and therefore as small-scale proto encyclopedias. The question is how he would adjust the template to whatever subject he undertook. By his fortieth year, Ibn Sina's competence in at least eight fields was widely acknowledged: law; finance; medicine; astronomy; mathematics; cosmology; logic; and metaphysics. The first two he would have dismissed as mere practical skills. And during the confrontation with Biruni he had acknowledged his rival's superior competence in math-based studies. Logic and metaphysics were clearly Ibn Sina's passion. But medicine had two distinct advantages over all the other fields. First, though Ibn Sina dismissed it as a mere craft, almost on a par with woodworking,[10] medicine could nonetheless be subsumed under a grand framework of logic, and this was Ibn Sina's forte. And second, its status as a practical enterprise assured that anything he would write in that field would elicit broad interest and support.

And so, Ibn Sina, stuck in Gorgan without a royal patron and supported only by an amateur whose interests were limited to basic topics in science, decided to write an encyclopedia of medicine and to base it on a logical structure of his own devising. He may also have considered a similarly comprehensive study of metaphysics and logic, but that would have to wait.

Challenging Ibn Sina was his knowledge that readers of Arabic already had access to a vast array of classical works on medicine. Aristotle had included seminal passages on medicine in many of his books. I've already noted Galen, whose 3 million words of surviving text is less than a third of his total *oeuvre*.[11] Pertinent for Ibn Sina, Galen had spelled out Hippocrates's theory of the four humors; stressed the links between medicine, logic, and philosophy; and even written a book entitled *That the Best Physician Is Also a Philosopher*. Two centuries before Ibn Sina, the Christian translator Hunayn ibn Ishaq had rendered numerous works by Galen into Arabic and also written his own *Introduction to Medicine*. Finally, a century before Galen, there was the first-century AD author Dioscorides, author of the five-volume work on pharmacology that Ibn Sina's own tutor back in Bukhara, Abu-Abdallah al-Natili, had edited. Ibn Sina, in short, was advancing on well-trod ground.

The first medical encyclopedia in the Arabic language was the work of Ali ibn Sahl al-Tabari, a ninth-century physician from the Caspian region near Gorgan. Many other experts in Central Asia and the Middle East followed suit, seeking to build on ancient Persian, Indian, and more recent Byzantine medical treatises as well as Greek sources. The best known of these was by Tabari's student, Razi, the same restless polymath who had so intrigued Biruni during his stay in Rayy. For Ibn Sina, Razi's vast guide to medical knowledge presented a formidable challenge. But it also posed an opportunity, for Razi's great posthumous work was poorly organized and confusing.

Razi was by no means the only hurdle to be overcome. Just before Ibn Sina began to study medicine, one of Razi's students, a Muslim convert from Zoroastrianism named Ali ibn al-Abbas al-Majusi, issued his own *Complete Book of the Medical Art*. The conciseness of Majusi's book made it more appealing than Razi's sprawling work, while its utter practicality posed a further challenge to Ibn Sina. Under these circumstances, anyone purporting to add yet another medical encyclopedia to the list of those already available must surely be seen as delusional. Yet Ibn Sina had good reasons to proceed. None of his predecessors had accomplished what he set out to do. Galen's sixteen volumes were unwieldy; Tabari's lacked depth; and Razi's were too disorganized for easy use. Only Majusi's more disciplined work came close to being a precedent, but it was thin on the philosophical side.

Thus Ibn Sina discovered a niche for himself. In seeking to fill it, he could call on three formidable assets. First, he had a prodigious memory. His seemingly total recall enabled him to draw at will on the contents of all prior studies he had read. Second, he could write—or, to be more precise, dictate—with exceptional speed and clarity. Third, and arguably most important, thanks to the rigor of his studies in logic and philosophy, Ibn Sina would be able to impose an orderly rational structure on the mass of details he would present. The combination of these assets was the key to the stupendous eventual success of Ibn Sina's project.

Why Ibn Sina decided to name his compendium *Canon of Medicine*, on the other hand, is a bit of a mystery. His title exudes the unbounded ambition that gave rise to the project. "Kanon" is a Greek word that was imported unchanged into Arabic as "Qanun." In its original Greek meaning it referred to a straight rod used for measuring, but it also had the cognate meaning of a standard, rule, or the law itself. The latter was its sole meaning in Arabic. When Ibn Sina made the decision to appropriate it, he knew full well that the title of his book signified nothing less than the Law of Medicine.

Ibn Sina undertook the writing of the *Canon of Medicine* when he was forty years old, living in a borrowed house in a backwater, with a dull bureaucratic job, only one or two paying students, and no prospects for the future. He could not claim to have discovered the laws of medicine. But he could gather them, organize them in a rational structure, correct them with his own clinical experience, enrich them with his insights on the interaction of body and soul, and in this form offer them to the world. In the *Canon of Medicine* he presents himself as nothing less than the prophet of medicine. His book, which numbers some 2,500 pages in modern translations, was to become for half a millennium the single most influential medical work in the world.

10

Expanding the Known World

In 1017, Biruni's world collapsed. The strategies he proposed as vizier to the shah of Khwarazm had, as noted, failed. That shah, who was also Biruni's patron, had been murdered and his capital ransacked. Countless men and women with whom Biruni had lived and worked perished or were taken captive in the fighting and ensuing chaos. He himself was now a captive. Driven by Mahmud's victorious army, Biruni now faced an arduous trek, one that would have taken a normal caravan sixty days had it made the trip without a break. But with a column of thousands of captives, all of whom had to be fed, with uncounted camels piled high with loot and requiring fodder, and with tens of thousands more of Mahmud's troops to watch over it all, this mass of people would be lucky if it reached central Afghanistan in under six months.

Mahmud may have valued Biruni as one of the world's two greatest thinkers, but Biruni was now the sultan's hostage—the highest living official of a government that had failed Mahmud and then been defeated in battle. To make matters worse, Biruni was accused of heresy. Someone had tipped off Mahmud that Biruni, in his *Chronology of Ancient Nations*, had written sympathetically (or without adequate condemnation) of the Qarmatians, a group of radical Shiites who, in the minds of the orthodox Sunnis around Mahmud, epitomized all that was evil about the Shiite schism. Mahmud's mullahs blamed the Qarmatians for stealing the Black Stone from the Kaaba in Mecca and throwing the corpses of its defenders into the holy well of Zamzam, from which the Prophet himself had drunk.[1] There was no way they could turn a blind eye to a scholar and captive who had failed to brand such people apostates.

According to the early thirteenth-century Arab chronicler Yaqut al Hamawi, Mahmud was so outraged that he condemned Biruni to death. The same sentence was passed on another captive scholar from Gurganj, Abd as-Samad Auvali. Under the custom of the day, this meant either stoning or beheading. Auvali was duly executed. The death sentence was Mahmud's means of advertising his bona fides as an orthodox Muslim. But he was not about to let this cost him the addition of such a prize thinker as Biruni to his stable of court poets and intellectuals. Instead of being beheaded, Biruni was spared and sent as a convicted criminal to a remote fortress called Nandana, high atop a mountain in the Salt Range in what today is Pakistan.[2] The valley it commanded was of such strategic importance that Alexander the Great had chosen it as his army's route to India. Mahmud had only recently captured Nandana but had no use for it other than as a place for incarcerating criminals.[3]

Biruni, having failed as a diplomat and been indirectly responsible for the death of his ruler, was deeply depressed. The fighting in Gurganj had destroyed his library and all his scientific instruments. He would later compare his distress at this time to that of the prophets Noah and Lot.[4] In spite of all this, when he found himself briefly in a town near Kabul he managed to improvise a simple instrument, called a counting board, with which he could fix the coordinates of that spot. That occurred on September 15, 1018, fourteen months after the burning of Gurganj.[5] In spite of his depression, Biruni was back at work. While at Nandana, Biruni carried out the project that would result in the most precise measurement of the earth before modern times. But aside from one mention of having once lived at Nandana,[6] Biruni never spoke of his presence there.

After Biruni had spent nearly a year at Nandana, Mahmud brought him back to the capital at Ghazni, where he joined the thousands of captive members of the old elite of Khwarazm who were now working in Mahmud's government. Biruni's old mentors, Ibn Iraq and the doctor Khammar, were also among the newly arrived captives. Their presence must have consoled Biruni, although the fact that both vanished from history thereafter suggests that neither survived long in Ghazni.

Mahmud and Biruni somehow worked out a *modus vivendi*. Several anecdotes indicate that Mahmud came to respect Biruni, if not like him. For example, travelers from the far north told Mahmud about sunlit summer nights in the polar region. Mahmud branded this as heresy, but Biruni stepped in to explain the phenomenon and Mahmud meekly accepted his account.[7] On another occasion Mahmud bragged that he was so rich that it would take a lifetime just to give it all away. Biruni reminded him that fate had been kind to him and that if fate were to turn against him he could lose it all in a day.[8] This bold admonishment brought no negative consequences.

Mahmud's respect for Biruni may have been qualified by lingering suspicions as to his religious views, but it did not prevent him from providing his court astrologer with an impressive astronomical observatory. The heart of this complex was a square building housing a large wall quadrant that featured a bronze arc 4.5 meters (15 feet) in diameter that was calibrated to an accuracy of one minute.[9] Thanks to Mahmud, for the first time in his life Biruni was able to design and use an observatory modeled directly after Khujandi's great instrument in Rayy.

By late 1018, Biruni was able to withdraw into his own work, complying with Mahmud's demands as they arose but otherwise keeping both the sultan and his court at arm's length. As a result, he could focus single-mindedly on his great (and awkwardly titled) study, *The Determination of the Coordinates of Positions for the Correction of Distances Between . . . Cities*. Biruni began work on it in 1018, completing it only in the year 1025.

This short but densely packed treatise marks the foundation of the modern field of geodesy, the discipline that measures the earth's geometric shape and orientation in space. This is precisely what Biruni was up to, but he went beyond that. Building on his earlier work, he used astronomy to measure distances on the curved surface of the earth. He wanted to determine the earth's precise dimensions. But he also sought to devise a rigorous process for measuring all terrestrial distances, to identify the latitude and longitude of all points on earth. The Russian translator of this book chose to rename it *Geodesy* (*Geodeziia*). While a fitting tribute to what Biruni managed to accomplish, this was not Biruni's title, which, for the sake of convenience, we will shorten to *The Determination of the Coordinates of . . . Cities*.[10] Biruni conceived geodesy as the master science of earth studies, built on the foundations of astronomy, mathematics, geometry, geography, and cartography. Its origins trace to Aristotle, Euclid, and Ptolemy, though the ancients did little more than provide a starting point.

Biruni used his introduction to *The Determination of the Coordinates of . . . Cities* to get something off his chest, and—very exceptionally—begins it with a cri de coeur, one that parallels Ibn Sina's lament from Gorgan. "I behold how people of our time in different parts of the world reflect such forms of ignorance, and how proud they are of it; how antagonistic they are to people of virtue; [and] how they plot against a learned scholar [e.g., Biruni himself] and inflict on him all sorts of harm and persecution."[11] In an oblique reference to his own recent troubles, he attacks the "extremists, who stamp the sciences as atheistic and proclaim that they lead people astray." He then denounces all forms of "primitive worship that do the soul no good because they are not based on intelligent knowledge that discriminates between good and evil." True knowledge, which Biruni equated with reason and science, acquaints people with their Maker and enables them to discriminate between genuine prophets and pseudo-prophets. In a paraphrase of Razi's denunciation of prophets and prophesy, he cautions, "The pretenders to revelation are many. Since they do not agree among themselves, it is certain that some of them are false prophets who would lead people astray."[12] The choice, therefore, is either to accept religion as a mere story and tradition or to investigate it scientifically so as to grasp and affirm its core truths.

Biruni then proceeds to set forth his views on society. Human beings, he writes, are social animals, and the division of labor among them is inevitable. But since labor and needs are not in balance, they are valued differently. Mankind therefore developed systems for pricing labor and goods based on the cost of rare metals and jewels. Prices are thereby set "on the just basis of the labor involved," which even thieves and oppressors acknowledge. Adam Smith, David Ricardo, and Karl Marx would all have applauded this pioneering expression of the "labor theory of value."

After that he offers a personal aside. Some people amass great wealth, Biruni explains, which they seek to pass on to their heirs. But "the air [people] breathe carries various kinds of infections" and natural cataclysms beset them. These gave rise to the field of medicine. Though people have benefited from its development, the achievements of medical science remain "insignificant" compared with those of "absolute science."

One wonders whether Biruni was echoing Ibn Sina's own dismissal of medicine as a lesser art, or indeed making another sly attack on Ibn Sina, who had just begun writing his *Canon of Medicine*. By comparison, he continued, the arts and other sciences have given rise to far more elevated studies. Music, for example, may be a passion of the rich, but mathematicians have managed to "investigate and discover the true principles of the science of music." And because human beings rely on nature for food and since food depends on climate and weather, the noble science of astronomy, too, serves both practical ends and humanity's yearning for knowledge.

After this Biruni defends the ancient Greeks against their modern critics. Someone at Mahmud's court had apparently denounced Aristotle as a heathen. In response, Biruni reminds his readers that the Greek thinker "was a theoretician, not a theologian."[13] At the same time Biruni insists that he himself was no worshipper of the ancients and rebuked Ptolemy for his numerous errors. He also rebukes those who seek to answer fundamental questions with frivolous logic. In one of the most sharply worded passages in *The Determination of the Coordinates of . . . Cities*, Biruni attacks those who seek to grasp the concept of time through the use of wrong-headed syllogisms. Such core issues, he insists, "cannot be realized in any way by minds reasoning [only] by syllogism."[14] Valid conclusions, he averred, must be based instead on careful measurement and on mathematics. In a key statement of his basic philosophy, he declares, "All that exists is denumerable," "beginning with the number one and ending in a finite number." Thus Biruni, without naming names, lobbed yet another attack on Aristotle and on his own adversary, Ibn Sina.

The final section of Biruni's introduction is devoted to the impact of astronomical conditions on the geology of mountains, lakes, deserts, and tides. He shows how the sun's rays decrease in intensity from the equator to the poles and how this defines the character of human societies in each climatic zone. In these passages Biruni reveals himself as an evolutionist. He believed that after God created the world, it underwent profound changes, leading to the upsurge of mountains, the drying up of seas, the creation of deserts, and the transformation of deserts into forests. In subsequent works he would return many times to the question of geological and social evolution.

In demonstrating the relevance of astronomy to geodesy and how geography shapes natural life and human societies, Biruni affirmed his own bona fides as a determinist. The tone of these passages reveals an opinionated and combative side that contrasts with his usual measured tone. Nonetheless, Biruni's treatise on determining the location of cities was the most comprehensive study to that time of latitude and longitude, offering insights on the interconnections between astronomy, geography, and mathematics. For example, he presented his method for measuring the distance between two points by simultaneously observing a lunar eclipse at both spots. His theses all turn on precise astronomical data, some of which he had brought from Gurganj but much of it resulting from fresh research he had conducted at Nandana and Ghazni.

Biruni's studies under Ibn Iraq and his own earliest experiments had helped launch this new approach to geodesy. Due to his early involvement with the Baghdad-Kath project, Biruni had acquired the necessary astronomical knowledge. In his first study of spherical trigonometry, written twenty years earlier at Gorgan, he had demonstrated an understanding of conical and cylindrical forms. This entailed the use of sine law, which was only then being adopted from the work of Indian mathematicians, in part thanks to Biruni's own mentor, Ibn Iraq. Biruni did not invent sine law but was the first to use it to solve the central geodesic problem, namely, to measure the earth's diameter. In *The Determination of the Coordinates of . . . Cities* and later in his *Masud's Canon* he also employed mathematical "chords" (a line connecting two points on the circumference of a circle), another Indian method that antedated the law of sines.

Biruni divided *The Determination of the Coordinates of . . . Cities* into four sections. These address the determination of longitudes; the obliquity of the ecliptic and its bearing on geographical studies; the problem of latitudes and declinations; and the coordinates of selected cities and the distances between them. Biruni had touched upon each of these issues in earlier studies, and they were all to emerge again in later works. However, they appear here in the most developed form to date and with a full presentation of the relevant astronomy and trigonometry. To facilitate his research, Biruni had developed three novel instruments, all of which combined precision with simplicity. None called for materials aside from long, straight wooden poles, cones, and a diopter, a basic but ingenious tool for measuring the radii of curved surfaces. All of these could be easily constructed and were highly portable.[15] The attention he lavished on these devices reflects Biruni's ability to define problems with precision and then to develop the necessary intellectual and physical tools to solve them.

The language of Biruni's work on geodesy is not graceful and his presentations are difficult to follow. He had a tendency to use the written word to record and reproduce his own reasoning process rather than as a tool for broader communication. Rarely did he feel it necessary to summarize a line of thought or argument. As a result, even his most significant works have the opaqueness that one would expect to find in a work in progress. They all seem to be awaiting an editor.

Still, what Biruni was trying to achieve in his *The Determination of the Coordinates of . . . Cities* was considerable. First, he considers all the various chapters and headings as parts of a single whole and not as separate research reports on vaguely connected topics. Second, his main focus is squarely on human societies and economies and their diverse characters in different parts of the world. The astronomy and mathematics were enlisted solely to serve this end. His great achievement was to appreciate the extent and manner in which different modes of human development are molded by geography and climate, which are in turn shaped by astronomical realities. Astronomy keenly interested him, and he was to make enduring contributions to that field, but in this work on geodesy his goal is to lay bare the processes through which movements of the sun and moon affect terrestrial life.

Third, and most important, Biruni wanted to enlarge our understanding of the earth itself. He bowed to the authority of Aristotle but considered the Greek master's conception of a single world island surrounded by a great ocean to be a dubious hypothesis, just short of fantasy. Nor did he consider Ptolemy's *Almagest* to be the last word in geography. Ptolemy was a stay-at-home geographer whose maps were limited to what he could find in gazetteers from the Roman and Persian empires and by what an earlier cartographer, Marinos of Tyre, had included on his charts. Biruni, by contrast, relied mainly on his own research. As a young man, he had pored over the pioneering geographical studies of Abu Zayd al-Balkhi from the Afghan city of Balkh, and the *Book of Routes and Kingdoms* by Balkhi's student from Bukhara, Abu Abdallah Jayhani. Biruni also consulted merchants who had spent their lives moving among the world's commercial centers. These travelers told him of distant cities that were unknown to Ptolemy and, with Biruni's help, provided measures of distances that were far more accurate than Ptolemy's.

Biruni's innovative mathematical and astronomical techniques enabled him to measure terrestrial distances with a precision greater than that of his predecessors. Some of the calculations he made on the basis of his data from Nandana ran to a dozen decimal points. This in turn opened a path for him to develop maps of unequaled precision. Modern scientists have discovered occasional errors in Biruni's calculations, but these barely affected his conclusions.[16]

The significance of Biruni's geodesic study emerges in his demonstration of how to determine longitudes. No question of practical and theoretical science had proven more vexing over the centuries. Latitudes are a simple matter because they run in circles that are parallel to the equator and equidistant from each other. The problem with determining longitude arises from the fact that they all come together at the North and South Poles. As a result, the span between longitudes increases or decreases depending on the distance from either pole. Biruni devised a way to use mathematics and spherical trigonometry, along with precise data gleaned from astronomical observations, to determine longitude. He was not alone in developing the mathematical tools needed to address this issue. More than a century before him Habash al-Marwazi from Merv and al-Khwarazmi had begun to develop spherical trigonometry and cotangent tables. But Biruni brought these efforts to fruition, pulled them all together, and applied them to geodesy.

The full extent of Biruni's contribution will only become known if and when copies of his major lost works turn up and are made available. Still, barring that, Biruni was without doubt the father of geodesy, the field that was to engage so many sea captains, scientists, and cartographers in the centuries to come during the Age of Exploration. Biruni's role in developing these studies was central, for he provided the key to cartography and, potentially, to navigation on the open sea. Had Biruni's work been known earlier it would have accelerated exploration. The fact that Biruni was a desk-bound explorer and not a sailor obscured his achievement. Not until the sixteenth century did Europe and the Mediterranean world catch up with him.[17]

Biruni's preeminence in the world of exploration is solidified by his effort to measure the earth. The ancient Greeks had launched this quest. Biruni's era, however, advanced matters significantly. Biruni knew that the Baghdad astronomer Buzjani had suggested the possibility of determining the earth's radius by a two-step process of triangulation that involved the measurement of the angle from a mountaintop to a point on the horizon, and from that point on the horizon to the bottom of the same mountain. With these in hand, he was able to construct a further triangle from the base of the mountain and the point on the horizon to a hypothetical point at the center of the earth. This possibility of triangulating from a so-called dip angle had first been proposed by a Baghdad colleague of Buzjani's, Abu Tayyib Sind bin Ali, but remained as yet unproven. This technique called for a mountain adjacent to a plain, thus affording an unimpeded view from the mountaintop to the far horizon. During his involuntary internment at the Nandana fortress in the Salt Range, Biruni found just such a site. His choice was a mountaintop just west of Nandana (not Nandana itself, a fact ignored by all but two of the several scientists who have recently attempted to replicate his research).[18]

Biruni constructed the necessary equipment and set it up on the mountaintop he had selected. His main instrument consisted of a long pole that could be suspended in a well to assure that it would be exactly vertical, and a very precise compass-like gauge to measure the dip angle between the vertical pole and the horizon. This instrument was, in effect, a simple but very precise theodolite, a rotating telescope used for surveying. We know from Biruni's own calculations that his home-made instrument was capable of reading minutes to within a degree by interpolation.

Beyond this, Biruni needed both a way to measure the distance between the base of the mountain and the point on the horizon—as well as a very clear day, without which neither the person on the mountaintop nor the person at the horizon could see the other. Since the distance is slightly over 62 kilometers (40 miles) and the climate at Nandana dry and dusty, this proved difficult. When the Pakistani scientist Saiyid Samad Husain Rizvi attempted to replicate Biruni's calculation in 1965, he had to wait weeks before the dust settled to the extent that two-way sightings were possible.[19] No less serious a problem was to locate a spot in the rolling terrain that would be on a precise level with the base of the mountain. Moreover, the process of triangulation depended for its accuracy on the precision with which he calculated the height of the mountaintop. Biruni's final calculation, which he made with the help of an astrolabe, turned out to be off by less than a fifth of a percent.

The final stage in the process again involved triangulation and the use of sine law to provide the length of the third side of the triangle formed by the point on the mountaintop, the point on the horizon, and the earth's center. It was for this last process that Biruni brought into play his skills at trigonometry, which he used to determine the distance from the mountaintop to the center of the earth. In this calculation he employed, again, the law of sines. The challenge was to find a precise value of the cosine of the angle of dip of the horizon. The importance of this calculation is clear when one considers that an error of 0.000001 in the value of the cosine of the angle of dip to the horizon would cause an error of 121 kilometers (72 miles) in the resulting calculation of the earth's radius. For this crucial calculation Biruni used sine tables he himself had developed.[20]

In the end, he measured the earth's diameter with stunning precision. His calculations resulted in a figure that differs from the modern calculation by only 34.62 kilometers (21.51 miles) or .003 percent. His calculation of the earth's circumference is only .007 percent less than the modern figure, while his measurement of one degree of longitude at the equator is a mere .085 percent less than the modern figure.[21] Just as Buzjani's estimation was an improvement over that of Eratosthenes of Cyrene in the third century BC, so Biruni's calculation far surpassed Buzjani's in accuracy. And all three of Biruni's calculations differ far more from Buzjani's than from the modern figures. Not until the seventeenth century did European scientists achieve measurements more precise than Biruni's. His measurement of the earth opened the way to similarly precise measurements of the distance between longitudes, the size of continents, and the distances between points too distant from one another to be measured by more conventional means. It was the single most momentous act of discovery in the fields of geography and geodesy up to that time.

The blunt yet conversational tone of Biruni's introduction suggests that the introvert Biruni had developed a circle of sympathetic readers in Ghazni who could balance whatever demands the imperious Mahmud might place upon him. The name of only one of these figures has come down to us, Abu l'Hasan Musafir. Apparently a man of means and influence, he became Biruni's patron and the dedicatee of four significant works, only one of which has survived.[22] That book dealt with the important but unexplored issue of the use of shadows in astronomy and related areas of mathematics. The analysis of shadows led Biruni to the concept of tangents and cotangents, which, along with sines and cosines, are fundamental trigonometric functions.

Astronomers since ancient times had employed the shadows generated by the gnomons of sundials to develop astronomical insights. Shadows were in fact the key to predicting solar and lunar eclipses, telling time, and determining geographical locations. However, no one before Biruni had subjected shadows themselves to detailed analysis. Like the ancients, he distinguished various types of shadows: direct (*umbra recta*); overturned (*umbra versa*); and so forth. Unlike his predecessors, however, Biruni analyzed the different calibration systems by which the Greeks, Indians, and Arabs measured them. He also resolved the trigonometric questions of whether projected shadows and light are cylindrical or conical in shape, by proving they are cylindrical. And he offered up shadow tables based on their tangents and cotangents.[23]

Another work of these years was entitled *Corrections to the "Elements" by al-Farghani*. Although this book is lost, we know enough about it to say that it cast in sharp relief Biruni's fundamental approach to the scientific enterprise. Abu al-Abbas Farghani was a ninth-century astronomer and scientist from the Ferghana Valley in present-day Uzbekistan who designed the "Nilometer," which was used for measuring the flow of the Nile at Cairo. Notwithstanding the fact that Farghani lived two centuries before Biruni, his efforts to measure the Earth's diameter and his book summarizing the astronomy and geography of Ptolemy's *Almagest* made him Biruni's direct intellectual forebear. Biruni respected his fellow Central Asian, though he had also discovered errors of omission and commission in Farghani's volume. He therefore penned a 400-page tome to correct them.

Biruni's achievements in astronomy were historic but have only recently been subjected to close study.[24] Biruni's work largely supplanted Ptolemy's *Almagest* and set the field onto a new course. Yet in this and many other instances, he opted not to replace a predecessor's system with his own but rather to correct his forerunner's work. This came naturally to someone of

Biruni's methodical turn of mind. It also reflected his convictions about science as such. Biruni was a practitioner of slow and deliberate science, not "Eureka" moments. In a later work he would caution that, given the limits of astronomical instruments, "the life of an individual or of whole generations will not suffice to determine the true length of the year."[25]

This was the spirit in which he returned to the same issues in astronomy, geonomics, minerology, and scientific instrumentation. For example, he mulled over the problem of heliocentrism in four major works and in an entire special volume, now lost. Biruni's readiness to revisit issues in light of new evidence or new methodologies attests to his view that science is constantly evolving. He saw himself as but one link in a chain extending through the centuries. As a consequence, he believed that any attempt to freeze scientific knowledge in a static encyclopedia or to force our existing knowledge of the world into an all-embracing system was futile. Foolish to its core, any such project would be doomed to failure.

11

Ibn Sina's Adventures

News of Ibn Sina's prowess in medicine had spread from his native Central Asia into Persia and especially to the city of Rayy, the same entrepot where the impoverished young Biruni had spent several productive years. Sometime around 1014, Ibn Sina pulled up stakes in Gorgan and moved there. Rayy, once a center of culture, had been in decline even before Biruni's brief stay there. By the time Ibn Sina showed up, the city was in crisis.

Why, then, would he have made such a move? The surviving evidence remains sketchy. The most widely cited account, and a colorful one indeed, is by the writer and Central Asian chronicler Nizami Aruzi. The events he describes in the account actually took place several years later than he claims they did, however, and in a different city.[1] Nonetheless, his report is believable in part because it is so bizarre.

"Fahr al-Dawla" or "Pride of the Realm," the emir of Rayy who had supported the astronomer Khujandi, died in 997. His rightful heir was his four-year-old son, Abu Taleb Rustan, who had already been dubbed "Majd al-Dawla" or "Exalted of the Realm." In spite of his tender years, this young boy was duly installed as emir. However, his mother, Shirin, known to history simply as "The Lady" ("al-Sayyida"), assumed actual control as regent. Sometime around 1007 The Lady's enemies attempted a coup in favor of her son, who was by then fourteen years of age. However, Majd al-Dawla's brother, the Buyid ruler of Hamadan, laid siege to Rayy and quashed the mutiny. Meanwhile, young Majd al-Dawla came down with what official documents described as a "severe bout of melancholia" but which was obviously something more serious. Considering himself unworthy to lead, Majd al-Dawla fantasized that he was a cow and demanded that he should be slaughtered to provide meat to feed more worthy souls.

The Lady contacted Ibn Sina in hopes that he might cure the young man. Rushing to Rayy, Ibn Sina sized up the situation. He ordered the lad to be bound up with ropes and readied for the butcher. He then called in a genuine butcher, who entered the room wielding his long carving knife. But on instruction from Ibn Sina, the butcher declared that Majd al-Dawla was far too thin to be edible and gave orders for him to be fattened up. Nourished by a rich diet, the young emir quickly recovered. His new doctor was appointed court physician, and Majd al-Dawla ruled for another fifteen years. Ibn Sina later wrote a treatise entitled *Cures of the Heart*, with a long opening section dealing with the treatment of emotional disorders and mental illness.[2]

During the two years he spent in Rayy, Ibn Sina continued to work on the first volume of the *Canon of Medicine* and found time also to compose two more treatises on the soul, known variously as *The State of the Human Soul* or simply as *The Destination*.[3] Acting on an *idée fixe* dating from his boyhood, Ibn Sina devoted the sixteen chapters of this work to the question of the soul's fate after the death and decay of the physical body.[4] After complaining once more about the hardships he was enduring, Ibn Sina summarized this work in his introduction. It dealt, he explained, with the "state of the human soul" and was an exploration into its "resurrection and circumstances that lead it in the afterlife."[5]

Though they read like a publisher's copy, these lines exude the confidence Ibn Sina had in his own philosophical method. Properly conducted, logic, together with philosophical analysis, reveals truths that cannot be challenged and must therefore correspond to reality. The American philosopher Lenn Goodman aptly summarizes Ibn Sina's thesis as this: "Our knowledge of universals betokens the immortality of the rational soul and its hegemony over (rather than dependence on) the body."[6] Ibn Sina held that intellect, with its potential to attain "knowledge of universals," is an instrument through which the soul can attain immortality. Given its grounding in logic and syllogism, the treatise on physical death and the soul's survival in the afterlife was, simply, true. To discover its truth the reader needed only to exercise reason and logic. Ibn Sina would use the same argument to dismiss the possibility of a soul migrating from one body to another through what we now call metempsychosis.

It has been said that *The Destination* reflects Ibn Sina's mature psychology. This may be true in a theoretical sense, but it says nothing about his own psychological state at the time. Having drawn a sharp distinction between body and soul, he then wrote *Ode to the Soul*, an ecstatic work in impassioned verse that contrasts dramatically with his formal philosophizing. Ibn Sina speaks of the soul dwelling "in heavenly gardens and groves, which to leave it was loath," and then its descent to "the ruined abodes of this desolate world." Finally, after the physical death of the body, the soul "returns, aware of all hidden things in the universe, while no stain to its garment clings." It seems somehow hard to reconcile that the same person who could write these lines would also devote hundreds of pages of his *Canon of Medicine* to the impact of both physical and immaterial conditions on the human psyche—in other words, a work that treats those "stains" as real and treatable in the here and now.

That Ibn Sina could develop a system of logic that justified such an emotionally satisfying outlook on life is admirable. However, he insisted that this was only for the select few, those of "pure heart," whose minds were capable of soaring as high as his own. Fortunately, by this time the ranks of those of "pure heart" had expanded with the addition to his circle of a number of new acolytes. In addition to Juzjani there were several highly competent students, including a young Zoroastrian from Azerbaijan named Bahmanyar, who later converted to Islam and co-authored with his teacher a volume of dialogues.[7]

In spite of all this bonhomie, all was not well in Rayy. Majd al-Dawla, as unstable as ever, tried to free himself from his mother's regency. Shams al-Dawla from Hamadan, appalled by his brother's behavior, resolved to end Majd al-Dawla's capriciousness once and for all by intervening against him. This time, though, Majd al-Dawla's army managed to repulse his brother's attack, relations between mother and both sons were somehow patched up, and his brother Shams returned in humiliation to Hamadan. As this dynastic conflict raged, spies from Ghazni reported to Mahmud on every detail of the turmoil. Frustrated by years of being unable to do anything to dislodge the Shiite Buyids from that city, Mahmud began preparing an assault on Persia. However, The Lady had her own spies, who reported to her on Mahmud's mobilization. She immediately wrote to the tyrant that a war between the two of them could have only one of two possible outcomes: "If [my army] carries the day I shall write to the entire world that I have defeated Sultan Mahmud, who defeated a hundred kings. . . . But if you are the victor, what will you write? That you have broken the power of a woman?"[8]

Mahmud brushed off this threat. He informed The Lady that he knew that she had been protecting the renowned Ibn Sina at her court in Rayy and demanded that she send him at once to Ghazni, where he could add luster to Mahmud's court. The Lady promptly tipped off Ibn Sina, who fled Rayy, as did The Lady herself and Majd al-Dawla. Scarcely had they passed out of the gates than Mahmud's army swept into town. Mother and son headed directly to Hamadan, where her other son, Shams al-Dawla, awaited them. Ibn Sina fled first to Qazvin, 150 kilometers (93 miles) northwest of Rayy. When he failed to find a post there he again hit the road, this time following the route south for the 300 kilometers (180 miles) to Hamadan. The Lady once more welcomed him and offered him the job of managing her personal finances.[9]

Hamadan was, and is still, a pleasant city. Spread over a broad plain at the foot of the Alvand Mountains in west-central Iran, it had been a royal residence for a millennium before Ibn Sina's arrival. The ruler was of course Shams al-Dawla, Majd al-Dawla's brother, whose name meant "Sun of the Dynasty." In reality, Shams al-Dawla was a mere regional princeling, a struggling minor potentate in the Buyid family's decentralized and rapidly disintegrating empire. His credibility had recently taken a beating when his younger brother had stymied his effort to take control of Rayy. Further complicating things for Shams, his controlling mother, the formidable Lady, had joined him in Hamadan to get beyond Mahmud's reach.

Capping Shams's misfortunes, he was now debilitated by painful and seemingly untreatable colic. Today we associate colic mainly with crying infants. But a millennium ago it was a catch-all term denoting acute abdominal pain that can arise from anything, including appendicitis, obstruction in the bowel, urinary infection, even cancer. With her son suffering so grievously, The Lady sent her new accountant and doctor to his bedside. Ibn Sina's treatment for Shams al-Dawla's colic was lengthy and complex—he would later write an entire treatise on colic. While the emir was undergoing treatment, he and Ibn Sina got to know one another. Shams increasingly took the older Ibn Sina into his confidence and sought his advice on matters of state.

Hamadan was a small principality facing formidable threats from many sides, especially from the Kurds to the west. Having failed in his effort to dislodge his own brother from Rayy, Shams al-Dawla decided that a successful campaign against the Kurds could restore his standing and self-respect. But the resulting brief campaign was a disaster, and powerful figures in the army blamed the failure on the emir's new doctor. They accused Ibn Sina of having whispered bad advice into their ruler's ear. Shams was either unaware of this criticism or chose to ignore it, for shortly after this military failure, the Sun of the Dynasty asked his doctor to serve as his vizier. This was an astonishing offer for someone who had never held a more senior post than court lawyer and financial consultant. Nonetheless Ibn Sina had had the experience of watching at close hand the collapse of sovereignty in Bukhara, Gurganj, Gorgan, and Rayy, and, despite having defined "governance" as one of the less challenging skills, he accepted the offer. He did so against the advice of his assistant, Juzjani, who later groused that Ibn Sina's service as vizier "proved distressful to us and a waste of time."[10]

Upon learning of the appointment, the army erupted in rebellion. A large band of soldiers gathered before Ibn Sina's house, torched his belongings, arrested him, and threw him into prison. The mob of soldiers demanded that the emir behead Ibn Sina. Shams al-Dawla refused and instead removed Ibn Sina from office and "banished" him, which turned out to be nothing more than requiring him to hide for forty days in the home of a sympathetic friend. During that time Shams al-Dawla once more succumbed to colic and once more summoned Ibn Sina to his bedside. After offering his profuse apologies, Shams reinstalled Ibn Sina as vizier.

Throughout his years in Hamadan Ibn Sina pursued simultaneously four quite different careers: practitioner and theoretician of medicine; philosopher of science and cosmology; senior governmental official; and teacher of advanced students. Ibn Sina and Biruni were both polymaths in the sense that their knowledge spanned a range of diverse subjects. Ibn Sina, however, was a *homo universalis* in that he practiced all four of these professions simultaneously.

In his role as vizier, Ibn Sina would have written hundreds of official documents and letters, none of which survive. He also composed a lengthy study on public administration entitled *The Management and Provisioning of Slave Troops and Armies, and the Taxation of Kingdoms*, which is also lost.[11] That Ibn Sina devoted an entire book to explaining how to control, clothe, and feed armies of slaves scarcely burnishes his modern reputation as a humanist. Yet it was testimony to the seriousness with which he now devoted his energies to his administrative role. Ibn Sina followed a daily schedule that began with mornings devoted to his own scholarly writing or, more accurately, dictating to Juzjani or other assistants. This was followed by lunch. Then the vizier turned to official business at his government office. In keeping with the traditions of the region, his responsibilities as vizier included holding public audiences, or *majles*, at which petitioners would bring him requests of all sorts. Then Ibn Sina would respond to each matter or refer it to the appropriate office or to the emir.

His deft handling of such audiences, combined with his writings, spread Ibn Sina's fame. A number of aspiring intellectuals soon sought him out. He regularly gathered these acolytes and students for evenings at his home. As described by Juzjani, these sessions invariably began with the reading and discussion of texts newly drafted or dictated by the master. Subjects for a typical session might include both new passages from the *Canon of Medicine* or drafts of philosophical works. The evenings invariably ended with less formal interactions that carried on late into the night.

These "seminars" have presented a challenge to Ibn Sina's biographers. Some of the more pious among them pass over them in silence, but there was ample grist for the critics. It was no secret that Ibn Sina fueled the sessions with large quantities of red wine. A disgusted Juzjani dismissed them bluntly as "drinking parties."[12] He also reported on the presence of professional singers, who would have been accompanied by instrumentalists playing the three-stringed *dotar* or *kamanche*, the *nay* flute, or the *daf* drum. With an eye to the critics, Juzjani refers to other entertainers but carefully describes them merely as "singers of various types." In his magesterial *Renaissance of Islam*, first published in 1922, the great German scholar Adam Mez notes that most professional singers in the Persian world were enslaved prostitutes.[13] Besides evoking sharp criticism, their presence likely gave rise to medical problems. Following Ibn Sina's death, the meticulous Juzjani commented in his *Life of Ibn Sina* on the cause of his master's demise. He duly noted the wracking "colic" that wore down his master, but then directly ascribed his decline to his insatiable sexual appetite.[14] This indulgence, too, was a prominent feature of these late nights in Hamadan.

This routine rolled on until early in 1021. By then Shams al-Dawla's strength had returned and his confidence had revived. A Kurdish army once more threatened Hamadan from the west. What better way to assert one's renewed vitality and boldness as a leader than to launch a preemptive attack on the Kurdish invaders? And so Shams patched up relations with his officers, mustered the army, and marched westward to face the enemy, dreaming of the brilliant victory that fate had earlier denied him. The Kurds, however, pushed back hard and threw Shams's army into disorderly retreat. To make matters worse, the emir's colic returned, worse than ever. This time, however, Ibn Sina had remained in Hamadan, which proved to all and sundry that responsibility for the latest military setbacks lay solely with the ailing emir and not his vizier. The absence of his doctor also left Shams without medical care. Untreated, he died a painful death in the field.

Shams's young son Sama' al-Dawla—"Canopy of the Realm"—then acceded to the throne, and once again the army intervened. This time, however, the officers pled with the young and untried emir to reappoint Ibn Sina as vizier. His ambition now tempered by bitter experience, Ibn Sina declined the offer. He knew that this would be taken as a rebuke and put him at risk.

Foreseeing only trouble in Hamadan, Ibn Sina had secretly written to the emir of Isfahan. This step was riskier yet. Ala ad-Dawla, or "Blessing of the Realm," ruled Isfahan as a satrap of the Shiite Buyids, but by birth he was neither Persian nor Shiite. Rather, he arose from the Daylamite people of the Caspian coast who had defended their native Zoroastrian faith against the Arab invaders. When they finally converted, they embraced not the Buyids' mainstream Shiism but the Ismailis' form of Shiism that was being promoted in Cairo by rivals of the traditional Shiite Buyids. This caused Ala ad-Dawla's allies to distrust him. Few doubted that his real plan was to link up with the Kurds against other Buyids to advance his cause. This was especially clear to the people of Hamadan, where he had openly and often expressed his desire to gain hegemony over their city and was only awaiting the best moment to act. The death of Shams al-Dawla and installation of his young and hapless son provided the perfect opportunity.

It seems somehow unlikely that Ibn Sina, who for years had been the second-most powerful figure in Hamadan, could have been truly unaware that the government he served maintained a region-wide network of spies. Equally unlikely is that he would not have foreseen that these spies might intercept his secret letter to the emir of Isfahan and discover his treachery. Yet this is exactly what happened. The man to whom the young emir of Hamadan had just offered the post of vizier was found to be in secret contact with the emir's worst enemy. When his letter was exposed, Ibn Sina took refuge in the home of a local grandee and then with a Hamadan druggist, where he again immersed himself in writing. But when a servant in the druggist's household informed on him, the new emir immediately had Ibn Sina arrested and dispatched under armed guard to the fortress of Fardaqan. Situated in barren countryside 60 kilometers (36 miles) southeast of Hamadan, the castle at Fardaqan had once been a Zoroastrian fire temple.[15] Now this massive stone fortress offered the most secure jail imaginable.

No period in Ibn Sina's life has been viewed with greater awe by later chroniclers than his period of hiding in Hamadan and then the four months of his incarceration at the Fardaqan castle. The Egyptian writer Yousef Zaidan even turned it into the subject of a suspense novel entitled *Fardaqan Castle*. Juzjani made much of Ibn Sina's spurt of creativity during this period but minimized the hardships involved. Reading Juzjani's account, one might conclude that Ibn Sina's time at Fardaqan was a foundation-funded sabbatical spent at a retreat for scholars. This is certainly not how Ibn Sina saw it, as one of his rhymed couplets suggests:

My coming here was certain, as you can see.
But many will doubt my departure.[16]

Ibn Sina had painted himself into a corner, and he understood that his incarceration could last a lifetime.

Then a stunning chain of events unfolded. Ala ad-Dawla in Isfahan had concluded that this was the moment to strike.[17] He had earlier helped both Majd al-Dawla in Rayy and his brother Shams al-Dalwa in Hamadan to suppress internal revolts, which he had done at the prompting of the ubiquitous dowager Shirin, "The Lady,"[18] to whom he owed his own appointment. Now Shams was dead and The Lady was dying. Ala ad-Dawla therefore marched on Hamadan, quickly overwhelmed its garrison, and began searching for the young emir. Sama' al-Dawla had meanwhile fled—amazingly, to the castle at Fardaqan. One can only imagine Ibn Sina's utter astonishment at seeing the man who had incarcerated him walk through the door of his own jail.

From this point matters assumed the madcap character of a Viennese operetta. The emir again apologized to Ibn Sina for having arrested him. Forced to coexist in the same fortress, they bonded to the point that Sama' al-Dawla once more pleaded with Ibn Sina to serve as his prime minister or vizier.[19] We might wonder how he was in a position to make such an offer, for by this time Ala ad-Dawla had completed his conquest of Hamadan, imposed reparations on the defeated city, and withdrawn his troops. All this rendered the young emir utterly powerless but at least enabled him to return to his city. His plan was to do so with Ibn Sina, his cellmate, as it were, in tow.

Once freed, Ibn Sina knew that if he refused the emir's offer, he would be sent back to Fardaqan, and this time with no hope of reprieve. But if he accepted, he would condemn himself to years of toil on behalf of a powerless and incompetent emir. In the end he chose a third course: to feign readiness to return to his post as vizier in Hamadan, then seize the first opportunity to flee to Isfahan.

12

Biruni's Masterpiece

In the Ottoman Archive in Istanbul and in a private archive in Paris are preserved manuscripts of one of the most significant works in the development of the social sciences globally: Biruni's *India*. It is a voluminous book. Modern editions run to some 700 pages. Unlike a great number of texts in Biruni's hand, it is actually quite readable. And yet its contribution to fields as diverse as mathematics, astronomy, cultural anthropology, geography, geology, and the comparative study of religions remains largely unacknowledged by all aside from a handful of specialists.

In its way, Biruni's *India* is also a monument to the rapacious empire builder, Mahmud of Ghazni. For had it not been for the campaigns of conquest and plunder Mahmud waged against India, the book would never have been written. These wars were what Germany's nineteenth-century chancellor, Otto von Bismarck, might have called a *Kulturkampf*, a battle of cultures and religions, pitting the massed and centrally controlled army of Islam against the decentralized and divided princely forces of Hindu India.

The two sides were grossly mismatched and the outcome never in doubt, which is why Mahmud waged his assaults so relentlessly. Mahmud's lifelong passion for conquest deep into the Indian subcontinent left a profound legacy that is felt even today in the volatile relations between Pakistan and India. It also defined Biruni's world from the day he arrived in Ghazni in 1018 to Mahmud's death in 1030.

Mahmud's father, Sebuktegin, had been a leader of vast ambition but without a country, having been rewarded by the Samanis for his service to them with the undeveloped territory of Ghazni and its hinterlands. As the Samanis' star faded, Sebuktegin decided to strengthen his hand through conquests in India. When he arrived in Ghazni on his march eastward he found that the city and surrounding territory were still controlled by local Hindu princes. Sebuktegin handily defeated them and captured their army, though at great cost to his own forces. Realizing the need to consolidate his rule in Ghazni and rebuild his army, he decided to suspend his planned assault on India. This left his grand Indian project to his son and successor, Mahmud, who embraced it as his lifelong passion. Mahmud's early campaigns, launched when he was twenty-nine after his father's death left him the throne, were directed against nearby Peshawar, Nargokot, and Multan. Along the way he took Nandana, the mountaintop fortress where Biruni would later carry out his measurement of the earth. Mahmud then overwhelmed the Punjab's major centers and moved on from them to attack the hilltop castles of Rajastan.

Late in the year 1025, Mahmud laid siege against the fort and Hindu shrine at Somnath, on the northwest coast of India in Gujarat. Somnath was, and is, of special importance to Hindus, for it is one of the twelve sites where Shiva, "the deity of deities," had appeared in a fiery column of light. Mahmud later boasted that his army butchered 50,000 of Somnath's defenders. His troops then hauled vast amounts of treasure, hundreds of war elephants, and thousands of prisoners back to Ghazni. Mahmud also sent a portion of these riches to the caliph in Baghdad, and also to both Mecca and Medina.[1]

These were the developments that brought Biruni to the Indus Valley. His presence there was as an expert on India whose fate was to observe atrocities. Modern analogies might be to a Japanese specialist on Manchurian studies in Changchung in 1933 or a German professor of Slavic studies in Warsaw in 1942. Yet Biruni's seriousness of purpose and deep knowledge won the respect of Hindu intellectuals in all the cities he visited. His first trip was in the role of Mahmud's personal astrologer. This was an important post, for it was thought that a good astrologer could foretell the best time to attack or withdraw as well as predict the fortunes and misfortunes of friends and foe alike. Biruni ridiculed astrologers' efforts to predict the future and would later criticize the entire enterprise in several book-length treatises. But he could not refuse the post, which gave him an opportunity to travel to India and pursue his own agenda, which was to explore Indian mathematics and astronomy. Specifically, he wanted to figure out how Indian scientists had been able to achieve pathbreaking results on some topics and abject failures on others. Such questions drew him into a deep encounter with Indian civilization at the very time the armies of his own master were laying waste to many of the centers of that great culture.

However unfortunate the timing of Biruni's trips to India, his quest itself had arisen naturally from his earlier studies. He had grown up in Khwarazm, where Indian traders were a common sight and where Indian art and culture brought glimpses into a distant but fascinating world.[2] Khwarazm's eastern links were ancient, dating to the first century AD. Trade flourished, bringing with it Buddhist monks, Indian art, and accounting based on the Indians' decimal system.

The rise of Islam and the Arab wars of conquest destroyed these links, but by the late eighth century they had been revived with new vigor when the Abbasids, who were mainly from Central Asia, took over the caliphate and moved its capital eastward from Damascus to Baghdad. Among the greatest cultural patrons of the new caliphate were the Barmak family, Buddhist converts from Balkh in Afghanistan, who served as a bridge between the cultures of India, Central Asia, and the Middle East. Al-Khwarazmi had celebrated the great Indian mathematical text *Sindhind*, while Muslim scholars in Baghdad had come to view the sixth-century Indian thinker Brahmaputra as a preeminent mathematician and astronomer, on the same level as Euclid, Pythagoras, and Aristotle.

Biruni's fascination with India began early. Both he and his teacher Ibn Iraq wrote treatises proclaiming the usefulness of the Indian system of numbers, and in his *Chronology of Ancient Nations* he had discussed Indian concepts of time.[3] He knew that the Indians were responsible for replacing "chords" (straight lines drawn between two points on a circle) with sines, and that they had explored the concepts of tangents and cotangents. But he was no blind enthusiast and also wrote a critical evaluation of the *Sindhind*, the same text his own teacher had praised.[4] No sooner had Biruni arrived in Ghazni than he began collecting books on India and Indian manuscripts, complaining bitterly whenever he could not locate a particular title.[5]

For two years, 1022–1024, besides acting as astrologer to the commanding general, Biruni managed to travel on his own in Sindh and parts of Punjab.[6] While he was unable to travel to Kashmir, he succeeded in obtaining many books from contacts there.[7] One stop in Sindh was the ancient city of Multan, where Alexander the Great was struck by a poisoned arrow, an event that came to symbolize the collapse of his Indian campaign. Arabs had conquered the city in the eighth century, but when Biruni arrived, Multan's population remained largely non-Muslim, and a significant number of its Muslims were Ismaili Shiites. Several major Ismaili scholars resided there, as did others who were deeply informed about Indian culture. Biruni met them all and interviewed them at length. In the city of Lahore, a major center of learning, he made contact with distinguished Indian intellectuals and even undertook the study of Sanskrit.[8] He would later translate two books from Sanskrit into Arabic and one book from Arabic into Sanskrit.

By the time he returned to Ghazni, Biruni could draw on his now-comprehensive library on India and also consult the Indian scholars and captive intellectuals and translators who now resided there. Indeed, the latter were as important as the former in shaping Biruni's understanding of Indian civilization.[9]

Beyond satisfying old curiosities, the purpose of all this travel and research was not to write a mere travel guide. Biruni knew that the Samanis' vizier and geographer, Jayhani, had described parts of India in his *Book of Routes and Kingdoms* and that several other recent books by Arab writers had touched on Indian geography, religion, and culture. But all of these were tainted by the authors' superficial knowledge and eagerness to pass judgment on whatever they suspected of being incompatible with Islam.[10] Biruni's purpose instead was to find answers to the specific questions about Indian mathematics and astronomy that had long been forming in his mind. His project, in other words, was analytic, not descriptive, and certainly not an exercise in cultural judgment.

In addressing his questions, Biruni did not assume that the analytic tools he had employed in the past would suffice. He was a mathematician, of course, but when issues would not yield to mathematical analysis, he was prepared to adopt completely different tools. Where Ibn Sina strained mightily to apply to medicine his single logical and metaphysical system, Biruni, when studying human societies, easily shifted to historical, cultural, sociological, and linguistic approaches. Not only that, he used each system of analysis to elucidate the others. This opened the door to advances in fields as diverse as cultural anthropology, the history of science, and comparative religion.

Biruni would denounce witchcraft, fortunetellers, and incantations and yet announce that all such matters were worthy of study because they reflect the cultures that produced them. His readiness to go beyond his usual analytical toolkit distinguished him from nearly all thinkers of his era. Applied to the study of India, it led to his pioneering several fields in the physical and social sciences. In the process he ferreted out heretofore neglected aspects of Indian civilization and assembled a body of information on India that remains invaluable even today.

The three areas in which Biruni pursued his enquiry were first, the Indians' views on mathematics and astronomy; second, their views on the measurement of time and distance; and, third, their views on the earth itself, that is, on geodesics. He wanted to know which Indian thinkers had addressed each topic, how they had done so, and the assumptions and cultural givens that shaped their findings so that he could determine which were valid and which were not. Accordingly, Biruni entitled his study of Indian science, "An Accurate Description of All Categories of Hindu Thought, Those Which Are Admissible, as Well as Those Which Must Be Rejected."[11]

As his patron was engaged in a holy war in India, Biruni knew that in touching on religion he was on highly sensitive ground. In his introduction he acknowledges the mutual hostility between Muslims and Hindus: "We recognize nothing that they believe and they recognize nothing that we believe. . . . In all manners and usages they differ from us to such a degree that they frighten their children with us and with our ways and our customs, and declare us to be the devil's breed."[12] In this same spirit, he included a whole section on Hindu practices that were bound to seem alien to Muslim readers.[13] They have red teeth from chewing arecantha nuts with betel leaves and chalk; they wear turbans and trousers; they let their hair grow long "in order to glorify their idleness"; on festive days they smear their bodies with dung rather than perfume; and they do not cut the hair of their genitals. He assures his reader that he is "well aware of all this, but there is still something there worthy of study." In the same effort to shield himself from criticism, he bluntly warns that "the holy books of the Indians contain a series of assertions concerning the form of the earth which are exactly opposite to the truths of science that are known to astronomers."[14]

Further distancing himself from the fray, Biruni then insists that the purpose of his book is not to criticize or praise. Rather, his goal is simply to enable readers better to understand a world that was radically different from their own. To this end, he would "make no unfounded attacks on my enemy." His book, he argues, will be "a simple historic record of facts." "I shall place before the reader the theories of the Hindus exactly as they are."[15] For these reasons, Biruni declares that he will not hesitate to quote at length the Hindus' own words.[16]

Turning to astronomy and mathematics, Biruni appreciated the fact that on many points the Indians were more advanced than their counterparts in Central Asia and the Middle East. When he arrived in India, Biruni admits, he considered himself the student and the Indians his masters, even if over time he perceived flaws in their analyses, usually in their mathematics. Far from turning their backs on him, the Indian scholars came to appreciate Biruni's analyses of their work, and even sought his views on astronomy "as if, he said, '[I] were some kind of a sorcerer.'"[17]

The Indian thinker who presented the single greatest challenge was Brahmagupta, the seventh-century mathematician and astronomer from Rajastan whose translated works had stunned Arabic readers and inspired Biruni in his youth. Biruni reminded readers that the concept of zero, the decimal system of counting, negative numbers, sine tables, and the most precise determination of *pi* down to that time were among Brahmagupta's contributions. He then proceeded to scrutinize Brahmagupta's measurements of the distances to the moon and the radii of both the moon and earth, correcting them where necessary with his own data.

So great was Biruni's initial enthusiasm for another Indian polymath, the sixth-century Varahamihira, that he actually translated one of his works into Arabic.[18] Varahamihira knew Greek science as well as Indian science and had gathered data on many issues of interest to Biruni, including planetary motion, the measurement of time, geography, and eclipses.[19] But in the end Biruni found Varahamihira's reasoning sloppy and his mathematics worse. A French scholar has suggested that Biruni's disparagement may have been due in part to Biruni's reliance on his own translation from the Sanskrit, which at several points was garbled.[20] In any case, toward another commentator named Balabhadra he was even more harsh: "All that Balabhadra produces is foolish in both words and substance, and I cannot find why he felt himself called upon to write a commentary if he had nothing better to say."[21]

Biruni's disdain for Varahamihira and his contempt of Balabhadra were more than offset by his praise for Aryabhata. A sixth-century native of Patna in northeast India, Aryabhata had done work on spherical trigonometry and sine laws. In fact, the English terms "sine" and "cosine" are the product of double mistranslations of Aryabhata's terms, first from Hindi into Arabic and then from Arabic into Latin. Aryabhata earned Biruni's respect for his analyses of solar and lunar eclipses and for his estimates of the earth's diameter, as well as for his measurement of the so-called sidereal year, which denotes a year as measured in astronomical rather than solar time. Biruni knew that Aryabhata's method for computing astronomical tables had already gained acceptance among Central Asian and Middle Eastern astronomers, but he was particularly intrigued by Aryabhata's thesis that the earth rotated daily on its axis.[22] Neither here nor in his later and more definitive *Masud's Canon* did Biruni embrace this concept. Nonetheless, in *India* he acknowledges that the notion of the earth rotating on its axis accorded with mathematics and hence the laws of astronomy. He would later challenge it on other grounds relating to physics. Brushing aside Brahmagupta's personal dislike of Aryabhata, which Biruni ascribed to petty jealousy,[23] Biruni concludes that Aryabhata and his followers "give us the impression of being truly men of great scientific attainments."[24]

Biruni was fascinated by the assumptions on astronomy to be found in popular religious literature, notably the *Puranas*, the Hindu sacred writings that brought together insights from ancient texts and more recent folklore. He began with what he termed the "enigmatic" concept of "the egg of Bhraman," a symbolic representation of the earth and heavens.[25] In *India* he subjects each assumption of popular belief to close (and usually devastating) analysis. Presenting a table of astronomical data drawn from diverse religious sources he concludes that "the differences of the traditions as exhibited by this table cannot be accounted for in a rational way."[26]

Biruni then turns to the Brahmins. The role of these members of the highest caste was to protect the sacred. As such, he explains, they had a vested interest in opposing the new knowledge generated by Brahmagupta and his ilk. Biruni found such willful ignorance and dogmatism contemptible. But he is far more damning of those Indian men of learning who censured themselves in order to avoid the charge of religious heresy. By so doing, he argued, the scientists themselves contributed to the society's general ignorance of astronomy and science.[27] Indeed, this topic elicits from Biruni one of the sharpest statements in all his writing. He focuses his attack on Brahmagupta, who had meekly backed down when confronted with the Brahmins' religious explanation of solar eclipses. According to them, the sun disappears because it has been swallowed by the severed head of a deity who was punished for attempting to steal nectar. This was too much for Biruni, who asks if Brahmagupta's craven concession to Hindu orthodoxy arose from ignorance, weakness, or a cynical contempt for the beliefs themselves.[28] In all the medieval era it is hard to find a more stark and damning juxtaposition of science and religion.

Biruni had long since demonstrated his passion for measuring and counting everything. He chides Indians on some of their absurd measures of time and distance but notes with admiration that the Indians are unique in having specific arithmetical terms for numbers beyond a thousand.[29] And having noted with surprise that many Hindu scientific texts were written in metrical verse, he then proceeds to construct a numerical grid for their poetic meters and to show how Indian scientists utilized each of them in their writings.[30] Biruni devotes an entire chapter of his *India* to systems of measurement, covering lengths, weights, liquids, and, of course, time.[31] This discussion is a continuation and expansion of his earlier research on time in his *Chronologies*. Rather than take the Indians' notions of time as a threat to what he'd written earlier, Biruni takes delight in the new insights. This notion of research as an ongoing process driven by new evidence reflects Biruni's understanding of science and learning as such.

We see the same understanding reflected elsewhere in Biruni's *India*, where he reports on new research on geography and cartography. He methodically lists the eleven cities whose latitude and longitude he had himself measured and dozens of others on information he had gleaned from travelers. He notes down the direction of roads and rivers but abstains from providing precise data on their lengths unless he himself had confirmed them.

Biruni sought information from scores of Indian travelers. He himself did not venture south, but those who had done so confirmed to him that the southern point of India extended well to the south of the equator. Independently he had confirmed the same for Africa. These findings contradicted Aristotle and Ptolemy, both of whom held that continents existed only in the northern hemisphere. In *India*, he also approvingly cites Varahamihira to the effect that "mountains, seas, rivers, trees, cities, men, and angels are all around the globe of the earth."[32] This insight, which further contradicted the ancient Greeks and their more recent Muslim followers, was to play a role in Biruni's later hypotheses regarding the existence of what came to be known as North and South America.

In addition to providing a mass of new geographical information, *India* offers findings in the areas of geology and paleontology. It provides details on sediments in several large alluvial plains and also describes regions where Biruni had discovered the fossilized remains of both vertebrate and invertebrate creatures. From such evidence it draws the conclusion that large parts of India had once been submerged beneath an ocean and that some cataclysmic event had lifted them upward, at the same time shaking rocks loose from the nearby mountains.[33] Combining these findings with his earlier discoveries in Gurganj and Ghazni, Biruni infers that such cataclysmic events were a normal feature of the earth's evolution over time. But rather than ask whether these phenomena cast doubt on religious explanations of Creation, Biruni deftly sidesteps the question, using a ploy he had first developed in an earlier work. Namely, he notes that the Creation had occurred so far in the past that it would be impossible to determine its dating or to prove or disprove the validity of how this subject was treated in holy writ.[34]

In a similar spirit, Biruni speculates on the process by which living organisms adapt to their environment. He observes, for example, that various animal species could proliferate to such an extent that they compete for food and resources. This, he realizes, could lead to overpopulation and crisis. But then other natural processes would intervene: "If the earth is ruined or near being ruined by having too many inhabitants, its ruler—for it has a Ruler and His all-embracing care is apparent in every single particle of it— sends a messenger for the purpose of reducing the too great number and of cutting away all that is evil."[35]

He implies, but does not state, that the "messengers" that cause the population of animals or other organisms to plummet and thereby reestablish demographic balances are epidemics and natural disasters. Whether due to limitations of time or to fear of offending the religiously orthodox, in *India* Biruni does not pursue further the question of geological cataclysms or of the destruction of species through overpopulation. But he shows beyond doubt that he was closely attuned to the kind of evidence that would later lead evolutionary geologists like Humboldt, biologists like Darwin, and demographic pioneers like Malthus to their epochal findings. In fact, Biruni directly presaged these scientists' provocative contributions to human understanding.

India embraces a huge scope, and Biruni does neglect questions about the earth as a whole. He devotes a chapter to Indian notions of the two poles[36] and another to the intractable problem of measuring longitude.[37] And in a striking passage, he notes that Indians clearly understood that tides are somehow related to the moon and had even erected seaside temples to deities that reflected that understanding. But neither he nor they could account for what was clearly a causal relationship.[38] Further passages are devoted to Indian methods for measuring the earth's circumference and the conclusions they reached,[39] and the location of the meridian at specific points.[40] The latter leads him to an extended discussion of Mt. Meru, the mountain that figures so centrally in Hindu thought but which Biruni dismisses as a figment of imagination.[41]

Overall, Biruni congratulates Indian thinkers for their work on geography but ends by observing wryly, "As the reader will observe, these theories of the Hindus are based on a correct knowledge of the laws of nature but, at the same time, they practice a little deceit [with respect to] their traditionalists and theologians." Indeed, Biruni traces many of the most serious flaws in Indian science to Hinduism itself, as noted with the explanation for the lunar eclipse. Given this, it is the more surprising that he devoted major sections of *India* to a close analysis of Hindu beliefs, both as the Brahmans expounded them and as the common people of India perceived them. This is precisely what he intended when he announced, "I shall place before the reader the theories of the Hindus exactly as they are."[42]

To orient his readers, Biruni argues that change through time compels us to acknowledge the importance of time as such.[43] He also believes that it "compels us to assume the existence of a Creator, who is wise and intelligent, who establishes and arranges everything in the best possible manner, and inspires people with the force of intelligence for the purpose of liberation."[44] Biruni offers this both as a statement of the obvious and as a profession of faith that embodied his own worldview. He was quite aware of philosophers who sought to prove these statements through argumentation, and specifically mentions Aristotle and Galen in this context. But in *India* Biruni himself affirms simply that one can confidently *assume* the existence of the soul, and *assume* the existence of a Creator.

On this basis, Biruni evaluates Hindu beliefs concerning their gods, asserting at the outset that "the theory of the Hindus on this subject is rather poor and very little developed." He pored through the Vedas to detect how Hindus proceeded, but in the end he confesses that it is "not within our grasp" to perceive their deepest thinking because it is expressed through highly abstract poetry that was written in languages that would require a lifetime to master.[45] Notwithstanding this disclaimer, Biruni shows so great an interest in one such difficult work—Patanajali's *Yoga Sutra*—probably the work of several authors between the second and fifth centuries AD—that he went to the considerable trouble of translating long passages from the Sanskrit into Arabic and offering his own commentary. Centering on the processes by which the soul can emancipate itself from earthly concerns, Patanjali's masterpiece bears comparison with the thinking of Muslim Sufis and Christian mystics. Indeed, as the scholar Mario Kozah has shown in his writing on Patanjali, Biruni drew together many strands of Hinduism and presented it in a way that was accessible to Muslims.[46] It is hard to imagine that Biruni's labors, while advancing his comparative study of religions and cultures, did not also reflect his personal interests.

At one point in his translation of Patanjali's *Yoga Sutras* Biruni observes that language itself presents a barrier to understanding, for words and phrases, even when accurately translated, have quite different meanings in different cultures. As an example, he notes how differently Christians view the simple words "Father and Son."[47] Similarly, there are diverse understandings among Hindus, with some being materialists and others who oppose that view.[48] Under the circumstances, Biruni argues, the best an outsider can do is to study the *customs* that embody Indian religion. But even here he encountered difficulties, given the caricatures advanced by Muslim writers on the subject. Typical, he said, were those of the ninth-century Persian philosopher Abu al-Abbas Iranshahri, who ended up describing Hindu doctrines that were purely his own invention.

In his translation Biruni therefore takes a different tack, explaining Hindu doctrines by comparing them with the beliefs of the early Greeks. Thus, he draws a parallel between the views of Hindus and early Greeks on the "intelligibles" and "sensibles," and between Hindus and Muslim Sufis, both of whom held that only the First Cause, that is, God, has existence. He cites further parallels between Hindus and Sufis on the connection of the soul with the material world,[49] their view of nature,[50] and their shared notion of a dual soul—one side human and perishable and the other transcendental.[51] Further, he suggests, the benevolent supernatural beings of the Vedas are strikingly reminiscent of angels in Islam.[52] In the same vein, Biruni notes that Hindus and Muslims are at one in their definition of virtuous behavior[53] and that Hindus also recall Plato in claiming that religious and civil law came ultimately from the gods.[54]

Comparisons and analogies identify fundamental points of difference between the two faiths. The first of many Biruni citations is the Hindu concept of metempsychosis, or the migration of souls after death into a new body.[55] After struggling to explain it, Biruni gives up, positing instead that it is comparable, in its centrality, to the Muslims' confession of faith ("There is no god but Allah") and the Christians' concept of the Holy Trinity.

However critical he was of the Brahmins for their censorship and for their muzzling of scientific enquiry, Biruni acknowledges that the Brahmin caste was indeed the bearer of Hinduism's intellectual heritage. By contrast, the mass of the population gained access to the essence of their religion only through the practice of rituals and customs. Rather than turn his back on the unsophisticated mass of Indians, however, Biruni plunges headlong into their rites and practices, describing them in detail, while knowing full well that his readers might find them utterly abhorrent. Are not religious sculptures and images "a foul and pernicious abuse," banned in Islam? Of course, writes Biruni, but we should understand that such images have their origin in the very human desire to commemorate the dead and console the living.[56] And isn't it characteristic of common people everywhere to welcome pictorial representations of abstract principles? If, for example, someone were to draw a picture of the Prophet Muhammad, Mecca, or the Kaaba, would not uneducated Muslims be quick to embrace them?[57] Moreover, Biruni opines, the holiness of idols derives not from supposed divine intervention or the value of the material from which they are made but from their having been worshiped through the centuries.[58] Even the sophisticated ancient Greeks turned to sculpture as a means of mediating between their daily existence and the realm of the divine.

One extended passage of Biruni's translation raises topics as diverse as pilgrimages, female self-immolation, alms, food, lawsuits, matrimony, fasting, burial, festivals, inheritance, crime, punishment, and the grooming of hair and fingernails. Along the way he even drops in the rules for a form of four-player chess played only within the borders of India. Throughout he explains Hindu practices, provides analogies where appropriate, and generally strips away the distorting veil of exotica that prevented his readers from understanding Hinduism. Biruni concludes this passage with a damning review of "those Hindu sciences that prey on ignorance."[59] By this he meant witchcraft in general, though his focus was on alchemy and astrology. As he turned to address these pseudo-sciences, he knew full well that both were widely practiced throughout the Muslim world and, indeed, at the court of his own patron, Mahmud. Here and elsewhere the often-blunt Biruni revealed himself as a master at saying indirectly what could not be stated directly.

One is hard-pressed to think of any other thinker of his day, and even of our own, who devoted as much effort as Biruni to exploring and understanding a culture or religion other than his own. Biruni made a huge effort to grasp another cultural world *on its own terms*, analytically, and in a manner that could be verified or rejected on the basis of evidence. No one could bring to the task a broader array of analytic tools. It is therefore useful to take note of the methods that Biruni applied to his task. Since it was Indian achievements in mathematics and astronomy that first drew him to study the Hindu world, it was inevitable that mathematics would be the first tool he would employ in his quest. Indeed, in his translation he makes clear that all assertions regarding astronomy and geodesy that were not subject to quantitative verification were ipso facto invalid.[60] No one before Biruni had made such broad use of quantitative data in the study of human culture, his own or another.

At the same time, Biruni was quick to acknowledge the limits of quantitative methods in the study of human societies. He realized what his usual method could not grasp and developed other methods that could advance his enquiry. What he sought was a way to trace the social and cultural roots of ideas. In this quest he advanced what we now call the fields of cultural anthropology and the sociology of knowledge. His depiction of the content and interaction of ideas and values at different levels of society also broke new ground, as did his treatment of oral history. Continuing a tradition dating back to Herodotus, Biruni gathered evidence from oral sources and folk tales. But he was far more cautious than his predecessors about the possible distortions and outright errors in folk sources, not to mention falsifications arising from old animosities or ignorance. Stated in terms of modern anthropology, he was remarkably cautious in his choice and handling of "informants."

When he began his study of Indian achievements in mathematics and astronomy, it is doubtful that Biruni had any idea how deeply it would involve him in the study of Hinduism and religion in general. But he followed his evidence and adjusted his methods in order to solve the problem at hand. By doing so, he created an entirely original work and pioneered in the analysis of religions on a comparative basis.

Biruni's *India* is permeated with the theory and practice of comparison as a method of research. Groping forward, Biruni came to distinguish between those general *functions* that all religions and societies need to fulfill and the specific *structures* with which each society actually fulfills them. Biruni did not employ these modern terms, of course. But by drawing this simple distinction he advanced the comparative study of human societies and cultures everywhere.

In his effort to apply this principle, Biruni encountered every manner of impediment, including the refusal of some Hindu divines to share secrets with a foreigner. He judged other informants as deliberate deceivers or fools. By far the biggest challenge Biruni faced, however, was language. Though he learned Sanskrit—as noted, to the point that he could translate both from it and to it—Biruni had no illusions that he really knew the language. He also knew that the Indians have countless other languages, each with its own body of literature and thought, none of which were accessible to him. Beneath this is Biruni's realization that language *is* culture, and that it is nearly impossible to unlock its secrets. He could discover that the Hindu term *Dvipa* denoted an island in the ocean of outer space and that it had no counterpart in Arabic.[61] But he realized that to grasp a single word like this was not the same thing as grasping Hindu culture as a whole. Far more than anyone up to his time, Biruni understood the intimate link between the specifics of language and thought, and therefore the fundamental challenge this poses to human communication.

Beyond all these considerations, the heart of Biruni's method in writing his *India* was to maintain sufficient distance from his subject that he could remain nonjudgmental. He occasionally worked himself into a lather of condescension, as when he confides that "the Hindus believe there is no country but theirs, no nation like theirs, no kings like theirs, no religion like theirs, no science like theirs. They are haughty, foolishly vain, self-conceited and stolid."[62] But Biruni employed these dyspeptic outbursts with a tactical purpose in mind, namely, to assure Muslim readers that he, the author, was safely part of their own world and had not "gone native." In short, that his readers could trust him.

In his *India*, as in all his works, Biruni was determined to speak the truth. He would employ a variety of tactics, but his goal was unchanging. He declares this in his introduction, supporting his words by quoting both the *Quran*: "Speak the truth, even when it is against yourself"; and the *Gospel of St. Luke*: "Do not mind the fury of kings in speaking the truth before them. They only possess your body, but have no power over your soul."[63] Along with his commitments and his doggedness in honoring them, Biruni was bracingly self-critical, especially when reporting the failure of a particular line of enquiry. This, too, may have been a tactic, for he made clear at the outset that he wanted Arabic readers actually to read his book. To a greater extent than any of his earlier or later writings, most of which had the character of research reports, *India* reaches over the head of his patron to the educated public at large.

Little wonder it achieved the success that it did. Edward Sachau, the scholar who rediscovered the book and translated it into both German and English, declares Biruni's *India* "is like a magic island of quiet, impartial research in the midst of a world of clashing swords, burning towns, and plundered temples."[64]

13

The *Canon of Medicine*

As noted earlier, Ibn Sina conceived of the *Canon of Medicine* in Gorgan shortly after he turned forty. He worked on the first volume in Gorgan and at Rayy, labored feverishly on the next three volumes while serving as vizier in Hamadan and as a captive in Fardaqan, and then finished the final volume at Isfahan. The work took him almost two decades to complete. Given its central place in his total oeuvre and subsequent fame, the work deserves close analysis. This is no easy task, since the *Canon* covers both the theory and practice of medicine and comprises thousands of separate entries. Nonetheless, we can describe the process by which it came into being, outline the general features of both its theoretical and clinical sections, and give a sense of its encyclopedic treatment of pharmacology.

The first volume consists of two main sections. The first offers a detailed presentation of the philosophical basis of medicine and the general themes of anatomy, psychology, the causes of disease and health, and gerontology. The second concludes with a detailed account of therapeutic procedures and the relief of pain. In splitting this volume between sections on theory and practice, Ibn Sina was following the structure devised by his immediate predecessor, Al-Majusi, in his *Complete Book of the Art of Medicine*.

Volume II provides a detailed listing of medical substances and their properties. Volume III covers the diagnosis and treatment of illnesses specific to single organs of the body, while Volume IV deals with illnesses that affect the body as a whole. Volume V returns, as noted, to the theme of pharmacology, offering formulas for the preparation and testing of hundreds of medical compounds and specific information on their use. While the second and fifth volumes are presented as practical handbooks, the third and fourth volumes were clearly intended for medical practitioners, teachers of medicine, and their students.

Ibn Sina launches his *Canon* with a definition of medicine drawn straight from Galen. "Medicine," he notes, "is the science by which we learn the various states of the human body in health and when not in health and, when lost, is likely to be restored back to health."[1] He then presents his reason for covering both theory and practice, arguing that "it is a truism of philosophy and a dictum of the exact sciences that knowledge of a thing is attained only through a knowledge of the causes and the origins of the causes—assuming there to be causes and origins." "Consequently," he continues, "our knowledge cannot be complete without an understanding both of symptoms and of the principles of being."[2] In other words, the study of medicine cannot proceed without a thorough understanding of both physics and metaphysics. Medicine is a subordinate field within physics, which in turn gains its founding principles from metaphysics. On his opening pages Ibn Sina thus plunges deeper than his ancient predecessors, Hippocrates and Galen, both of whom focused their attention above all on immediate causes and on the "temperaments" and "humors" through which they are manifest. For Ibn Sina, these were necessary but not sufficient.

Continuing his presentation of theory, Ibn Sina dutifully explains the four causes of health and disease as Aristotle defined them: "material," "efficient," "formal," and "final." He may have thought these necessary for the sake of logic, but they were distressingly vague when he applied them to medicine. What, for example did Ibn Sina actually mean when he defined "efficient causes" as those capable of "preventing or inducing change in the human body"? Without pausing to elaborate, he proceeds to the two "elements" that define causation in the medical field: the "humors" and the "temperaments." In doing so he falls back on his ancient masters and above all on Galen.

The humors were thought to be liquid substances that affect the body's functioning. When in balance with one another they produce a normal body temperature and therefore health. In a tradition dating back to Hippocrates, Galen and other Greek physicians agreed that there were four humors: blood, phlegm, yellow bile, and black bile. These corresponded to the four qualities in the physical world, that is, heat, cold, moisture, and dryness. These in turn were all emanations of the primal elements of earth, air, fire, and water, all of which had existed since Creation. Manifesting the four humors were the four types of human personalities, or "temperaments." Galen and his predecessors had identified these as sanguine, phlegmatic, melancholic, and choleric.

The ancient Greeks' framework of humors and temperaments enabled Ibn Sina to trace the state of a person's health to what we now call metabolism. Like some of his predecessors, he believed that the cause of most diseases were imbalances between the various humors and temperaments. This causes him to dispute Galen, who considered blood alone to be the most important bodily fluid.[3] So when Galen attributed hard bones to a good supply of blood, Ibn Sina counters with the argument that hardness in bones is a consequence of the presence in the blood of "hard and black bile material," in other words, of the humors. Here Ibn Sina sticks with Aristotle, even at the price of contradicting his other Greek masters.

In the same spirit, Ibn Sina explains the role of the four temperaments in health and sickness. Having divided them between heat and cold, moisture and dryness, he then indicates which bodily organs belong to each category. Throughout the remaining sections of the introduction, which covers anatomy, physiology, breath, and psychology, he is at pains to apply the doctrine of temperaments and humors. He then draws logical distinctions between what he calls "simple" and "compound" organs. Having done so, he abruptly sets them aside and instead offers straightforward descriptions of everything from the jaw to vertebrae, in every case speaking purely as the medical practitioner he was.

When Ibn Sina finally came to the heart, however, things become complicated. He points out that there is "great disagreement between the philosophers and the physicians." Aristotle saw it as the "root of all the faculties or drives," and physicians thought that this drive stemmed from a number of organs, such as the liver or brain.[4] He sides with Aristotle, calling his view "valid." However, he doesn't explain why and, having offered this pronouncement, moves on.

In the section devoted to the breath, Ibn Sina again falls back on the medical experts of ancient Greece. Citing "the sages and those physicians who agree with them,"[5] he asserts that joy, sadness, fear, and anger all arise from the "breath of the heart." But then he flips cause and effect, claiming that each emotion generates its own type of breath, and that specific medicines can stimulate and focus the breath. This is another of the many instances where Ibn Sina the logician, theoretician, and disciple of Aristotle comes into conflict with Ibn Sina the clear-eyed observer and diagnostician. In this case the tension goes unrecognized. But in the section on psychology that followed, he first presents an elaborate categorization of passions and drives and then simply backs down, concluding, "The validity of these conclusions should be left to the philosophers for necessary consideration."[6]

If Ibn Sina was indebted to Galen and his predecessors for the notion of humors and temperaments, on another important point he parts company with Galen. For Ibn Sina believed that the basic reality of the universe and of human life is Spirit, not matter; further, he held that it was Spirit or God that brought about Creation, and which inheres in every human being as consciousness, mind, or soul. While he did not state it in the *Canon of Medicine,* Ibn Sina held that while the universe, as macrocosm, embodies both matter and spirit, each human being is a microcosmos, combining both material and spiritual elements. The correspondence between these two concepts is based on the harmony and inner sympathy between them. In the words of scholar Seyyed Hossein Nasr, "The sympathy, which is hidden to most men, becomes more evident as the soul increases in purity until, in the case of the prophets, the inner harmony between man and the cosmos becomes universally manifested."[7] These concerns might have led Ibn Sina to consider in greater depth the nervous system, but such was not the case. The Greek physician Herophilus of Chalcedon had been the first to focus on the nervous system, as early as the third century BC, However, Herophilus's works were unknown to Ibn Sina, as indeed they remained unknown to everyone else until the 1980s, when an enterprising American scholar edited and translated surviving fragments of them.[8]

Ibn Sina's cosmological views are fully on display in the *Canon,* in which he asserts that the link between body and soul or spirit is the breath, and that "the beginning of the breath is as a divine emanation."[9] Indeed, he writes, "God created the left side of the heart and made it hollow in order that it should serve as a storehouse for the breath and as a seat for the manufacture of the breath."[10] In other words, breath *is* life, and is implanted in us by God through the left side of the heart. This is a far cry from Galen's materialism. The difference is fundamental, yet in the *Canon* Ibn Sina refrains from engaging in a polemic on this issue. Instead, he simply states his view on the role of breath and the heart and then passes on to other subjects. This has led to more than a little frustration on the part of scholars whose main concern is with Ibn Sina's philosophy and cosmology. They assert that the *Canon* is so thoroughly saturated with philosophy that it overwhelms the countless instances in which Ibn Sina presented clinical evidence, which they largely ignore. His apparent stress on the metaphysics has led some skeptics even to question whether Ibn Sina had much clinical experience at all.[11]

In support of this more cynical view is a case involving Ibn Sina's search for the cause of a young woman's illness. Throughout a series of detailed conversations, he held the woman's pulse while he spoke on a variety of topics. Only when he raised the topic of love did her pulse rate jump, which led Ibn Sina to conclude that she was literally lovesick. Some champions of Ibn Sina's diagnostic skills cite this case as evidence not only of Ibn Sina's clinical experience but also of his pioneering role in psychoanalysis. And so it was believed, until a diligent scholar from Spain pointed out that he lifted his account of this case directly from Galen's great compendium.[12]

In spite of this, it seems undeniable that Ibn Sina had accumulated a formidable amount of clinical experience. In the *Canon* he often cites cases drawn from his own practice. On some issues, such as his discovery of the antiseptic qualities of alcohol, he introduces significant innovations that derived from his hands-on practice.[13] Further, his amanuensis, Juzjani, reported on a large collection of Ibn Sina's own clinical notes that he had hoped to use some day in the *Canon*, but which were lost in the sandstorm as he crossed the desert to Gorgan.

Only on the basis of his own clinical experience could Ibn Sina have insisted so vehemently on the need for the clinician himself to be free of medical conditions that could affect his judgment. To diagnose a problem, doctors themselves must "have no disharmony of functions." Specifically, they must have normal urinary and bowel functions, be free of fatigue and emotional preoccupations, and have regular breathing, which must remain "under control of the will."[14] Yet Ibn Sina spent far less time in clinical work than others, including his contemporary, Majusi; a main reason that Majusi's *Complete Book of the Art of Medicine* emerged as the main competitor to Ibn Sina's *Canon* is that Majusi cites his own clinical experience in support of practically every point.

A yet more formidable clinician, towering over the entire field, was Razi. Ibn Sina could never have outdone the vast knowledge of medical practice that Razi accumulated over a long lifetime. What he could do, though, was to impose a comprehensive structure onto the mass of issues and evidence discussed by Razi: in other words, to subject medicine to the logical categories that Ibn Sina had drawn from Aristotle and which he was seeking to impose on all branches of knowledge—hence the significance that Ibn Sina himself assigns to the dense and often confusing "theoretical" parts of his *Canon of Medicine*.

And yet the *Canon* revises clinical insights of both ancient and contemporary experts, even while remaining staunchly loyal to Aristotle. With the exception of his stress on the role of God and Creation, Ibn Sina accepts nearly all of Aristotle's theory of medicine, notably his concept of humors and temperaments. In cases where Galen modified these notions, Ibn Sina sides firmly with "The Philosopher." No wonder that Biruni, in their exchange of letters, had asked Ibn Sina why he so doggedly clung to Aristotle.

Fig. 1 Map showing regions relevant to the lives of Ibn Sina and Biruni.

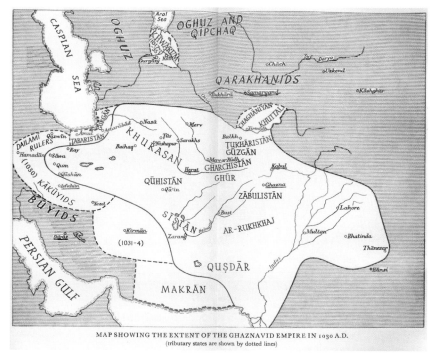

MAP SHOWING THE EXTENT OF THE GHAZNAVID EMPIRE IN 1030 A.D.
(tributary states are shown by dotted lines)

Fig. 2 Mahmud of Ghazni's empire at its zenith.

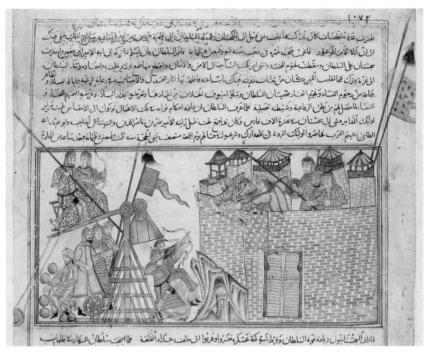

Fig. 3 Mahmud on the attack, from a fourteenth century manuscript.
Source: University of Edinburgh Library.

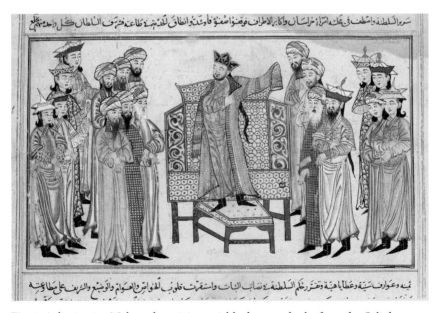

Fig. 4 A diminutive Mahmud receiving a richly decorated robe from the Caliph al–Qadir, in 1,000, from an early fourteenth century miniature.
Source: From a miniature from Rashid al-Din's Jami' al-tawarikh. University of Edinburgh Library.

Fig. 5 Gold dinar 998–1030 citing Mahmud and Caliph al-Qadir as overlord of his sultanate.

Fig. 6 Coins of Mahmud of Ghazni with Islamic declaration of faith and name of Caliph al-Qadir.

Fig. 7 Interior of tomb of Mahmud, by the English artist James Ratray, 1842.
Source: Asia and Pacific Collections, The British Library.

Fig. 8 Ghazni and thirteenth century citadel walls in 1939.
Source: Graphische-Sammlung, Helvetica Archives.

Fig. 9 Plate from Khwarazm, eleventh century, depicting ruler and female attendants surrounded by Bactrian camels and merchants in Sogdian hats.
Source: Getty Images.

Fig. 10 Image of Hamadan in the medieval era.
Source: https://www.wikiwand.com/en/Hamadan.

Fig. 11 Image in brass of Persian leader al-Dawla.
Source: National Museum of Asian Art, Freer Gallery of Art.

Fig. 12 Muhammad prohibiting intercalation, from early fourteenth century manuscript of Biruni's *Chronology of Ancient Nations*.
Source: Centre for Research Collections, Main Library, University of Edinburgh.

Fig. 13 John the Baptist baptizes Christ, from early fourteenth century manuscript of Biruni's *Chronology of Ancient Nations*.
Source: Centre for Research Collections, Main Library, University of Edinburgh.

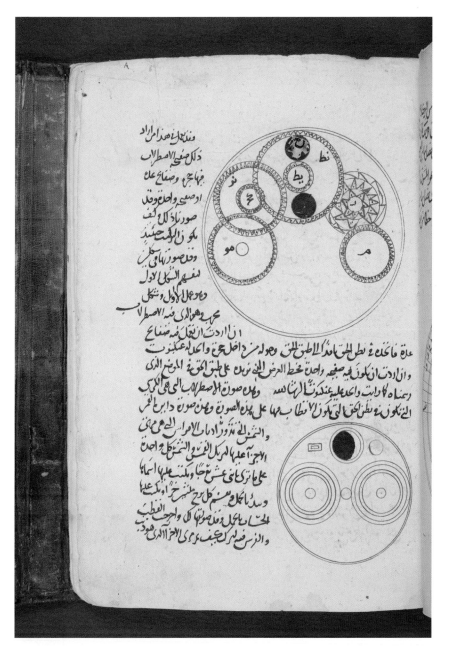

وفلك إذا هذا أراد
ذلك صنع الاصطرلاب
فيها خرج وصناعة على
أوضعي واضاع وقد
صور بلاد كل كف
يكون الصفيحة حسب
وقد صورنا هاي شكلين
لنفهم التبل أول
وبرعمل الأول وتشكل
محبة وهو الذي فيه الاصطرلاب

ان اردت ان انقل منه صناعة
عدة ماكانت ة بطول الحق ماذا الاطبق الحق وهولا من دا أضا عح واعلم عكنت
وان اردت ان يكون فيه صفيحه واحدا خط العرض الذي نرى على طبقة الكون ة الموضع الذي
رسمناه لا رابت واحد عليه عندنا الرباس وهن صور الاصطرلاب الى هي الكبرى
الذي يكون ة بطن أكن الى يكون الا نظا بها على هذه الصوير وهن صور دا بر الثقب
والنش الى نقربه وز أدان الاعراس الحجى هي
الحج آعليها لكل الفمى والنشركل واحد
على ما نرى بانى عش حجا ونكنته عليها اسماها
وسدها كل ومنه كل رح ملن رح او نكته علنا
لحنا باجل وقد صورتها الى واحدة القطب
والرسم فيه لبر كحف عمى الاخ الذي هود

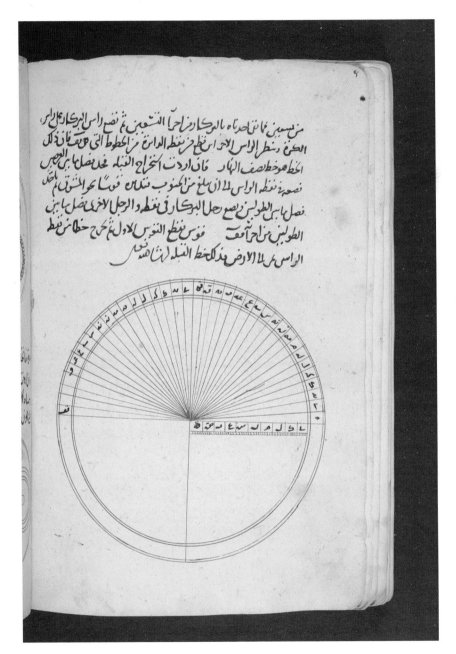

من قسمين فما بقي احدناه بالبركار من احدا التسعين ثم نصف راس البركار على راس
الخط ونقط الراس الاخر على نقط من نقط الواقع من الخطوط التي وقعت بان ذلك
الخط هو خط نصف النهار فان اردت استخراج القبلة مدد فضلا بين الحبس
نصفه نقط الواس لما ان بلغ من الجنوب نقطا قوسًا نحو المشرق ثم
بصل ما بين الطرفين بصع رجل البركار في نقطه والرجل الاخرى بصل ما بين
الطرفين من احر آوقت ◊ قوس نقط النوس لاول ثم تخرج خطا من نقط
الراس على لا الارض من ذلك الخط القبله ابنا فصل

Fig. 14.1 and 14.2 (Continued)

Fig. 15 Mountain atop which stands Nandana Fort, Salt Range, Pakistan, where Biruni measured the earth.

Source: By Amir Islam (Own work), CC BY-SA 4.0, https://commons.wikimedia.org/w/index.php?curid=42816597.

Fig. 16 Fourteenth century copy of Biruni's world map showing distribution of land and sea. The south is at the top.

Source: © akg-images/Roland and Sabrina Michaud.

Fig. 17 Indians celebrating the autumnal equinox, from an early manuscript of Biruni's *India*.

Source: Biblioteque nationale de France, Gallica.bnf.fr/ark.

Fig. 18 Ancient medical equipment excavated near Bukhara, Uzbekistan.
Source: Anvar Iliasov, Aiphoto, Uzbekistan.

Fig. 19 Ibn Sina as crowned teacher.

Source: Hulton Fine Arts Collection, Getty Images.

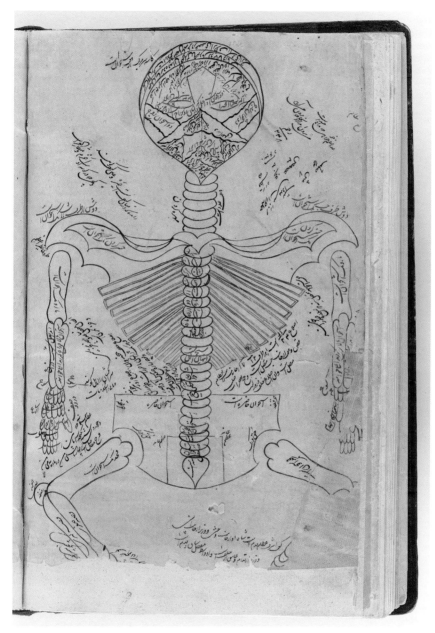

Fig. 20 Anatomical illustrations from a fourteenth century copy of Ibn Sina's *Canon of Medicine.*

Source: Avicenna, Canon of Medicine. Wellcome Collection.

Fig. 21 Medicinal iris plant, from Volume V, *Canon of Medicine*.

Source: Science History Images, Alamy Stock Photo.

Fig. 22 A seventeenth century Turkish follower of Ibn Sina treats a patient for measles.

Source: Bridgeman Images.

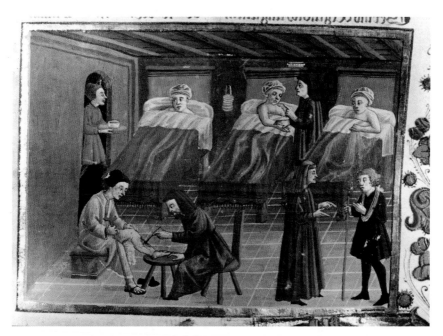

Fig. 23 A hospital from a fourteenth century translation of Ibn Sina's *Canon of Medicine*.

Source: Granger tps://www.granger.com/results.asp?image=0494281&itemw=4&itemf=0001&itemstep=1&itemx=27. Image 0024636.

Fig. 24 Fortress of Fardaqan, Iran, where Ibn Sina was incarcerated.
Source: Dr. Vali Kaleji, Tehran.

Fig. 25 An elderly Ibn Sina (left) in discussion, from a fourteenth century painting.
Source: fineartamerica.com.

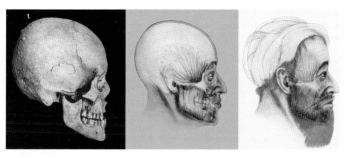

Fig. 26 What did the elderly Ibn Sina look like? When Ibn Sina's grave was opened in the1940s, a photograph (left) was made of his skull. In 2012, experts at the Centre for Anatomy and Human Identification at Dundee University used it to reconstruct his appearance.
Source: International Journal of Cardiology, September 1, 2013.

Fig. 27 Nasir al-Din Tusi and colleagues at the observatory in Maragha, Persia.
Source: British Library.

Fig. 28 Tusi's observatory and compound at Maragha, as reconstructed on the basis of archaeological research.
Source: Khabaronline.

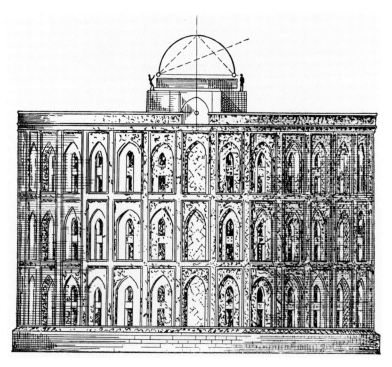

Fig. 29 Hypothetical reconstruction of Ulugbeg's observatory at Samarkand based on archaeological excavations by Vasili Viatkin, 1908.
Source: Smith Archive, Alamy Stock Photo.

Fig. 30 A Renaissance image of Ibn Sina seated between Galen and Hippocrates.

Source: Science History Images, Alamy Stock Photo.

Fig. 31 Thomas Aquinas, by Rafaelo Botticelli, 1482.

Source: Digital Commons.

Fig. 32 Nicolaus Copernicus (Mikołaj Kopernik), 1473–1543, completing the work of Biruni.

Source: Sheila Terry/Science Photo Library.

Fig. 33 Biruni (center), Ibn Sina (right), and Omar Khayyam (left) at the United Nations' headquarters, Vienna. The government of Iran, donor of these statues, claims both Biruni and Ibn Sina as "Iranians."
Source: Daily Sabah.

Fig. 34 Statue of Biruni in Khiva, near site of his home town of Kath, Uzbekistan.
Source: Agephotostock.

Fig. 35 Tomb of Biruni at Ghazni, Afghanistan; badly damaged by an earthquake in 1974, it was restored with American aid. The Taliban then destroyed it, leaving only the gravestone, but it is again being restored.

Source: Taha Aamir Nizami, Flowers Magazine.

Fig. 36 Mausoleum complex of Ibn Sina, Hamadan, Iran.
Source: Cultural Institute of Islamic Republic of Iran, Rome.

Fig. 37 Ibn Sina Hospital, Rabat, Morocco.
Source: Ibn Sina Hospital, Rabat, Morocco.

Fig. 38 Campus of Biruni University, Istanbul.
Source: Biruni University, Istanbul.

In other respects, however, Ibn Sina leaned heavily on Galen. His deep respect for that Greek physician stands in sharp contrast to his dismissal of Razi. Though respectful of Aristotle and a self-proclaimed disciple of Galen, Razi bolted at his ancient predecessor's notion of bodily fluids as independent variables that define health and disease. To make his point, Razi injected liquids of different temperatures into a patient's body and observed how quickly the fluids would heat up or cool down.[15] This and other challenges to Galen arose from Razi's direct knowledge of the impact of chemical agents on the human body. He based his objections not on logic but on empirical evidence.

Razi humbly acknowledges that Galen is the "Master and I am the disciple," though this does not prevent him from "doubting" what he considers "erroneous" in Galen's theories. Even then, Razi grieves at his own criticism of a master "from whose sea of knowledge I have drawn so much."[16] This is the same man whom a younger Ibn Sina had accused of exceeding his competence by meddling in metaphysics, who should have stuck with setting bones and doing urine and stool samples. Ibn Sina's disparagement of Razi seems to have arisen from seeing him as a rival and threat. Though Razi had died half a century before Ibn Sina's birth, he looms over the *Canon* like a specter.

Ibn Sina labored mightily to make his own medical study an alternative to Razi's work and not a mere supplement to it. He clearly succeeded. Yet it was inevitable that Ibn Sina would draw heavily from Razi, as well as from Majusi and other authors going back to Galen. This, after all, was common practice in an era when borrowings were both common and rarely acknowledged. Even in the West the concept of deliberate plagiarism (from the Latin *plagiarius*, or "kidnapper") did not elicit general condemnation until recently and even remains legal in most countries. A definitive estimation of the extent of Ibn Sina's borrowings from Razi would require thousands of close comparisons. However, it is difficult to avoid the conclusion that Ibn Sina's general failure to acknowledge the existence of Razi's *Comprehensive* belies his profound indebtedness to his predecessor.

However great Ibn Sina's borrowings from Razi, they were strictly limited to clinical and diagnostic matters, not the philosophy of medicine. Ibn Sina held that medicine presents two faces to the world, one practical and the other theoretical. What is striking in the *Canon* is how much effort it devotes to identifying the links between the two. For example, rather than simply present the humors and temperaments and leave it at that, Ibn Sina offers tables listing all bodily organs in terms of their degree of heat, cold, moisture, and dryness.

Even more striking in this respect is his discussion of embryology. Here he confronts the question of when and how the semen, which he conceived as both male and female, is transformed from being *potentially* human to being *actually* human. One historian of science points out that Ibn Sina generally argues for discontinuous change that occurs all at once, a position that is grounded in his metaphysics.[17] But in this case he confronted his own practical observation that the change appears to take place gradually. This issue, which echoes today in debates over when and how a "person" emerges from a few cells, posed a problem for Ibn Sina. No wonder that in his later *Book of Animals* he devotes a lengthy passage to embryology. There, however, he argues the case for abrupt and discontinuous change, and claims, in contrast to his presentation in the *Canon*, that this conclusion is confirmed by observation.

In the end, Ibn Sina fully embraced the Greeks' theory of humors and temperaments. The question is what relevance, if any, Aristotelian concepts and his own underlying philosophy had at the operational level. They gave Ibn Sina the intellectual armature he needed to proceed, and to that extent they were crucial. But whether they provided him with more than the *appearance* of order and structure as he addressed the infinite complexities of medicine is a separate issue. A summary review of the four subsequent volumes of the *Canon of Medicine* might provide insight into this core question.

In the second and third sections of Volume I, Ibn Sina offers a classification of diseases, their causes, symptoms, and diagnosis.[18] Among many causes, he lists traumas, hot baths, tight bandaging, excessive food, strenuous activity, lack of sleep, moroseness, violent evacuation, and coitus. These sections were clearly the heart of the medical section of the *Canon* as Ibn Sina initially conceived it. He mentions a possible further volume on "simple drugs" and speaks vaguely about still other volumes in which he might address other neglected topics.[19] But then nothing more. This indicates that the *Canon* evolved by stages and not according to a comprehensive architecture conceived at the outset.

After his densely philosophical opening, Ibn Sina explains the difference between diseases that are the result of external factors and those that arise from within the body. But while his explanations of the former are focused and concrete, his treatment of the latter roll out the concept of humors and temperaments in a formulaic manner. In some places of Volume I, though,

Ibn Sina's invocation of temperaments and humors is more convincing. For example, when discussing eating, drinking, and bathing, the concepts of dryness and moistness fit the evidence. His prescriptions for those whose temperaments are excessively hot or cold are also practical and designed to address the identified symptoms.[20] In these passages one senses—yet again— the complex interaction between Ibn Sina the abstract thinker dwelling on first principles and the eagle-eyed physician offering prescriptions for actual patients. While the former helped Ibn Sina impose order on the confusing welter of diseases and conditions, the latter gave rise to much of what readers found most valuable in the *Canon of Medicine*.

A striking feature of the practical sections of the *Canon*'s first volume is the amount of attention it accords to preventive medicine. In today's parlance, Ibn Sina would be called a "wellness" expert. He offers advice on such everyday topics as diet, exercise, childcare, bathing, massages, and travel by land (in summer and winter) and by sea. Having never seen an ocean, he relied on Galen for information on seasickness and vertigo. Some of these brief entries are gems. Concerning travel, for example, Ibn Sina recommends that anyone taking a long trip begin by purging his bowels, wrapping a warm fabric around his mid-section, and smearing his feet with warmth-inducing oils. He also warns of travel fatigue, offers recommendations for skin care, and suggests that travelers bring along snacks that are appropriate to their temperament and unlikely to cause thirst.[21]

The same sense of practicality suffuses his discussion of childcare. He launches his discussion with pointers on prenatal care, then advises that the umbilical cord be cut to a length of four fingers, and gave a recipe for the powder to be applied to the cut surfaces: equal parts of turmeric, dragon's blood (a dark red powder made from the resinous plant of the same name), sarcalla, cumin seed, and lichen.[22] He turns next to the selection of a wet-nurse, who should be of healthy complexion, with a strong neck and broad chest, and a well-developed, muscular body. It was also important that she "should not have suffered from any abortions or miscarriages and should always have had full-term babies."

No passages in Ibn Sina's *Canon* have attracted more comments than those involving wine.[23] The *Quran* condemns "strong drink and games of chance" as Satan's handiwork (Sura 5:90), though its description of Paradise includes "rivers of wine that are delicious to the drinkers" (Sura 47:15). Ibn Sina considered wine to be medically beneficial when consumed in moderation. Thus, he recommends wine for its ability to stimulate digestion, dissolve phlegm, cause yellow bile to exit the body in urine, and also help black bile to leave the system.[24] Since black bile was believed to be a harmful byproduct of intense mental activity, this point was quite relevant to Ibn Sina personally. Yet more relevant, if not blatantly self-serving, is his claim that "wine does not inebriate quickly a person of powerful brain, for the brain [of such a person] is not susceptible to ascending harmful vapors, nor does heat from the wine reach it to any degree beyond what is appropriate." Far from clouding exceptional minds, a good tipple actually stimulates them, and they "become clear to a degree unequalled at other times." Then, with lordly condescension, he concludes that "the effect is different on persons who are not of this caliber." The derision that such views elicited from his early readers caused him later to issue a full treatise on alcohol, tellingly entitled *On the Benefits and Harm of Wine*.

Three further groups whose medical needs Ibn Sina addresses are the lean and the obese, those especially prone to disease, and the elderly. Nearly all of Ibn Sina's recommendations for better health are non-invasive, calling for changes in lifestyle that would meet with approval from any medical expert today. Those medicines he called for were mainly preparations made from medicinal plants and herbs, to which he devotes the entire second volume of the *Canon*. Throughout he is at pains to show how the value of some medications stems from their ability to neutralize an excess of the same or some opposite chemicals. The term "homeopathy" was not coined until the late eighteenth century, but something akin to it had existed since the era of Hippocrates. Ibn Sina not only stands in that tradition but contributed significantly to it.

Ibn Sina was, of course, passionately devoted to categorization. In the *Canon* he catalogues no fewer than twenty-three different types of fevers. Had an instrument for measuring temperatures existed then, he might have carried his analysis further, but this had to await Galileo's invention of the thermoscope in the sixteenth century and Daniel Fahrenheit's thermometer two centuries later. In Ibn Sina's day, the main analytic technique was to observe and categorize, not to measure. Addressing future doctors, Ibn Sina counsels them to be attentive to everything, including hair, complexion, and musculature. Countless passages in the *Canon* attest to Ibn Sina's alertness also to nonverbal cues and to his ability to gain valid information even when the patient was stressed, reticent, or even silent.

Beyond interviewing and carefully observing the patient, Ibn Sina relied heavily on the pulse as a diagnostic tool. Close attention to the pulse was nothing new, for physiologists at least since Galen had placed great stock in this simple method of gauging the speed and regularity of heartbeats and of determining the systolic blood pressure (diastolic pressure being unobservable by tactile methods). In his *Canon* he offers his readers a thirty-page disquisition on the subject. Out of respect for the patient's modesty, Ibn Sina recommends that the pulse be taken only at the wrist and not at the neck or groin. Based on his own analysis and in keeping with his passion for categorizing, he presents ten aspects of the pulse that could provide diagnostic insights. Nine of them were diastolic indicators while the tenth focused on such traits as "meter, rhythm, harmony, measure, and accent."[25] More than any of his predecessors, Ibn Sina sought to turn the medical doctor's hand into a subtle diagnostic instrument.

The only other matters to which the *Canon* assigns the same diagnostic importance as the pulse are urine and feces. Having once declared that Razi should have stuck with examining urine and stool samples, Ibn Sina himself now accords their study a prominent place in the *Canon*. And rightly so. Sumerian doctors studied urine samples 6,000 years ago, while Hippocrates wrote that "no other organ of the human body provides so much information by its excretion as does the urinary system." Ibn Sina looked to urinalysis to identify malfunctions of the liver, kidneys, and blood vessels as well as the presence of abscesses, fevers, and infections. In an aside, he also draws comparisons between urine and feces from males, females, and animals.

The *Canon* reveals that Ibn Sina understood full well the problem of pain. He first shows how the doctor can employ psychological factors to the patient's benefit, among them being "anything that exalts the sensitive and vital drives: for instance, joyfulness."[26] A change of venue could also help, or a smaller mirror to prevent someone with a facial deformity from fixating on it. Above all, he counsels the doctor to avoid all strong measures, including purging, cautery, and surgery.

Having duly admonished medical experts to avoid "strong measures," the *Canon* then spells out the treatments that comprise that group of therapies. The chapter titled "The Use of Eliminants: Purgation, Emesis, Cupping, Venesection [e.g., phlebotomy], Leeches," is one of the longest in the first volume. All these "eliminants," as well as the application of leeches, had been in the doctor's toolkit since ancient times. Ibn Sina merely counsels caution in their use. This brings his *Canon* to the subject of incisions. Ibn Sina's very modest list of surgical interventions can only evoke surprise, for surgery was by no means unknown in his era. Trepanations to relieve intracranial pressures were not uncommon in ancient Mesopotamia and Egypt and had been carried out by Hippocrates;[27] other practices were the removal of tumors, draining of lungs, tracheostomies, and operations to remove kidney and bladder stones. Muslim practitioners embraced all of these. Cataract surgery was also practiced throughout the East, while circumcision was universal for male Muslims and Jews.

There are two reasons the *Canon* limits its discussion of surgical interventions to seven pages and does not even mention the operations enumerated above. First, though surgery existed, it was mainly for emergency care, as on the battlefield. Second, a division of labor relegated surgeons to a separate and lower order of medical practitioners. In Ibn Sina's day, broken bones were handled not by medical experts but by the lower order of "bonesetters," and this subject has no place in the *Canon*. Razi too did not practice surgery and offered only a few comments on the subject. Admittedly, there were other experts in the Muslim East and in Andalusia who were soon to make extensive use of surgery, and with important results.[28] But in his silence on surgery Ibn Sina was simply following the practice of his day.

Had Ibn Sina expected the first volume of his *Canon* to be an immediate sensation he would have been disappointed. "Publishing" meant copying, an arduous and slow process. Also, Majusi's convenient two-volume study remained very popular, while many specialists still preferred Razi's ubiquitous treatises. To achieve its success, the *Canon* would require time. Meanwhile, one can imagine a frustrated Ibn Sina leafing ruefully through the pages of Razi's old essay, "Why Most People Turn Away from Excellent Physicians and Towards the Worst Ones."[29]

To promote the *Canon* and his views on medicine and life, Ibn Sina wrote several short and accessible pieces and even two poems.[30] His *Discourse on the Principles of Cardiac Medicine* gained a wide readership because it reflected the popular view that emotional and mental states trace to the heart. Another work designed for a broad readership was *A Poem on Medicine*, which summarized the entire contents of the *Canon* in seventy pages of versified text.

In Hamadan, Ibn Sina used his evening sessions with senior students as a sounding board for fresh drafts of his *Canon*. He also set to work on Volume II, a comprehensive guide to medicines, the *materia medica*. Such "Formularies" had been a feature of medical treatises since ancient times, and a broad range of sources was readily available. However, merely to compile this voluminous evidence posed an immense challenge that could be met only while Ibn Sina was in Hamadan, where he had acolytes and students whom he could draft as research assistants. His own role in this volume was as editor, not author, but it enabled him to insert his own often pointed views on dosages and effects.

Ibn Sina's researchers drew from more than two dozen sources, ancient and modern, including works by Romans, Byzantine Greeks, and Indians. They also had ready access to the knowledge of practicing apothecaries. Judging by the measures, mortars and pestles, scales, bottles for fermentation, and retorts for distillations that archaeologists have found, this was a sophisticated profession, rich with experience and lore. Yet for all their diligence, the research team missed some important sources. For example, Abu Mansur Muwaffaq Harawi, a contemporary of Ibn Sina from Herat in Afghanistan, had just issued a medical collection that included important pharmacological and diagnostic material drawn from Indian sources. But it found no place in the *Canon*.

Ibn Sina focused his second volume on the pharmacology of those plants, minerals, and animal products that were employed on their own and in pure form. This left medical compounds to the fifth and final volume. Ibn Sina's understanding of "pharmacopoeia" covered not just what today might be considered medicines but also stimulants for athletes, drugs to prevent memory loss, as well as cosmetics and products for coloring hair. Besides thousands of obvious substances, his tome covers an amazing range of what today would be considered exotica, including oyster shells, smoke of burning frankincense, scorpions, and salamander excrement. Brushing aside taboos, it also provides advice on the clinical use of wine, beer, opium, marijuana, and hashish. Each entry is carefully identified by its name in Arabic, followed by details on its preparation, use, and dosage.[31]

The second and fifth volumes on pharmacology came into wide use, but some of those who drew from them would have come up against a serious challenge. In drawing so heavily on the works of ancient Greek, Roman, and Byzantine writers, Ibn Sina focused mainly on plants, animals, and minerals of the Mediterranean world, many of which did not exist in the lands to the east, where most of his early readers lived. Where, for example, could a reader in landlocked Bukhara find a horned sea poppy? Further complicating the situation, many plants and animals bore completely different names in Arabic, or worse, a single name could refer to quite different plants in different places and languages. Was Ibn Sina even aware of this issue? There is no evidence that he was.

As a philosopher, Ibn Sina regularly tested hypotheses advanced by his predecessors. But as a medical practitioner he was often content to borrow from the works of his forebears. One key exception is his interest in validating claims advanced for new drugs through what we now call clinical trials. Though Razi had preceded him in this practice, as in so many others, Ibn Sina's contribution was nonetheless significant. The *Canon* lays down eleven rules to be followed in testing the effectiveness and strength of medicinal compounds. It was in the form advocated by Ibn Sina rather than the proposals of his forebears, that clinical trials became part of the doctor's toolkit.[32]

The entirety of Volume III is devoted to diseases affecting only one organ of the body, and Volume IV to those affecting the body as a whole. Ibn Sina's coverage in both volumes is impressive for its range and detail. Thus, in discussing the treatment of respiratory diseases he reviews the typology and multiple sources of pulmonary malfunctions, advises on the type of examination appropriate for each, and recommends both pharmacological and environmental treatments. Similarly, for edema Ibn Sina starts by distinguishing three types of water retention and their causes and then suggests specific treatments for each.[33] The few times in this extended presentation that he draws on his own clinical experience were to issue warnings such as "This medication is dangerous. I would never prescribe it."[34] And in spite of his general aversion to surgery, in the case of edema of the liver he details various surgical interventions, identifying the risks and dangers of each.

Volumes III and IV are written in a straightforward, almost chatty style, often posing questions and then answering them. Their accessibility is the very opposite of the abstruse discourse of his theoretical introduction in Volume I. So striking is this difference that the reader involuntarily asks what, if any, is the relationship between them. It is a commonplace to characterize Ibn Sina's worldview as unitary and fully integrated beneath the umbrella of metaphysics. As Seyyed Hossein Nasr puts it, Ibn Sina perceived the natural and physical worlds "in the light of cosmological doctrines which derive from intellectual intuition, not from nature by itself." A related thesis is that Ibn Sina's concern for the actual practice of medicine was secondary. In the words of Dimitri Gutas, "Clinical observation, independent of all philosophical presuppositions, as one finds them with Razi, are assigned a quite secondary place" in the *Canon*.[35] In the same vein, one noted student of Islamic medicine tartly observes that the actual practice of medicine "is not a topic with which [Ibn Sina] concerns himself in the *Canon of Medicine*."[36] Lending further authority to this view are Ibn Sina's own words on the second page of Volume I, informing readers that the theory of medicine is not what the doctor actually does but what enables him to decide what to do.[37]

This perspective is surely relevant to the important "cosmological" sections of Volume I. Yet for all their significance, these comprise only a small fraction of the *Canon* as a whole. Meanwhile, it is the second half of Volume I and the entirety of Volumes III and IV that constitute the medical heart of the work. In the third and fourth volumes the philosophical structure that is said to underlie the entire *Canon* is scarcely evident. To the extent that it appears at all it mainly reminds the reader of its existence. Ibn Sina does not invoke it either to explain clinical phenomena or to suggest or defend his prescriptive responses. Indeed, one can grasp nearly every detail in the volumes on diseases without reverting to the extended "theoretical" introduction to Volume I.

Ibn Sina did not intend the *Canon* to be a research report. It offers no innovations comparable to Razi's pioneering distinction between smallpox and measles or his identification of alcohol and sulfuric acid as discrete substances. Nor did Ibn Sina pause to identify issues that had stumped him or that might become the subject of future research. His aim was to enumerate questions for which his *Canon* could provide answers and not to confuse practitioners or general readers with questions that would go unanswered or are unanswerable. Acknowledging this, clinical sections of the *Canon* nonetheless present more than a few noteworthy advances. To cite but one example, Ibn Sina traces a wide range of neurological issues to the brain. He ascribes strokes to blockages of the arteries leading to the brain and devoted careful attention to vertigo, epilepsy, and dementia, offering his views on the causes and treatment of each. Nor does he ignore what today would be considered psychiatry, including such conditions as insomnia, nightmares, paranoia, and hysteria.

The *Canon of Medicine* was a product of its times. As such, it is no surprise that many of its prescriptions are ineffective and some even highly dangerous. Among the latter are Ibn Sina's recommendation that certain diseases of the eyes be treated with highly toxic blue vitriol (hydrated copper sulphate), which causes blindness. Yet in that same passage on the eye, he coins a term which, translated later into Latin, gave us the word "retina."

All these considerations greatly complicate the task of assessing the work as it is. Still, we can start by noting what the *Canon of Medicine* was *not*. In the eleventh century, there were other approaches to medicine that differed radically from Ibn Sina's. His *Canon* was, for example, not a book of astro-logical medicine, a popular approach that purported to trace both the causes and cures of maladies to the positions of the heavenly bodies. Nor was it a book of "Islamic" medicine, although the idea of deriving a body of con-crete medical knowledge from the *Quran* and the *Sayings* of Muhammad was gaining currency at the time. Nor, finally, was it a compendium and study of folk medicine, though the vast majority of patients at the time were treated under that system.

The *Canon* may not have been inherently superior to its predecessors, but it nonetheless was to dominate medical learning for centuries to come. It did so because of what Ibn Sina himself summarized as his ambition to discover by means of pure theory the universal traits of the ailments of the human body and the causes that produce them and then to offer the philosophically informed "universal rules governing treatment."[38] This remarkable state-ment crystallizes Ibn Sina's intentions in writing the *Canon of Medicine* and his own assessment of what he had achieved. Implicit throughout the *Canon* is Ibn Sina's belief that we live in a rational world that came into being when the Prime Mover created the universe and which, by its wholeness and com-pleteness, could give confidence to medical practitioners immersed in the vexing minutiae of diagnoses and treatment.

Yet there remains the disconnect between the two sides of the work, the cosmological and theoretical versus the practical. It is hard to escape the conclusion that the former was like an architect's schematic drawing but one that the architect failed to put into the builder's hands. Instead, the architect turned over only a sketch, leaving the builder to proceed on the basis of his own experience and instincts. In his *Canon of Medicine* Ibn Sina was both the architect and the builder. In the end, he himself had to acknowledge that it is difficult to grasp, for instance, how heat and cold, dryness and moistness, might account for conditions of the bowels, or the difficulty of applying some of his cosmological notions to the specifics of health and disease.[39]

In spite of this, Ibn Sina's *Canon of Medicine* inspired confidence in its readers. It offered structure and coherence where previously there had been a bewildering mass of disconnected facts. The confidence it engendered was doubtless a boost to overwhelmed doctors and a balm to their patients. As such, I would argue that Ibn Sina's *Canon* did more than any other single work to forge the medical profession and became the most important text in the history of medicine.

However, that confidence came at a high price. For the *Canon* advances no open-ended questions for later readers to explore, no hypotheses that could lead to counterhypotheses and yet more questions. This is scarcely surprising, for it was not in Ibn Sina's character to pose questions he could not himself answer. He invites readers to master his system rather than challenge and possibly supersede it.

That Ibn Sina's *Canon* provides more answers than questions and places no premium on enquiry and innovation led eventually to the downfall of the system it espouses. For all the enthusiasm it engendered over the course of half a millennium, that system proved in the end to be more stultifying than invigorating.

14

Biruni's *Canon* for Masud

While Ibn Sina was composing—or navigating his way through—the *Canon of Medicine*, Biruni was writing up a dozen further projects, few of which have survived. He had completed *India* while Mahmud was still alive, but he prudently chose to keep it under wraps. Instead, he seized on the respite created by Mahmud's annual campaigns in India to write four additional works dealing with technical issues involving Indian mathematics and astronomical tables. The longest of them is said to have run to 1,100 pages.[1] All are lost, but we know that they were neither restatements of earlier work nor spin-offs from more important projects. Rather, each addressed fundamental questions of Indian astronomy that Biruni had not covered in his *India*.[2]

All that is known of seven further writings from this period are their titles, but they nonetheless shed light on how Biruni interacted with valued colleagues and on his restless and ever-broadening curiosity. In separate papers he responded to astronomical and mathematical questions posed to him by scholars in India and Kashmir. He also wrote a story about water lilies adapted from a Persian tale, and a treatise on the great Buddhist statues in Bamiyan, Afghanistan.

Meanwhile, the geopolitics of Central Asia were once more in turmoil. By the late 1020s, Mahmud's empire controlled far more of Eurasia than had any other empire since the peak of the Abbasid Caliphate two and a half centuries earlier. Yet Mahmud was not done. He had hit all the obvious targets in India but had yet to conquer the decentralized holdings of the Buyid family in Persia—and beyond that lay the grandest prize of all—Baghdad. Mahmud dreamed of placing himself at the head of a great Sunni crusade to liberate Persia from the despised Shiite Buyids and put an end to the Shiites' control of the caliphate. This would be the crowning achievement of his imperial project and also his apotheosis as the protector of Sunni Islam. These are the aspirations that led to Mahmud's bloody conquest of Rayy in 1029, which he saw as the first stop on the road to Baghdad.

If the lands to the west of Mahmud's core territory presented an opportunity, they also posed a threat in the form of the Turkmen nomads. Mahmud's earlier efforts to push the Turkic tribes out of Khorasan and Khwarazm had brought unintended consequences. In search of pasture, the nomads began attacking Mahmud's own territories in what today is western Afghanistan, Turkmenistan, and eastern Iran. Their internal organization improved in the process and their ambitions soared. Soon the Turkmen tribesmen, who now called themselves "Seljuks," were also dreaming of conquering Baghdad. Thus, Mahmud's campaigns gave rise to a highly mobile and battle-hardened rival.

None of this affected Mahmud's daily life. He continued to hold court, wallow in praise from his army of poets, and not bother Biruni when his house "astrologer" wrote texts that neither he nor anyone else at court could understand. Mahmud even developed a grudging respect for the astrologer whose mind was in the clouds. When Mahmud received a diplomatic mission from remote and unknown China, he asked Biruni to sit in on the meetings and evaluate what he heard.[3]

Over time a strange bonhomie developed between them. Half a century after Mahmud's death, the historian Beyhaqi heard a story about Mahmud and Biruni sitting together in a roof garden with two exits. Mahmud, poking fun at Biruni's renown as an astrologer, asked him to write down on paper the door he, Mahmud, would use to exit. When Biruni had written his answer Mahmud called in workmen, who cut open a third door. But when Mahmud read Biruni's note he saw that his astrologer had anticipated the Sultan's trick. Angered, he had Biruni thrown from the rooftop, but Biruni landed safely in a net, and when Mahmud read a second note from his astrologer he saw that Biruni had foretold that outcome, too.[4] Irked at being outplayed, Mahmud briefly confined him in the Ghazni fortress. This did not end the matter. According to a near contemporary, Mahmud continued to be peevish until his vizier pointed out that Biruni had twice correctly foretold the future. Only then did Mahmud acknowledge his own foolishness, release him, and renew their curious relationship.[5]

To his credit, Mahmud supported Biruni's request to build a globe larger than the one that had been destroyed in the sack of Gurganj and to use it in his research.[6] However, when Biruni then constructed a mechanical calendar clock for the cathedral mosque, Mahmud had it ripped down, because it was based on the Roman calendar rather than the Muslim system. Biruni groused that the measurement of time is a purely secular matter and that convenience and utility alone should prevail with respect to clocks. But he did this privately.[7]

Some have tried to shift blame for Biruni's continuing travails at Mahmud's court onto Mahmud's viziers. Biruni served under three of them and all three came to bad ends.[8] When Mahmud accused the first of extortion, the poor man voluntarily went to prison, where he died. The second, Ahmad bin Hasan al-Maimondi, was a foster brother of Mahmud and a man of considerable learning.[9] This vizier protected Biruni from 1013 to 1025, but Mahmud then packed him off to prison. The third, Abu Ali Hasan ibn Muhammad, known as "Hasanak," harassed Biruni until Mahmud accused his brazen and ignorant official of heresy and had him put to death.[10] The first and third of these unfortunates may well have been responsible for Biruni's hardships during their brief terms in office. But the fact remains that over the twenty-two years he spent in Ghazni, Biruni did not dedicate a single work to Mahmud, as would have been normal. And when he deigned to acknowledge Mahmud in *India* he referred to him not as the sultan, the title Mahmud had claimed for himself, but merely as the emir. In spite of all this, Biruni acknowledged that at a later stage of their relationship "He [Mahmud] pardoned my ignorance and began to appreciate me, and his appreciation improved my looks and dress."[11] This was the grudging praise of a servant who knew how to handle his master, and not the words of a free man.

In spite of his new clothes, Biruni's mood was gloomy. "It is quite impossible," he wrote, "that a new science or any new kind of research should arise in our days. What we have of science is nothing but the scanty remains of bygone better times."[12] Fortunately, Biruni was long accustomed to filtering out the external world and focusing on his work. And work he did. Having completed *India* and other shorter projects, he conceived the idea of a single comprehensive study that would update and present his life's work in mathematics, astronomy, geometry, trigonometry, geodesy, geography, and further topics as interested him.

It was the right time to undertake so massive a project. Biruni was fifty-five years old. Though he had suffered some kind of medical crisis in 1023,[13] he was once again in good health. He would call this work his *Qanun*, or *Canon*. He would later dedicate this work to Mahmud's son and successor, Masud, for which reason it is still called *Masud's Canon*.

The fact that Biruni chose the same title that Ibn Sina had used for the first volume of his *Canon of Medicine* five years earlier immediately raises suspicion. Did Biruni launch his own *Canon* as a provocative response? A few years later the old rivals would once more work in parallel, with Biruni writing a book on medicinal plants at about the same time Ibn Sina released the fifth volume of his *Canon* on the same subject. If so, the question is how Biruni might have learned of Ibn Sina's activities. Did copies of Ibn Sina's writings reach Ghazni, or did Mahmud's spies report on them? When Masud's troops pilfered Ibn Sina's camel bags at the gate of Isfahan, they came across many of his books and dispatched them to the great library at Ghazni.[14] It is tempting to assume that Biruni read them. But the destruction of that entire repository a century and a half later removed the evidence on which a conclusion might be based.

Biruni's *Canon* is a large and demanding work, spread over eleven "books" that treat a broad range of highly technical subjects. Its core concern, however, is with observational astronomy, the measurement of time, and the mathematics needed to analyze both. To this end, Biruni rigorously analyzed the full body of mathematics on which the Ptolemaic system was based.[15]

Only twice does Biruni deviate from this focus. The first time is early in his tome, when he felt it necessary to refute those holdouts who still believed the earth to be flat. By Ptolemy's time ancient Greek astronomers had agreed that the earth is round. Muslim astronomers, too, accepted this as a given. But Biruni knew there were still holdouts, mainly Muslim theologians. Anticipating criticism from those whom he called "*kalam* imams," he therefore ran through the familiar evidence of the earth's spherical shape. Then he returned to the subject at hand.

Biruni's other deviation from this focus occurs in the last section, when he turns to the body of astronomical knowledge advanced by astrologers. Though he himself was formally employed as an astrologer, Biruni, as noted, considered astrology to be an absurd pseudo-science. However, on the pages of *Masud's Canon* he wastes no time refuting its practitioners, since his interest at this point was solely in garnering whatever useful astronomical data astrologers might have gained in the course of their studies.

In approaching *Masud's Canon*, as was the case with Ibn Sina's *Canon of Medicine*, it is useful to bear in mind what that work is not. First, in spite of its being divided into "discourses" or books, as was commonly done with medieval encyclopedias, it was not intended as an encyclopedia of scientific knowledge. Throughout his life Biruni assumed that each sphere of science demanded exhaustive analysis in its own right. Without such rigorous study, generalizations would be little more than the glib repetitions of old shibboleths, with some unproven hypotheses thrown in for good measure. An encyclopedia full of such half-baked information would be worthless. Moreover, the notion of an encyclopedia implied a fixed system. Biruni, however, considered that all the sciences were constantly evolving, and that any encyclopedia would scarcely outlive the moment. All this was in sharp contrast to Ibn Sina and his *Canon*.

Second, Biruni's *Canon* is in no sense a passive summary of the work of previous thinkers. While it includes countless references to both ancient and modern astronomers as well as to the principal Indian astronomers and mathematicians, Biruni accepted nothing simply on authority. Thus, while he reports approvingly on many aspects of Ptolemy's overall system, on issue after issue he also subjected Ptolemy's formulations to withering criticism. His treatment of recent Muslim astronomers from the Middle East and Central Asia is even less reverential. He cites relevant works by all these predecessors, sometimes to praise them but more often to identify and correct their errors.

Third, Biruni's *Canon* is not a reference work, nor was it intended for educational purposes, as is implied by the Greek term "encyclopedia" (ἐγκύκλιος παιδεία). Biruni's students at Ghazni, if he even had any, were very few in number and he did not consider them his primary audience. With its generous use of spherical trigonometry and its innovative treatment of sines, Biruni's *Canon* was meant for that handful of experts who commanded the same level of knowledge as Biruni himself.

Fourth, Biruni did not aspire to present a comprehensive view of any field of science or philosophy. His sole focus was on knowledge in any fields that he had personally verified mathematically. In covering geodesy, Biruni refers to the same broad range of Greek, Jewish, Christian, Zoroastrian, and Muslim systems for the measurement of time as he had done in *Chronology*, adding masses of information on India for good measure. But these were there simply to elucidate his mathematical and astronomical arguments, not as ends in themselves. For the same reason, Biruni's *summa* left out most of the religious and cultural issues that were the focus of *Chronology* and *India*. And while its contents are rich with implications for metaphysics and cosmology, Biruni did not address them in *Masud's Canon*, leaving the reader to pursue them on his own.

If Biruni's *Canon* is not an encyclopedia, an intellectual history, a reference work, or an educational treatise, what is it? The modern reader can best approach it as Biruni himself did, namely, as an extended and open-ended report on a lifetime's research on the earth, moon, sun, stars, and cosmos. How do we know that this was Biruni's intent? One indication is the frequency with which he confesses that he has been unable to pursue further a given line of research. For example, after studying the fire-like flares emitted by the sun, he corrects ancient and recent astronomers who considered them to be a metaphysical entity and argues instead that the sun is an actual substance subject to the usual laws of nature. But when it came to measuring the sun's diameter and distance from the earth, Biruni throws up his hands. He offers a definitive critique of Ptolemy's process of estimation, which led to a gross underestimation of distances,[16] but reports candidly that he was unable to proceed further.

Biruni had continued to ponder the sun's diameter since writing his *India*, when he dismissed it as not measurable by existing instruments. Now, in *Masud's Canon*, he added an interesting alternative to better instrumentation, by demonstrating that he could calculate the sun's diameter if he had the opportunity to observe a total solar eclipse.[17] Unfortunately, he then calculates that several centuries would have to pass before such an event would be visible in Afghanistan. On several equally important issues Biruni draws no conclusions because, as he explains, to do so he would require astronomical observations extending centuries into the future.

Since *Masud's Canon* embraces the whole field of observational astronomy and the measurement of distance and time, along with the associated mathematics, it is possible here only to touch on some of its high points. I'll do so by moving from the solar system to the sun, moon, and finally, the earth.

Biruni accepted Ptolemy's general notion of a spherical universe with the planetary orbits or spheres stacked atop each other. But when it came to measuring the very gradual eastward movement of the fixed stars on what appeared to be a central axis, he challenged all his predecessors. Ptolemy calculated the rate to be a degree every century while two of Biruni's Arabic predecessors pegged it at between sixty-six and seventy years. Biruni's figure—seventy and a third years—is closest to the modern measurement.[18] He also measured the sun's apogee more precisely than anyone before him, in the process faulting Ptolemy for carelessness.[19] His measurement of the solar year remained the most precise until the twelfth century when the astronomer Omar Khayyam improved its accuracy by two minutes. And he used highly sophisticated optical and mathematical techniques to measure the sun's dip below the horizon at sunset.[20]

With regard to the measurement of the moon's diameter and distance from the earth, Biruni confidently concludes that Ptolemy's figures were more accurate than those of recent Arab astronomers. But when it comes to calculating the moon's orbit, he is at a loss to explain the irregularities he has himself observed. Astronomers since Ptolemy had known of these, but neither Biruni nor anyone else could explain them until astronomers challenged the prevailing assumptions regarding the circularity of the moon's orbit and the earth's immobility. Instead, Biruni calls for continuous observations over time. He himself launches this process by making extremely precise measurements of the daily movements of the moon vis-à-vis the sun.[21]

Turning to the earth, Biruni offers geodesic information on more than 600 cities worldwide.[22] This grand compilation far surpassed all previous efforts at charting the earth's surface and fixing precisely those places inhabited by humans. It represents a striking improvement not only over Ptolemy and the ancients but over the compilation a century earlier by the astronomer Abu Abd Allah Muḥammad al-Battānī, who had listed only a hundred sites. Taking this body of Biruni's research as a whole, it is clear that few of the many later shipboard explorers did as much as the earth-bound Biruni to expand our knowledge of the globe we inhabit.

By including his own measurements and those he had commissioned others to make, Biruni's map of the world covered all of Eurasia except China and Japan, India as far south as the Deccan, and Africa down to the Equator. He had no authoritative data beyond these borders. During Biruni's time at Mahmud's court, he had had the opportunity to interview Chinese diplomats, but they had been unable to provide precise geodesic data on their country. Similarly, Biruni knew of the existence of Japan, but it remained for him a cartographic *terra incognita* for lack of precise data. However, based on evidence gleaned from sailors, he succeeded in correcting Ptolemy's assumption that India and Africa were connected, and indicated instead that the Indian and Atlantic Oceans met one another off southern Africa.[23]

Of particular importance is the fact that in *Masud's Canon* Biruni takes care to present the mathematical processes he employed to make each of these determinations. By so doing, he renders all his data reproducible and thus verifiable, an important step forward in the development of the scientific method.

Biruni surpassed all his predecessors in his passion for measurement. He saw in it a source of concrete knowledge that made possible precise comparisons between known phenomena and, through mathematics, the generation of new insights on the unknown. But measurement could not resolve all the problems Biruni addressed. The measurement of the sun's angular path across the sky as seen from earth had challenged astronomers through the millennia. In his usual meticulous manner, Biruni measured it with great precision and corrected errors in previous calculations dating back to ancient times. What he failed to grasp was the possibility that the obliquity of the ecliptic is itself slowly moving, due to the influence of the moon.[24]

Biruni's passion for precise measurement occasionally hit other impediments, but it more often led him into new territory. It was his zeal for quantification that had earlier caused him to trace to their underlying assumptions all known concepts of time, to identify the astronomical and mathematical foundations of each, and then to unify them under a single global system. It was this same zeal that now led him to hypothesize the existence of what we now call North and South America as inhabited continents.[25]

In his *Canon* Biruni reports once more on the research at Nandana that enabled him to calculate the earth's diameter and radius more precisely than anyone before him.[26] But he did not stop there. Whereas in his book on geodesy he confined himself to the earth's radius, diameter, and circumference, he now speculates about the possibility of calculating the earth's surface area and even its weight, as measured in gold. These were by no means fantasies, and he would doubtless have carried out these calculations if he had not been so absorbed with other issues.

First among these was his project to combine his measurement of the earth with his voluminous data on longitudes and latitudes. This was facilitated by the large new globe Mahmud had allowed him to construct in Ghazni, replacing the one that had been destroyed in Khwarazm. On it he located every spot for which he had data on its longitude and latitude, probably marking each location with a pin. It was then an easy matter to identify the westernmost and easternmost points for which he had precise knowledge. These would have been at the longitude of the Azores in the West and of the Sea of Japan in the East.

To this point Biruni's *Canon* was simply showcasing its author's voluminous data on longitudes and latitudes in a new, three-dimensional form. The next step was to calculate the distance between his easternmost and westernmost points. This calls upon one of the several innovative methods of calculating longitude that Biruni had himself devised. He had realized that the distance between the two points comprised only about a third of the earth's circumference. This brought him face to face with a question that was as puzzling as it was provocative: what was out there in the two thirds of the globe that extended between his easternmost and westernmost known points? Aristotle had confidently proposed a simple answer: water. He believed that the known lands, which for him included northern Africa, Europe, the Middle East, and parts of India, were surrounded by what he called the World Ocean. Biruni realized that this was at best an unproven hypothesis and at worst utter nonsense. From his knowledge of geological processes, Biruni knew that the existence of terra firma in the known world had to be the result of specific geological conditions and processes. As such, land would have to have been in conformity with the laws of nature. On what basis, then, could Aristotle have claimed that those same laws would have been suspended on the other two thirds of the globe?

Absent concrete information to the contrary, Biruni concludes that the only defensible hypothesis is that the same geological conditions that gave rise to land in the known part of the globe would also have created one or more land masses or continents in the unknown part. Biruni, in short, had found both evidentiary and logical grounds for affirming the existence of what we now know as North and South America. "There is nothing to prohibit the existence of inhabited lands in the Eastern and Western parts," he writes. "It is therefore necessary that the supposed regions do exist beyond the [known] remaining regions of the world [and are] surrounded by waters on all sides."[27]

Biruni is not yet done. He then poses the obvious follow-on question: if there are unknown continents on the opposite side of the globe, are they inhabitable? Here he calls on his earlier research on latitudes and weather that he had reported in *Determination of the Coordinates of . . . Cities*. In that work he had explained why the earth's northern polar region was uninhabitable by humans and why the same factors would cause the southern polar region to be similarly devoid of life. This meant that for the unknown continents to be uninhabitable, they would have to be situated either in the very far North or the very far South.

To address this, Biruni turns once more to the large body of data on latitudes that he had assembled on the known worlds of Eurasia and northern Africa. He notes that the inhabited lands are confined to a broad east-west belt across the earth's middle section. This concentration of land in the earth's mid-section clearly conformed to physical laws. He then asks again why laws of geology would prevail in one of the globe's hemispheres and not the rest? Barring contradictory evidence, Biruni concluded that the only defensible hypothesis is that the one or more unknown continents in the World Ocean would have to be situated somewhere near the earth's middle, like the known continents of Eurasia and Africa. This being the case, they would therefore have temperate climates and would be inhabitable. As he put it, "neither extreme heat nor cold stand in the way."[28]

Thus, almost five centuries before Columbus, a mathematician-astronomer who had never seen an ocean, correctly hypothesized the existence of what became known as North and South America as inhabited continents. It was a remarkable feat of discovery that was, for the time being, only a hypothesis, unconfirmed by evidence and data from the other side of the globe. Biruni fully acknowledges this. Unlike Ibn Sina, he did not equate logical proofs with physical proofs. Instead, he demanded both. Seeing no way to gain physical confirmation of his hypothesis about the existence of unknown continents, Biruni merely reports on it and then turns to other questions that are more amenable to the kind of proofs he demanded.

Another question that Biruni addresses in *Masud's Canon* concerns the nature of the solar system and the place of the earth and sun within it. Once more he found himself balancing the insights of mathematical astronomy with physical evidence. In both the Muslim and Christian worlds the questions of whether the earth rotated on its axis and whether the earth or sun lay at the center of the solar system were heavily freighted with religious concerns. However, Biruni and his predecessors in Greece and India all viewed such questions as purely technical and theoretical issues.

When Biruni was a young man in Gurganj, the local vizier had asked him why the earth remained stationary and why it did not turn on its axis. Biruni's answer is lost, but he presumably repeated the views of Aristotle and Ptolemy and left it at that. But the issue would not go away, and he turned to it again in his large compendium on Indian astronomy, now lost. Biruni had also taken it up in his great study of India, where for the first time he opened himself to the notion that the earth rotates on its axis, which, he argues, "does not in any way impair the value of astronomy."[29]

Biruni proved mathematically that the earth could rotate on its axis, but that was not enough for him. Once more he demanded physical proof as well, and it was here that problems arose. He was aware of the Greeks' argument that if the earth rotated on its axis, then anything in the air, including birds and clouds, would appear to be whirling around in the stationary atmosphere. Working on the basis of this flawed hypothesis, he went so far as to calculate the rate at which such whirling would occur. But he observed no physical evidence of such movement in the sky, so he rejected as unproven the hypothesis that the earth rotates on its axis.

The flaw in Biruni's conclusion derived not from his mathematics, which were correct, but from an erroneous assumption about physics that he could readily have corrected without recourse to modern telescopes. In fact, this is precisely what Galileo did in 1632. Replying to a critic who defended the same view as Biruni, Galileo pointed out, first, that an object dropped from the top of the mast of a ship under sail and the same object dropped when the ship was at anchor would both land at precisely the same spot; and second, Galileo explained why this was compatible with the hypothesis about the earth's axial rotation.

Until he could come up with physical evidence to support the notion that the earth turns on its axis, Biruni was forced by his own rigorous standard of proof to reject the hypothesis. The same evidentiary issues emerged again as he took up yet another great question: did the sun revolve around the earth, or did the earth move around the sun? This gave rise to the renowned confrontation between advocates of geocentrism and heliocentrism.

This great question had vexed Biruni since his youth. It was among the core questions he brought to the study of Indian science. Now he returns once more to this issue in *Masud's Canon*. Biruni knew that the issue had been raised in the third century BC by Aristarchus of Samos, whose lost work on the subject had been summarized by the mathematician and physicist Archimedes, and that other ancient thinkers had also pondered the issue. He knew, too, that the Indian astronomer Aryabhata had explored the question—indeed to such an extent that Biruni had devoted a whole book, now lost, to assessing Aryabhata's heliocentric theory. In *Masud's Canon* Biruni falls back on Ptolemy, stating almost in passing that the earth is the center of the universe and that it has no motion of its own, that is, that it neither revolves on its axis nor in an orbit around the sun.[30] This may have been a bow to religious orthodoxy, for he knew full well that the orthodox Muslim theologians around Mahmud would be deeply upset if he proposed that the earth is not the center of God's universe. Yet even having written this, Biruni did not consider the matter closed.

At this point a nearly forgotten contemporary of Biruni's enters the picture. What little we know of Abu Sa'id al-Sijzi comes from Biruni's own brief account of their contact. Sijzi was a mathematician, astronomer, astrologer, and first-class tinkerer from Sistan, a desert region lying along the western border of Afghanistan.[31] This province had long been a bastion of independence in both thought and action. The last Persian ruler fled there to escape from the Arabs, and the entire population repeatedly rose up in arms against the Muslim conquerors. After the rise of Islam, Ismaili Shiism found fertile soil there, and it was from there that Abu Yaqub al-Sijistani, the zealous Ismaili theologian and proselytizer whose works influenced Ibn Sina's father, launched his crusade against both Sunni and Shiite orthodoxy.

Sijzi's expertise in astrology and astronomy had earned him the patronage of a Shiite emir in Persia and the support of leaders in the Afghan city of Balkh, the ancient Buddhist center now ruled by Mahmud. Through channels that are as yet unknown, Sijzi had gained a knowledge of how to express astronomical and astrological processes with metal devices using precisely calibrated gears. This technology traced at least to the third-century BC Greek astronomer Archimedes of Syracuse, who had designed and built the Antikythera device that, as noted earlier, anticipated in some respects the modern analog computer. Though lost during Roman times, knowledge of how to use complex observational techniques and gearing mechanisms to describe astronomical phenomena survived among the Byzantine Greeks, who passed it to the Arabs and Persians. By the 800s, a Persian astronomer and tinkerer in the city of Fars had developed a way of using a geared mechanism to combine and integrate data drawn from precise astronomical observations.

By Sijzi's time, ever more precise and complex instruments were being developed. Sijzi's achievement was to apply these technologies to a mechanism that replicated the movements of all known planets. Featuring a series of intermeshed gears, this complex device, which modern students have concluded was a type of spherical astrolabe, had one innovative and astonishing feature: rather than showing a stationary earth with the planets revolving around it, it presented the earth as rotating on its axis and both the earth and planets as revolving around the sun.[32] In other words, deep in what is now Afghanistan, an obscure thinker and tinkerer offered what since the sixteenth century we have known as a Copernican view of the solar system.[33]

Sijzi had learned of Biruni's interest in heliocentrism and traveled from Balkh to Ghazni to discuss the matter. He brought with him the remarkable instrument of his own design. After carefully examining the instrument and quizzing Sijzi at length, Biruni wrote that he admired it immensely "because it rested on an independent foundation" and that its conclusion, that the "motion lies in the Earth and not in the Sky [e.g., Sun]," could not be refuted by "Geometricians and Astronomers who depend merely on the [data] resulting from their own measurements."

In other words, Biruni, as a mathematician, upheld the hypothesis of a heliocentric universe. But once again this did not end the matter. Instead, he compounded the complexity of the issue by framing it in different terms. In what is surely the most provocative but prescient statement in the entirety of his *Canon*, Biruni declares that it doesn't matter whether the Sun or the Earth moves. "In neither case does it affect the science [i.e., the mathematics]. If it is possible to contradict this belief and resolve the uncertainty, then it should be above all the concern of the physicists to do so."[34] In other words, all motion is relative. That the earth revolves around the sun or the sun around the earth are merely two ways of saying the same thing, like saying that A marries B or B marries A.

In these sentences, concise but frustratingly laconic, Biruni anticipates by half a millennium the core thesis that Galileo employed to confirm the heliocentric nature of the solar system. Proceeding further, he then plunges into the nature of motion itself. In doing so he anticipated a problem that Newton, Descartes, and Leibniz would all ponder at length and which received its ultimate formulation at the hands of Einstein in his General Theory of Relativity.[35] Typical of Biruni, he tossed out these notions as postulates that any thinking person would accept, and felt not the slightest need to elaborate or defend them further. Nor did he. As a result, his statement escaped the notice of most of those few readers who, over the following ten centuries, had access to *Masud's Canon*.

That Biruni qualified his embrace of a heliocentric solar system has led some to deny that he—or Sijzi—beat Copernicus to the mark. This robs Biruni of the place he deserves in the history of science. In Biruni's case it seems doubly unfair. Not only did he embrace the hypothesis on mathematical grounds but he was prepared to embrace it also because of his belief that all motion is relative.

Proceeding rationally, *Masud's Canon* enumerates the various methodologies by which astronomers might either confirm or deny heliocentrism by observing the heavens. Here he was forced to report that the astronomical observatories of his day were simply not up to the task. He showed that existing observatories could confirm the hypothesis by closely observing a specific type of solar eclipse. But his calculations revealed that such an eclipse would not occur for another two centuries. Biruni was stuck, forced to be content with an astonishingly bold hypothesis that remained, according to his own exacting standard, only half-proven. Yet his qualified embrace of this hypothesis and his insistence on the need for both mathematical and observational confirmation of the heliocentric hypothesis only confirm his stature as a scientist.

Biruni's astronomical research as reported in *Masud's Canon* produced mixed results. On the issue of the earth's axial rotation, his acceptance of false Greek notions about what would constitute observable evidence led him down a wrong path. But on the question of the sun's central place in the solar system and the earth's revolving around it he achieved a remarkable advance over his predecessors. On purely mathematical grounds he embraced a conclusion that anticipated the great astronomers of the Renaissance.

No less impressive was the distinction he drew between proofs attained through mathematics and those confirmed by physical observation. He did not prioritize either of these but instead insisted that both must be brought to bear for a hypothesis to be considered valid. Typically, he observed that the flames from the sun that are visible during a total eclipse indicate that the sun is a physical entity and not the spiritual body envisioned by astronomers through the ages. Yet because he was unable to express this phenomenon mathematically, he did not affirm this point. Once again Biruni emerged as the cool-headed, analytic, and impressively modern scientist.

The stress on both observation and mathematics suffuses Biruni's *Canon* as a whole and accounts for its important contribution to science. Yet another step forward was Biruni's embrace of elliptical rather than circular orbits. He had touched on this issue in his early polemic with Ibn Sina and explored it further in his treatment of Indian astronomy. Now, in *Masud's Canon*, he addressed it frontally, charging Ptolemy and others with "straining the evidence" to support the concept of circularity. He challenged his predecessors by advancing precise mathematical evidence in defense of elliptical movement.[36] In doing so he advanced toward the laws of planetary motion that Johannes Kepler would propound in the seventeenth century.

The eyes of all but the most specialized readers may glaze over when confronted with page after page of Biruni's observational data or when he lays out complex equations in multiple forms. Yet it is precisely on such pages as these that trigonometry first stepped forth as a fully independent field of study. The entirety of the third section of *Masud's Canon* is devoted to it. These extended passages constitute a full-blown practicum of the field, including the first proof of the spherical theorem of sines, the important subfield of spherical trigonometry.[37]

As I've noted, Biruni was by no means the first mathematician outside India to employ sine law. But he did more than anyone else to validate it, explain its value, and extend its use. Thanks to him, sine law came to supersede the old Greek methods for calculating chords. He was the first to prove the spherical theorem of sines,[38] while the sine tables he developed were unrivaled at the time. And in a different area, one twentieth-century mathematician credits Biruni with the first use in classical mathematics of the calculus of finite differences.[39]

Biruni's mode of expressing mathematical formulae again reflects the clarity he brought to bear on all problems. Drawing on a practice employed two centuries earlier by Khwarazmi in his classic work, *Algebra*, Biruni explains trigonometric processes not with numerical examples but with words. Take, for example, the following formula:

$$S_8 = \sqrt{\gamma^2 - \gamma\left(\gamma\sqrt{2} - \gamma\right)}$$

Rather than express it in this manner, Biruni presented it with equal precision using everyday language. "If we wish to find the chord of an octagon," he writes, "we should multiply the radius by the difference of the radius and the chord of a square, and subtract the result from the square of the radius, and then extract the square root."[40] Only in the late twentieth century did a few professors of mathematics seek to revive this demanding practice as a teaching tool. They did so because it fosters a conceptual grasp of the points at issue and not the mere ability to manipulate formulae.

Biruni was no less meticulous in his use of empirical data, much of which came from his own observations carried out with instruments of his own design. Typically, he compared his own instrument for measuring the solstice and equinox with that of Ptolemy and found the latter wanting.[41] But he rarely relied on only one tool, mathematical or observational, and acknowledged and applied methods developed by others.

Taken as a whole, *Masud's Canon* is a compendium of original findings, refutations of flaws in the works of other astronomers, past and present, and also frustrated explorations. While Biruni could respect some of his predecessors' mistakes, with others he could be unforgiving. Typically, on an issue of geography he acknowledged that "Ptolemy understood what he did but Yaqut [Yaqut al-Hamawi, a ninth-century geographer] did not know what he was doing."[42] No wonder that a contemporary could write of *Masud's Canon*, "It wiped out the traces of all prior books written about mathematics and astronomy."[43]

Biruni's writings tend to leap from issue to issue as he sought to incorpo-rate into his presentation all relevant dimensions of a problem. However log-ical, this practice gave rise to confusion and frustration among his readers. In *Masud's Canon*, however, Biruni narrowed his focus. Cultural and social issues find no place in it unless he considers them essential to his explication of mathematics and astronomy. Though a Muslim, he barely mentions God in the *Canon* except to affirm His role as the Prime Mover. Biruni's *Canon* is by no means an anti-religious work, but except for the initial invocation, it remains free of theology, metaphysics, and mysticism. Biruni's God is defi-nitely the Creator, but He does not interfere with His own laws of nature.

Biruni intended his *Canon* not as a final and closed system, one embracing all aspects of mathematics and astronomy, but as a time-bound research report based on his own explorations and those of his Greek and Indian predecessors whose work he judged to be sound. No previous figure in any of the fields that comprise *Masud's Canon* revealed nearly as broad a reach as Biruni. Yet his conclusions were purely his own, the fruit of days spent poring over his scrolls, notes, and sheafs of data in Ghazni, Afghanistan.

Though understandable, it is astonishing that Biruni had no contact with the handful of scholars in Egypt and Spain who were seeking to advance mathematical and astronomical knowledge in the same years. And yet he far surpassed them all. No wonder that George Sarton, who, as I noted in the introduction, founded the history of science as a field of study, concluded that Biruni was "one of the very greatest scientists of Islam and, all things considered, one of the greatest of all times."

15

The Cure

I've noted that Ibn Sina solved his dilemma of whether to serve the emir of Hamadan or refuse his offer by using the same combination of reason and intuition he had employed to arrive at the middle element of a syllogism. To avoid both of the obvious possibilities, he decided instead on a third: flee Hamadan and seek refuge with the emir Ala ad-Dawla of Isfahan, where he finished the fifth volume of the *Canon of Medicine*.

This was to be the last of five escapes Ibn Sina made during his life-time: Bukhara to Gurganj; Gurganj to Gorgan; Gorgan to Rayy; Rayy to Hamadan; and now Hamadan to Isfahan. It was also the only change of venue in Ibn Sina's long life that was not defined largely or in part by the actions of Mahmud of Ghazni. But if the tyrant from Afghanistan did not create the sit-uation in Hamadan from which Ibn Sina fled, the tyrant's son, Masud, would soon pose a danger to the philosopher's new home, Isfahan, and to Ibn Sina himself. That Biruni dedicated his *Canon* to this same Masud was mainly because that autocrat was temporarily out of his hair. Thus, the sinister and aggressive force from Ghazni that had first darkened the skies for Ibn Sina and Biruni in Gurganj continued to cast its long shadow over Ibn Sina, 800 kilometers (500 miles) away in Isfahan.

I also noted that the meeting of captive and captor in the jail at Fardaqan had about it the air of an orchestrated farce. Ibn Sina's flight from Fardaqan and Hamadan in 1023, however, was a full-blown melodrama. He risked being discovered and recaptured by the willful young emir of Hamadan and his spies. Members of his party therefore disguised themselves as Sufi pilgrims. The rough woolen robes covering most of their bodies provided camouflage and at the same time signaled to other travelers their desire to keep to themselves. His party consisted of five people: Ibn Sina; his aman-uensis, Juzjani; Ibn Sina's brother, Mahmud (who shows up at this time in Juzjani's biography without any explanation); and two slaves. The slaves were either Slavs captured on the northern frontier or Indians who had been sold to Persian buyers in the market at Ghazni. There would also have been a train of camels loaded with books and manuscripts. As was customary throughout

Central Asia and Persia, the party did not travel alone but instead attached itself to a caravan of many hundreds, or even thousands, of camels and their trader-owners.

The 550-kilometer (300-mile) trip to Isfahan would have taken nearly a month. However, when the weary and outlandishly attired band of five finally reached the gates of Isfahan they were met by a large delegation of local officials presenting the honored guests with ceremonial robes and offering trays of sweets. For the first time since leaving Bukhara, Ibn Sina could feel safe. He must have experienced a sense of relief and hope as he made his grand entrance into the city. Given the chaos that had engulfed his world over the preceding six years, this was fully warranted. His first years there lived up to his expectations. Isfahan had been known since the time of Cyrus the Great as a tolerant city, with a large and productive population of Jews, Christians, and Zoroastrians among its diverse population. It had stagnated for several centuries but was now reviving under Ala al-Dawla.

The people of Isfahan treated Ibn Sina as a celebrity, as indeed he was. When he showed up one day at an official event, a crowd numbering in the thousands was there to greet him.[1] At the Friday soirees of Emir Ala al-Dawla, Ibn Sina, clothed in brocaded robes, was always seated beside the ruler at the place of honor. These events, at which every manner of subjects was discussed, also featured poets declaiming their works and musical performances.

Though Ibn Sina reveled in the lordly trappings, his new status did not apparently bring him much peace. Hypersensitive as always, he was quick to take offense and took delight in wreaking vengeance on those who offended him. An oft-told tale has another attendee at the emir's levee named al-Jabbar making a derisive comment about Ibn Sina's imperfect command of archaic Arabic. Stung by this accusation, Ibn Sina plunged into the study of rare early texts written in it. He then forged three odes that were barely intelligible to a reader who knew only contemporary Arabic, and made the manuscript look old by having it bound in deeply weathered leather. He brought Ala al-Dawla in on the prank. With much ceremony the emir presented the forgery to al-Jabbar, describing the dusty tome as something he had been found during a hunting expedition in a remote desert. Al-Jabbar took the bait, and took Ibn Sina's forgery for the real thing. Revealing the truth, Ibn Sina reveled in his little triumph.

Chroniclers of Ibn Sina's life look on his time in Isfahan as his Golden Age, when he could concentrate fully on completing the *Canon of Medicine* as well as contemplate work on another grand project. But this was by no means the case. For no sooner had Ibn Sina arrived than Ala al-Dawla asked him to serve as his vizier, the same post he had held in Hamadan. Since it was the emir who had rescued him from Hamadan and now supported him in Isfahan, Ibn Sina was in no position to refuse. Nor is there necessarily any reason to think that he wanted to, for he had by now fully grown into his third career as a statesman and senior administrator, having performed the role before.

Shortly thereafter, the emir asked Ibn Sina to write a concise summary of the most important knowledge—a one-volume encyclopedia—in the Persian language. Once more Ibn Sina could not refuse. To write this volume, known as *The Salvation* (Najat), he mined his own earlier writings and filled them out with his more recent thoughts on each topic. Curiously, he entirely ignored mathematics. Ibn Sina dictated this work on the fly while traveling with the emir and his army, which was putting down a Kurdish rebellion.

In spite of his official responsibilities and the emir's increasingly bold military ventures, Ibn Sina also managed to dictate what remained to be done on the Physics section of an ambitious new project that had long been taking form in his mind. This was in 1027, when he was about fifty-four years old. This means that his celebrated period of "respite from conflict" had lasted a mere three years. For the next decade, Isfahan would be in a constant state of conflict with enemies near and far, and Ibn Sina was in the thick of it. An initial expedition against the Kurds was so successful that Ala al-Dawla and Ibn Sina decided to press their advantage by launching several more punitive strikes against Kurdish forces. Their goal was to strengthen Isfahan's hand regionally.

That many of the Kurds were dissident Ismailis added a religious element to the project. As if parodying the actions of Mahmud of Ghazni, Emir Ala al-Dawla sought to legitimize his rising status by issuing golden coins with his own name on one side and the caliph's on the reverse. The message was clear: Isfahan, under the banner of the caliphate (which the Buyids still controlled) was leading the battle against Ismaili dissidents loyal to the rival caliphate in Cairo.

Ibn Sina's remarkable capacity for multi-tasking was on full display during this period. While playing a central role in all the political and military turmoil, he managed simultaneously to direct his intellectual energies to what would be his most ambitious project to date, the work that would do more than any of his other writings to establish his lasting fame as a thinker. The genesis of that initiative is curious. During his several previous moves, Ibn Sina had lost most of his early writings, while others existed only in single copies owned by bibliophiles and collectors. Recognizing this loss, his assistant, Juzjani, had suggested that he rewrite the lost works, setting down in definitive form his views on Aristotle's entire oeuvre, covering logic, physics, chemistry, botany, zoology, mathematics, astronomy, meteorology, music, and metaphysics. Quite reasonably, Ibn Sina refused, on the grounds that he had "neither the time nor the inclination to occupy himself with close textual analysis and commentary." But then he countered with a proposal of his own: to write a "comprehensive work arranged in the order which will occur to me."[2] In other words, Ibn Sina proposed to write a book on the same broad range of topics, without constant resort to Aristotle. The demands of such a project would be far greater than simply rewriting his lost studies of Aristotle.

Ibn Sina gave this grand synthesis the Arabic title, *al-Shifa*, which is variously rendered as *The Healing*, *The Book of Healing*, *The Book of the Remedy*, and *The Cure*. His aim was to cure ignorance, which he considered an illness, and to heal the soul. I will follow Dimitri Gutas and refer to it as *The Cure*.

Though not referring to Aristotle's work, Ibn Sina divided his project into sections corresponding to Aristotle's categories of knowledge. Thus, the "mathematical sciences" included geometry, arithmetic, music, and astronomy. Several of these main categories were subdivided into other fields. Since Ibn Sina wrote them separately, I'll start with the section to which he himself devoted far the most attention—that involving philosophy and metaphysics.[3]

Ibn Sina had no doubt that human beings lived in an orderly world that somehow emanated from God. The task of humanity, he believed, was to understand that world and come to grips with the Power that ordained it. This should be done not by fixating on one or another part of the world around us—for instance, on communicable diseases, sine law, or the physics of music—but on the whole of creation. Mortals can grasp the hierarchy of the cosmos and locate their own place within it only by affirming the Creator that gave rise to it all. Reason alone offers a window onto eternity. The goal of knowledge is not to study its separate elements but to master everything that is knowable and thereby discern the grand order that gives meaning to its parts. Human beings are endowed with reason and intellect, which enable them to grasp the underlying realities and to distinguish between what is true and what is false. Indeed, it is only through the exercise of reason that the human soul can fulfill its immortality.

Ibn Sina had started on the new project while still in Hamadan, when his students were pushing forward with the second volume of the *Canon* on their own. He cut back on his usual mass production of shorter pieces and concentrated fully on *The Cure*, starting with the section on physics. Here and throughout *The Cure* he drew extensively on his own earlier digests and commentaries, lifting whole sections from pieces he had written decades earlier and plugging them unchanged or with only slight revisions into his text. This would all have been a perfectly routine project had Ibn Sina's own thinking not evolved in the meanwhile. The deeper Ibn Sina immersed himself in the writing, the more he found himself rethinking many of his earlier positions. In many cases the changes were mere nuances or adjustments. But in others the changes were fundamental.

Ibn Sina was, and would remain, the greatest medieval representative of the Peripatetic school of philosophy founded by Aristotle's interpreters. But by the time he completed *The Cure* he had respectfully declared his selective independence from all his ancient mentors, including the Peripatetics and Aristotle, and had struck out on his own.

Having laid the foundation of *The Cure* in Hamadan, Ibn Sina then found himself incarcerated for those four months at Fardaqan. During those days he turned out a number of minor pieces. In response to the condition of someone imprisoned with him or in memory of Shams, he wrote a brief study on colitis[4] which eventually found its way into the *Canon*. For his brother, Mahmud, five years younger than Ibn Sina and by then a fellow inmate (as we've seen, Mahmud would join his trek to Isfahan), he wrote a pedagogical allegory, *The Guidance*, in which he summarized his own philosophy.[5] A second allegory, *Alive, Son of Awake*, also appeared at this time. In these pieces Ibn Sina was seeking to build bridges between his usual mode of logic and the hidden meanings that could best be encapsulated in allegory. To this end he even composed a short treatise on the allegory of the Prophet Muhammad's ascent to heaven.

During those months, Ibn Sina allowed his mind to wander into new territory. In this spirit he set down the results of a curious thought experiment that he had conducted with himself. "The Floating Man" is a hypothetical being conjured up by Ibn Sina at Fardaqan as he pondered the great question of the immateriality and immortality of the human soul. The experiment asks the subject to imagine himself as being suspended in space. Lacking a physical body, it is completely deprived of sensory perceptions and has no contact with the physical world. Ibn Sina then asked: in what sense can such a being affirm its own existence?

Incarcerated in a remote castle and with ample time to ponder the question, Ibn Sina reached a stark conclusion. Such a being would be utterly incapable of affirming itself as a *physical* reality. However, it would be nothing more, and nothing less, than an incorporeal being which, in Ibn Sina's words, finds itself "fluttering over the abyss of eternity."[6] Nonetheless, he argued, such a being would still be conscious of itself. Even unembodied, the conscious soul is able to perceive its own existence. Awareness, in other words, exists independently of the physical world. Critics have countered that such awareness can exist only thanks to the existence of a physical brain and mind. For Ibn Sina, the Floating Man resolved the mind-body conundrum in favor of the former. And since the incorporeal mind or consciousness is not subject to physical decay, it survives death. It is, in short, immortal.

In his youth, Ibn Sina's first venture into philosophy had focused on the soul, its reality, non-material nature, and immortality. It was to form a central issue not only of *The Cure* but of several later works, including his final writings. All his many works on the subject were written in a tone of utter certainty. However, the deep seriousness with which Ibn Sina treated his Floating Man experiment, the fact that it arose in his mind at a moment when he was without a path forward yet briefly freed of external pressures, suggests a very different state of mind: uncertainty rather than certainty; anxiety rather than confidence. Far from being another brick in an already solid conceptual edifice, the parable of the Floating Man arose from Ibn Sina's uncertainties over one of the keystone elements of his entire intellectual construct. Whether or not they had existed earlier, these ruminations gained urgency during his incarceration at Fardajan and continued thereafter to challenge him. Their existence implies that Ibn Sina had come to consider the non-corporeal nature of the Soul (or human consciousness) and its immortality not yet as confirmed truths but as hypotheses that required further proof.

The anxiety that gave rise to "The Floating Man" bears comparison to Descartes who, 600 years after Ibn Sina, faced a similar dilemma. Descartes found resolution when he hit upon the famous formula, *cogito ergo sum*, "I think, therefore I am."[7] On an absolutely central issue, both Ibn Sina and Descartes embrace simple and seemingly common-sense arguments as the foundation upon which they built their entire systems. Yet whereas Ibn Sina's cosmology asserts that "God is not involved in the creation and destruction of specific events or objects, but has knowledge of events in a universal manner," Descartes argued that God simultaneously understands, wills, and accomplishes everything.[8]

As I've noted, the sections into which *The Cure* is divided stemmed ultimately from Aristotle. Its four main divisions cover *Logic, Physics, Mathematics,* and *Metaphysics.* These in turn are divided into sub-headings, each of which covers an entire sphere of knowledge. Metaphysics, from the Greek term signifying the "core," involves the study of the fundamental nature of reality and included mathematics, astronomy, and related sciences, which are commonly grouped together as "cosmology." Ibn Sina covers all of these in *The Cure.* His treatment of these subjects largely follows well-known paths, but he also offered some surprises, such as when he proposed that a mathematical relationship exists between the weight of an object in motion and its velocity—in other words, that velocity is directly proportional to weight.[9] Underlying and supporting all these studies, however, was epistemology, which considers the processes of cognition and reasoning that enable us to know what we know. This had always been Ibn Sina's deepest passion and figured centrally in his thinking at both the beginning and end of his career.

By Ibn Sina's own account, he acquired the tools he needed when he "discovered" the discipline of logic and epistemology, which took place, he claimed, thanks to that chance purchase from a Bukhara bookseller of a second-hand copy of a treatise by al-Farabi. It was by studying Farabi that Ibn Sina discovered logic and epistemology as a universally applicable means of reaching truth, and it was also thanks to Farabi, as we've seen, that Ibn Sina gained an understanding of Aristotle's metaphysics.

Ibn Sina was around seventeen years of age at the time of his encounter at the Bukhara bookseller's,[10] but he had already written his first work, the short treatise on the soul. He addressed this issue many times in later writings. It was the nature of the human soul that was at issue in "The Floating Man," and he returned to it one last time in his final treatise, entitled simply *The Soul.* It is clear, then, that Ibn Sina's primary and deepest concern was with the nature of the human soul or consciousness, and the soul's relationship to God. He considered logic to be the essential tool for plumbing these issues. But in the end, it was merely a tool, a treasured means but not an end in itself.

How did the "God question" gain its central place in Ibn Sina's thought? The standard account has him drawn to it during his early teenage years after discovering al-Farabi, drifting away from it for several decades, but then focusing on it with single-minded intensity in Isfahan. That metaphysics and theology gained such urgency during his later years may not be so noteworthy, as this often happens with older people. But in Ibn Sina's case it was indeed remarkable, for it led him to fresh understandings that would profoundly affect the world of thought.

To understand Ibn Sina's path to metaphysics and hence to his most important philosophical writings, we need to look back again at his boyhood, less to emphasize the influence of al-Farabi and more to focus on the effect of the Ismaili branch of Shiism. As we've seen, his father had been a convert and invited several Ismaili missionaries to live with his family and use his home as a base for their subversive proselytizing. Ibn Sina recorded that as a boy he had listened in carefully as they discussed God and metaphysics.

Founded in the Middle East and now prospering in their own caliphate in Cairo, the Ismaili Shiites were considered the main threat to orthodox Sunni Islam. Thirty years earlier, Ismaili missionaries had managed to convert to their cause the ruler of Bukhara and the Samani state. This conversion caused a geopolitical earthquake. Nor was this merely a political event, for the Ismailis' head missionary in Bukhara had been a leading thinker of the Shiite world at the time, Muhammad al-Nasafi. A native of nearby Nasaf (now Karshi, in Uzbekistan), Nasafi was a follower not only of Aristotle but of the Neo-Platonists, with their disconcerting—to orthodox Sunni Muslims— passion for mysticism. Drawing on the writings of late Greek writers like Plotinus, Nasafi saw the human soul as having become estranged from the Eternal. He then charted a path by which it could be reunited with the transcendent One, that is, God. He and his fellow Ismaili's spearheaded the recovery of the Neoplatonists' mysticism in the Shiite world.

Nasafi's main work, now lost, gained a following among the intelligentsia of Bukhara but evoked the fury of the solidly Sunni local clergy (ulema). In 943 the clergy unleashed a bloody revolt that brought down the emir, Nasr bin Ahmad, and ended with the massacre of Nasafi himself and all of his fellow missionaries. But the Ismailis did not give up. Though banned, they soon began once more to send underground missionaries to Bukhara. Nasafi himself had two sons who continued their father's work. It is even quite possible that these heirs of Nasafi were the very missionaries living in Ibn Sina's household.[11] Moreover, his ideas were being elaborated by another native of the region, Abu Ya'qub al-Sijistani. Drawing on texts he attributed (wrongly) to Aristotle, Sijistani posited a deity that is absolute, and quite unknowable through reason alone.[12]

All this took place immediately before and during the lifetime of Ibn Sina's father. Though a newcomer to the capital, he was aware that he was playing a risky game, one made yet more dangerous because he was a senior civil servant. We can be sure that he and his missionary-guests—whoever they were—were closely acquainted with the banned works by Nasafi and Sijistani, and that their ideas on God, the soul, and on cosmology were at the heart of those private discussions which young Ibn Sina listened in on.

Ibn Sina insisted, of course, that he "remained unconvinced" by Ismaili ideas, a statement that has led most subsequent writers to dismiss Ibn Sina's early contact with the Ismailis as irrelevant to his intellectual development. But as the Ismailis had been banned as heretics in Bukhara and the entire world of eastern Islam, it would have been suicidal for Ibn Sina to have expressed the slightest sympathy for their views. Yet Ibn Sina himself admitted that he had listened carefully to the discussions among the Ismaili missionaries and his father. As senior figures, the missionaries would have carried great authority in a movement that emphasized the role of lineage and authority. They would have exposed the young Ibn Sina to their quest for that higher, direct, but hidden knowledge of God and the soul that was unattainable through the everyday practice of the faith. Farabi, whose book on metaphysics introduced the teenage Ibn Sina to Aristotle's logic, provided a method for pursuing that quest but not the quest itself, the origins and passion for which seem to date to an earlier and deeper stratum of Ibn Sina's consciousness.

These speculations are difficult to prove or disprove. However, we can say that Ibn Sina's contact with the Ismailis is likely responsible for one aspect of his thinking, namely, the possibility of philosophizing on the most important questions in a way that was neither Sunni nor mainstream Shiite. Henceforth he would go his own way, following the path that led him finally to write *The Cure*. Over the years, Ibn Sina returned repeatedly to the issue of the soul, offering several descriptions of it. Aristotle had done so as well, using the Greek term for the soul, *psyche*. Aristotle's work on the soul, which was translated into Latin as *De Anima*, is a book not of theology but of psychology and the nature of consciousness. This was to be Ibn Sina's approach. His passion for bringing everything under one umbrella equaled or even surpassed that of Aristotle. But unlike the severely rational Aristotle, and in line with both the ancient Neo-Platonists and their Muslim heirs, the Ismailis, Ibn Sina also embraced elements of mysticism that were beyond the reach of logic and rational proofs.

This caused him to make his analysis of the soul a kind of dependent variable to his exposition of what Aristotle called "The Prime Mover" and Ibn Sina called Allah or God. In pursuing this enquiry, Ibn Sina encountered a problem. On the one hand, he was as committed as Aristotle had been to the notion that matter, that is, the universe, was eternal. On the other, he fully accepted the Old Testament's account of how God created the world out of nothing. Were the universe eternal, what need was there for God's creation? Ibn Sina adroitly distinguished between what he called *potentiality* and *actuality*. This distinction, which he borrowed from Aristotle, separated the ability to have something from actually having it. The first state refers to an abstract reality, a potential or an essence—the philosophical term for this is "quiddity." The second refers to an actuality that has existence. In other words, Ibn Sina's concept juxtaposed the abstract concept of something from its material reality. This enabled him to ascribe to the universe a timeless existence as potentiality but not as actuality, which it attained only with God's act at Creation.[13]

As to creation, it came about not as an act of volition on God's part but as a necessary act deriving from God's very nature.[14] In *The Cure*, Ibn Sina defines God as the force that transforms potentiality into actuality. God is the agent that imparts *existence* to what was heretofore merely *essence*. For this to happen, the Agent must itself have existence that precedes its transformative actions and which continues to coexist with what it has transformed. God, in short, has both essence and existence. This line of thinking, Ibn Sina believed, proved with certainty both the prior and continuing existence of God and His abiding role in human life.

The reasoning behind all this is more complex than related here. Readers who seek a more precise and thorough exposition should refer to the many works by scholars of Ibn Sina's thought. The outcome, however, is clear. Aristotle's notion of a Prime Mover or Giver of Forms came from his tracing causal chains back to the beginning, which called for some force to get the process moving. Ibn Sina's contribution was to have defined more precisely the relationship between eternity and creation. Creation, he posited, was that which gave existence to what heretofore had been non-existent but which nonetheless had the potential for being.[15]

Ibn Sina, in short, squared the circle of creation and eternity. In so doing, he responded to the seemingly incompatible claims of reason, science, and theology. Concluding that God and the world are thereby co-eternal, he validated the study of both the sciences and of God as understood by Islam and by the other peoples of the Book.

This was merely the beginning of Ibn Sina's line of thought. God, the "Necessary Being," created an order that is intelligible to reasoning people. This First Intelligence then expanded, by a process which Ibn Sina called "emanation," to create further spheres, a multiplicity of being. He held that this process proceeds indefinitely, with every succeeding sphere of existence embodying the same underlying order. And every emanation has its own inner being or "soul," which is able to cause change in its own immediate realm of existence, though not in the whole of creation. It is thus soul or consciousness that makes a living thing live and makes it capable of action. It is what makes possible activity in any form of living organism. The soul utilizes the senses but remains independent of them.[16] In human beings, it is the cause of all activity, yet in its essence it does not need or have a body.

In *The Cure*, Ibn Sina argues that this process ceases only when the "Active Intelligence" establishes "order and the good of the material world."[17] This order does not come about through God's constant and direct intervention in every detail of worldly life but because the process as a whole emanates from God. He affirms that we live in a universe that is both comprehensible and benign. God is not merely the Prime Mover who then steps aside but an ongoing though general presence in the larger order of existence. And it is that larger order which is, in the deepest sense, providential. God is the *Necessary* Being, while all parts of the universe are merely "possible beings" until they gain full existence through the power of divine Creation.

But what actually is that "soul," Aristotle's *psyche*? Both Aristotle and Ibn Sina found souls wherever life exists. Plants have souls, animals have "animate souls," and, of course, human beings are endowed with souls.[18] The human soul is unique because of its ability to make deductions through reason and to perceive universals. In Aristotle's formulation, "The soul is to the body as a pilot is to a ship."[19] Implied in this formulation is the corollary that a human being who does not engage in these activities has merely the unused capacity of a soul but not its living reality.

Several modern scholars have argued that this conception of the universe and of humankind's place in it owed less to Aristotle than to Plato and his explanation of the origins of the universe with its rational and benign orderliness. As interpreted by Greek writers in the Hellenistic era and by Ismaili thinkers, this universe is the work of a *Demiurge* or divine craftsman. This reality challenges humans to understand it and, in the process, exercise the soul with which they are endowed. Ibn Sina incorporated all this, though he parted company with the Platonists on the nature of specific parts of that universal order, including human faculties, for which he relied mainly on his own insights.

Ibn Sina's consideration of human perceptions led him into the realm of psychology. Perception arises from the senses, from imagination, and from the exercise of reason. These form a natural hierarchy, with the senses on the lowest rung of the ladder due to their being limited to the material world, and with reason on the highest. The exalted status of reason arises from its capacity for perceiving "*universals*" rather than merely "*particulars*" deriving from the senses. And while the senses gradually decay over the course of a lifetime, reason, precisely because of its ability to rise above the senses and grasp the *intelligibles*, gains strength. Reason employs the senses, but it benefits even more from the imagination, which enables it to grasp universals that are otherwise unintelligible. Accordingly, Reason, informed by imagination, is the very core of the soul.

This brought Ibn Sina to a fundamental question: if reason is inseparably part of the soul, one that can be strengthened through rigorous exercise over a lifetime, does it perish with the body? Following earlier religious thinkers and also Plotinus and other Hellenistic followers of Plato, Ibn Sina insists in *The Cure* that the soul is independent of the body. The senses, unlike consciousness, imagination, and reason, are earthly and corruptible. But the reasoning soul is independent of the physical body and hence free and incorruptible. The sense-bound soul perishes with the body but the rational soul lives on, surviving the body's death.

The soul is thus immortal. Each soul is also specific, having been informed over a lifetime by impressions and thoughts. However, Ibn Sina argues that the physical and earthbound part of the soul cannot migrate after death into another body. The transmigration of souls, as embraced by Pythagoras, the Hindus, and Buddhists, was hence impossible.

Beyond all these carefully formulated propositions, *The Cure* offers a number of judgments that were bound to raise eyebrows. For example, it discusses an *estimative faculty*, the ability to make judgments based on prior experience, which it divides into favorable and unfavorable, dangerous or safe, good or bad. In one intriguing passage, it postulates that animals, too, possess this faculty. Aristotle had tiptoed around this issue, but Ibn Sina plunged into it headlong, even though it would seem to dilute his own argument about the uniqueness of the human psyche. It also raises the issue of accounting for Ibn Sina's deviations from his own main thesis. Soheil Afnan, a Palestinian philosopher who wrestled with such questions over the course of his long career at Cambridge, concluded that it shows Ibn Sina at his best, challenging his own arguments with evidence that could potentially qualify or change them.[20]

In its treatment of God and the soul, *The Cure* relies not only on Ibn Sina's beloved logic but also on imagination and what has been called "rational mysticism."[21] In acknowledging the endless complexity and richness of human consciousness, it opens a door also to more immediate and less rational perceptions of reality, including the flashes of insight that were possible through mysticism. During the last years of his life Ibn Sina ventured increasingly into that realm, enriching his otherwise austerely rational theory of knowledge.

In his presentation on God and the soul, Ibn Sina frequently paused to lay down careful definitions and to employ logic to advance his arguments. But in those sections of *The Cure* that deal with God and the soul, he is concerned more with metaphysics than logic. Ibn Sina's passion for plumbing the primary mysteries of existence only grew with the passage of time. Here, in his poem entitled *Ode to the Soul*, we sense the intensity of that passion, as the soul descends to earth from heaven and pines for its return.

> It descends upon thee from out of the regions above,
> That exalted, ineffable, glorious, heavenly Dove.
> 'Twas concealed from the eyes of all those who its nature would ken
> Yet it wears not a veil, and is ever apparent to men . . .
> Until, when it entered its downward descent,
> And to Earth, to its center, unwillingly went,
> The eye of Infirmity smote it, and lo, it was hurled
> Midst the sign-posts and ruined abodes of this desolate world.
> It weeps when it thinks of the home and peace it possessed,
> With tears welling forth from its eyes, without pausing or rest . . .
> Now, why from its perch on high was it cast like this
> To the lowest Nadir's gloomy and drear abyss?[22]

Acknowledging that Ibn Sina was at bottom more metaphysician than logician, it is nonetheless important once more to stress the intensity of his commitment to logic. From the moment he discovered Aristotelian logic as a young man, it became his principal tool for investigating all questions of science. In his late work *The Salvation*, he still spoke of logic as "an instrument common to all the sciences. It is a method for discovering the unknown from the known."[23] Logic itself was for Ibn Sina a science with its own demanding system, a method of proof and reasoning not touching religion.[24] So important was it to his intellectual tool box that over the course of his long career he devoted to it at least fifteen works.[25] As philosopher Tony Street aptly put it, the syllogism assumed a "totemic" role in Ibn Sina's thinking.[26]

By Ibn Sina's day, logic was no longer simply a method for deriving new truths out of the existing propositions that Aristotle had codified, seemingly for all time. During the previous century it had been thoroughly worked over by the orthodox followers of the Baghdad theologian Ali ibn Ismail al-Ashari. Ashari weakened the strict system of the Aristotelian syllogism by introducing into it a hypothetical or conditional element, that is, instead of the concrete formulation, "a cat is orange," they allowed, "*if* a cat should be orange." This seemingly innocent change opened the door to those who disallowed a role for independent human volition in worldly affairs and buttressed their claim that all activity, by both animate and inanimate objects, comes directly from God. By Ibn Sina's day, a mere three generations after Ashari's revision of the syllogism to include hypotheticals and conditionals, it had been embraced as a central element of Sunni Muslim orthodox theology and remains so today.

This "adjustment" in the logical syllogism was not itself the cause of Ashari's counter-revolution against the concept of independent powers in the natural world. That arose instead from Ashari's effort to prove that God directed all events on earth and, as a corollary, to limit severely the sphere of independent human action. In Ibn Sina's mind, the effect of this feature of Muslim theology was to rip out of the thinker's hand a priceless and God-given tool for reaching truths independent of theological dogma. In opposing it, Ibn Sina could not simply exhume Aristotelianism, since on this point it had already been irrevocably distorted. Instead, in *The Cure* and later works he champions a very different manner of conceptualization. Rather than accept hypothetical and conditional statements, he combines more complex propositions or statements in a single element of the syllogism. This so-called propositional logic became Ibn Sina's essential tool for the analysis of all phenomena of nature. It is no overstatement to declare, as Lenn Goodman does, that Ibn Sina thereby emancipated logic both from its Aristotelian past and from its theological present.[27] But as so often happens, what began as a revolutionary insight or technique can harden over time to become a formalistic ritual. As we will see, this was to be the eventual fate of Ibn Sina's logic.

Ibn Sina's theses on God, the soul, and logic lay at the heart of his thoughts on the physical universe, the natural world, and all its contents. For instance, his analysis of what he called "essences" and "existence" spoke to his effort to bridge logic and science.[28] Such were the foundations upon which he grounded his analysis of phenomena as diverse as geodesics, astronomy, mathematics, music, and even medicine. In fact, he dwells on all these and other sections of *The Cure* not as ends in themselves but as manifestations of the divinely instigated reality we know as nature. It delves into each area in order to show how God interacts with humankind not just through Creation but in the ongoing world.[29]

This is not to say that Ibn Sina's interest in the elements of the natural order per se was any less intense. In the *Canon of Medicine*, as we saw, he had brought together masses of specific information about causes, diagnoses, and prescriptions. For whole pages and sections he carries on as if his deeper concerns have somehow been pushed into the background. Yet they are there, in the first "theoretical" volume, his most ambitious project prior to writing *The Cure*. God, the soul, and the role of logic had been his main preoccupation from youth. But his views on them were not static and did not reach their full development until he wrote *The Cure*. Indeed, they continued to evolve thereafter. They were like the diapason notes of the organ in a Bach fugue, always present and sounding at the deepest level of his writings.

Ibn Sina's thoughts on God and the soul and on the logical system with which one can grasp the natural world do not lend themselves to simple conclusions. Indeed, modern specialists on Ibn Sina's philosophy debate virtually every point in the brief overview offered above. Moreover, questions have even been raised over whether surviving texts of the metaphysics section of *The Cure* came from Ibn Sina himself or were revised versions reworked by his followers.[30] Nonetheless, I would argue, several points can be affirmed. Thus, his proof of the existence of God was without precedent in antiquity, the Muslim world, or in the West. St. Anselm, bishop of Canterbury from 1093 to 1109, propounded a roughly similar line of reasoning, but that was three generations after Ibn Sina wrote *The Cure*.

Employing both reason and intuition, Ibn Sina set forth an ontological argument for the existence of God. In doing so, he offered a reconciliation of the positions of Aristotle, the Neoplatonists, and the theologians of his day. At its core, the ontological argument is based not on observation of the world or the cosmos but purely on reason:[31] using its premises and proceeding analytically to their conclusion, in this case to God's existence. In this instance, the key element is the distinction between potential and actual, between essence and existence. Al-Farabi had begun to address this issue a century before Ibn Sina, but it was Ibn Sina who fully delineated it, and it is what makes his ontological argument a major innovation. No less an innovation was his argument for the eternity of the soul, though followers of Plato and Plotinus in late antiquity and early Christian thinkers had all wrestled with the same issue.

With this foundation in place, *The Cure* addresses, one by one, all the sciences except medicine, which Ibn Sina had already covered in his *Canon*. Along the way it engages with mathematics, astronomy, chemistry, geology, biology, geodesy, and even music, which he placed under the rubric of mathematics. While these sections of *The Cure* are not devoid of innovations, they were also not Ibn Sina's major concern. Rather, it was to demonstrate the relationship of each of them to the cosmic order that he had set out in such detail in his Metaphysics. His whole system, in short, was oriented upward, toward the skies. In his study of Islamic cosmological doctrines, Seyyed Hossein Nasr summarizes this core feature of Ibn Sina's science, in which "both reason and the senses have a legitimacy on their own level." He adds, "The science which derives from them, however, finds its meaning and legitimacy only in light of the wisdom, or *sapientia*, which lies above the domain of the senses as well as that of reason."[32] Far from being a neutral enterprise, science—like everything else in nature—has a purpose, which is to manifest the harmony, order, and equilibrium that govern the universe.[33] Its goal is to lay bare the natural sympathy between the earthbound microcosm and the eternal macrocosm. To truly "do" science, the individual must engage all available faculties, those capable of dealing with matter and those which deal with abstract forms.[34]

This is possible, Ibn Sina believed, because there exists a natural sympathy between humankind and the universe, a harmonious relationship which, he asserted, is based on love.[35] In asserting divine providence, Ibn Sina was updating and integrating into science the visionary passion of the later Greek Neoplatonists, Christian and Jewish Gnostics, and Muslim Sufis.[36]

One further note regarding Ibn Sina's scientific method is called for—namely, his skeptical attitude toward induction as a tool for the investigation of nature.[37] On this important point he parted company with Aristotle. One prominent historian of science, drawing on several of Ibn Sina's other writings as well as *The Cure*, pinpoints Ibn Sina's objection to the fact that syllogisms resulting from induction are necessarily flawed, because the first premise, based on observation, always differs in kind from the less specific second premise.[38] This, according to Ibn Sina, is a condition that cannot lead to the establishment of truth.

The Cure is more likely to strike awe than attract readers. The section on physics alone would fill a modern volume. The mountain of knowledge that it amasses has given rise to a thriving academic industry devoted to analyzing Ibn Sina's views on just about everything, with monograph after monograph comparing his assertions with those of his ancient predecessors and of later thinkers in Central Asia, the Middle East, and Europe.[39]

A skeptic might point out that a large part of *The Cure*'s length derives from its summaries of what Ibn Sina deemed to be the best of past thinking in the various areas of knowledge. In other words, it was yet another encyclopedia, with entries consisting of carefully selected, edited, or rewritten material drawn from other sources, both ancient and modern, and from his own earlier compendiums.

For his treatment of mathematics, astronomy, and physics, Ibn Sina indeed drew heavily on Euclid's *Elements* and Ptolemy's *Almagest*.[40] He fully acknowledges that the section on geometry is an abridgement of Euclid's *Elements*. On mathematics, he drew on Euclid, Archimedes, the Indian Aryabhata, and al-Khwarazmi but makes no mention of the contemporary breakthroughs achieved by Buzjani, Ibn Iraq, and notably, Biruni. In astronomy *The Cure* draws above all on Ptolemy, with his forthright affirmation of a geocentric universe. In all these borrowings Ibn Sina freely rearranged arguments to make them more coherent and sometimes added his own inputs as, for example, his mention, but not acceptance, of the possibility of irrational numbers, which he drew from the Indian Brahmagupta.

At several points in *The Cure* and later works, Ibn Sina refers to claims in Ptolemy's *Almagest* that had long since been refuted on the basis of observation. Some of the refutations were drawn from more recent sources. For example, he criticizes Ptolemy's method for determining eccentricities in the orbits of Jupiter, Mars, and Saturn, and the inclination of the earth's obliquity. However, the corrections he proposes are based on well-known observations conducted in Baghdad 200 years before Ibn Sina's time. Even though he assures his reader that he himself has confirmed this observation, it is clear that in these sections of *The Cure* Ibn Sina is out of his depth.

But Ibn Sina's aim was less to provide the most up-to-date insights from every area of knowledge than to indicate how each separate field of enquiry was subordinated logically to the metaphysical core, that is, to the deeper realities of God's relationship to the universe and to humankind. Happily, this did not prevent him from opining on a host of topics ranging from meteorology to music.

Some assertions in these areas strike modern readers as quaint. Among his seven causes for thunder, for example, Ibn Sina lists hard stones banging into each other. And one of his four causes for lightning compares it to the spark that occurs when steel strikes a hard rock.[41] Yet in other areas his speculations are insightful, and none more so than in geology and paleontology.[42] He carefully notes that the presence of deep sediments in many places indicates that large areas of the earth were once covered by water. He observes that the existence of different layers indicates that many such floods had occurred in the remote past. Rocks, he hypothesizes, have diverse origins. Some arose from the congealing of watery sediments, while massive stone outcroppings had been formed by earthquakes accompanied by the most intense heat. He draws on his own observations to conclude that metals and stone-like formations could also be formed through lightning strikes, and even by large meteors. He also reports on his (unsuccessful) attempt to melt a meteorite and concludes that it had been formed through greater heat than could be produced by any earth-bound fire.[43]

Like Biruni, Ibn Sina saw the Earth as constantly evolving, changing in some eras through slow processes over prolonged periods of time and in others through violent cataclysms. Between cataclysmic change and slow processes of evolution extending over eons, Ibn Sina places greater emphasis in The Cure on the latter. Calling on his own boyhood observation of hills along the river Oxus (Amudarya), he applies the erosion thesis to explain even the formation of mountains, which he attributes to the elimination of softer soils over long periods of time, and the vitrification of what remained.[44]

In a final bow to Ptolemy's Almagest, Ibn Sina includes music in the section of The Cure devoted to mathematics. Why music? Because, as he explains, it is "a mathematical science in which there is discussed the state of melody in so far as it is harmony or in discord, and the state of the intervening periods."[45] Ptolemy's works on music had long since been translated into Arabic, but it was al-Farabi who, three generations before Ibn Sina, transformed such study into a science with his Grand Book on Music.[46] Ibn Sina followed Farabi in all details. Farabi, an accomplished lutenist, could write as an insider about melody, pitch, and rhythm, and as a result he produced a book that became for centuries the standard text throughout Central Asia, the Middle East, and Europe as well. By comparison, Ibn Sina's section on music is schematic, which is quite appropriate, since its purpose was to show its place in knowledge as a whole rather than to present an exhaustive study of music as such.[47]

The Cure reveals two ambitious goals. First, Ibn Sina wanted, through syllogistic logic, to demonstrate the inter-relatedness of all knowledge and its dependence ultimately on God. To do this he had to clarify the nature of human consciousness and the intellect and their relation to the immortal soul. Second, he wanted to correct and thereby update the entire legacy of ancient learning and recast it in terms of these principles.

For much of his career, Ibn Sina viewed himself as a humble acolyte of Aristotle, "The First Teacher," and of his followers, the Peripatetics. By the time he finished writing *The Cure*, however, he had not merely updated Aristotle but had in many respects supplanted him. *The Cure* addresses the main issues of knowledge and faith confronting thoughtful people in the eleventh century. No mere encyclopedic compilation, it presents knowledge in terms of an all-encompassing structure. As happened in the *Canon of Medicine*, there are many long sections of *The Cure* that unfold without explicit reference to that structure. But it is nonetheless there. The fundamentalist Asharites severely criticized Ibn Sina's logic, but his passion to understand human consciousness not only accorded well with Muslim law (*sharia*), but it also directly echoed the words of the great Sufi Abu Zakariya Yahya al-Razi who, preaching in Afghanistan and Khorosan, had proclaimed, "He who knows himself knows the Lord." Ibn Sina's writings also stand in the direct line of descent from the inscription on the Temple of Apollo at Delphi, which called on Greeks to "Know thyself," while his stress on the sanctity of human consciousness captures the essence of numerous passages in the Jewish *Book of Wisdom* and *Psalms*, and also the writings of Christian theologians like Clement of Alexandria, who exhorted his readers to "Know yourself so you can know your Lord."[48]

The Cure was not intended for the general reader, whether a resident of Bukhara, Gurganj, or Isfahan. Ibn Sina observes with disdain that the intellectual reach of common folk does not extend beyond symbols and allegory.[49] This might have ended the matter. But had not Plato's own followers defended allegory as a branch of logic, and had Ibn Sina himself not written several allegories to express what he could not communicate simply through syllogisms and logic?[50]

For the thoughtful reader thirsting for knowledge of the earth and cosmos, *The Cure* was truly a healing of confusion and ignorance. It completes the vast project that began when the first works by ancient Greek thinkers were translated into Arabic. As such, it marks an ending, a culmination. But it was also a beginning, a salvo in a fresh debate that was to extend for more than half a millennium into the future.

16

Biruni's Encore

A pall of uncertainty had always hung over Biruni's life at Ghazni. In 1025 Mahmud fired his long-serving vizier, Maymandi, who had quietly protected Biruni. By 1028 the decline of Mahmud's health caused a cloud of fear to descend on his capital. His two sons, Muhammad and Masud, actively maneuvered to succeed him. When Mahmud showed signs of favoring Muhammad, Masud's champions at court plotted a coup, which was thwarted only when Masud himself intervened against it. Mahmud, ever more paranoid and irascible, even turned against his faithful young partner, Asad.[1] Responding to court gossip, he also abruptly disinherited Masud, thus assuring that power would fall into the hands of Muhammad.

Muhammad was crowned sultan in 1030. This infuriated Masud, who mobilized his army at Nishapur and set out on the long march across Afghanistan to Ghazni. Along the way he proclaimed himself sultan. Learning of this, and fearing Masud's larger forces, the officers of Muhammad's army revolted and declared their fealty to Masud. This averted a dynastic war and left Masud fully in charge of the empire. He immediately launched a purge of all those who had supported his father and brother and rehabilitated Maymandi, whom his father had fired seven years earlier.

All acknowledged that Masud was physically brave. He also liked to meet with scholars, had a professional understanding of architecture, and in his own hand could turn out elegant works of penmanship.[2] But he was by all accounts wine-soaked, self-indulgent, and capricious. One scholar, Vasili (Wilhelm) Barthold, said of him that "he inherited only his father's faults." Among those was "cupidity" in which "he yielded nothing to Mahmud; the overburdening of the inhabitants by forced levies was carried in his time to an extreme degree."[3] Another scholar, C. E. Bosworth, the greatest modern authority on Ghazni, noted, "As Masud's reign progressed, observers noted a decline in his character and resolution." And, Bosworth might have added, his strategic judgment.

The two greatest threats to the empire that Masud inherited arose from the tribes of Oguz Turkmen (now known, as noted earlier, as Seljuks) to the west and north and from rebellious Indian subjects to the east. Rather than focusing on these, Masud decided instead to settle old scores with the Persian Buyids, who were failing to pay the tribute they had promised and scheming to claw back their old possessions. This is what led him in 1034 to send yet another army into the Buyid lands. His aim was to punish Ala al-Dawla in Isfahan for his disloyalty and greed and, inter alia, to prove that he, Masud, was truly his father's son. This was the invasion that resulted in the seizure or destruction of Ibn Sina's books and the collapse of his health.

Just as Masud was plunging headlong into this project, Biruni approached him with the completed text of his *Canon*. His own life having greatly improved under Masud's rule, Biruni dedicated his masterpiece to the new sultan, not least because Masud was now out of his hair. Hence it is known as *Masud's Canon*. Somewhat earlier he had also dedicated his *India* to Masud—a wise move, considering the barely veiled criticisms of Mahmud he had slipped into that work.[4]

Masud honored Biruni's gestures with a camel-load of silver. Biruni declined the gift, asking only to be allowed to continue his work in peace for the rest of his days and to visit his homeland, Khwarazm, which he did shortly thereafter. He also tossed off for his new patron several short and non-technical treatises on astronomy.[5]

Just prior to reaching his understanding with Masud, Biruni had complained to friends of being lonely and depressed.[6] As soon as he came to terms with Masud, however, his mood brightened. He set down a further work on the region of Khwarazm, now lost. And he was emboldened to write a history of Mahmud's father, Sebuktegin, and even a detailed *History of Sultan Mahmud's Days*. Both works are lost, but we know that in the latter book he recorded his own bitter memories of Mahmud's nefarious conquest of Khwarazm and poured out tales of Mahmud's hypocrisy and brutality.[7] He also described Mahmud's endless maneuvers in behalf of religious orthodoxy.[8]

Thus disburdened of the past, Biruni allowed himself the enjoyment of reading and even translating poetry. Biruni's eight poetic translations warranted a thirteenth-century writer to list Biruni among the great men of letters of his age.[9] One of these poems, a romantic tale (now lost, alas) translated from the Sanskrit, was so compelling that one of the greatest Persian poets and a fellow member of the court at Ghazni, Abu Hasan from Balkh, took it as the basis for a major work of his own. Another was Biruni's translation into Arabic of an ancient Persian epic, *Vamik and Azra*, a tale of star-crossed lovers.

We don't usually think of bibliographies as major cultural statements. But Biruni took advantage of the security he gained under Masud to create one that is: by compiling a complete listing of Razi's works and then appending to it a bibliography of his own writings. The compiling of bibliographies in Arabic was not new; a generation earlier, Ishaq al-Nadim, the ambitious son of a Baghdad bookseller, had compiled a giant bibliography comprising 10,000 works and 2,000 authors. But no one before Biruni had exploited bibliography as a cover for biography.

A cover, because Razi, for all his reputation in medicine and science, was known to have harbored highly controversial views on religion. One of his tracts denounced most prophecy as bunk because prophets contradicted one another, while another ridiculed the mutually contradictory notions propounded by many faiths. The ultra-orthodox and powerful Sunni establishment dismissed all this as the ravings of a heretic, yet suspect works by Razi circulated sub rosa in many quarters.

Biruni esteemed Razi more highly than all his other scholarly and scientific predecessors, including Aristotle and Ptolemy. Indeed, some have argued that it was only Biruni who grasped the full importance of Razi's scientific legacy.[10] Biruni drew on Razi's atomistic theories, borrowed many of his arguments against Aristotle and the Peripatetics, emulated his austere lifestyle, and admired his dispassionate and fact-driven mode of research. And he was also in sympathy with some of Razi's heterodox views on religion.

Yet to issue a biography was out of the question. So Biruni instead compiled a bibliography of Razi's works. But even this could be seen as subversive. As Biruni put it, "I [was] afraid that such an undertaking would bring down on me the hatred of his [Razi's] opponents and cause them to think of me as a supporter who approved his ideas."[11] He therefore announces blandly in the foreword that he has not undertaken this project at his own initiative and agreed to proceed only when a student insisted that he do so. He further covers himself by including prominently in his list two works in which Razi defends God's existence and role as Creator.[12] Finally, as an *homage* to the man he considered his own teacher, Biruni appended to the bibliography a full listing of his own writings to date.[13]

The caution with which Biruni approached the Razi project mirrors how he dealt with two other sensitive subjects: astrology and alchemy. Biruni was no stranger to these esoteric fields. As a young scientist in Gorgan he had devoted an entire book and several shorter treatises to astrology. He had also written about astrology in his *Chronologies* and in the *Determination of the Coordinates of . . . Cities*, and produced a volume, now lost, on the astronomical basis for Indian astrology, in which he inveighed against those who refused to take the Indians seriously.[14] During his later years he was also to compose a compendious volume of questions and answers concerning astrology for a woman named Rayhannah Bintul al-Hasan, who was among the former members of the Khwarazm elite who were marched to Ghazni after the tragedy of 1017.[15]

Biruni's highest official function since arriving in Ghazni had been to serve as court astrologer. By all accounts he did it with distinction. His rooftop falling out with Mahmud (recounted above, p. 13) arose from the accuracy of his prognostications, not his failures. But this does not explain his long-term interest in the subject. Astronomy had always been an inseparable part of astrology. Plying their trade, astrologers had amassed vast observational and computational data that were directly relevant to Biruni's own research. It was natural, then, for him to utilize the astrologers' data, even as he ridiculed their prognostications.[16]

In fact, Biruni's innovation was to draw a sharp semantic distinction between astrology and astronomy,[17] to separate the useful data amassed by astrologers from their conclusions and thereby lay the foundations upon which astronomy could stand forth as an independent science. Astrology, he wrote, was based on "totally absurd principles, weak deductions, and contradictory guesses." In contrast, "The science of astronomy, to which this book is dedicated, is absolutely self-sufficient in its own excellent principles."[18]

Biruni advanced astronomy as an independent science by treating the astrologers' data with respect and ridiculing their prognostications. In this spirit he extolled the astronomical findings of the renowned astrologer from Balkh, Abu Mashar, and even wrote down questions he would have put to Mashar, who died in 886, had he been able to meet him. Similarly, he devoted an entire treatise to a respectful treatment of astrologers' views on the transit of the planets, that is, the process by which one planet crosses in front of the moon or sun, and he wrote four other tracts on astrology, none of which have survived.[19] These led one recent enthusiast to claim that Biruni was "one of the great Muslim astrologers."[20]

This would have infuriated Biruni. He flatly rejected the astrologists' claim to be able to predict the future. Sometimes he did this politely. In *Masud's Canon* he calmly explains that astrologists use their prognostications for self-aggrandizement, "by dangling before their patrons the possibility of predicting the future."[21] Far more frequently, though, Biruni expressed his criticism with savage bluntness. He called the writings of one astrologer "nonsense," and said that any effort to reason with another was like "trying to converse with someone who is speaking a foreign language."[22] He particularly loved to undermine those astrologists' who "ascribed to divine wisdom whatever in the physical sciences they don't understand. They justify their ignorant claims by declaring that God is all powerful."[23] And in a final word on the subject in *Masud's Canon.* he states that astrology "rests on totally absurd principles, weak declarations, contradictory guesses, and the merest assumptions, as opposed to certainties."[24] Biruni loved to recount his experience of when, suffering an illness, he called in two astrologers and asked them to tell him how much longer he would live. When he managed to outlive their prognostications, he dismissed them both as fools.[25]

By the time he reached his sixties, Biruni's health showed signs of failing. His eyes, never good, now deteriorated to the point that he had to abandon making astronomical observations. An assistant read to him texts he could no longer see clearly. Around the year 1038 more serious problems arose. "Grave diseases are now consuming me," he wrote. "My bones have grown fragile, my body weakened, I have difficulty walking, and my senses are deadened."[26]

Even as Biruni's health was declining, so was Masud's empire. The downward spiral began with Masud's decision to shift his capital from Ghazni to India in order to keep a closer watch on his most valuable possession. This emboldened the Seljuk Turkmen to launch a full-blown assault on his second-most valuable possession, Khorasan. Masud's rule there had been brutal. In a verse that eventually reached Masud himself, a local poet complained that Masud's governor had "alighted on the people for hospitality and left not one timber on another in their houses."[27]

The settling of scores took place in May 1040, at Dandanaqan, near the city of Merv in what is now Turkmenistan. Masud's army of 50,000 faced a Seljuk force of only 16,000. The battle should have been a pushover. But Masud's army was slow and burdened with a huge baggage train and a mass of camp followers, while the Seljuks traveled light. Moreover, the local populace viewed the Seljuks as the lesser of two evils. In the Battle of Dandanaqan, the Ghazni army was obliterated and soon thereafter Masud was murdered by his own brother. Amid the ensuing chaos, Masud's young nephew, Maudud, seized the throne. Though a military man with no interest in learning, the new sultan continued to honor his father's commitment to Biruni, who dutifully dedicated his next book, *Minerology*, to Maudud.

Supported and left alone, Biruni in his final decade was highly productive, especially in two fields, minerology and pharmacology, which seemed far removed from his lifelong passions. Nonetheless Biruni's interest in minerals dated to his boyhood in Kath and Gurganj. Ibn Iraq had introduced him to the challenge of weighing minerals, and the young Biruni actually wrote a treatise on the subject.[28] While in Rayy, as we've seen, Biruni had roomed with two young dealers in gemstones, who further sparked his interest in rare minerals and metals. In Gorgan he composed a speculative piece, *On the Relationship of the Masses of Gemstones and Metals*.[29] And, finally, both *Determination of the Coordinates of . . . Cities* and *India* contained scattered tidbits on minerals and their relation to geological history and modern economics.

Many writers at the time were issuing books on quasi-scientific topics, and some of them contained highly original insights. For example, a popular *Book of Animals* by an Arab writer from Basra named al-Jazih (meaning "Goggle Eyes") includes a prescient exposition of the theory of evolution in animals. Wrote Goggle Eyes, "[Animals] engage in a struggle for existence and resources in order to avoid being eaten and to breed." Their environment causes them "to develop new characteristics in order to ensure their survival, thus transforming them into new species."[30]

Gemstones were a popular subject, and Biruni was well acquainted with the literature on them. Among this was a translation of the Roman writer Vitruvius's writings on rare stones and a study of minerals by the ninth-century philosopher al-Kindi, whose broad typology Biruni borrowed. Biruni pored through these and other earlier tomes, did considerable primary research of his own, and produced *A Collection of Information on the Recognition of Jewels*. In this neglected volume he developed the concept of specific gravity, devised a remarkably precise instrument for measuring it, and published the specific gravity of the most highly valued minerals and metals.[31] And lest the reader's interest flag, he enlivened his study with relevant poetry drawn from eighty-four authors and even included some verse of his own.[32]

The book begins by inquiring into the attitudes toward specific gemstones and rare metals of peoples from India to the Mediterranean and Africa. Although he was a confirmed cultural relativist, Biruni nonetheless detected commonalities underlying the economic function of gold and diamonds everywhere. Impatient as ever with sloppiness, he skewers the unfortunate author of a recent book on gemstones who, among other "nonsense," reported on an *engraved* diamond.[33] He also ridicules all the magic associated with gems even while relishing the colorful fables about diamonds and gold offered by poets and folklore. The subject of fakery also appears frequently in the book, as it surely did in bazaars of the day. Most of the cases Biruni cites arose from the claims of Indian alchemists, whose enterprise he dismisses as "witchcraft."[34]

In all, Biruni's book describes some hundred minerals, setting forth the characteristics, cost, and sources of each. From his detailed descriptions of jewel-bearing veins, mining machinery, and refining processes, it is clear that Biruni himself had descended into actual mines, probably in Badakhshan in what is now northern Afghanistan and Tajikistan. Otherwise, he relied on an army of informants. To bring order to his mass of information, Biruni refines Kindi's typology based on hardness and density. Moving beyond the bazaar merchants' simple tests and his own use of scales and a magnifying glass, he then devises an original method for determining specific gravity. Inspired by Vitruvius, he had perfected a scale for weighing mineral specimens by measuring the water they displaced. This enabled him to arrive at measurements of specific gravity that were accurate to the fourth decimal point—an achievement not surpassed until the eighteenth century. A team of scientists under the Russian physicist B. A. Rozenfeld has reconstructed on paper the simple equipment Biruni designed and built, and which enabled him to achieve these results.[35]

Biruni himself realized that his work in mineralogy would make possible precise evaluations of the gems and minerals that were the basis of economic value and currencies. However, his discovery of specific gravity had implications that would reverberate far beyond the realm of economics. This research, which Biruni conducted in remote Afghanistan, would turn out to be essential not only to the development of metallurgy, but also to the fields of chemistry, physics, mechanics, and engineering.

By now, Biruni's health was declining precipitously and he was barely able to see or walk. Making no concessions to mortality, however, he undertook one last research project, this time a 400-page compendium on pharmaceutical plants. It is quite possible that he had been inspired, or goaded, to undertake this by reading the volumes of Ibn Sina's *Canon of Medicine* devoted to that topic, though there is no firm evidence for this. Biruni does not mention his old rival by name in the book. Nor need he have done so, because

Biruni's approach to pharmacology differed fundamentally from Ibn Sina's. While Ibn Sina's main concern had been with the medicinal properties of named plants, Biruni's was with the plants themselves.[36]

In his two volumes on pharmacology, Ibn Sina accepted at face value the entire existing nomenclature of plants. He lists plants from Greece to India, but without probing to find out what each name actually refers to.[37] Biruni, by contrast, digs into the precise terminology in each language and compares each with known descriptions of the plants themselves. By so doing, he demonstrates that plants bearing the same name might diverge sharply in different countries and geographical zones. And by closely comparing the actual properties of plants, he demonstrates that plants with different names in different countries could in fact be the same. Finally, his work demonstrates that plants bearing the same name in different countries and geographies and which to all appearances were actually the same could in fact differ in their medicinal properties.

In carrying out this research, Biruni even plumbed the terminology of local dialects. By doing so he shows that the name of a single plant could vary in separate regions extending from Oman to Afghanistan. A student of Biruni's pharmacology has shown how he extended this study to 900 plants from Persia and Central Asia, 700 from Greece, 400 from Syria, and 425 from India.[38] Moving beyond mere terminology, Biruni's book cites local poetry to indicate how specific plants were perceived by each culture.

Whether intentional or not, Biruni's work presented a fundamental challenge to Ibn Sina. By showing how profoundly language and culture can distort our perceptions to the point of causing outright errors, Biruni undermined the very foundations of Ibn Sina's pharmacology. Continuing his analysis, he then offers a philological evaluation of the relative value of Greek, Syrian, Arabic, Persian, and Indian languages as vehicles for scientific communication. Biruni criticizes Arabic for its bewildering system for marking inflexions[39] but then offers his famous *mot*—that he'd "rather be criticized in Arabic . . . than praised in Persian."[40] He even placed himself in the mirror by asking whether and how his own use of Arabic might distort his analyses.

The research that led to these contributions to the study of philology and culture exceeded Biruni's flagging energies. He therefore engaged a medical doctor named Ahmad ibn Nahshai to assist him.[41] Unfortunately, Biruni was to die before completing the book, leaving Nahshai to finish it. One can assume that had Biruni lived he would have removed the repetitions that mar the surviving text. Nonetheless, Biruni's book transformed and expanded the field of pharmacology. As an example, while his main source, Dioscorides, enumerated 570 medicinal plants and Ibn Sina 400, Biruni's compendium examines 1,116 medicinal plants and their products.[42] Arguably he did more to advance the taxonomy of plants than anyone down to the Swede Carl Linnaeus in the eighteenth century. And he challenged his readers to undertake the comparative study of languages.

Biruni's later works present other contributions. Scattered through them are trenchant observations on subjects as diverse as politics, economics, ethics, and the origins of human societies. He had done this before, of course, but now he allowed himself to range further afield. Notable among them were his notes on governance. Prior to Biruni, most writers in the Muslim East had focused mainly on the rise and fall of dynasties. An exception was Farabi, who offered his thoughts on the "good society," but in the highly abstract manner of Plato's *Republic*. Farabi hadn't read Aristotle's more practical-minded *Politics*, which had yet to be translated into Arabic. When Biruni launched his inquiry into the origins of society and of wealth, he was treading new ground.

In his book on geodesy and in his book on mineralogy,[43] Biruni argues that human beings are by nature unequal. Among other evidence for this he points out that even Adam's sons Cain and Abel were unequal in their abilities. The advent of money provided a measure of wealth in general and of inequality in particular.[44] Humans, he argues, are also highly individualistic. Differences in people's abilities brought variations in wealth. Many of those who amass wealth hide it away in their homes in hopes of passing it on to their offspring. Biruni rails against inherited wealth and privilege, warning that those who receive them are "dead." Worse, the withdrawal of wealth from circulation impoverishes society, which cannot exist without the productive exchange of goods and services. To preserve themselves from dangers posed by their environment, people had to band together and collaborate. The sciences arose not just from some inborn quest for knowledge but as a means of addressing the practical needs of existence.[45] Labor, when voluntary, gave rise to the arts and industries.

Turning to the valuables that signified wealth, Biruni explains that human beings were initially attracted to gold and jewels by their beauty, but soon realized that their value and compactness made them uniquely useful as proto currencies. Besides providing predictable value, they could be used for storing wealth, making distant purchases, and even for evading customs duties. Changes in their value over time, he suggests, are due less to the actions of governments or changing tastes than to increases or decreases in their supply. Biruni, in short, was an eleventh-century monetarist. He was also an exponent of the labor theory of value, a champion of equal opportunity, and a defender of unequal results, provided that governance was in the hands of strong and just leaders. Only with these provisos did he defend inherited monarchy and a powerful state.

One might ask why, given Biruni's long-standing interest in these issues, he never devoted an entire work to them. Two reasons stand out: first, because he was so deeply preoccupied with the great scientific issues that were his first passion; and second, because to have done so at any prior time in his life would have been dangerous. It appears that he wrote his early work, *Determination of the Coordinates of . . . Cities*, "for the desk drawer" and not for Mahmud's censorious eyes. Only in his old age could he afford to take up these issues and even announce his desire to write a major study on ethics and moral philosophy.[46]

Though a succession of illnesses sapped his strength, Biruni remained an optimist. He continued to conduct research, to write, and to plan for future projects. He continued to rail against spurious science and sloppy thinking. Withal, he remained true to his conviction that science is an unending process extending deep into the future. To this extent, Biruni believed devoutly in progress.

Back in 1034–5, when he was sixty-one, Biruni wrote a friend saying his one wish was for a long life and sufficient strength to continue his work.[47] He was granted this wish for another fourteen years, during which he completed several studies and maintained contact with a few old colleagues and friends. Among them was Abu-l Hasan al-Valvalidji, a jurist from the palace administration in Bost, Afghanistan, whom Biruni had gotten to know during court visits to Mahmud's grand palace in Helmand. Valvalidji was the last to visit Biruni, on September 11, 1048. By then Biruni, nearly blind and unable to walk, was confined to his room, and bedridden. He nonetheless plied Valvalidji with questions about a detail of Muslim contract law on which his visitor was an authority. When Valvalidji expressed amazement that a man in Biruni's condition would be concerned with such quotidian matters, Biruni is reported to have replied, "Is it not better for me to leave this world knowing the answer to this question than not knowing it?"[48] Scarcely had Valvalidji left the room than he heard women sobbing from within. Biruni had died.[49]

17

Ibn Sina's Encore

It was Ibn Sina's good fortune, by his early fifties, to be ensconced in a comfortable home in Isfahan and with the title and pay level of the second-most senior official in the land.[1] His job as vizier entailed serious and time-consuming responsibilities, but it also left him time to think and write. It helped that he had at his beck and call a team of eager acolytes to whom he could entrust the time-consuming tasks of culling old books for material, rewriting, editing, and copying.

During his stay in Isfahan Ibn Sina completed the last three volumes of the *Canon of Medicine*, which alone comprise nearly 3,000 pages of fine print in modern translations, and also the final sections of *The Cure*, which number a further thousand pages. Then there were further treatises, essays, poems, and letters. Ibn Sina completed his *Canon* about the same time he finished the final section of *The Cure*, on astronomy, in which he again offers his abridgment of Ptolemy's *Almagest*. As we've seen, his patron, the emir Ala al-Dawla, intrigued by that field, funded some observational instruments, several of which Ibn Sina himself designed.[2] Ala al-Dawla, however, was not prepared to plow through *The Cure*, so he charged Ibn Sina with preparing a shorter version—in other words, an abridgement of a summary of a compilation. Ibn Sina passed most of this task to his secretary, Juzjani,[3] but saved the section on philosophy for himself.[4] In these years Ibn Sina also drafted for Ala al-Dawla a treatise on the benefits and harms of wine and one on colitis, both of which presumably pertained directly to the emir's own condition.

If we are to believe Juzjani, Ibn Sina continued the drinking and carousing that had become a fixture of his life during his time in Hamadan.[5] Yet for all his frenetic socializing, he remained a curiously solitary figure. Even after holding years of evening "seminars" at his home in Hamadan, he had few committed disciples. A diligent recent scholar came up with only four, counting Juzjani.[6] And in every case except Juzjani, their relationship with Ibn Sina went downhill.

If it was difficult to be Ibn Sina's friend, it was painful to be his enemy. His bitterest conflicts tended to be with senior officeholders who had intellectual aspirations of their own. One who remained on Ibn Sina's "enemies" list for decades was Abu Ali ibn Miskawayh, a second-level bureaucrat, sometimes writer on ethics, bookman, and overall a respectable mediocrity. Ibn Sina encountered him first in Rayy and again in Isfahan, where Miskawayh had made the unfortunate decision to spend his retirement. Ibn Sina never missed a chance to ridicule the man.

Miskawayh had had a friend in Hamadan named Abu l-Qasim al-Kirmani, whom he forewarned of Ibn Sina's arrival and primed for combat. It was Kirmani whom the emir paired with Ibn Sina for the traditional debate by which a newcomer would be presented to the court and local intelligentsia. The exchange went badly.[7] In a private letter Ibn Sina fumed that Kirmani was "strange and outlandish. . . . As for his logic, it was another logic, his natural science some other natural science."[8] Elsewhere Ibn Sina referred to him as a "dung beetle" and "shit-eater."[9] Most offensive to Ibn Sina was Kirmani's repeated claim that members of the most influential circle of thinkers in Baghdad supported his own and Miskawayh's dialectic mode of analysis and not the syllogistic reasoning of Ibn Sina. Knowing that these men also claimed to be the true heirs of Aristotle and the Peripatetics, Ibn Sina wrote them a challenging letter and then ordered copies of all their works from a Baghdad book dealer. Upon reading their writings he was so disgusted that he sent back the entire bunch without seeking repayment.

Ibn Sina was adept at sustaining grudges: typically, he extended the feud with Kirmani over several decades. Even a victim's death did not end matters. The philosopher and theologian Abu al-Hassan Muhammad al-Amiri died in 992, but thirty years later Ibn Sina was still ridiculing him as a "muddler" who did not deserve to be called "the foremost of modern philosophers,"[10] as some had done. Some of his most ferocious attacks were doubtless defensive in nature, as when he forbade his Azerbaijani disciple Bahmanyar from showing the manuscript of his last major work, *Pointers and Reminders*, to any of the "ignoramuses," "deviants," "parasites," "shit eaters, and anyone else who is not worthy of the truth."[11] The same should be said of the boasting that often accompanied Ibn Sina's belittling of others.

Ibn Sina himself was by no means above criticism. As noted, he lifted passages of his autobiography from a Greek biography of Aristotle.[12] That he would brazenly pilfer this work, which was well known in its Arabic translation, attests to his grandiose—and perhaps even delisional—view of himself. Most of his contemporaries respected his intelligence but thought, as poor Miskawayh put it, that he should "amend his own character."[13] A modern

Muslim biographer who deeply respects Ibn Sina's philosophy nonetheless points out that contemporaries were full of praise for his knowledge but "had not a single kind word for the man himself."[14]

Despite being handsome, engaging, and supremely intelligent, Ibn Sina had never been at peace with himself. Throughout his life he yearned for company. And down to his last years he always fell short of his own expectations. Some of his most sustained outbursts of vanity are to be found in the autobiography he dictated to Juzjani. This took place in Gorgan, as we've seen, when Ibn Sina was in his forties and in the midst of his third failure to establish himself in any job or profession. Even while enjoying his most secure post, in Isfahan, he felt compelled to write a self-pitying letter to Emir Ala al-Dawla, in which he bemoans his fate, saying, "I don't know what to do, on which course I can rely, or how I can achieve a return to service."[15] A quatrain attributed to his pen contains this revealing cri de coeur: "How I wish I could know who I am, and what it is in this world that I seek."[16]

Yet Ibn Sina persisted, with dogged determinism and boundless energy. He remained a seeker to the end. He was also a prolific one and still capable of offering profundities that would maintain their significance over the centuries. No sooner did he complete writing *The Cure* than he began drafting several "follow-on" works, in which he clarified, amplified, and even modified positions he had adopted over the years. None of these explanatory texts survives, but we know of their contents because later authors embedded brief passages from several of them in their own works. In all these successor studies Ibn Sina continued to dwell on metaphysics. The attention that he lavished on these final works shows that his views on human consciousness and on God remained in flux down to his final days.

The first of these, *The Easterners*, is thought to have grouped Aristotle and his most loyal Muslim followers as the "Westerners," and juxtaposed them to the "Easterners," that is, the several philosophers from Khorasan and Central Asia who were most active in revising the Aristotelian tradition.[17] Ibn Sina implied that he himself was the leading Easterner and champion of revisionism. This argument opened the door to Ibn Sina's final and most mystical thoughts on the relation of mankind to God.[18] As such, this text became Ibn Sina's "manifesto of philosophical praxis."[19]

In the second of Ibn Sina's final works, *Fair Judgment*, he offers his responses to the multitude of questions that had been posed to him by students and correspondents after they read *The Cure*. It is in this compendium that Ibn Sina, for the first time, comments on Aristotle's *Theologia*, thereby demonstrating his deepening interest in theology per se. That commentary, like the whole of *Fair Judgment*, was in fact a further step toward Ibn Sina's final emancipation from Aristotle and from the Peripatetics. In yet another of his final works, *Pointers and Reminders*, Ibn Sina declares his full independence from Aristotle.

In these works, Ibn Sina addresses a number of issues that had challenged him throughout his career. Thus, he ponders once more the relationship between metaphysics and science and the psychological processes underlying them, the relation between logic and science, and the role of such cognitive processes as induction and abstraction in addressing such issues.[20]

A major theme in these last writings was Ibn Sina's ongoing effort to separate the soul from all physicality, discussed in *The Cure*. I noted that these could well have been the thoughts of an old man who was observing the decline of his body and ruminating over the fate of his soul. The rational soul, of course, had been the subject of Ibn Sina's youthful philosophizing fifty years earlier. It now figures centrally in these late works and in his last known work, an essay entitled simply "On the Rational Soul." In that short piece he offers this profound and revealing description of the soul:

> Know that human beings alone, to the exclusion of all other living beings, possess a faculty highly capable of grasping the intelligibles. This faculty is sometimes called the rational soul, sometimes "the soul at peace," sometimes the sacred soul, sometimes the spiritual spirit, sometimes the commanding spirit, sometimes the good word, sometimes the word that unites and separates, sometimes the divine secret, sometimes the governing light, sometimes the chief commanding light, sometimes the true heart, sometimes the core of the self, sometimes the understanding, and sometimes the brain. It exists in every single human being, young and old, adolescent or adult, insane or sane, sick or sound.[21]

Here Ibn Sina steps forth as his own Aristotle. He does this not simply by drawing on Plato and his followers, as some have contended. Indeed, in a typical barb, Ibn Sina accuses Plato of peddling "paltry wares."[22] Rather, he accomplishes this by introducing into his system of metaphysics original, logically essential, and hence verifiable, elements drawn from his own thinking.

Ibn Sina's Isfahan writings culminated a lifetime spent using reason and logic to ponder God, the soul, the heavens, and earth. In so doing, he extends the reach of these tools beyond what Aristotle had conceived possible. However, Ibn Sina was not at peace with his own achievement. It was well and good for the mass of thoughtful people to content themselves with the logic of *The Cure*, but Ibn Sina himself came to view this method as cold and insufficient. Several experts date the shift to *The Easterners*, in which he is supposed to have contrasted "Western" thought as dealing only with matter and the shadows of reality, to "Eastern" thought, which directly grasps the Light.[23] This is a tidy hypothesis but unprovable, since the work itself is lost.

What cannot be denied is that during the last phase of his life, Ibn Sina's ruminations drew him increasingly toward mysticism. This was reflected in his increasing use of mystical terminology and symbolism, and in the allusive and poetic style of his final works. It was in this vein that he composed three visionary narratives or "recitals," all of which are also lost, and his final piece on *The Soul*, in which he asserts that love pervades the cosmos. Ibn Sina seems to have foreshadowed the words of the American essayist H. L. Mencken, who suggested that "Religion is not a syllogism but a poem."

One expert has detected in these late works the influence of mystical Sufism.[24] We have seen that during Ibn Sina's grim flight from Gurganj to Gorgan in 1012 he spent three days with the Sufi sage and poet, Abu Said. During one session the mystic apparently threw a pot into the air and it remained there, levitated. When Ibn Sina asked why this had occurred, the sage replied that the pot was Abu Said's soul, and that if Ibn Sina were to purify his own soul it could do the same. Arguing against Ibn Sina's supposed Sufism is his distaste for renunciation in any form. He continued his worldly and voluptuous life down to the end—scarcely the mark of a would-be Sufi. I've noted the mystical elements in the doctrines to which he had been exposed as a boy. He claimed in his autobiography to have found them "unconvincing." The question is whether this is actually so, or whether he had suppressed these esoteric thoughts over most of his adult life, only to return to them in old age. Whatever the case, one thing is clear: Ibn Sina shared his mystical and visionary writings with only a handful of people whom he judged to be truly enlightened, and not with the general public, to whom he recommended only his "official" works. He forbade his acolytes to share his esoteric writings with outsiders.

Discussing Ibn Sina's late turn toward the esoteric and mystical, I would note that there had always been a strain of "rational mysticism" running through Ibn Sina's thought.[25] Even in his most rigorous philosophizing about the relationship between man and God, angels, for example, played a role as intermediaries. Leading this band of Ibn Sina's mediators between God and man was Gabriel, the angel of revelation. Belief in angels is one of Islam's six articles of faith, but Ibn Sina seems to have taken that faith into the realm of philosophy. Moreover, Ibn Sina's deepening orientation toward mysticism replicated the evolution of one of his mentors, the philosopher Kindi, who, for all his rationalism, had increasingly felt pulled in the opposite direction. These considerations make Ibn Sina's late embrace of angelology and mysticism less anomalous than it may at first appear, and more as part of a continuum—or perhaps a tension—in his life and thought.

The same equivocation regarding the unknown and unknowable can be detected in Ibn Sina's treatment of alchemy and astrology. On the one hand, he acknowledged that "it is not within the power [of alchemists] to bring about a true change [of minerals]."[26] As I've mentioned, he wrote an entire book denouncing the astrologers' claims to foretell the future. Yet at the same time he considered silver and gold so generically similar as to make it possible to transform one into the other. And he accepted the astrologers' core belief that cosmological events somehow affect earthly affairs and human life.

Life in Isfahan may have brought a welcome pause in the stressful confusion of Ibn Sina's life, but, as I've suggested, the interlude did not last. Barely five years after Ibn Sina arrived at the gate of Isfahan in 1023, Mahmud of Ghazni again emerged as the critical factor in the life of the Shiite Buyids. This time, however, the first step in the chain of events that led to war traced not to Mahmud but to the Buyids themselves, specifically to Sayyida, "The Lady," cousin of Ala al-Dawla and mother of Majd al-Dawla of Rayy, whose death had destabilized the entire region.

This opened the way for Ala al-Dawla to move against Sayyida's son, whose case of melancholia had first brought Ibn Sina to Persia. Having watched from afar the growing might of Isfahan, the feckless Majd al-Dawla panicked. He knew that his uncle's expanded Isfahani forces would soon be at the gates of Rayy. Desperate, he made the most foolish decision of his hapless career: he turned for help to the head of the yet larger force that threatened him, Mahmud of Ghazni.

From Mahmud's standpoint, the timing of this request could not have been better. A Buyid himself had asked for help, a plea that empowered Mahmud to launch the anti-Buyid and anti-Shiia crusade of which he had long dreamed. Mobilizing manpower and Indian war elephants, he readied to launch the attack. But after thirty years of ceaseless campaigning, Mahmud's strength had run out, so he named his son Masud to lead the army. Masud's strategic goal was to capture Baghdad and liberate the Sunni caliph from the Buyid Shiites. What could be more convenient than for Masud's army to pause on the way to Baghdad, seize Rayy, and take control of its government? Masud and his motley but well-trained army of Turks, former Samani soldiers, Indian draftees, and slaves quickly mobilized and marched across western Afghanistan into Persia.

The ill-fated Majd al-Dawla sent a party of dignitaries to receive Masud, who promptly arrested the delegation and both Majd al-Dawla and his son for good measure. After sending them all back to Ghazni as captives, he turned to sacking Rayy. Acting as the sword of Sunni orthodoxy, he launched a bloody purge of Shiites, Ismailis, Christians, Zoroastrians, and all others who rejected the Afghans' form of Sunni Muslim orthodoxy. Masud's troops then turned on the emir's library, a priceless storehouse of learning. It took some fifty camels to haul the emir's collection of manuscripts from the library building onto the street. They then set fire to the mound. Countless texts by Razi, Khujandi, and other savants went up in flames. With gruesome attention to detail, Masud's troops piled the books along the roadway in such a way that the conflagration raged "at the feet of the corpses of the Ismailis, Rejectors [i.e., Shiites], philosophers, and other unbelievers that hung from the trees."[27]

In January 1030, Masud's forces made the ten-day march from Rayy to Isfahan and easily took the city. Ala al-Dawla, Ibn Sina, and most of the government barely managed to escape Masud's onslaught by fleeing southward into the sparsely populated region of Ahwaz. In their panic to get out of Isfahan they abandoned the caravan with their baggage just outside the main gate—the same gate at which Ibn Sina had been so fulsomely welcomed six years earlier. In a vain search for valuables, troops from the Ghazni army pillaged Ibn Sina's camel bags, pitching aside whatever lacked value. Among the losses was the manuscript of *Fair Judgment*.[28] Whatever books remained were packed off to the library at Ghazni.

Had fate not intervened at this moment, it seems all but certain that Masud would have captured Ibn Sina and sent him to Ghazni as a prize hostage. By so doing, Masud would have ornamented his father's court with the one intellectual Mahmud had most wanted to attract and whom he had tried unsuccessfully to capture over the preceding quarter century. But this was not to be. Only a few weeks later, in May 1030, Mahmud of Ghazni died at the age of fifty-nine. Informed of this by courier, Masud raced back to the capital in Afghanistan.

Taking advantage of Masud's sudden departure, Ala al-Dawla regrouped his forces and headed to Rayy in hopes of filling the political vacuum created by the death of "The Lady" and the departure of Masud's army. Ibn Sina was with the invading party from Isfahan and spent several months in Rayy renewing old acquaintances. But his celebrations were premature and ended with the news that Masud had triumphed over his brother and now ruled in Ghazni. Masud wasted no time in sending an army to recapture Rayy and Isfahan and consolidate his earlier gains. As a result, Ala al-Dawla of Isfahan now became Masud's liege, with the obligation to send 200,000 gold dinars annually to his overlord.

This costly respite was to last less than four years. Ala al-Dalwa and Ibn Sina, who still served as vizier, made plans to expand Isfahan's fortifications but otherwise resumed their usual routine. This was the final brief interlude in Ibn Sina's life, but a very productive one, resulting in the completion of his final body of treatises and papers. Yet it was overshadowed by political realities. Now Ibn Sina, as well as Biruni, though separated by 1,500 kilometers (900 miles), were both under the direct control of the all-powerful regime that Mahmud had built and of its new ruler, Masud. Yet more ominous was the fact that Ala al-Dawla, whether from overconfidence or poverty, failed to make the annual payments that Masud had imposed upon him.

Meanwhile, Masud in Ghazni and his liege Ala al-Dawla in Isfahan were both being threatened by the Turkic Seljuks to the west of Isfahan. These tribesmen would eventually conquer much of the Middle East and the Byzantine lands in Anatolia and threaten Constantinople itself. They now posed the most serious threat to Masud's rule and, potentially, to Ala al-Dawla as well. Instead of addressing this threat, however, Masud rushed to India in an effort to crush a Hindu rebellion there. Only in the late spring of 1034 did he send an army of his own Kurdish forces to quell the Seljuk tribesmen and, incidentally, remind Isfahan's ruler of his unpaid debts to Ghazni.

Ibn Sina was now sixty years old. Against Juzjani's advice he continued to drink and carouse in his usual manner. But by 1030 his health began to give way. First he complained that his handwriting had deteriorated.[29] Then he began suffering from a condition he described as "colic." This self-diagnosis could have referred to nothing more serious than problems in the upper digestive tract. Had this been the case the regimen he prescribed for himself—a compound of ground celery seeds administered through an enema—might well have worked. Interestingly, though, celery seeds are not mentioned in the second volume of Ibn Sina's own *Canon* devoted to natural pharmaceuticals, and they were certainly not listed as a treatment for colic. The "colic" persisted, and clearly signified something more serious than a digestive disorder. Modern specialists, reviewing the evidence, suggest that Ibn Sina suffered from a severe blockage of the intestines or, worse, stomach or colorectal cancer.

By 1034, when the emir of Isfahan and his vizier were again forced to flee, Ibn Sina's condition had worsened. In spite of the frequent enemas Ibn Sina administered to himself, he could barely limp back to Isfahan. He then recovered enough to resume some of his old duties and routines. After a further brief respite, Isfahan once again came under threat from the army from Ghazni. This time, however, Ala al-Dawla planned a brazen countermove, marching his army across the open countryside toward Hamadan, his vizier in tow. Ibn Sina's condition had deteriorated to such an extent that he had to be carried on a litter. He barely made it back to Isfahan alive. He began to experience epileptic seizures and added doses of mithridatum to the enemas. Compounded from forty herbal substances including frankincense, wild poppy, and balm of Gilead, mithridatum had been a revered but much feared element of the pharmacopeia since antiquity and widely prescribed by Galen, among others, for a variety of the most serious conditions, including rabies and poisoning. It was a medicine of last resort, and one that neither Galen nor Ibn Sina, in the fifth volume of his *Canon*, prescribed for either epilepsy or cancer.

The ailing philosopher continued to attend court functions and to plug away at his own writing. He even managed to accompany Ala al-Dawla in 1037 when the emir launched a campaign against Masud's general Tash Farrash and the Kurds. But as the emir's army proceeded from Isfahan toward Hamadan, Ibn Sina's condition further deteriorated. The mithridatum and celery-seed enemas (eight daily) left him so weak that he again had to be carried on a litter. Then, one of his internal organs ulcerated, causing an abscess that would soon have led to fatal peritonitis. Having long since declared that he would prefer an expansive life to a long one,[30] Ibn Sina gave up. In his own words, "The governor that used to rule my body is too weak to rule any longer, so treatment would be of no further avail."[31]

At this point a slave added opium to the concoctions of celery seed and mithridatum that Ibn Sina was administering to himself through enemas.

While acknowledging that this might have been an accident on the slave's part, Juzjani strongly suggested that the slave had acted deliberately because he had been stealing money from his master and feared punishment.[32] Thus, according to Juzjani, Ibn Sina was likely murdered. He was sixty-four years of age.[33]

18

Biruni and Ibn Sina through the Ages

When Biruni and Ibn Sina died, whether their works would endure was unknown. Even the physical survival of their texts was at risk. The destruction of their writings had begun when Ibn Sina abandoned his bags as he fled across the Karakum desert back in 1012. Seven years later Biruni lost his entire library and equipment when Mahmud sacked Gurganj. Ibn Sina lost what remained of his writings when he fled Hamadan and, again, when Masud's troops ransacked his luggage outside Isfahan. Most of the manuscripts were destroyed, though a few of them may have ended up in the imperial library at Ghazni.[1]

Having served three Ghazni sultans as court astrologer and in-house astronomer, Biruni would have been expected to place all of his post-Gurganj works in that same institution, which also housed manuscripts by the great Persian poets who served at the court of Mahmud, including Ferdowsi. Tragically, this priceless collection survived for only a century. In the year 1151 an army from the rising Afghan power of Ghor sacked Ghazni and burned its famed library.[2]

For a book to escape this fate, someone would have had to commission a scribe to make a copy, and that copy would have had to have been made accessible to readers and not squirreled away by a collector as private treasure. Few books were so fortunate. Ibn Sina was well aware of this. He and his secretary had been deeply concerned about the future of his life's work. That is one reason he had written accessible spin-offs for some of his more demanding longer works. His versified synopsis of the *Canon of Medicine* and of his *Logic* were also disseminated widely.[3]

Ibn Sina's status as a public official and colorful *persona* generated interest in his writings. He also had at least a couple of students and correspondents who preserved his memory, while in Juzjani he had a publicist who was dedicated to documenting his every move. Another factor that favored Ibn Sina's legacy was that he wrote on medicine. After his death, the *Canon* was being copied and emulated wherever there were readers of Arabic. Its very success invited challengers who sought to outdo Ibn Sina, and in so doing they further spread his fame.

Biruni enjoyed none of these advantages. Stuck in an imperial court that championed poetry over science, he avoided publicity. He did not seek to be a public figure, and no one bothered to chronicle his deeds, aside from Beyhaqi, whose information, while uniformly positive, was fragmentary. Nor did Biruni have students or a large circle of correspondents.[4] Biruni's home was Ghazni, a geopolitical center, but its main trade was in military equipment and slaves from India, not books. Few intellectuals visited Ghazni, and few cultural goods found their way from there to the Middle Eastern cities that boomed as the Central Asian centers passed their peak. Then in the thirteenth century came the Mongols, whose role was everywhere destructive, but especially in the Central Asian centers that defined the geography of Biruni's life. On the eve of the Mongol invasion, the chronicler Yaqut could consult a sixty-sheet listing of Biruni's complete works that were preserved at a mosque in Merv.[5] But a few short years later they had all gone up in flames.

By fleeing to Hamadan and then Isfahan, Ibn Sina had placed himself in active centers of trade and places where the ranks of merchants included more than a few booksellers. When caravans departed for the Middle East, it was an easy matter for traders to include a few manuscripts in the saddlebags. The fate of the *Canon of Medicine* offers an example and deserves particular attention. The book reached an ambitious young physician in far-off Arab Andalusia named Ibn Zuhr, later known in Europe as Avenzoar.[6] Ibn Zuhr took an immediate dislike to it because of what he considered its needless and prolix philosophizing. Not only did he refuse to put a gift copy in his library, but he also cut off the margins of his own copy of the text and used them for writing prescriptions.[7] Eager to make his mark, Ibn Zuhr entitled his handbook a *Book of Simplification Concerning Therapeutics and Diet*. Borrowing heavily from Ibn Sina but stripping away the philosophy, the *Book of Simplification* gained popularity by focusing on "how to" questions. Ibn Zuhr's concentration on practicality was one of the reasons the great Ibn Rushd (Averreos) would later praise him as the greatest physician since Galen.

To some extent such praise was warranted, for Ibn Zuhr not only led in the development of surgery but appears to have been among the first to speak of cancers as a distinct category of disease. On the whole, however, Ibn Zuhr and the Arabs in Andalusia lagged behind the Central Asians and Persians in medicine. Moreover, Ibn Zuhr's criticism inadvertently publicized Ibn Sina's

Canon as a compendium for experts and philosophers, thus reinforcing Ibn Sina's status as the leader of the field throughout the Muslim world.[8]

Meanwhile, in the thirteenth century, a young Syrian doctor named Ibn al-Nafis further enhanced the visibility of the *Canon*, also by attacking it frontally. He challenged the account of the heart's functioning, which Ibn Sina had borrowed from Galen and propagated in his *Canon*. Ibn Sina had maintained that the two ventricles of the heart were connected by a hole, thus enabling them together to cleanse the blood. Nafis demonstrated that no such hole existed and that the cleansing occurred when the blood passed between the right ventricle and the lungs. He then proposed a whole list of further corrections to Ibn Sina's anatomical claims, which simultaneously enhanced Nafis's reputation and drew further attention to the *Canon* itself. Not content with his critique of the *Canon*, Nafis announced that he would outdo Ibn Sina's five volumes with a staggering 200 volumes of his own. He managed to complete eighty volumes before his death in 1288.

The westward shift in the main locus of medicine and science that began in response to the Mongol invasion carried the works of Ibn Sina in its wake. Medical experts first in Cairo and then in Andalusia continued to ground their work in the *Canon*. A similar geographical displacement took place in an eastward direction. It took another two centuries, but the shift that had led to the activation of medical studies in Andalusia had its counterpart in India. The center of this eastward intellectual migration was the Delhi sultanate, which emerged as northwest India recovered from the Mongol onslaught. Mahmud's cultural wars had left much of the region Muslim. Thousands of migrants from Central Asia had emigrated to the Indus Valley, and for a period Arabic gained acceptance there as the language of government and culture. Among the imports that arrived with the migrants were copies of the *Canon*, which immediately found an enthusiastic audience, inspiring the Indian medical community to gather Arabic texts by other medical experts, notably Razi.

The Indians were well aware that Ibn Sina, Razi, and other writers had drawn from the wellsprings of ancient Greek medicine. As a result, the system of medicine propounded by Ibn Sina's *Canon* came to be known in India as "Unani" or Greek medicine. Along with works by the prolific Galen, the *Canon* became the cornerstone of this new school of Indian medicine. Systematized during the Mughal period, Unani medicine was also institutionalized, with numerous hospitals, universities, and medical schools devoted to its propagation and further development. In today's India, Pakistan,

Bangladesh, and South Africa, many of the most prominent centers of Unani medicine still bear Ibn Sina's name.[9]

Even from this brief survey it is clear that the Muslim world, with notable exceptions, embraced Ibn Sina's *Canon*. Even critiques of it did not prevent the integration of much of its contents into everyday practice. The same cannot be said, however, for Ibn Sina's philosophy as a whole, and especially for his metaphysics and cosmology. These elicited jeers from some quarters and a determined defense from others. Together, the contending forces went far toward defining the factional dynamics of Muslim philosophy as a whole and even exerted a powerful influence on Jewish and Christian thought.

The central figure in this extended drama was Abu Hamid Muhammad al-Ghazali, known in the medieval West also by his Latinized name, Algazel. This lifelong student of philosophy and theology was a Persian from Tus, the city near the border between Iran and Afghanistan where Ferdowsi had composed most of the Persian national epic.[10] Ghazali had benefited from a thorough grounding in the kind of philosophy that al-Kindi and Ibn Sina himself had practiced. The ruling powers singled him out for his quick wit and invited him to Baghdad to head the first of a new type of religious school, called a *madrassah*. It was the goal of the caliph and his vizier that these schools would become furnaces of piety in which a new and strictly orthodox Sunni Islam would be forged.

At the time Ghazali arrived in Baghdad in about 1089, combat between Sunnis and Shiites had reached a fever pitch. Ghazali, still in his mid-thirties, was enlisted to lead the Sunnis' ideological front. His first action was to pinpoint and define the enemy—namely, Ibn Sina and the other philosophers who used Aristotle to defend their views. He set down his case in a treatise, *The Incoherence of the Philosophers*, which he presented before a Baghdad audience packed with hundreds of students from his madrassah.[11]

Ghazali focuses his attack on twenty points, each of which he addressed in detail. He pays special attention to three in particular. First, he rejected Ibn Sina's concept of Creation, which, as we've seen, turned on the distinction between *potentiality* and *actuality*. Ghazali considers this distinction to be adroit but false, for it left intact at least the shadow of Aristotle's notion of the universe's eternity—which Ghazali called the "pre-eternal" existence of substance and which he flatly rejects.[12]

Second, Ghazali challenges Ibn Sina's assertion that "God's knowledge does not encompass the temporal particulars among individual [existents]."[13] Was God's concern confined only to the generality of humanity, as Ibn Sina seemed to suggest, or did it extend also to the details of individual lives? Similarly, can God's will not be detected in every movement and action in the physical universe or is it manifest only in the overall order in which they all exist? And third, Ghazali asks how the human soul, which Ibn Sina believed to be immaterial, could possibly appear bodily at the Day of Judgment and be capable of achieving physical resurrection, both of which were specified in holy writ?[14] On all three issues he concludes emphatically that Ibn Sina was wrong and that his views were incompatible with Islam.

Curiously, *The Incoherence* does not include what was later to be widely seen as his most inflammatory charge: his thoroughgoing attack on causality as Ibn Sina perceived it. While Ibn Sina followed his ancient mentors in treating physical laws as universals, Ghazali (who did not actually deny that position) wanted also to reserve the possibility of God's acting independently of physical laws, such as, for example, making water run uphill.[15]

Ghazali presented his arguments in full-throated attack mode, accusing Ibn Sina and his followers of "tricks" and willful deception. From first to last his goal was to expose Ibn Sina's misguided fealty to Aristotle, Plato, and other ancients with "high sounding names." He also accused Ibn Sina of slavishly borrowing from Christianity and Judaism.[16]

Ghazali's venom was as much personal as philosophical. Barely had he finished dedicating his book to God than he launches his *ad hominem* attack. *The Incoherence* accuses Ibn Sina and "the philosophers" of rejecting the Islamic duty regarding acts of worship, disdaining religious rites pertaining to the offices of prayer and the avoidance of prohibited things, and belittling the devotions and ordinances prescribed by the divine law.[17] In plain language, Ibn Sina drank, didn't pray, and scoffed at the pious. By piling up such personal accusations even before he launches his analysis, Ghazali seeks to cap his case against Ibn Sina even before he lays it out, and to dispose of everything in the thought of his predecessor of which he, Ghazali, disapproved.

Bombast aside, Ghazali was sophisticated and makes his case in a lawyerly manner. Far from rejecting "philosophy" out of hand, he gladly embraces the use of mathematics, observation, and logic to reach conclusions about the heavens and physical world. Indeed, *Incoherence* argues that anyone who attacked these essential tools "harms religion and weakens it."[18] In the same spirit, not only did he embrace Ibn Sina's mode of reasoning, but he also intended, as he had announced in an earlier work, to employ it himself in order to disprove Ibn Sina's conclusions. *The Incoherence* therefore presented

Ibn Sina's positions so faithfully that it would later become a vehicle for transmitting them to readers who could not bother to read Ibn Sina himself.

This blending of personal attack and declared commitment to moderation must have caused Ghazali's audience to hold their breath as they awaited his final judgment. While in *Incoherence* he claims to have dismantled Ibn Sina's arguments on all twenty counts, he focuses his main accusation on just three he had singled out. On these, he declares that Ibn Sina was not only guilty as charged of "manifest infidelity," but that his views "do not agree with Islam in any respect."[19] Ibn Sina was trying to rehabilitate the views of the Mutazilites, the arch-rationalists whom Sunni Muslims had long since drummed out of their camp. Anyone advancing such views must be pronounced an apostate from the faith.

Having declared Ibn Sina an apostate and having reminded readers that "the killing of those [who] hold such views is obligatory," Ghazali then adroitly pivots and declares in *The Incoherence* that he will leave to others the final judgment on Ibn Sina's infidelity. Ghazali would let the jury decide on the appropriate punishment. However, since the accused had been in his grave for sixty years, the punishment would have to be directed not against the man himself but against his ideas. And how does one behead or stone to death an idea?

Scribes and copyists went to work disseminating Ghazali's case against Ibn Sina. The fact that this intellectual purge bore the imprimatur of the Sunni Caliphate, now controlled by the Seljuk Turks, only added to its authority. Anyone who would dare challenge Ghazali's accusations would have faced serious risks. A recent scholar, Robert Wisnovsky, has shown that few at the time dared to refute or even elaborate upon Ghazali's charges.[20] It is not surprising that Ghazali's attack on Ibn Sina and on philosophy in general had a deeply chilling effect on intellectual discourse.

Ghazali was not to bask in his triumph for long. Shortly after he delivered his infamous Baghdad speech, the caliph died and then Ismaili Shiites murdered Ghazali's home-town friend and protector, the vizier Nizam al-Mulk. Crushed and disoriented, Ghazali suffered a nervous breakdown. He left his family and began the long trek to the Holy Land, where he remained for many years. His garb thereafter was the rough woolen cloak of a Sufi pilgrim. This choice is revealing, for when Ghazali had first arrived in Baghdad it was said that he brought with him a collection of richly embroidered robes that were the envy of all who saw them.

After the deaths of his patrons, Ghazali's life changed[21] radically. The young philosopher may have been a showman in a highly politicized world, but he was also an acute thinker. His abrupt abandonment of a narrow Sunni orthodoxy for the life of a Sufi ascetic was the turning point of his life. His later writings, which have been the subject of several recent studies, combined all the main elements of his thought, early and late, and attracted appreciative readers throughout the Muslim world and, later, among Jews and Christians.

In spite of Ghazali's diatribe, many thinkers in the Muslim world embraced Ibn Sina's legacy. Omar Khayyam, the great mathematician and astronomer (and putative author of *The Rubaiyat*), translated one of Ibn Sina's treatises into Persian. A severely rationalist theologian from Central Asia named Fahr al-Din Razi also took notice of Ibn Sina. Known by the sobriquet "The Sultan of Theologians," Razi was one of the most interesting but neglected polymaths of that era.[22] Deeply conservative in his theology, Fahr al-Din Razi launched a sustained attack on Ibn Sina's theodicy while at the same time embracing many of Ibn Sina's ideas.[23] This had the paradoxical effect of legitimizing them among the more rationalistic of the Asharite practitioners of *kalam*. Contrary to Aristotle and Ibn Sina, however, Fahr al-Din Razi also championed atomism, rejected the centrality of the earth, and championed the existence of "thousands" of universes.[24]

The one thinker to issue a rejoinder to Ghazali's charge that Ibn Sina was both incoherent and a heretic was Muḥammad Ibn Aḥmad Ibn Rushd, later known to Latin readers as Averroes. By the twelfth century Andalusia had fallen under the rule of fundamentalist emirs from Berber North Africa who were known as the Almohads. The Almohad emir of Cordoba had a doctor who read Ibn Sina in his spare time. This doctor introduced his ruler to his friend, Ibn Rushd.

Ibn Rushd was a polymath of the old school, a respected judge in the religious court and the author of books on mathematics, medicine, philosophy, astronomy, and, of course, law. His point-by-point rejoinder to Ghazali, which bears the polemical title *The Incoherence of the Incoherence*, is systematic and thorough. But he waged his defense not to defend Ibn Sina but to rehabilitate Aristotle. In fact, elsewhere he offered a systematic and scathing critique of Ibn Sina's work. One scholar notes that Ibn Rushd's criticisms were "wide-ranging, in so far as they address all the main areas of Avicenna's philosophy, from logic, to the different sections of natural philosophy, to metaphysics." His attacks on Ibn Sina "are not occasional and incidental diversions, but represent a leitmotiv and a concentric target of these works.

The tone of the criticisms is derogatory: [Ibn Rushd] tends by all means to stress the gravity of Ibn Sina's errors, and he employs to this end a style that is direct, emphatic, and polemical."[25] The pointed juxtaposition that Ibn Rushd drew between Ibn Sina and himself was to echo down through the centuries among the defenders of both thinkers.

Meanwhile, the writings of Ibn Sina were finding new champions in other quarters. By the late twelfth century, leadership in the world of thought had shifted from the polymath philosophers to practitioners of *kalam*, the special-ized study of Muslim doctrine and its defense against critics. Whether Sunni or Shiite, theologians of *kalam* were a sophisticated lot and during the twelfth and thirteenth centuries enjoyed a kind of golden age. In their own way they embraced—some say "appropriated"—Ibn Sina and launched a many-sided effort to integrate elements of his thought into Muslim theology. Sunnis and Shiites competed to claim his legacy, in a struggle that the scholar Robert Wisnovsky has characterized as a "tug of war."[26] Mainstream theologians on both sides viewed Ibn Rushd and his undiluted Aristotelianism as a voice from the past.[27] In the end, it was the conservative Asharite school that showed most commitment in claiming Ibn Sina as its own, assuring his place within strict orthodoxy. Poring through the extant corpus of Muslim writings from the eleventh through the sixteenth centuries, Wisnovsky found only two systematic commentaries on *The Cure*. This did not mean that nobody read it. Clearly, many did so, from the Pamirs to the Pyrenees.[28] But rather than drown in its immensity, most early readers chose instead to ferret out its meaning by reading Ibn Sina's concise *Pointers and Reminders*. As noted, it was precisely in this very late—and now lost—work that Ibn Sina most thor-oughly emancipated himself from Aristotle.

Within a century after Ibn Sina's death, people as far afield as Bursa and Cairo were copying out his surviving texts, above all *Pointers and Reminders*, and writing commentaries on them. The process began with a couple of Ibn Sina's students, then extended to *their* students and eventually embraced a multitude of specialists who not merely explained but expanded and even transformed Ibn Sina's thoughts. Among the many topics they repeatedly chewed over was the old distinction between essence and existence that was so essential to his understanding of God and Creation.

The reach of Ibn Sina's ideas stretched far beyond the circle of those who actually read them. This was due in good measure to Ghazali; although he was among Ibn Sina's harshest critics, he adopted Ibn Sina's view that human beings could judge the validity of the claims of prophets and did not need to rely on revelation alone. Indeed, Ghazali became one of the most influential disseminators of Ibn Sina's philosophy, after Ibn Sina himself. Ibn Rushd, for example, absorbed Ibn Sina's metaphysics by reading Ghazali. Another who followed this route was the Jewish polymath Moses ben Maimon. Maimonides, as he is known, was born in Cordoba in 1213, a century after Ibn Sina's death. The Almohads' intolerant regime had already repressed the highest manifestations of Andalusian culture in the name of Sunni orthodoxy. Now they were forcing Christians and Jews to choose between conversion or exile. Maimonides fled to North Africa, then to the historic lands of Israel, and finally to Egypt. By his fortieth year he had completed his fourteen-volume *Mishneh Torah*, the most authoritative code of Talmudic law.

In his *Guide for the Perplexed* and elsewhere throughout his voluminous writings, Maimonides sought to find common ground between Aristotle and the Peripatetics and Jewish learning.[29] His accomplishment, as Lenn E. Goodman put it, was to effect a fusion of two civilizational concepts that had heretofore been considered to differ radically from one another: "the Hebraic idea of holiness as transcendence and the Greek ideal of reason as insight into genuine value."[30] Like Ibn Sina himself, Maimonides's purpose was not to undermine the pillars of his faith but to strengthen them, especially as they define and defend the virtuous life. Again quoting Goodman, he did this by "defending and reestablishing the integration of act, virtue, and outcome that is unquestioned in the Torah."[31]

The intellectual solvent that made possible Maimonides's compound was Muslim philosophizing of the preceding centuries, principally by Farabi,[32] but also by Ghazali and Ibn Rushd. In a letter to a rabbi friend, Maimonides made clear that he considered Ibn Sina's writings of lesser value than Farabi's, yet praised them as "subtle," "exacting," and "worthy of study." Maimonides made good use both of Ghazali's overview of Ibn Sina's work and of Ibn Rushd's critique of Ghazali and Ibn Sina.

Maimonides's main concern was with the virtuous life. To achieve clarity on that issue he had to delve deep into questions regarding God, creation, the soul, and eternity. Following Ibn Sina, he squared the circle of God's creation and the eternity of the universe by drawing a distinction—just as Ibn Sina had—between possible and necessary existence.[33] Though barely citing Ibn Sina, he embraced his view of God as the final cause, of a God that provided a space for human choice and hence for ethics, and of the human soul as immaterial and eternal. On many points he sided with Razi and Ghazali, but even on these issues the role of Ibn Sina's agenda is manifest. By contrast,

Maimonides had little good to say about the Muslim theologians of *kalam*, even though they, too, had by now embraced those of Ibn Sina's positions that appeared compatible with their project of codifying their faith.

This brief survey does not touch upon the many other Arabic and Persian language authors whom Ibn Sina influenced, either directly or indirectly. The fact that prominent later thinkers both championed Ibn Sina's views and sparred with them by citing them at length shows how widely his works were disseminated throughout the region. By the seventeenth century, Persian theologians were not just studying Ibn Sina's ideas but were appropriating and transforming them.[34] The fact that many later writers often incorporated his ideas without citing his writings and without even knowing their source attests to the extent to which his thought had come to penetrate the culture.

This cannot be said of the posthumous fate of Biruni's writings in the Muslim world. An Afghan-born historian named Abu Said Gardizi, who may actually have met Biruni, did write briefly about him. And more than a century after Biruni's death a learned Syrian proclaimed that "there was not in his lifetime or even down to the present a more accomplished scholar in the science of astronomy than Biruni." By contrast, a thirteenth-century author from near Samarkand issued a biography in which he claimed that Biruni was a native of Sind in India.[35] Adding insult to injury, during the centuries following Biruni's death, the only one of his books that consistently found readers was his late treatise on astrology.[36] Overall, Biruni's writings generated so limited a resonance that they bring to mind the conundrum posed by the eighteenth-century Irish bishop-philosopher George Berkeley: "If a tree falls in a forest and no one hears it, does it make a sound?"

The first among several causes of this situation was the sacking of Ghazni and its library in 1149, which was followed after 1218 by the Mongols' destruction of many other great libraries. For them to survive this onslaught, copies of Biruni's writings would have to have reached the Mediterranean world prior to the Mongol onslaught. Most didn't. Many of the few that did were considered treasures and vanished into private collections.

Nor did Biruni's subject matter attract eager readers. It is not surprising that many lay readers pored through his books on astrology rather than his other works, since wading through his *Determination of the Coordinates of . . . Cities* or *Masud's Canon* demanded a sophisticated knowledge of mathematics, spherical trigonometry, and astronomy. Few could meet that challenge.[37] The disappearance of Biruni's *India* from the consciousness of educated people in the Middle East and Central Asia was due to different factors. By Biruni's death, large parts of the Indus valley had become just another part of the Muslim realm. Because of this, both *India* and Biruni's further studies of Hindu learning lost their timeliness and urgency. As to the *Chronology*, its bewildering blend of cultural history, the beliefs of strange religions, and highly technical astronomy may have put off potential readers. And his immense *Pharmacology* remained incomplete and unknown.

I noted above how a westward shift of the intellectual center of the Muslim world affected the writings of Ibn Sina. The changing intellectual geography also shaped Biruni's legacy. Intellectuals in Syria, Egypt, and the Maghreb who knew of Biruni were few and far between. And the few astronomers who emerged in Andalusia after 1100 AD carried on as if Biruni had never lived. Typically, a twelfth-century astronomer from Cordova, Nur ad-Din al-Bitruji, was quite unaware of Biruni's existence.[38] Yet it was Bitruji's very partial revision of Ptolemy's system of the universe, not Biruni's much more thoroughgoing version, that was translated into Latin and spread across Europe in the thirteenth century.

Two writers whose work preserved Biruni's memory were both originally from Central Asia. One was Abdu l-Fadl al-Alami, who in sixteenth-century India served as vizier to the great Akbar, Mughal emperor, general, and patron of culture. Alami not only made extensive use of Biruni's *India* but explained and applied Biruni's method for determining the specific gravity of minerals.[39] Another worthy but undistinguished Central Asian scholar, Mahmud ibn Vali from Bukhara, wrote of Biruni's mineralogy as well as of his several works on astrology.[40]

It took several generations after Biruni's death for anyone to produce original works based on the foundation he had laid. All were distinguished from the rest of the educated populace by their high competence in mathematics and astronomy. The texts that attracted their attention had been passed down through the generations, in the process becoming so familiar to the astronomical and mathematical avant-garde that it was no longer necessary for them to mention the original author by name. This is just as Biruni himself would have preferred, given that he saw mathematics and sciences as an ongoing process based on ideas and data, not personalities.

One of the major scientists who was intimately acquainted with Biruni's research and who devoted serious attention to advancing his agenda was Omar Khayyam, the mathematician and astronomer to whom, as I've noted above, was long attributed also the immensely popular collection of verse, the *Rubaiyat*. Such was his renown as an independent intellectual that poets who composed quatrains that flew in the face of religious orthodoxy or everyday morality appended his name to their works and used it as a cover.[41] This is how Khayyam's *Rubaiyat* arose.

After studies in his native Nishapur, Bukhara, and Samarkand, Khayyam served the Seljuk sultans in Baghdad and Merv before returning home. Besides taking the first steps toward a non-Euclidian geometry and the acceptance of irrational numbers, Khayyam focused his attention on the full range of problems in trigonometry that had preoccupied Biruni, gratefully acknowledging the pioneering work of his predecessor. Inspired by Biruni's book on mineralogy, Khayyam composed a treatise on the specific gravity of minerals and metals.[42] He also drew on Biruni's reports on Indian mathematics for his proposals regarding the extraction of square cubic roots and his development of a general theory of cubic equations. When a sultan assigned him the job of building an observatory, Khayyam found guidance in Biruni's detailed analysis of Khujandi's facility at Rayy. Reverting to Biruni's study of calendrical systems, he also devised so precise a calendar that modern Iran still uses a slightly modified version of it today.

Above and beyond Khayyam's debt to Biruni for advancing the understanding of specific mathematical problems was his overall approach to research, which closely parallels Biruni's. Laying studies by the two of them side by side, one is struck by the similarities, even of their language. Both began by precisely defining the problem and then evaluating relevant prior research. Only then did they set forth their own solutions, to which they appended a final discussion of relevant objections. The writings of both were concise, even telegraphic, and accessible mainly to experts.

Khayyam's final post was as astronomer to the Seljuk Sultan Sanjar, who briefly assembled at the great academic center of Merv in what is now Turkmenistan a band of the most talented scientists of the day. One of them was Abu al-Fath Mansur al-Khazini, known simply as al-Khazini. An emancipated slave who was as self-effacing as he was brilliant, Khazini devoted his life to elaborating Biruni's research on weights and measures and to exploring issues in mathematical astronomy that Biruni had pioneered. Even more than Biruni, Khazini was a mechanic and tinkerer, who laced every section of his *Treatise on Astronomical Wisdom* with plans for research instruments of his own design. For the Sultan's treasury he constructed a balance along the lines of Biruni's, adding to his instrument innovations introduced by a fellow researcher from Herat in Afghanistan. Khazini also advanced Biruni's studies on hydrostatics and metallurgy and reported his findings in a treatise entitled *A Book of the Balance of Wisdom*. Like Biruni, he wrote on diverse calendar systems, determined precisely the longitude and latitude of his hometown, Merv, and wrote highly sophisticated astronomical tables on the basis of his own research. And like Khayyam, Khazini, who died in 1130, advanced Biruni's research agenda while introducing important innovations of his own.[43]

The most significant burst of posthumous interest in Biruni's work took place not in Central Asia but at the city of Maragha in the Azerbaijani region of what today is northwestern Iran. Hulagu Khan, a grandson of Chinggis Khan, had established his capital at Maragha in order to keep watch over his vast empire, which stretched from what is now Turkey to Pakistan. Maragha's location also made it a convenient launching site for invading the north Caucasus and the one land he had failed to conquer, Egypt.

Along the way to Maragha, Hulagu had conquered and despoiled Baghdad, laying waste the city and destroying its priceless library. In spite of perpetrating this crime, Hulagu had a certain sympathy for learning, to the extent that Maragha eventually became a center for the study of Muslim theology or *kalam*. Like most rulers of the day, he yearned to foretell the future, which meant his keenest interest was in astrology and its scientific twin, astronomy.

On his way to Baghdad, Hulagu had crossed the mountains of northern Persia, where he defeated the Ismaili "Twelver" Shiites at their last and seemingly impregnable mountain stronghold, Alamut. At this remote and forbidding spot, he encountered among the defeated defenders a remarkable and entrepreneurial mathematician and astronomer named Nasir al-Din al-Tusi.[44] Curious about science, the Mongol heir got on well with Tusi and was swayed by Tusi's self-serving argument that all existing astronomical tables had to be recalculated so as to reflect the location of Hulagu's new capital. On this slim basis, Hulagu became Tusi's patron. Six years later, in 1259, Tusi inaugurated at Maragha the greatest observatory of the age. With long-term funding from the charitable foundation (*waqf*) Hulagu had set up, the Maragha facility included a large wall quadrant based on Biruni's description of Khujandi's, and also an azimuth quadrant of Tusi's own design. The complex also contained a library that was said to have housed several hundred thousand volumes, a research center, and staff housing.

A Shiite and an Ismaili, Tusi also took a sympathetic interest in Ibn Sina's philosophy and even wrote a treatise in which he clarified unclear points in Ibn Sina's *Logic*.[45] He focuses on the ever-contentious question of Ibn Sina's doctrine on God's most basic attribute, that is, the old issue of essence versus existence. Elsewhere Tusi denigrated Fakkhr al-Din Razi's attack on Ibn Sina as "a calumny."[46] In his forthright defense of Ibn Sina's metaphysics, Tusi went far toward reclaiming his predecessor's legacy from the Asharites and other traditionalist thinkers who had until now monopolized Ibn Sina's heritage. Moreover, as Robert Winowsky has shown, in doing so, he made generous use of Ibn Sina's *The Cure*, which had largely escaped close attention until that time.

In spite of these passionate works in defense of Ibn Sina's metaphysics, Tusi's passion for mathematics and astronomy drew him, above all, to Biruni. Indeed, Tusi was one of the very few later Muslim thinkers with the breadth of knowledge and interest to embrace the work of both Ibn Sina and Biruni. Building on the foundation that Biruni had left, Tusi produced what was to then the most precise chart of the heavens, developed an array of new instruments, and conducted research leading to a new model of lunar motion.

On the basis of these studies, he then propounded his renowned "Tusi Couple." This geometrical technique enabled astronomers to calculate the linear motion of the moon or planets from two circular motions measured by observation. Tusi aimed to replace Ptolemy's model of planetary movement based on irregular motion with precisely calculable circular motion. Biruni had put this problem on the scientific agenda, and it was Tusi who now solved it. Three centuries later Copernicus would employ Tusi's breakthrough concept in his proof for the heliocentric model of the solar system.

Tusi followed Biruni in treating trigonometry as an independent field of enquiry. He capped Biruni's studies with a comprehensive exposition of both plane and spherical trigonometry, for which he again drew heavily on his great predecessor.[47] In the same spirit, Tusi embraced Biruni's research on minerals and added his own method for calculating densities. He also followed Biruni in elaborating new design features for that scientific workhorse, the astrolabe.[48]

Unlike Biruni, Tusi enjoyed the means to assemble a team of talented collaborators. First among them was Fao Munji, a Chinese astronomer whom Hulagu had brought from Beijing. At Maragha, Fao introduced further modifications to the Ptolemaic system. Another critic of Ptolemy's

Almagest was Qutb al-Din al-Shirazi, who advanced his own model of planetary motion. In all, we know of nine Tusi associates at Maragha. They hailed from as far afield as Afghanistan, China, and the Maghreb. All of them worked in Biruni's shadow and all left their mark on science.[49] For all Tusi's personal brilliance, his greatest attainment lies in his creation of a genuine scientific institution at Maragha that offered mutual stimulation and support to its participants. Together with Tusi himself, this team of astronomers and inventors for a time made the Maragha observatory, in historian's Stephen Blake's words, "the most advanced scientific institution in the Eurasian world."[50]

That the Muslim East was otherwise so impoverished in this respect goes far toward explaining the eventual withering of science throughout the region. Tusi's greatest heir, and therefore a direct intellectual descendant of Biruni, was Mīrza Muhammad Taraghai from Samarkand. Mirza Muhammad visited Maragha only once, and then as a boy. Moreover, his visit came 200 years after Tusi's death in 1274, by which time the observatory lay in ruins. Mirza Muhammad's tour guide for what remained was his grandfather, who was none other than the conquering tyrant Timur, or Tamerlane. The boy was deeply impressed by what he saw and vowed to himself that he would someday build his own observatory. To this end, once he was back in Samarkand, young Mirza Muhammad studied under a leading local astronomer, who gave him Biruni's works to analyze and critique. By the time Mirza Muhammad was in his mid-thirties he was finally able to build his dream of a new Maragha on a low stone outcropping outside Samarkand. By then he had become Ulugbeg, "The Great Ruler," Tamerlane's heir, and the supreme leader of all Central Asia.

Ulugbeg's massive circular observatory featured a giant brass mural sextant with a radius of thirty-six meters (110 feet). Its design was a lineal descendant of Khujandi's observatory at Rayy that Biruni had described and analyzed in such detail. Nearby stood a fifty-meter-high (160 feet) gnomon which, again following Biruni's lead, enabled Ulugbeg to determine the length of the year with a precision that surpassed even the calculation of Copernicus a century later. In most respects Ulugbeg's team of astronomers and mathematicians followed Tusi's agenda. Their star tables were as much an advance over Tusi's as Tusi's had been over Biruni's.

Ulugbeg's greatest contribution, however, was less his research than his decision to translate his commitment to science into a network of highly innovative madrassahs.[51] These differed sharply from the narrowly sectarian institutions that Ghazali had established and which were now spread across the region. While respectful of religion, the classics, and art, the curriculum at Ulugbeg's madrassahs gave priority to scientific learning in all its dimensions. For the first time, the values that Biruni had so persistently espoused were translated into institutional and pedagogical terms. In a rare exception to the general neglect of *Masud's Canon*, this demanding work became the core text for students at all of Ulugbeg's madrassahs.

Just as all this innovative activity was at its peak, Ulugbeg's ability to pursue his dual careers as ruler and scientist came to a gruesome end. In 1449 he was murdered by his own deranged son, who had powerful backers among Ulugbeg's enemies in Samarkand. Moving swiftly, they closed down the observatory and all the madrassahs and fired the scientific staff and teachers. This marked the last time a major scientific institution was created in the premodern Muslim world. The fact that it ended so badly signaled to many potential successors throughout the Muslim East that their efforts, too, might end in disaster. Why should they even try?

The most talented member of the staff at the Samarkand observatory was Ulugbeg's deputy, the Persian-born Ala al-Dīn Ali ibn Muhammed, known as Ali Qushji. Following his leader's death in 1449, Qushji fled to Istanbul, newly conquered by the Ottoman Turks. There he briefly managed to set up an observatory of his own until it, too, was closed down at the order of the Ottoman sultan. In spite of setbacks, Qushji managed to write a highly polemical work, *Concerning the Supposed Dependence of Astronomy on Philosophy*, in which he attacked those who dared base their science on religious dogma.[52] In so doing, Qushji further advanced Biruni's lifelong effort to emancipate astronomy from philosophy and metaphysics.

Scholars in many countries have seen Ghazali's screed, *The Incoherence of the Philosophers*, as signifying the waning of the great age of thought in the Muslim world. With such notable exceptions as Tusi, the successors of Biruni and Ibn Sina were for the most part epigones, followers rather than initiators. Other more generous observers date the end of the age of innovation to the murder of Ulugbeg. Still others defend the importance of developments after that date, but they have garnered little support, for the main focus of that later activity was the endless piling up of facts, with only superficial analyses.

Whatever one's position on this question, all sides agree that the debates about Arabic language works on philosophy and science that began in Central

Asia and the Middle East eventually leaped across the Mediterranean to Europe, where they gained a new life in the Latin language. Curiously, these works might also have reached Europe instead via the Byzantine Empire, where there were skilled linguists who translated major important Arabic scientific works into Greek. But so bitter were relations between Orthodox Christian Constantinople and the Catholic West that very few of these translations found their way to western Europe. As a result, the Europeans' main source of Arabic texts was not Christian Byzantium but the Muslim-ruled Maghreb of North Africa. From that source came manuscripts that resulted in Latin translations of some 130 Arabic texts by dozens of authors.[53]

The reception of Arabic language texts in the Latin world was often glacially slow, but in the case of some of Ibn Sina's philosophical writings it took place swiftly. At the same time that leading thinkers in the Arabic-speaking world were butting heads over Ibn Sina's legacy, a parallel storm of debate arose in Europe, thanks to Latin translations. At times, the Europeans' debates replicated the philosophical disagreements that had emerged in the Muslim world. At other times, though, they were shaped by Europeans' effort to adapt Ibn Sina's thought to the doctrines of their Christian faith. They also exuded the distinctive intellectual style that came into being with the rise of scholasticism at universities in Paris, Oxford, and elsewhere.[54]

Translators Latinized Ibn Sina's name as Avicenna and rebranded Ibn Rushd as Averroes. The two were often juxtaposed to one another in the centuries-long disputation that ensued. Also figuring in the polemics were other leading Muslim writers, especially Kindi and Farabi. Looming over the entire European debate was Aristotle, whose works remained the benchmark against which Europeans measured the writings translated from Arabic. It took several centuries, but in Catholic Europe it was the Muslim Ibn Sina–Avicenna who finally edged out Ibn Rushd–Averroes and, at least partially, Aristotle himself, "The First Teacher" from polytheist Greece.[55]

European readers gained early access to Latin versions of three sections of *The Cure* that had been translated in Toledo and Burgos, Spain. These included the texts on metaphysics, natural philosophy, and logic. No one at the time questioned the authenticity of the Arabic texts from which they worked, but recent research has shown that at least one of them was probably the work of Ibn Sina's followers rather than Ibn Sina himself.[56] Eventually the remaining scientific sections were also translated, but none of these elicited much interest.[57] The mathematics section of *The Cure* was never translated into Latin.

Not long after Ibn Rushd's assault on Ibn Sina's metaphysics, the Muslim debate over these two figures was reenacted in Europe, this time casting the purportedly atheist Ibn Rushd–Averroes against the "pious" Avicenna–Ibn Sina.[58] These disputations were suspended when the bishops of Paris twice condemned Ibn Rushd's works, in 1270 and 1277. The change of venue and passage of time could also soften old polarities, to the extent that many Latin-speaking scholars of the thirteenth century presented Ghazali and Ibn Sina virtually as teammates. Some even concluded that Ghazali had been Ibn Sina's student! This was less preposterous than it may seem, for Ghazali himself had acknowledged that there was much common ground between the two of them. More important, because Ghazali had so faithfully summarized Ibn Sina's views in his *Incoherence of the Philosophers*, his text could be considered an authoritative source on his old opponent's positions.

If there were those who saw Ibn Sina as a bearer of wisdom about eternal things, many others saw him as almost a wizard bearing dark tidings, a kind of Dr. Faustus. As the Reformation approached, many European thinkers took umbrage at the important place Ibn Sina accorded in his later writings to angels as mediators between God and man, and especially to Gabriel, the angel of revelation.

The intense interchanges over Ibn Sina's philosophical legacy that took place in Europe between the twelfth and sixteenth centuries have been closely studied by a formidable international corps comprised mainly of philosophers and theologians. Their research shows how an initial and sweeping enthusiasm for Ibn Sina's metaphysics in the thirteenth century gave way later to questions and doubts. These ranged over such diverse issues as the eternity of the world, human psychology, chemical compounds, spontaneous generation, prophesy, and miracles.[59]

Rather than attempt to plumb once more these abstruse polemics, I'll merely take note of two of the many issues on which they focused: the interrelation of God's will and human freedom, and, closely related to this, whether divine will deals only with universals or also with individual phenomena and souls. On both points Ibn Sina had proposed innovative solutions that had affirmed God's omnipotence while at the same time reserving ample space for "particulars" and for human agency.[60]

The principal players in this intense interchange were Franciscan and Dominican friars at the University of Padua in Italy, then at the University of Paris, and finally at Oxford and the higher school at the Cathedral of Santa Sabina in Rome. The process was launched by the strong-willed William of

Auvergne, who maneuvered to get himself appointed Bishop of Paris in 1227 and then backed the reforming leadership at the University with such vigor that he provoked a student uprising. Amid these dramas, the busy prelate managed also to turn out commentaries on nearly all of Aristotle's works (which he knew mainly from Latin translations of Arabic translations), and finally plunged directly into the study of Ibn Sina and Aristotle's other heirs in the Muslim world.

One of William's prize young professors at Paris was a young Bavarian named Albert, later known to the world as Albertus Magnus. A Dominican friar and ardent student of Aristotle, Albert wrote thirteen treatises on "The Philosopher," which led him to the careful study of both Ibn Sina and Ibn Rushd. By bringing the pair to the fore, he launched a century-long debate between partisans of Ibn Rushd, who was seen as Aristotle's most loyal champion, and Ibn Sina, who was viewed as more independent-minded and more pious.

The rising star in Albert's classes, in turn, was a well-born fellow Dominican from Italy, Thomas Aquinas. Incarcerated by his family for wanting to join the Dominicans, Thomas eventually found his way to Paris and then to Rome where, between 1265 and 1273, he composed his great but uncompleted monument of Western thought, the *Summa Theologiae*. To write this immense work, Thomas followed directly in Ibn Sina's footsteps. Like Ibn Sina, he had examined Aristotle's works and even produced twelve studies on his metaphysics, astronomy, meteorology, and the soul. These were enriched by material drawn from Ibn Sina's writings on the same subjects, which he explicitly cited ten times and paraphrased in many other places.[61] Indeed, parts of Thomas's *Summa* were nothing less than redrafted and transformed chunks of *The Cure*, now restated in Christian terms.

There were important points on which Aquinas and Ibn Sina parted company.[62] Yet in his *Summa*, Aquinas presented an account of the eternity-creation issue as it had been framed in the metaphysical section of Ibn Sina's *The Cure*.[63] Aquinas, however, argued that creation had been an act of volition on God's part, whereas Ibn Sina had posited that it derived inevitably from God's very nature.[64] Like Ibn Sina, Aquinas's frame of reference was at once utterly rational and profoundly religious. His beginning point was Ibn Sina's assertion that metaphysics could not prove God's existence because no science can establish the existence of its own subject. No wonder, then, that the third of Thomas's several arguments for the existence of God was largely a restatement of Ibn Sina's ontological argument.

Unlike his predecessors in Paris, Thomas was no fan of Ibn Rushd, but this did not save him from the charge of "Averroeism." For this sin he was twice suspended from the office of regent master or rector of the University of Paris, and twice had to defend himself by writing tracts attacking Ibn Rushd, whom he charged with following Aristotle in asserting the eternity of the world and in rejecting the eternity of the soul.[65] On both points and many others besides, Thomas girded himself with arguments drawn from Ibn Sina. Thanks largely to Aquinas, Ibn Sina's star, which had otherwise been eclipsed by Aristotle, rose again in the skies of Europe.

We might compare Thomas's great project with the writings of Muslim theologians and practitioners of *kalam*, the so-called *mutakallimun*. Two points stand out. First, the Muslim practitioners of *kalam* opposed Aristotle but accepted his teachings to the extent they had been acceptably adapted by Ibn Sina. Similarly, Christian scholastics in Europe used Ibn Sina to merge Aristotelianism with Christian theology.[66] Second, for all their precision, the Muslim theologians never succeeded in providing for Islam what Aquinas did for Christianity. Shiites came closer than the Sunnis, many of whom persisted in holding Ibn Sina at arm's length. Neither succeeded in endowing their faith with its own grand synthesis incorporating what they found valid in Ibn Sina and other thinkers and rejecting the rest. This said, what the church fathers and Muslim practitioners of *kalam* had in common was to have affirmed God's Creation and centrality in human affairs and the eternity of the soul, while at the same time reserving a meaningful sphere for human volition and responsibility.

Most modern readers would gasp at Thomas Aquinas's boast that he wrote his *Summa* "in a way that is fitting to the instruction of beginners." Ibn Sina had made no such claims. His writing was generally clear and accessible, but he cast his later works in ever-more abstruse language and then announced that he intended them only for the initiated few. One of those few was John Duns Scotus, a brilliant Scotsman from Oxford who taught at Paris during the decades after Aquinas departed for Rome. Duns Scotus's exposition on the existence of God made Aquinas's seem simple and accessible by comparison but he, too, had thoroughly mined the works of Ibn Sina.[67] Meanwhile, accessible or not, many passages of Thomas's *Summa* became the subject of heated debate that continued down to Martin Luther and beyond. It was through such indirect channels that an important part of Ibn Sina's philosophical legacy was passed to the modern world and even today stands as a monument to human reason, human freedom, and human responsibility before God.

So different were the Western receptions of Ibn Sina's metaphysics and the way Europeans received his *Canon of Medicine* that one might have thought they were the work of different authors. Whereas his metaphysical texts reached Latin readers one-by-one over an extended period,[68] a Latin version of much of the *Canon* arrived early, the work of a single translator. And where the philosophical works were studied only by erudite churchmen, the *Canon* immediately found a large audience among Europe's medical experts and even among the literate public.

Shortly after Ibn Sina died, a North African Christian known as Constantine Africanus pioneered the translation of Arabic medical documents into Latin. With institutional support from what became Europe's first medical school, at Salerno in Italy, and also from the Catholic Church, Constantine issued translations of major sections of Ibn Sina's *Canon*, as well as selections from Hippocrates, Galen, and Razi. Sometime later, Gerard de Sabloneta,[69] laboring in Palermo at the court of the erudite Holy Roman Emperor, Frederick II, translated most of the remaining sections of the *Canon*, and also works by Ibn Sina's predecessor, Razi. Other translations followed, the best of them by Jewish scholars who were fluent in both Arabic and Latin, as well as Hebrew.[70] Thanks to this, by the time the full text of the *Canon of Medicine* appeared in Europe, it was immediately juxtaposed not only to the ancient Greek doctors but also to Razi, whom Ibn Sina had so arrogantly dismissed during his exchange with Biruni. The battle was on.

The main setting of this centuries-long feud were the new medical schools that cropped up in Italy and France during the thirteenth century, the oldest of them being at Padua and Montpelier. Because the learned doctors at these institutions all needed authoritative and accessible texts for teaching, there was a continuing demand for Latin translations of the *Canon*.

Over the several centuries that framed the rise of European medicine, Ibn Sina's *Canon* was everywhere the most widely cited sourcebook. Its rational organization, clear exposition, and digestible length assured its use as the main teaching tool over more than half a millennium. Scholastic doctors embraced the theoretical first volume, hands-on practitioners concentrated their attention on volumes three and four, while pharmacists took up volumes two and five. Neither group knew anything about Ibn Sina himself, who was variously thought to have known St. Augustine and to have been a native of Cordoba.

The widespread use of the *Canon of Medicine* for teaching earned its author an honored place in European culture. Dante's *Divine Comedy*, for example, lists Avicenna/Ibn Sina, along with Plato, Socrates, and Aristotle, as residing in Limbo, saved from eternal damnation by their status as "virtuous pagans." In the field of medicine, Dante places him squarely between Hippocrates and Galen. In far-off England, the narrator in the Prologue of Geoffrey Chaucer's *Canterbury Tales* recalls a meeting with a "Doctour of Phisyk" who, besides having mastered the four humors:

> Well knew he the old Esculapius
> And Deyscorides, and eek Rufus,
> Old Ypocras. Haly, and Galyen,
> Serapion, Razis, and Avycen.[71]

Inevitably, Ibn Sina had his critics among Europe's medical specialists. It was his posthumous fate again to be paired with Razi and, just as often, with his later critic, Ibn Rushd. Far more serious was the rising competition between the *Canon* and the medical writings of Aristotle, Dioscorides, and Galen, which were gradually becoming available in Latin translations. Whether because of the sheer length of Galen's encyclopedic work on medicine or because he, unlike Ibn Sina, was one of the honored ancients, it was Galen who most often triumphed in these sweepstakes. Prejudice also came into play. Typically, the thirteenth-century doctor and astrologer Arnold of Villanova, who left no evidence of having so much as glanced at the *Canon*, dismissed Ibn Sina as "a professional scribbler who stupefied European physicians by his misinterpretation of Galen."[72] Arnold, we should note, also predicted that the world would end in 1378.

Far more numerous than such dyspeptic reviews were the many grateful readers who praised the *Canon of Medicine* as a priceless resource in its own right but also for being a window to all the wisdom contained in those ancient texts that had yet to be translated into Latin. It is no exaggeration to say that the translated works of Ibn Sina were principally responsible for a medical renaissance that preceded the Renaissance, an era when Arabic texts served as surrogates for the books by ancient writers that had yet to appear in Latin.

The momentous rise of movable type printing transformed this situation overnight. Suddenly full Latin translations of the works of Galen, Dioscorides, Hippocrates, and Aristotle became widely available in printed editions. Why study Ibn Sina when one could read Galen himself? Holding forth at Padua in the sixteenth century, Professor Gianbattista Da Monte asked his students why they would want to eat acorns when bread was available?[73] The snide Da Monte went on to opine that "I don't think any of you . . . can say he has learned anything from [Ibn Sina]." In the minds of some, Ibn Sina was reduced to the status of a mere transmitter and not a particularly good one at that. Da Monte was among many European humanists who also criticized what they considered their colleagues' overdependence on Muslim writers in general.

In spite of these concerns, demand for the *Canon of Medicine* continued to soar and zealous printers continued to satisfy it. One scholar, Nancy G. Siraisi, records sixty European printed editions of all or parts of the *Canon* that flowed from the presses between the years 1500 and 1674, as well as a full printed edition of the Arabic original, which was issued by a Venetian publisher in an astounding print run of 1,750 copies.[74]

As these many editions of the *Canon* flooded the market, critics began chipping away at Ibn Sina's edifice. None of these were more colorful than Theophrastus von Hohenheim, the Swiss physician, alchemist, and bumptious critic of elitist learning known as Paracelsus (1493–1541). Claiming he wanted an entirely new pharmacopeia, Paracelsus stunned his students at University of Basel in 1527 by publicly burning Ibn Sina's *Canon*, along with works by Galen.[75]

By the seventeenth century, fresh discoveries in physiology, anatomy, and surgery gradually rendered the *Canon* obsolete. Evidence for this is the shift of those writings about the *Canon* from medical practitioners to students of language and culture. These new enthusiasts were based not in Italy but at Leiden in Holland. Nonetheless, the *Canon* remained in the medical curriculum for at least another century. In the seventeenth century, John Harvey, who discovered the circulation of blood, advised a student to "goe to the fountain head, and read Aristotle, Cicero, and Avicenna." As to those whom he called "neoteriques" [i.e., moderniziers], they were, in Harvey's view, mere "shitt-breeches."[76] Following Harvey's advice, the *Canon of Medicine* and its Aristotelian doctrine of the humors continued to figure prominently in European medicine until germ theory overtook it in the late nineteenth century—eight centuries after Ibn Sina.

Where were the works of Biruni during the years when Europeans were gaining access to the translated works of Ibn Sina? Sadly, nowhere to be seen. To be sure, his *India* had been known and consulted at the court of the

Norman king Roger II in Sicily, but that had been back in the twelfth century.[77] A century later, when the great thirteenth-century English polymath Roger Bacon began mining Arab sources for his studies on physics, he had at hand the work of Ibn Sina, Kindi, and Farabi, but not of Biruni.[78] Diligent research might still turn up passing mentions of Biruni in other writings from medieval and early modern Europe, but the trail is faint and not likely to grow much stronger. Suffice it to say that not a single text by Biruni was available in twelfth-century Toledo, the fountainhead of the translation movement, and none of his works were rendered into either Hebrew or Latin by the tireless band of translators working there.[79]

Nor did this situation change for the better thereafter. George Saliba, author of an authoritative analysis of *Islamic Science and the Making of the European Renaissance*, mentions Biruni only three times and never in connection with mathematics, astronomy, geodesy, or mineralogy. Poor Biruni was not alone. Neither Omar Khayyam nor Khazini earned a mention, while Ulugbeg rated only three references. This was not due to negligence on Saliba's part but because Biruni and his heirs were all but unknown in the Maghreb, which meant that their books were not among those shipped across the Straits of Gibraltar to Andalusia or from other North African ports directly to Christian Europe. One can only imagine what might have happened had it been otherwise. Seyyed Hosein Nasr, with his deep knowledge of both Arabic and Latin scientific literature, may not have exaggerated when he suggested that had Biruni's grand *Masud's Canon* been translated into Latin, it would have become as famous in Europe as Ibn Sina's *Canon of Medicine*.[80]

The works of many mathematicians and astronomers from the Muslim world who came after Biruni were faithfully translated into Latin and figured prominently in European discourse on astronomy and mathematics during both the late Middle Ages and the Renaissance. However, most of these writers were hardworking followers rather than leaders, elaborators rather than pacesetters. Meanwhile, the earlier generations of scientific innovators from Central Asia and the Middle East, Biruni among them, remained unheralded or unknown.

Fortunately, a couple of those whose works found their way into Latin were major figures in their own right, and the most notable among them were conscious heirs of Biruni. Consequently, it was the works of these heirs of Biruni, rather than those of Biruni himself, that transmitted at least some of Biruni's legacy to Europe.

First among this small group was Nasir al-Din Tusi and members of the remarkable team that he assembled in Maragha. All had studied Biruni's legacy and added to it. Selected works by Tusi himself were translated, as were studies by three of his students and successors. While Tusi's text on his seminal important "Tusi Couple" never appeared in Latin, knowledge of the concept circulated widely, eventually reaching Mikolaj Kopernik at the castle of Frombork on the distant Baltic coast.[81]

Recent research has turned up convincing evidence that Kopernik, known to history as Copernicus, had direct knowledge of the Tusi Couple and employed it in his revolutionary account of celestial motion, *On the Revolutions of the Celestial Spheres*.[82] The mathematician Otto Neugebauer proved that Copernicus borrowed directly from Tusi but failed to acknowledge his debt. As evidence, Neugebauer showed that the specific letters Copernicus used to designate features on his technical charts were the same ones Tusi had employed for his diagrams.[83]

While this curious point does not pertain directly to Biruni, it illustrates the difficulty of tracing the indistinct path of unattributed ideas through time. The fact that it turns on such minutiae helps explain the extreme difficulty in pinpointing Biruni's impact. So much of Biruni's oeuvre has been lost. Most of those works that survived left few traces. As is common in science, later Muslim astronomers and mathematicians rarely bothered to note the source of every concept they employed. They in turn passed this silence on to their successors in Europe. Due to this process, it would take another half millennium before Biruni's achievements came to be widely known and appreciated.

The change in Biruni's fate took place in 1845, the year a Parisian scholar named M. Rainauld included several brief passages from *India* in his *Fragments arabes et persans inedite relatifs a l'Inde*. Then in 1866 a Russian orientalist and diplomat, Nicolas de Khanekov, issued a plea for attention to Biruni.[84] This inspired Eduard Sachau to publish the Arabic text of *India* in 1910, as well as his own German and English translations. Sachau then issued editions of *The Chronology of Ancient Nations* in the same three languages. This was possible only because copies of the manuscripts had recently been discovered in archives in Turkey and Europe. Almost nothing was known of Biruni's life until Sachau issued a brief biography as a foreword to his *Alberuni's India*.

Sachau's landmark editions triggered a boom in Biruni studies led by another prolific German scholar, Eilhard Wiedemann from Leipzig. Thanks to

Wiedemann, Europe gained its first inkling of Biruni's findings on the size of the earth, trigonometry, mathematics, geodesy, meteorology, and the construction of astrolabes. Thanks also to Wiedemann, material drawn from *Masud's Canon* first came to light. Other scholars in Germany, Italy, France, Belgium, and Iran quickly climbed aboard Wiedemann's bandwagon.

Beginning in the 1930s, the center of research on Biruni shifted to the Soviet Union, where a group of Arabists in Tashkent, Dushanbe, Leningrad, and Moscow translated, edited, analyzed, and published all of Biruni's known works. These dedicated scholars brought to their task not only a thorough command of medieval Arabic but also a deep knowledge of mathematics and of the other branches of science in which Biruni labored. During the same decades, other Soviet historians carried out groundbreaking research on the social and cultural milieu in which Biruni and Ibn Sina lived and worked.

Many of these scholars were Jews who had taken refuge from Stalin's terror by fleeing into the safe world of fundamental research. Russia's colonial expansion into Central Asia had brought the birthplaces of Biruni and Ibn Sina within the boundaries of the tsarist empire and its heir, the USSR. Because of this, the study of the history and culture of the region became a safe refuge for scholars working in Russia and Central Asia itself. It is mainly through their dedication that Biruni's central role in the history of science came fully to light.

As I noted in the first chapter, even today the works of these scholars in the Soviet Union remain largely unknown in the West. The reason for this is simple: they wrote mainly in Russian, and few Western scholars knew that language. As a result, few Western scholars tapped, or even acknowledged, the vast fund of new knowledge about Biruni and his world issued in Russian. Still less did they avail themselves of research published in Uzbek, Tajik, or Farsi.

The linguistic divide between Russia and the West faced in both directions, however, and coincided with an intellectual divide for which the Soviet government was responsible. For in the same years in which the Russians were issuing their translations and startling new studies of Biruni, study of the history of science underwent a quantitative and qualitative boom in Europe and America. This innovative research in many fields inspired Western thinkers to reassess the very process by which learning advances. Their efforts were known in the USSR, but few Soviet scholars dared incorporate them in their published studies.

The Viennese-born Karl Popper, who fled Nazi Austria and eventually settled in London, rejected the entire tradition that held that science advances through a steady and cumulative process of induction. Instead, he proposed in *The Logic of Scientific Discovery* that science advances through bold *Conjectures and Refutations*, to cite the title of another of his studies.[85] He added an epigraph drawn from the German poet Novalis that declared, "Theories are nets: only he who casts them will catch." Working scientists welcomed this salute to their creative imaginations, but historians of science were skeptical.

Biruni had two methods of work, neither of which conformed to Popper's schema. One was to identify a problem like the earth's diameter and then devise methods for solving it. The other was to test some existing hypothesis against data he himself had gathered. He would then either accept, modify, or reject the hypothesis. This is how he proceeded on the question of heliocentrism versus geocentricism. It bears repeating that Biruni accepted the heliocentric hypothesis proposed by his friend al-Sijzi on the grounds that it made mathematical sense. But his acceptance had been conditional. Instead of embracing the heliocentric hypothesis solely on mathematical grounds, he had insisted that it had also to be verified through observation. This process was less poetic than Popper's bold leaps of conjecture, but far more rigorous.

Further developments in twentieth-century Europe and America helped rescue Biruni from oblivion. First, between 1927 and 1948, George Sarton published his epochal *Introduction to the History of Science*, a massive work that not only established that subject as an academic discipline but focused fresh attention on the works of Biruni, Khayyam, and other medieval Eastern scientists.[86] Sarton was a Belgium-born chemist who emigrated to America in 1915. His decision to study Arabic sources in the original launched what became a widespread approach. By the end of the twentieth century, members of a new generation of European and American scholars were bringing a high level of skill to the study of Biruni's most abstruse mathematical and astronomical works, and also of Ibn Sina's most impenetrable philosophical writings. Thanks to them, the heritage of both thinkers is slowly being reintegrated with the mainstream of world thought. Symbolizing the renewed interest in their work globally were the celebrations of the thousandth anniversary of the births of Biruni and Ibn Sina in both India and Pakistan.

19

Biruni and Ibn Sina, a Millennium On

How we view the world is in constant flux. Sometimes our perspective shifts when we find fault with things that we previously considered certain. At other times new ideas cause our outlook to change. And then there is the relentless passage of time, which causes our perspective to alter in ways of which we ourselves are usually unaware.

Tracing how the world viewed Biruni and Ibn Sina over the centuries makes it clear that all these processes were hard at work. Broadly speaking, Ibn Sina's star shone bright for most of that period, then waned in recent times. This stems from the rise of modern medicine and science, the spread of secularism in the West, and a surge of religious traditionalism in the Muslim world. Biruni, after having been neglected for half a millennium, has only recently come into his own, though mainly among specialists. However, in a millennial reversal, both men's stars are once more rising.

The Taliban tried to destroy Biruni's tomb in Ghazni in May 2019. However, a crater on the far side of the moon bears his name, as does an asteroid, "9936-Al-Biruni," and also a university in Istanbul and other learned institutions worldwide. Ibn Sina's gleaming mausoleum dominates a plaza in Hamidan, Iran, and features a pencil-like tower patterned, ironically, after the tomb of Qabus, the ruler to whom Ibn Sina turned for help but who died before providing any. More than a dozen hospitals and medical schools worldwide bear Ibn Sina's name. They also take a joint bow at the United Nations' office in Vienna. At the center of the main courtyard stands the "Scholars' Pavilion," which features large modernistic statues of both Biruni and Ibn Sina, and also of Razi, and Omar Khayyam.

With the passage of time, our two subjects have emerged today as avatars of intellect, remembered only vaguely but blending together as the greatest minds of their region and era. But if we view them on the basis of what we now know of their lives and work, a more complex picture emerges, one that brings each one individually into sharper focus.

After his early encounter with public life, Biruni avoided it. Shortly after arriving in Ghazni, he wrote, "Here, if I can control myself, I will work [only] on that which is still in my soul, and that is [astronomical] observation and scientific projects."[1] He succeeded at this, remaining immersed thereafter in solitary research and writing. In arguments he was relentless but maintained no grudges and hence had no serious enemies. To the very end he was a loner, a soloist, with few correspondents, fewer friends, and no students to carry on his work after he was gone.

Ibn Sina was born to socialize or, more precisely, to exhibit his many talents in social settings. His long-suffering assistant, Juzjani, wrote about organizing soirees at which earnest discussions with students were followed by drinking and carousing with slave concubines. Juzjani also claimed that Ibn Sina's hyperactive sex life hastened his death. However, one scholar has now suggested that this passage was inserted into Juzjani's text by later critics.[2] Whatever the case, Ibn Sina's boundless ambition and domineering personality left him with few friends and many enemies. At the same time, his manifest skills and ardent temperament also attracted appreciative patrons and admirers.

In intellectual debates, Biruni patiently dissected arguments he considered flawed and, in most cases, treated the authors with respect. But for those who seemed to be willfully ignoring the dictates of reason he had an inexhaustible fund of invective. He did not differentiate between fools who were living or long dead, but he did not nurture grudges. Most contemporaries considered him to be modest and earnest to a fault.

Ibn Sina bowed to no one in his mastery of pungent invective. He was also a self-promoter who bragged about his youthful triumphs over one of the learned scholars his father had hired to teach him—and then went on to pilfer that same scholar's work for his own writings.[3] Blithely ignoring those who are now known to have been his teachers in medicine, he claimed to have quickly mastered that field on his own, to the point that even as a teenager "distinguished physicians" came to watch as he opened up what he termed "indescribable possibilities of therapy."[4] A distinguished modern scholar has rushed to Ibn Sina's defense. Focusing on the part of his autobiography that Ibn Sina himself dictated, this apologist claimed that what strikes most readers as "the self-congratulatory bombast of a megalomaniac"[5] was in fact his systematic effort to set forth a theory of knowledge and to demonstrate how he himself had acquired it. One can only smile at such loyalty.

After his brief stint as head of foreign affairs for his native land, Biruni foreswore public service and avoided official duties. Ibn Sina, by contrast, after backing in to his first assignment as a prime minister or vizier, gladly continued in that line of work through the rest of his life. And why not? He was obviously good at it and relished the platform and benefits it afforded him. Thus, Ibn Sina immersed himself in the life of every society in which he lived, while Biruni, after tasting public service and the worldly life, retreated to his field research, his scientific instruments, and his study.

Early in life both thinkers identified a small number of analytic problems and focused on them throughout their careers. However, Biruni added to his list throughout his life, pursuing new topics as they came to his attention and as he discovered in them a fresh challenge. In this sense he was an opportunist. Ibn Sina, too, focused on a short list of major issues but expanded their number only when he came to understand how each new issue bore on his original concerns. As a result, his focus was more specific than Biruni's, and his oeuvre as a whole far more integrated.

One of the sharpest contrasts between them is reflected in their use of language. Biruni was a mediocre writer whose main interest was in getting his research findings down on paper. His *Chronology of Ancient Nations*, for example, forces the reader to shift frenetically between historical, theological, mathematical, and statistical modes of analysis. Biruni was aware of this problem and even apologetic about it, explaining that "the wish to embrace this whole field compels me to cause trouble both to myself and to the reader."[6] Half a millennium later Galileo, defending himself against the same criticism, wrote, "I do not regard it as a fault to talk about many diverse things, even in those treatises which have only a single topic."[7] Only in his *India* and his penultimate work on mineralogy did Biruni write as if he wanted to reach a non-specialized audience.

Ibn Sina's writings, on the other hand, were neatly organized, clear, and accessible. If his works on logic and metaphysics seem dense and off-putting, this is because he used a conceptual discourse that is familiar today only to specialists. That Ibn Sina dictated most of his works contributed to their clarity, as did his practice of vetting them orally before audiences of students and critics. For all his professional difficulties, Ibn Sina was fortunate to have as readers an immediate circle of patrons, colleagues, and students who welcomed whatever he wrote. Only during his last decades did he encounter sharp critics, to whom he responded by declaring that his writings were not for the ignorant and other closed-minded "shit-eaters."

Biruni's interactions with readers were rare or non-existent. Even had he been capable of writing in an accessible vein, he spent the second half of his writing life under the direct gaze of an ultra-orthodox, narrow-minded, and suspicious patron, Mahmud of Ghazni. The last thing Biruni would have wanted was for Mahmud and most members of his circle actually to read his work. Like many writers in repressive societies today, he was content to write "for the drawer."

At the heart of the divide between Biruni and Ibn Sina lies their very different methods of exploration. Each was convinced that he had found the key to knowledge. Ibn Sina's emphasis on logic and the syllogism gave all of his writings, including some of his medical works, an abstract and theoretical quality. This was their fundamental strength. We have already noted his boast to have "shown by pure theory the universal traits of the ailments of the human body and the causes which produce them." He went on to speak of specifics, but always, or so he thought, in the context of abstract theory. At the end of the day Ibn Sina was less interested in specifics than in what he called the "first principles" of all the knowledge, "access to which can be gained only through the science [of metaphysics]."[8]

How profoundly different is this from Biruni. In a process diametrically opposite to Ibn Sina's, he reveled in the specific and moved from the specific to the general. As he put it in his *Chronology of Ancient Nations*: "Our duty is to proceed from what is near to the more distant, from that which is known to that which is less known, and to gather the traditions from those who have reported them, to correct them as much as possible, and to leave the rest as it is, in order to make our work help him who seeks truth and loves wisdom in making independent researches on other subjects."[9]

Biruni was convinced that quantitative measures were the most reliable avenue to truth. "Counting," he wrote, "is innate to man."[10] As to geometry, he called it "the science of dimensions and quantitative relations as they relate to each other." "Thanks to [geometry]," he proclaimed, "the study of numbers is transformed from the particular to the general and the study of the sphere from guesses and hypotheses to Truth."[11] Counting is innate to man because numbers are innate to nature. Who but Biruni would notice that the petals of many flowers form a circle of isosceles triangles, their number always being 3, 4, 5, 6, or 18 but almost never 7 or 9.[12] Such was the mentality that enabled Biruni to achieve his breakthroughs in mathematics, a landmark achievement whose full extent is only now being appreciated.

While suspicious of all windy theorizing, Biruni nonetheless recognized that truth could be attained by various means. Among them he included the drawing of precise comparisons. "The measure of a thing," he wrote, "becomes known by its being compared with another thing which belongs to the same species and is assumed as a unit by general consent."[13] Such a frame of mind left Biruni comfortable with the attainment of knowledge that is solid but partial. He was convinced that science is not a fixed corpus (or canon) but a process of discovery extending from the past indefinitely into the future. Biruni's view of the world was open-ended and constantly evolving. Also, experience had taught him that observations of nature needed to be repeated again and again to assure accuracy.[14] He revisited three times the important body of data he had collected at Nandana to measure the earth.[15] Recognizing the inadequacy of his own instrumentation, he rued that "whole generations wouldn't suffice to measure precisely the length of the year.[16] This cast of mind also led him to suggest paths for future researchers and to spell out the instruments and methods they would need to pursue these leads.

Ibn Sina had a passion for certainty. Tortured by his own doubts even on matters he had previously considered settled, he believed that his mission as a thinker was to resolve questions, not leave them open for future researchers to address. His approach was more integrative than analytic, which enabled him to discern relationships between seemingly disparate phenomena and to build whole systems based on them. It was these systems rather than the specifics they embraced that constitute his chief intellectual legacy. From first to last, the binding force that held them together was logic. Biruni, too, sought certainty but was willing to admit when he couldn't judge between two hypotheses. He, too, sought to uncover relationships between disparate phenomena, but in contrast to Ibn Sina, his principal tool for doing so was mathematics. His temperament lacked Ibn Sina's passionate unease and enabled him, when necessary, even to admit that "I don't know." Ibn Sina would have considered such a conclusion unthinkable.

All of this helps explain the huge differences between Ibn Sina's two great syntheses, the *Canon of Medicine* and *The Cure*, and Biruni's *Masud's Canon* and his *Determination of the Coordinates of . . . Cities*. Ibn Sina offered his works as closed systems, whole and complete, while Biruni issued his landmark studies as reports on an unending process. Nowhere in Ibn Sina's vast writings can one find any statement comparable to Biruni's oft-repeated remark that what is known today is insignificant compared with all that is knowable, and that everything we know today is but partial and unclear.

For half a millennium, thinkers throughout the Muslim, Christian, and Jewish worlds were captivated by the wholeness and completeness of Ibn Sina's *Canon* and *The Cure*. They stood in awe of his claim to have united all knowledge under an all-embracing theory, and were consoled by the possibility that here, finally, all things knowable had been gathered under a single orderly system. They might vehemently reject his formulations on specific points and instead embrace those of Ibn Rushd or Ibn Sina's Christian critics. But for centuries they all followed Ibn Sina in believing that the core task of human thought was to achieve the kind of comprehensiveness that he had sought in his greatest works.

This process assured that Ibn Sina's thought, in its original form or as recast by his successors, would become deeply embedded in all three of the so-called Religions of the Book. A similar process took place with respect to the *Canon of Medicine*. Down practically to the discovery of the circulation of blood in the seventeenth century, the *Canon* reigned supreme and continued to dominate medical pedagogy in the East and West for another century.

Biruni never had such good fortune. Because he presented all his findings as open-ended hypotheses, the few of his writings that survived stimulated further research that built on Biruni's achievement and advanced beyond it. It was this open-ended quality of the best science that led Isaac Newton to say that he was merely "standing on the shoulders of giants." By contrast, the comprehensive but closed-ended quality of Ibn Sina's syntheses shut as many doors as they opened.

The French scholar Roger Arnaldez, in a brilliant comparison of the two thinkers, argues that Ibn Sina was the more speculative and systematic, gladly embracing practical evidence but only to the extent that it related to the truths of logic and metaphysics. At bottom, Arnaldez concluded, Ibn Sina was a Neo-Platonist. Biruni, by contrast, engaged passionately with each brute fact in its concrete singularity. Only on this basis, he believed, could one attain verifiable truths. Arnaldez concluded that Biruni was therefore the epitome of the anti-Platonist.[17]

Another way of expressing the difference would be to name Biruni the positivist and Ibn Sina, in spite of his tidy system of logic, more the idealist. As a positivist, Biruni turned his back on metaphysical explanations and embraced only what he could confirm by observation, computation, or experimentation. Ibn Sina also had phenomenal powers of observation. But from his youngest days his mind inclined toward the general rather than the specific, the abstract but logically verifiable rather than the concrete and quantifiable.

Ibn Sina and Biruni may have both striven for unity, but their paths for achieving it differed radically. Ibn Sina, proceeding from the general to the specific, stumbled over unexplained differences, while Biruni had no difficulty in acknowledging them and found in them a challenge. Where Ibn Sina tended to brush aside the diversity to which geography, culture, and the passage of time give rise, Biruni reveled in it and devised innovative methods for studying it. More than anyone before him, he also grasped the profound differences between high and popular cultures and sought the factors that shape such differences.

Stated differently, Ibn Sina gloried in the sublime unity of Creation, while Biruni, while also conceiving Creation as unified and complete, reveled in its endless diversity. This opened his mind to explorations that vastly expanded the borders of the known world. Such reasoning enabled him even to hypothesize the existence of unknown but inhabitable continents where North and South America were later discovered.

حبيب

Having dwelled on the differences between our two thinkers, we should also ask whether those differences ever led to similar ends. A definitive answer to this question would require exploring the daunting number of fields in which Ibn Sani and Biruni both worked, including geology, paleontology, mineralogy, geometry, and pharmacopoeia.

Short of this, however, we know that they had a great deal in common. They were both Central Asians and contemporaries, born under what was arguably the world's most intellectually advanced regime at the time, the Samani empire. As such, they both spoke Persianate languages or dialects of Persian and expected to make their way in the sophisticated Samani centers of learning. This did not happen, for just as they entered manhood, the last Samani rulers were swept from power. This geopolitical event condemned both of these rising geniuses to lives of wandering and improvisation.

Born to privilege, they received private instruction from the most knowledgeable teachers available. They received orthodox training on the *Quran*. By their time, readers of Arabic also had access to a wealth of translated works of ancient Greek philosophers and scientists. This prompted them not only to master what the ancient Greeks had to say but also to delve into the structure of their arguments in order to identify flaws and correct them. Not until the European Renaissance did anyone in the West subject the classical heritage to such rigorous scrutiny.

They pursued their goals through thick and thin. Neither enjoyed the collegial support that Newton found in the Royal Society. Indeed, the absence of institutions where thinkers like Ibn Sina and Biruni could be encouraged and challenged is a major failure of early Muslim intellectual life and a cause of its eventual decline. Their persistence is all the more notable in that both men suffered from the vengeful avarice of their lifelong common enemy, Mahmud of Ghazni. It was because he judged Ibn Sina and Biruni to be the two greatest living geniuses that Mahmud ordered them both to his court in Afghanistan. Mahmud succeeded in snaring Biruni, of course; Ibn Sina managed just barely to escape. At no point did either Biruni or Ibn Sina enjoy anything approaching normal support for their work. What a contrast with the many modern scientists who enjoy tenured research posts and secure funding. Biruni and Ibn Sina had neither; over the course of his career Ibn Sina labored under seven fickle rulers and Biruni under six. Yet they carried on.

Biruni and Ibn Sina were what we now call workaholics. Biruni is known to have worked every day of the year, taking breaks only for the winter and summer solstices. Ibn Sina's lifestyle was expansive, yet he never paused in his dictating. For both men this was possible because neither married and neither had a family. Biruni declared that "my books are my children."[18]

That these innovators were extremely competitive goes without saying. This became evident during their choleric exchange of letters and then continued through their dueling *Canons* and down to their final, if unacknowledged, clash over the nature of medicinal plants. It was manifest in Ibn Sina's rare but pointed ventures into mathematics and in Biruni's equally rare but well-informed venture into medical matters.

Finally, as is inevitable in science, Ibn Sina and Biruni equally made serious mistakes in their work. Later astronomers faulted Biruni for failing to understand the cause of the steady decline of the obliquity of the sun's ecliptic that he himself had measured so precisely. Critics also took him to task for errors in computing. As to Ibn Sina, later scientists in the Middle East and Europe pointed out the instances in which loyalty to his ancient mentors led him into error. Ferreting out flaws in the *Canon of Medicine* became a cottage industry.

At this point we could tally up their commonalities and their differences. But there remain two key areas on which their thought should be evaluated both individually and collectively, two touchstones that crystallize their outlooks on their world: one is their views on the good society; the second concerns religious faith.

To start with politics and society, the challenge is that neither developed his views in great depth. Ibn Sina said that he intended to write a book on political philosophy while Biruni claimed to have similar plans for a book on ethics. Neither book was ever written. In spite of this, numerous passages provide revealing insights on their political philosophies.[19] Their positions reveal serious differences between them but also striking similarities.

Ibn Sina draws on Plato's *Republic*, later writings of the Neoplatonists, on Farabi, and on the Baghdad philosopher Kindi to set forth his morality-based concept of the good society or, as he put it, the good city.[20] At the core of his concept stands his conviction that the goal of every human being is to live the contemplative life and to fulfill the immaterial and unworldly aspirations that are its essence. With Plato, he affirms, in the words of Jon McGinnis, that "one lives the virtuous or moderate life as a practice for death and dying, where 'death' is understood as the separation of the soul from the body."[21]

Ibn Sina holds that the growth of specialization meant that early humans had to band together in communities. In that condition they required laws, which must conform to the broader scheme of things that God revealed through His prophets. The purpose of such laws was to constrain physical desires and worldly passions. Such vices are evil in themselves but also because they distract people from their true mission, which is to perfect themselves as human beings.

It is no surprise, argues Ibn Sina, that ordinary people are incapable of formulating such laws on their own, nor are they able to do so through collective processes. Law, which is the essence of human society, can therefore arise only from God, his prophets, and those rare human beings whose wisdom enables them to fulfill this supreme function. Thus, Plato's Philosopher-King reemerges in Ibn Sina's *Metaphysics* as the Philosopher-Prophet, through whose wisdom alone the good society becomes possible.[22] Besides laying down the essential laws and regulations, the all-wise ruler also sets down the obligations of members of society and assures compliance with them. Prayer is first among these duties, for good deeds are as nothing until they are sanctified by worship.

Because mankind lives not for the here and now but for eternity, Ibn Sina considers the good city to be a moral community. This called for powerful and moral leadership, the Philosopher-Prophet, whose task is to prepare the community of mortals for their future by establishing firm laws against immorality. So focused is Ibn Sina on this moral agenda that he all but ignores the vast realm of economic, legal, social, and political interactions.

Biruni based his political philosophy on the practical need for human beings to protect themselves and their property against external threats. Not once did he suggest that the social enterprise had any purpose beyond its own welfare and betterment. Biruni believed that a good society depends on the moral qualities of its leader. Like Ibn Sina's, his state is a top-down and authoritarian system. Yet he acknowledged that leaders of the sort he calls for rarely appear. In all times and places, from Tibet to the Turks, leaders build fortresses to protect their wealth, become self-indulgent, make vulgar displays of vanity such as drinking water out of golden cups, and engage in all sorts of "mischief." Through their greed and hoarding, leaders lose sight of the sources of their wealth, causing all their gold and jewels "to vanish like smoke."

For all the differences between their political philosophies, however, the systems of government they espoused turned out to be strikingly similar. Ibn Sina's and Biruni's visions closely resemble what had long been accepted as the ideal of good governance in Central Asia and the Persianate world. This called for a powerful and wise leader, preferably but not necessarily with inherited power, who governs in accordance with divine law and exercises wisdom and firmness for the benefit of society at large. Ibn Sina and Biruni shuddered at the prospect of men and women managing their own communities. Instead, they placed their faith on the wise leaders who inspire awe . . . and fear. Explicit in Biruni and implicit in Ibn Sina is the assumption that respect and fear must go together. When either is lost, the economy collapses, people are unable to pay taxes, the poor die, and the good society is no more.

How utterly different all this was from what either experienced in his own lifetime. Experience had taught them that actual governments are based instead on vanity, avarice, insecurity, and greed. Under such conditions, the idea of the good society and its government was for both of them as remote a concept as Heaven itself. Could either have survived in the "good city" each envisioned? It is quite possible that the stolid and private Biruni could have managed to do so, although his impatience with fools and his sharp tongue likely would have done him in. Ibn Sina, by contrast, would surely have been censored by the Philosopher-Prophet for his dissolute and seemingly impious style of life.

No aspect of Biruni's and Ibn Sina's thought has been more persistently debated over the millennium since their death than that regarding God and religion. For their contemporaries, their intellectual heirs and enemies, and for those in the modern era who seek to gain a rounded picture of them, the question of their faith, or absence of faith, assumes great importance. Was either of them a Muslim or at least a believer, and if so of what sort? Or, alternatively, was either of them agnostic or even an atheist? Finally, did their views of religion unite or divide them?

On one point there is no dispute: neither is known to have been particularly attentive to the canonic duties of their religion. Neither made the pilgrimage to Mecca nor is known to have fasted. It is unknown whether they donated 2.5 percent of their income to charity, as is required of all Muslims, although it seems likely they did. Regarding the five-times-daily prayers, Biruni was silent. And while Ibn Sina spoke of praying at several critical junctions of his life, and while his amanuensis Juzjani refers once to his observing evening prayers, his critics lambasted him for not doing so. They also denied that a person who lived so dissolute a life as did Ibn Sina could be considered pious. This leaves the Declaration of Faith ("There is no God but Allah and Muhammad is His Messenger"). Whatever their degree of piety or impiety, for either Ibn Sina or Biruni to have provided even the slightest evidence that he questioned this central article of faith would have been unthinkable.

More than one writer makes the case that for all his writings about God, Ibn Sina was actually indifferent to religion, or at best a deist. This was the firmly stated view not only of some orthodox Muslims but also, in the modern era, of the East German scholar Ernst Bloch, who, in his 1949 volume *Avicenna and the Aristotelian Left*, argues that Ibn Sina's system was "above faith." The case for Ibn Sina's supposed indifference turns on the fact that his principal tool for establishing truth—logic—was free of theology. This led Bloch to argue that the line of descent from Ibn Sina leads not to Islamic theology, as Muslims maintain, or to St. Thomas Aquinas, as Christians argue, but to Giordano Bruno, the sixteenth-century pantheist monk who became an early disciple of Copernicus and who was martyred for denying core doctrines of his faith.

Even during Ibn Sina's lifetime, fundamentalist Muslim theologians cited the independence of his logic from theology as proof that he was irreligious. Ibn Sina was well aware of such criticism and wrote tracts and even a poem to deny it. At one point he became so exasperated by these attacks that he lashed out. "If I am a heretic then there is not a single Muslim anywhere in the world." Not everyone was convinced. But the fact remains that for Ibn Sina the fundamental source of religious truth is revelation, and he embraced religious prophets as philosophers par excellence.

The case for Biruni's indifference to religion was made with even greater vehemence. Such arguments turn on specific statements, such as his criticism of those "who ascribe to divine wisdom whatever they cannot verify in the physical sciences. They justify their ignorant claims by declaring that 'God is all-powerful.'" A generation of Soviet scholars, parroting their government's official atheism, touted Biruni as a secularist. Yes, they admitted, he made occasional bows to religion, but most of these were merely tactical moves to escape the wrath of his ultra-orthodox patron in Ghazni. There is truth in this, for Biruni sometimes stooped to using religious arguments for purely instrumental purposes. He would accuse astrologers of irreligion on the grounds that they placed a causal force—astrology—between God and man. In an opposite spirit, he sometimes launched his attacks as a materialist and religious skeptic. Needless to say, ideological zealots in Soviet times reveled in every such comment.

If a passionate concern over the existence and nature of the human soul is a test of faith, then Biruni fails. The most direct statement of his own views, cited earlier, could not have been more perfunctory, to wit, than "there are living beings in the existing world. Therefore, we must assume the existence of the soul."[23] Period. In *India* he quotes without criticism the Hindu view of the soul as merely "the will that directs the feelings," which it accomplishes "by gaining a physical body and acting through it."[24] In the same vein, he cites without criticism another Indian thinker who proclaimed that "*matter is the core*, and everything else is subservient to it and only helps it to consummate actions."[25]

Finally, those who see Biruni as essentially secular make much of the fact that in his *Chronology of Ancient Nations* he directly criticizes the prophet Muhammad for rejecting intercalation in favor of a system that caused all dates, including religious holidays, to shift throughout the year. In the same vein, in his book on geodesy Biruni points out contradictions between widely differing statements in the *Quran* concerning the length of a day. Several passages in his later writings are similarly harsh on religious practice. Typical is his observation that "to bow to a divinity is like flinging oneself into deception, since divinity takes so many forms around the world."[26]

Summing up, those who champion Biruni's secularism declare that Biruni was at best a deist by convenience and a Muslim by necessity. When one recent writer praised Biruni for freeing astronomy from the shackles of philosophy he meant, by implication, of religion as well.[27] On only one point do defenders of Biruni's secularism and of his piety agree: that he was relentlessly critical of all religions as practiced by the ignorant masses. In his *Mineralogy* he sharply ridicules "primitive worship," which he saw as pervading all societies, including the Muslim world. Such elemental belief, he argues, is based on "no knowledge" and was on the same level as unbelief.[28]

These arguments about their religious view cannot be denied, but by no means do they tell the whole story. For Ibn Sina, the counterargument typically starts with his confession that even as a boy he would often retire to the mosque when stumped by a problem of logic. It might more convincingly begin with the fact that his earliest exposure to "philosophy" was to the doctrines of deeply pious but independent-minded Muslim thinkers who advanced the doctrine that "intellect" is not merely a quality of the human mind but the work of the Supreme Being—in other words, that there can be no conflict between reason and faith.[29]

Like Biruni, Ibn Sina was a relentless critic of religious ignorance and bigotry. However, it would be a mistake to take his attacks as evidence of unbelief. Rather, they attest to his conviction that such attitudes drag true faith down to the level of superstition. Ibn Sina offers a rational alternative to the primitive faith of the masses, and devoted a lifetime to refining it. From first to last he focused on the human soul and its relation to God. It is revealing that his final works, *Fair Judgment* and *Pointers and Reminders*, were both saturated with his concern for mankind's relationship to divinity and that Ibn Sina himself considered his writings on theology and cosmology to be his most consequential works. Given this, it is the more regrettable that the text of *Fair Judgment* was lost during a military rout and that the dense and complex *Pointers and Reminders* has yet to appear in an authoritative edition or translation.[30] However, we might note that it was in this spirit of piety that during his last years he penned detailed exegeses of several Suras from the *Quran,* and that his surviving poetry is suffused with an ecstatic religious spirit which some consider akin to Sufism.[31]

Biruni, like Ibn Sina, rejected the Greeks' notion of the eternity of the world and the "foolish persuasion" that time has no terminus. Instead, he affirmed the concept of God's mastery over the whole universe.[32] Like Ibn Sina, too, he stood completely apart from the Sunni-Shiia controversy.[33] Rising above sectarianism, he declares in his masterwork on geodesy that Islam as a whole had "united all the different nations in one bond of love."[34]

Biruni was indeed a religious believer who conceived God as the Prime Mover and whose works are largely accessible to human reason. This did not mean that he accepted the syllogistic logic of Aristotle and Ibn Sina as a tool for understanding God's Creation. Nor did he accept the text-bound dogmas of Muslim traditionalists, even though Mahmud and his state were staunchly committed to upholding them. Nor, to repeat, did he align himself with either the Sunni or Shiia Muslims: Biruni himself records that he wore a ring with two stones, one of them venerated by Sunnis and the other by Shiites.[35]

Biruni traced the observable order and symmetry of creation to God. But what happens when things go wrong? He saw the possibility of a future crisis of overpopulation, which could cause famine and misery. He acknowledged that this could indeed occur. But were it to happen he declared that God would send a "messenger for the purpose of reducing the too great number."[36] He thus affirmed God's continuing and benign presence in human affairs and, incidentally, anticipated Malthus's thesis on overpopulation by eight centuries. Other such observations by Biruni are too numerous to enumerate.

While Biruni respected how every religion seeks answers to the great questions of existence, he affirmed Islam because of what he considered its rationality.[37] When he criticized Muhammad's rejection of intercalation he did so on purely rational grounds, and without expanding his critique to Islam as a whole or to religion as such. He acknowledges God as the Prime Mover and sees God as a beneficent presence in human affairs. Concluding his discussion of the danger of overpopulation, he stresses that the "messenger" of correction would be sent by God, whose "all embracing care is apparent in every single particle on earth."[38]

It is perhaps an exaggeration to say, as Hossein Nasr does, that Biruni "can be considered among the most Muslim of those in Islamic civilization who devoted themselves to the study of the intellectual sciences and who synthesized the achievement of pre-Islamic cultures and developed them in the spirit of Islam."[39] Yet to ignore his abiding religiosity would be to deny his own words, his personality, and his times.

Ibn Sina and Biruni considered themselves Muslims whose identities were inseparable from their faith. At the same time, they relied on reason to ferret out the truths of human existence and the universe. On this point Biruni was adamant, declaring that the *Quran* itself is totally accessible through reason, for it "speaks in terms that do not require an allegorical commentary."[40] Here, of course, Biruni was at odds with Ibn Sina in his later years.

Whatever the differences between their faiths, neither Ibn Sina nor Biruni felt compelled to soft-pedal his findings so as not to offend mainstream preachers and scholars from the *ulema*, the body of clerics who considered themselves the guardians of the faith. They stood shoulder to shoulder in their disdain for Muslim theologians who, in their practice of *kalam*, evaluated all thought solely in terms of their narrow definition of Muslim orthodoxy. But this did not qualify the fundamental faith of either man. They saw reason not as an alternative to religious faith but as its fulfillment. Both could have agreed with Isaac Newton's declaration that God "is supreme, or supremely perfect. He is eternal and infinite, omnipotent and omniscient. That is, he endures from eternity to eternity; and he is present from infinity to infinity; he rules all things, and he knows all things that happen or can happen." And both would also have concurred with Newton when he said, "As a blind man has no idea of colors, so we have no idea of the manner by which the all-wise God perceives and understands all things."

No issue has more consistently challenged the faithful than the presence of evil in the affairs of mankind. The Old Testament, Bible, and *Quran* all dwell on it. Thinkers of all three faiths have devoted seemingly endless exegesis and tracts to it. The lives of both Biruni and Ibn Sina were marked by evil. They endured under leaders who were certifiably malevolent. Yet in the end, neither viewed it as an inevitable driving force in human affairs and neither dwelled on it extensively in any of their writings. They agreed on the need for governments to exercise a strong hand to prevent crime and protect the civic order against malefactors. But beyond this, it is striking to see how dismissive both of them were of the problem of evil as such.

As Muslims, they had been taught that evil arose when Satan (Shaytan) refused God's order to bow down to Adam, and then spent eternity seeking to lead humans astray. Evil thus became an unavoidable presence in human affairs. Yet neither Biruni nor Ibn Sina accepted this. Evil may be everywhere, but not once did Biruni mention Satan or conditions arising from the days of Adam. Rather, in his *Determination of the Coordinates of . . . Cities, India*, and his book on mineralogy he argued that evil arises not from our inner nature but from ignorance. Ignorance is the sole cause of evil, and knowledge is its cure. Knowledge—not piety. Indeed, Biruni often attributed the most evil of deeds to those of all cultures were were pious but ignorant.[41]

Ibn Sina equally refused to accept evil as part of the divine order of human nature. Ignoring the Quranic account, he defined evil simply as "the absence of perfection."[42] Evil may infect individuals, but it isn't inherent to the species. And in a final strike against the pessimists, he argues that whatever evil exists is confined to earthly life and is therefore temporary, and that in the grand balance is far outweighed by the good.

Ibn Sina and Biruni based their arguments on different premises, but both denied that evil is part of the divine order of things, and both pointed out the path by which individuals could overcome it. They knew from bitter experience that rulers and individuals perpetrate evil deeds, but that society can survive if it is ruled by a wise but forceful leader. In spite of their own bitter experience, they were, at bottom, optimists. Neither believed that people can achieve perfection, and neither anticipated Rousseau's chilling assertion that "man is born free but is everywhere in chains." Yet they held that individuals could lead good and moral lives and, through enlightenment and divine providence, avoid evil.

All of this seems to call out for some kind of bottom-line assessment of Ibn Sani and Biruni. Yet how impossible this seems. Every age has viewed them and their work differently—the world being in constant flux—confounding any attempt to offer a truly objective balance sheet of their lives and work. We might ask instead what relevance their lives have for us today.

But such an evaluation cannot be made on the basis of their direct impact on our times, for the passage of centuries obliterated the memory of Biruni until quite recently and caused the memory of Ibn Sina to be preserved mainly among a small band of highly specialized philosophers, theologians, and historians of medicine. The best alternative, then, is to narrow the question still further by enquiring about the significance of the two lives and their written legacy as I have portrayed them.

A place to start is by exploring their respective roles in the history of science and knowledge generally. The framework proposed by Thomas S. Kuhn in *The Structure of Scientific Revolutions* holds much promise.[43] Reduced to telegraphic form, Kuhn proposed that most scientists practice what he called "normal science," in which the main parameters are set and accepted but which leaves open many unresolved questions. In the course of addressing these, researchers encounter "anomalies" for which the main thesis or "paradigm" cannot account. Eventually these anomalies mount up to create perplexity, confusion, and eventually a crisis. The crisis is resolved only when a new framework or paradigm is put forward and accepted. This, Kuhn argued, is how scientific revolutions come about.

Viewed in this light, Biruni and Ibn Sina both identified anomalies, though each of the two men addressed the anomalies he uncovered in his own manner. Ibn Sina began as a respectful disciple of Aristotle, correcting and refining the master's thoughts on specific points. Only later did he break free of the old paradigm and emerge as an Aristotle for a new age. By contrast, Biruni valued the work of his predecessors, yet only as a starting point. He declared his independence from the outset, and also his neutrality. He recognized many striking anomalies, explored them, and was definitely open to considering new paradigms, but only to the extent that they could be confirmed by solid evidence.

Ibn Sina may have offered new paradigms in the realm of logic, philosophy, and cosmology, but at bottom he was a conservative reformer, leaving intact and esteeming all that he didn't reformulate. Whether he was more than this in the field of medicine is at best doubtful. While he is rightly credited with many specific innovations, he left intact the Aristotle/Galen paradigm. Until specialists compare his treatment of scores of different medical issues with specific texts by his Greek and Muslim predecessors (Razi notable among them), it will be impossible to know the extent to which he was more than a diligent compiler and occasional corrector. Nonetheless, he refined the preexisting "normal" with such thoroughness and success that his system remained largely intact for centuries.

Ibn Sina's focus was above all on identifying the overarching frameworks that linked and explained all phenomena and knowledge. Only by such a process could he have arrived at writing the *Canon of Medicine* or *The Cure*. So broad was his vision that it comprehended such starkly different areas as philosophy, medicine, geology, and music. From first to last his goal was to lay bare first principles on which each is based and to identify the manner in which those principles lead upward to God.

Biruni always began with a specific problem, cataloguing and evaluating all prior efforts to address it, and then offering his own solution. When he failed to resolve the issue he would sketch out what had yet to be learned in order to solve the problem, thus mapping the way for future researchers. This process enabled Biruni to achieve incremental but important advances in a wide range of areas. And on several issues he achieved major breakthroughs. Thus, he proposed the first global system for measuring time, advanced a bold new way to study other societies, and introduced the transformative concept of specific gravity. Beyond all this stand his signal contributions to mathematics, geometry, trigonometry, cartography, geography, botany, and several other fields.

Finally, Biruni's treatment of the problem of a heliocentric universe deserves special note, not merely because he accepted the theoretical possibility that the earth rotated around the sun but for the method he employed to evaluate this hypothesis. He did not respond to some widespread discontent with the old paradigm, as Kuhn would have it, but to his own recognition of an anomaly. Using data he himself generated and employing mathematical tools that he himself had refined, he proved that a heliocentric universe was entirely possible, that is, an acceptable paradigm. In the end Biruni stopped short of embracing his own paradigm because he could not confirm it by observation. He left it to Galileo and his telescope to clinch the argument and validate the paradigm that he, as a mathematician, had defended. In this context, the recent discovery of the so-called God particle in particle physics seems relevant. Known as the "Higgs Boson," it accounts for the fact that elementary particles have mass. The "God-particle" was confirmed by observation only in 2019. However. a group of five physicists had earlier hypothesized its existence purely on the basis of mathematics. For this achievement, two members of that earlier group were awarded the Nobel Prize in 2012.

Even had most of Biruni's works been miraculously preserved, their impact might have been limited to that small group of scholars whose competence was on a par with his own. By the same token, the very comprehensiveness of Ibn Sina's systems in both medicine and metaphysics assured for him an audience of both specialists and generalists who would either reject them, as did some of his Muslim and Christian critics, or seek to refine and adjust them as a new round of "normal science." What is in the end most striking about both men is their readiness, when necessary, to take scientific, philosophical, or religious orthodoxies head-on. While not themselves full-blown revolutionaries, they were harbingers of the revolutions that gave rise to the modern mind.

The lives and work of Biruni and Ibn Sina challenge us to reconsider several of the comfortable dichotomies with which we describe our world today. By simultaneously embracing the past and breaking from it, they challenged the notion of Ancients versus Moderns that arose in the sixteenth-century West and persists in many forms today. By simultaneously embracing science (in the broadest sense) and religion, they confound those who see the world in terms of an eternal struggle between science and faith. Instead, they recast these and other dichotomies in terms of knowledge versus dogma, both religious and scientific, and dedicated their lives to knowledge.

Biruni and Ibn Sina were, as noted, avowed Muslims, yet their works rose above sectarianism. As a consequence, anyone could take intellectual sustenance from them. In both philosophy and science they ameliorated the juxtaposition of Muslim, Christian, and Jew, not by denying or avoiding differences but by engaging constructively with them. In the same spirit, while they were men of their place and time, their work came to be studied in both the East and West, again dissolving what many still consider a global clash of cultures. They rejected all forms of stodgy orthodoxy. By so doing, they ended up transforming the received intellectual heritage. In this they were not alone; others had already begun moving along this path, albeit more tentatively than either Biruni or Ibn Sina. At the same time, opponents of their project were also mobilizing and would score tactical victories over the coming centuries.

Whether or not one concludes that they were geniuses—and I do—it is undeniable that Biruni and Ibn Sina were both virtuosos of the mind, standing at the very peak of human achievement. The differences between them were profound. Yet these very differences attest to the breadth and depth of the Central Asian and Persianate culture from which both sprang.

This, too, is relevant to our own times. The new states of Central Asia are only now emerging from more than a century of colonial rule, a period in which important elements of their intellectual and spiritual heritage were destroyed. Iran remains stuck in a painful state, in which a people with a rich cultural and scientific heritage is controlled by religious zealots. As to Afghanistan, a country from which Ibn Sina's forebears sprang and where Biruni carried out his most important research, its government is now controlled by religious fanatics who would have been quite at home in the barracks of Sultan Mahmud in medieval Ghazni.

All of these peoples deserve to regain the memory of their multi-talented and complex geniuses, and to be inspired by them. The sharp distinctions between them—in character, interests, and modes of thought—bear witness to the importance of individuals in human history. Particular nations, regions, and religious factions deserve to claim each as one of their own. But in the end, Ibn Sani and Biruni stand forth as individuals, unique and incomparable. Their lives remind us that while advancements in knowledge can result from the progress of society as a whole, they can take place even in periods of regression and chaos.

Between them, Biruni and Ibn Sina created a two-man Renaissance. For all their manifest differences, they shared the conviction that God's Creation is orderly and in conformity with natural laws that are accessible to human reason. This was no mere working hypothesis but a ground truth. With Virgil, they affirmed, "Happy is the man who has learned the causes of things, and who trampled beneath his feet all fears, inexorable fate, and the roar of devouring hell."[44] By that standard, Biruni and Ibn Sina had every right to be happy.

Acknowledgments

Isaac Newton declared that he stood on the shoulders of giants. I, by contrast, have sat at the feet of great scholars, present and past, and have benefited from their rich and timeless research. First among them is the wise Seyed Hossein Nasr, one of the few thinkers to have analyzed and compared the work of both Biruni and Ibn Sina and to have offered insights on their mutual relations. It was my good fortune to have met Nasr sixty-four years ago, on my first day as a freshman at Yale. Thanks to him and his cousin, Hooshang Nasr, my roommate, I developed a lifelong interest in the Persianate world in which they both were born.

Many of my most valuable guides and teachers have long since passed from this world. The great nineteenth-century German scholar Edward R. Sachau heads this group, with his first-ever editions of two long-forgotten masterpieces by Biruni. C. L. Bosworth occupies a similarly noble place in the twentieth century, thanks to his studies of the Ghaznavids and of the historian Beyhaqi. It was my good fortune to have met Bosworth during his last year of life. He kindly paused in his own writing to encourage me to undertake the present study and urged me to focus on Biruni's and Ibn Sina's actual lives and the tormented era in which they lived. My debt to the late Avicenna scholar Dimitri Gutas also turned out to be immense, and it saddens me that I can thank him only posthumously. I owe a like salute to the tireless Tashkent historian P. G. Bulgakov for his classic studies of Biruni's life and several of his specific works. And to the Pakistan scholar Mohammad Farooq, for his pioneering translation and edition of Biruni's *Masud's Canon*.

It is a pleasure to thank more recent scholars for vastly expanding my understanding of both of our "geniuses of their age." To cite only a few of these heroes, the Scottish mathematicians John J. O'Connor and Edmund Robertson carefully analyzed Biruni's mathematics, while Edward S. Kennedy, in addition to editing a key work by Biruni, contributed meticulous analyses of his astronomical and trigonometric research and wrote the insightful overview of his oeuvre for the *Dictionary of Scientific Biography*. Meanwhile, thanks are due to the German Arabist Gerhard Strohmaier for his several biographical studies on Ibn Sina, and to the Russian scholar Iurii

N. Zavodovskii, whose life of Ibn Sina included material not found elsewhere, while his colleagues, B. Rosenfeld and B. Belenitskii, did the same for their study of Biruni's research on specific gravity and gems.

I have benefited greatly from studies in many languages of the impact of Biruni and Ibn Sina on later thinkers in both the Middle East and Europe. Modern studies of Ibn Sina's immediate impact reached a peak with Frank Griffel's research on Ghazali, which I gratefully culled, while I want also to acknowledge Robert Wisnowsky's pioneering research on Ibn Sina's impact on Nasir al-Din Tusi and the band of thinkers whom he assembled at Maragha in Iran. The list of scholars who have traced Ibn Sina's impact in Europe is long, but I want to thank particularly Dag Nikolaus Hasse from the Universitat Wurzburg and Amos Bertolacci from the Scuola IMT Studi in Lucca for their pioneering research.

I am deeply indebted to the many current scholars who have critiqued drafts of this book. Jon McGinnis, an insightful expert on Ibn Sina, toiled patiently to correct errors or clarify passages in my early drafts dealing with Ibn Sina's metaphysics, while Muhammad U. Faruque of the University of Cincinnati offered timely suggestions on passages on philosophy. Others, who were immersed in meeting deadlines of their own, led me to colleagues and advanced graduate students who were working on topics relevant to my book and offered generous encouragement for my effort to detail the lives of Biruni and Ibn Sina and to present the broad outline of their thought in a manner accessible to general, educated readers. In this context I wish to thank particularly Lenn Goodman of Vanderbilt University and Robert Wisnowsky of the Institute of Islamic Studies at McGill University, both of whom were quick to grasp the difference between my goal of a dual biography and the in-depth textual analyses at which they are premier experts, and to encourage me in my labors.

The list of others whose help made this book possible is long. Let me note just two members of this band of expert-enthusiasts: Vali Kaleji, a wise and dispassionate analyst of contemporary affairs at the University in Tehran, identified the site of the fortress-prison in which Ibn Sina was incarcerated, while Ismatulla Irgashev, Uzbek diplomat and formidable expert on Afghanistan, shared my enthusiasm for restoring Biruni's damaged tomb in Ghazni and has lent timely support to my effort to preserve the legacy of both Ibn Sina and Biruni in Taliban-ruled Afghanistan.

This book was made possible by the forbearance and support of my colleague and friend Svante Cornell, director of the Central Asia Caucasus

Institute in Washington and Stockholm, and of Herman Pirchner, the genial and wise founder and director of the American Foreign Policy Council, of which the Institute is a part. My gifted and endlessly patient editor at Oxford University Press, Timothy Bent, guided me through the intricate process of rendering the text accessible to educated generalists. And it is thanks to my friend Peter Frankopan, author of the justly acclaimed *The Silk Roads*, and to Zoe Pagnamenta that this manuscript found its way to Oxford University Press in the first place.

Finally, and above and beyond all these encomia, I wish to express my profound gratitude to my wife, Christina, for her deep understanding both of her husband and of his peculiar enthusiasms that led to the writing of this book. She uncomplainingly sacrificed relaxed meals, travels, and quiet times together, a debt that a further lifetime could never repay. And amid it all, Christina offered abiding encouragement. This same debt and gratitude extends to our lovely and talented daughters, Anna Townsend and Elizabeth Scharfenberg, their husbands, and their wonderful children.

S. Frederick Starr
Washington and New Orleans

Notes

Introduction

1. George Sarton, *Introduction to the History of Science*, Washington, 1927, vol. 1, p. 707.
2. Tony Booth, *Analytic Islamic Philosophy*, unpub. draft, ch. 5, p. 2, https://mail.goo gle.com/mail/u/0/#trash/WhctKJWQmrwDHgpJhCQGSgdxgnLVgkhpjwpgWntGf dPQhNLTssthmPXLMKVMLSCrVgtnPBg.
3. Seyyed Hossein Nasr, *Three Muslim Sages*, New York, 1976, p. 20.
4. M. A. Kazim, "Al-Biruni and Trigonometry," *Al-Biruni Commemoration Volume*, Calcutta, 1956, p. 167.
5. A. M. Goichon, *Introduction d'Avicenne*, Paris, 1933, p. xvii; Dimitri Gutas, *Avicenna and the Aristotelian Tradition*, p. 86. Lenn E. Goodman, in his *Avicenna* (Ithaca, 2006, p. 18), considers this claim "a bit excessive," noting the works of the Jewish philosopher Saadiah Gaon from seventy years before Ibn Sina's.
6. Abu Ali Ibn Sina (Avitsenna), *Sochineniia*, 9 vols., Dushanbe, 2021.
7. Biruni, *Sobranie svedenii poznaniia dragotsennostei (Minerologiia)*, A. M. Belenitskii, transl., Moscow, 1963, p. xi.
8. Yahya Mahdavi, *Bibliographie d'Ibn Sina*, Tehran, 1954; O. Ergin, *Ibn Sina Bibliografyasi*, Istanbul, 1956.
9. Bulgakov, *Zhizn I trudy Beruni*, Tashkent, 1972, pp. 288 ff.
10. The shrine of Muhammad Shah, ibid., p. 289.
11. Sayid Samad Husain Rizvi, "A Newly Discovered Book of Al-Biruni 'Ghurrat-Uz-Zijat' and Al-Biruni's Measurement of the Earth's Dimensions," in *Al-Biruni Commemorative Volume*, Hakim Mohammed Said, ed., New Delhi, 1973, pp. 605 ff.

Chapter 1

1. On Khwarazmian urbanism, see S. P. Tolstov, *Po sledam drevnekhorezemskoi tsivilizatsii*, Moscow-Leningrad, 1948, and V. A. Lavrov, *Gradostroitelnaia kultura Srednei Azii*, Moscow, 1950, chs. 2–3.
2. Not to be confused with the Mamun dynasty that had earlier presided over Baghdad's golden age.
3. *Wazir* in Arabic.
4. Also spelled as-Sahli and as-Sukhaili.

5. Soheil M. Afnan, *Avicenna: His Life and Works*, London, 1958, p. 55; Joel L. Kraemer, *Humanism in the Renaissance of Islam: The Cultural Revival during the Buyid Age*, Leiden, 1992, pp. 123–130.
6. Beyhaqi, *The History of Beyhaqi*, vol. 3, p. 384.
7. Dimitri Gutas, *Avicenna and the Aristotelian Tradition*, Leiden, 2nd ed., 2014, p. 79, fn. 2; also Gutas, "Avicenna's Maqhab, with an appendix on the question of his date of birth," *Quaderni di Studi Arabi*, vols. 5–6, 1987–1988, pp. 323–336, and Rudolph Sellheim, review of Ergin, *Ibni Sina Bibiyografyasi*, 2nd ed., *Oriens*, vol. 11, 1958, pp. 231–239.

Chapter 2

1. I. Iu. Krachkovskii, "Arabskaia geograficeshkaia literatura," *Izbrannye sochinennia*, Moscow-Leningrad, 1957, vol. 4, p. 245.
2. Gutas, *Avicenna and the Aristotelian Tradition*, p. 176.
3. Aristotle, *Prior Analytics*, A. J. Jenkinson, transl., Middletown, DE, 2016, p. 4.
   Dimitri Gutas, "Avicenna's Maqhab, with an appendix on the question of his date of birth," *Quaderni di Studi Arabi*, vols. 5–6, 1987–1988, Jonathan Barnes, ed., Venice, 1984.
4. Gutas, *Avicenna and the Aristotelian Tradition*, p. 207.
5. Nasr, *Three Muslim Sages*, pp. 42–43.
6. For a cogent discussion of this key issue, see Tony Street, "Avicenna and the Syllogism," in *Interpreting Avicenna: Critical Essays*, Peter Adamson, ed., Cambridge, 2013, ch. 3.
7. M. Ullman, *Die Medicin in Islam*, Leiden, 1072, p. 6 fn., pp. 260–261.
8. Gutas, *Avicenna and the Aristotelian Tradition*, pp. 180–181.
9. Victor Courteois, ed., Calcutta, 1951, p. 195.
10. J. J. O'Conner and E. F. Robertson, "Abu Ja'far Muhammad ibn Musa Al-Khwarizmi," MacTutor History of Mathematics Archive, https://mathshistory.st-andrews.ac.uk/Biographies/Al-Khwarizmi/.
11. S. P. Tolstov, *Po sledam drevnekhorezmiiskoi tsivilizatsii*, Moscow-Leningrad, 1948, pp. 189 ff.

Chapter 3

1. B. C. Law, "Avicenna and His Theory of the Soul," in *Avicenna Commemorative Volume*, V. Courtois, ed., Calcutta, 1956, pp. 179–186.
2. Dimitri Gutas, *Avicenna and the Aristotelian Tradition*, 2nd ed., Leiden, 2014, 86–93.
3. Ibid.
4. See above, ch. 1, fn. 3.
5. William F. Gohlman, *The Life of Ibn Sina*, Albany, 1974, pp. 92–93.

6. Avicenna, *The Metaphysics of the Healing*, Michael E. Marmura, transl., Provo, 2005, pp. 362–363.

7. The reference was in Biruni's important *Determination of the Coordinates of . . . Cities*. See Bulgakov, *Zhizn i trudy Beruni*, pp. 28–29.

8. Ibid., p. 32.

9. Biruni, *The Determination of the Coordinates of . . . Cities: Al-Biruni's Tahdid al-Amakin*, Jamil Ali, transl., Beirut, 1967, p. 14. See also E. S. Kennedy's *A Commentary upon Biruni's Kitab Tahdid al-Amakin*, Beirut, 1973.

10. Ernst G. Ravenstein, *Martin Behaim, His Life and His Globe*, London, 1908.

Chapter 4

1. Bulgakov, *Zhizn i trudy Beruni*, p. 35.

2. For a thorough discussion of Biruni and Khujandi's observatory, see Bulgakov, *Zhizn i trudy Beruni*, ch. 3.

3. Biruni, *Geodeziia, Izbrannye proizvedendii*, P. G. Bulgakov, ed., Tashkent, 1973, p. 137.

4. The French scholar Boilot found the sole copy of this paper at the Jesuit University in Beirut: D. J. Boilot, "L'Oeuvre d'al-Berumi: Essai bibliographique," Institut Dominicain d'etudes orientales du Caire, *Melanges*, vol. 2, Cairo, 1955, p. 237; but when the Soviet scholar Bulgakov searched for it he was told the paper disappeared during World War I. Bulgakov, *Zhizn i trudy Beruni*, p. 50.

Chapter 5

1. Bulgakov, *Zhizn i trudy Beruni*, pp. 61 ff.; Gutas, *Avicenna and the Aristotelian Tradition*, p. 449; Gotthard Strohmeier, "Avicenna und al-Biruni im Dialog uber aristotelische Naturphilosophie," in *Naturwissenschaft und ihre Rezeption*, K. Doering and G. Woehrle, eds., Bamberg 1992, pp. 115–130; Rafiq Berjak and Muzaffar Iqbal, "Ibn-Sina-Al-Biruni Correspondence," *Islam and Science*, 1, 2003, December, pp. 91–98; June, pp. 253–260; 2, 2004, June, pp. 57–62; December, pp. 181–187; 3, 2005, June, pp. 57–72; December, pp. 166–170; 6, 2006, pp. 126–141; December, pp. 53–60. The translation by S. H. Nasr and M. Mohaghegh is to be found at "al-As'ilah wa'lajwibah (Questions and Answers) Including the Further Answers of al-Biruni and al-Ma'sumi's Defense of Ibn Sina," High Council of Culture and Art, Tehran, 1973, pp. 74–85.

2. Avicenna, "Ibn-Sina-Al-Biruni Correspondence," *Islam and Science*, vol. 1, June, 2003.

3. Ibid.

4. Avicenna (Ibn Sina), "Ibn-Sina-Al-Biruni Correspondence," *Islam and Science*, vol. 1, December 2003.

5. Ibid.

6. Nasr, *An Introduction to Islamic Cosmological Doctrines*, p. 221.
7. Avicenna, "Ibn-Sina-Al-Biruni Correspondence," *Islam and Science*, vol. 5, Summer 2007.
8. Avicenna, "Ibn-Sina-Al-Biruni Correspondence," *Islam and Science*, vol. 1, December 2003.
9. Avicenna, "Ibn-Sina-Al-Biruni Correspondence," *Islam and Science*, vol. 2, June 2004.
10. Avicenna, "Ibn-Sina-Al-Biruni Correspondence," *Islam and Science*, vol. 3, June 2005.
11. Ibid.
12. Avicenna, "Ibn-Sina-Al-Biruni Correspondence," *Islam and Science*, vol. 3, June 2005.
13. Avicenna, "Ibn-Sina-Al-Biruni Correspondence," *Islam and Science*, vol. 1, p. 12.
14. Avicenna, "Ibn-Sina-Al-Biruni Correspondence," *Islam and Science*, vol. 5, January 2007.
15. Gutas, *Avicenna and the Aristotelian Tradition*, p. 450, suggests that the questioner in this series may not have been Biruni but either his friend and amanuensis Abu l'Qasim al-Jurjani or Avicenna's later archenemy, Abu l'Qasim al-Kirmani. In either case, the correspondence would have dated from at least a decade later. However, the continuity in substance and tone from the earlier exchange suggests that the questioner was indeed Biruni and that it was part of the same exchange. Mention of "Abu-l-Qasim" in the one extant manuscript from Egypt suggests that one of them may have written the early copy that is preserved in Egypt.
16. Nasr, *An Introduction to Islamic Cosmological Doctrines*, p. 166.
17. See below, Chapter 10 on Biruni's *The Determination of the Coordinates of . . . Cities*.
18. Seyyed Hossein Nasr, personal communication with the author, September 19, 2020.

Chapter 6

1. Gutas, *Avicenna and the Aristotelian Tradition*, pp. 7–8, incorrectly dates the death as 1005 and suggests that Ibn Sina reached Gurganj by 1002.
2. Afnan, *Avicenna: His Life and Works*, p. 62, hypothesizes that Ibn Sina's departure from Bukhara was caused by the Karakhanid Turks' hostility to the indigenous Persianate people. The only evidence he cites in support of this claim is a nonexistent work by Biruni entitled *A Warning against the Turks*.
3. Also known as Abu l'Husayn as-Suhayli.
4. *Autobiography*, reproduced in Gutas, *Avicenna and the Aristotelian Tradition*, p. 19. Cf. Gohlman, *The Life of Ibn Sina*, p. 41. The *taylasan* was a trapezoidal-shaped fabric of Jewish origin that had been adopted by the Samani lawyers. See Judith Klinginder, "Bid'a or Sunna: The Taylasan as a Contested Garment in the Mamluk Period," in *Al-Suyuti: a Polymath of the Mamluk Period*, Leiden, 2017, p. 74.
5. On Biruni and Qabus, see *Kabus name, perevod, statia, i primechaniia*, E. E. Birtels, transl., ed., Moscow, 1953, pp. 228–230.
6. Bulgakov, *Zhizn i trudy Beruni*, pp. 81 ff.

7. *Alberuni's India*, vol. 1, p. 277; Abu Raikhan Biruni, *Izbrannye proizvedenniia*, II *India*, p. 255.

8. Abd al-Rahman al-Sufi, known in the West as Azophi (903–986).

9. J. L. Berggren, "The Mathematical Sciences," in *History of Civilizations of Central Asia*, C. E. Bosworth and M. S. Asimov, eds., Paris, 2000, vol. 4, pt. 2, p. 192.

10. E. Wiedeman, "Allgemeine Betrachtungen von Al-Biruni in einem Werk uber die Astrolaben," in *Report of Physical-Medical Society of Erlangen*, vol. 52–53, Erlangen, 1922.

11. Muhammad Ibn Ahmad Biruni, *The Chronology of Ancient Nations*, C. Edward Sachau, transl. and ed., London, 1879.

12. Biruni, *The Chronology of Ancient Nations*, pp. 186, 189–194.

13. Ibid., pp. 16 ff.

14. Ibid., p. 178.

15. Ibid., p. 90.

16. Francois Clement de Blois, "'Al-Bayrouni, the Twelve Apostles and the Twelve Months of the Julian Year,' Winds of Jingjiao. Studies on Syriac Christianity in China and Central Asia," in *Orientalia Patristica Oecumenica*, Li Tang and Dietmar W. Winkler, eds., vol. 9, Zurich, 2016, pp. 155–160.

17. Biruni, *The Chronology of Ancient Nations*, p. 27.

18. Ibid., pp. 27, 121, 129, and 131.

19. Ibid., p. 29.

20. Ibid., ch. xiii.

21. Biruni, *The Chronology of Ancient Nations*, pp. 14, 36 ff.

22. Ibid., p. 349.

23. Francois de Blois leads the British effort. See his "The New Edition of al-Biruni's 'Chronology,'" "Al-Biruni and His World," Department of Hebrew and Jewish Studies, University College London, workshop of February 15, 2016. https://blogs.ucl.ac.uk/calendars-ancient-medieval-project/2016/10/03/al-biruni/.

24. This incident is drawn from E. E. Birtels's epilogue to his Russian translation of the *Kabus-name, perevod, statia, i primechaniia*, Moscow, 1953, pp. 228–230.

25. Yaqut al-Hamawī, *Irshad al-arib ila marifar al-adib (Dictionary of Learned Men)* (Russian edition), D. S. Margol, ed., vol. 6, p. 150.

26. E. E. Birtels, ed., transl., *Kabus-name, perevod, statia, i primechaniia*, Moscow, 1953, p. 82.

Chapter 7

1. P. G. Bulgakov discovered this date while translating Biruni's later *Determination of the Coordinates of . . . Cities* (Abu Raikhan Biruni, *Kitab Tahdid Nihayat al-Amakin Litashih al-Masakin*, Jamil Ali, ed., Beirut, 1967, p. 81).

2. Bulgakov, *Zhizn i trudy Beruni*, pp. 127–128.

3. D. J. Boilot, "L'Oeuvre d'al-Beruni: Essai bibliographique," Institut Dominicain d'etudes orientales du Caire, *Melanges*, vol. 2, Cairo, 1955, p. 192, no. 47.

4. The exception was "Averting General Harm to Human Bodies by Preventing Various Mistakes in Treatment," which contains material that Ibn Sina could use later in the *Canon of Medicine*; Gutas, *Avicenna and the Aristotelian Tradition*, p. 516.

5. Ibid., pp. 445–449.

6. Nizami Arudi (Abu'l Fadl Beyhaqi), *A Revised Translation of the Chahár maqála ("Four discourses") of Nizámí-i'Arúdí of Samarqand)*, Edward G. Browne, transl., London, 1921, p. 86.

7. Ibid., p. 66.

8. Ibid., pp. 86 ff.; see also Afnan, who implies that this demarche by Mahmud dates to the time of Biruni's departure, i.e., 1017, *Avicenna His Life and Works*, pp. 63–64.

9. Most of these cities had earlier been hotbeds of a politically ambitious sub-group of the Shiite movement, the Qarmatians. For an original and stimulating analysis of the religious geography of Ibn Sina and his family, see Guenter Lueling, "Ein anderer Avicenna. Kritik seiner Autobiographie und ihrer bisherigen Behandlung," *Zeitschrift der Deutschen Morgenländischen Gesellschaft*, vol. 3, no. 1, 1977, pp. 436, 496–513.

10. Slightly modified, from Gutas, *Avicenna and the Aristotelian Tradition*, p. 198.

11. That Ibn Sina exchanged several letters with the mystic was reported by the saint's grandson, Muhammad ibn Munavar. The saint lived near present-day Ashgabat, Turkmenistan. His tomb is now a shrine.

12. There is some question whether this was a full history of Khwarazm or merely biographies of its leaders. Beyhaqi says the title of this book was *Eminent People of Khwarazm*, Beyhaqi, *Istoriia Masuda (1030–1041)*, p. 808. See Frantz Grenet, "Al-Biruni as a Source for Choresmian History," "Al-Biruni and His World," Department of Hebrew and Jewish Studies University College London, workshop, February 15, 2016. https://blogs.ucl.ac.uk/calendars-ancient-medieval-project/2016/10/03/al-biruni/.

13. Abu l'Fazi Baykhaki (hereafter "Beyhaqi"): *Istoriia Masuda (1030–1041)*; A. K. Arends, ed., Moscow, 1969, p. 808,

14. Beyhaqi, *The History of Beyhaqi*, vol. 3, p. 387.

15. Beyhaqi, *Istoriia Masuda (1030–1041)*, pp. 808–814, and Nazim, *Life and Times of Sultan Mahmud of Ghazna*, pp. 56–59.

16. Beyhaqi, *The History of Beyhaqi*, vol. 3, p. 387.

17. Ibid., vol. 3, p. 381.

18. Muhammad Nazim, *The Life and Times of Sultan Mahmud of Ghazna*, Cambridge, 1931, p. 59, citing Beyhaqi.

19. Ibid.

20. Beyhaqi, *The History of Beyhaqi*, vol. 2, p. 382.

21. Ibid., vol. 2, p. 388.

22. Ibid., vol. 2, p. 386.

Chapter 8

1. Abu l'Fazl Bayhaqi, *Translation of the Tarikh-I-Sultan Mahmud-I-Ghaznavi or, the History of Sultan Mahmud of Ghazni*, G. Roos-Keppel and Qazi Abdul Ghani Khan, transl., Lahore, 1908, p. 4.

2. Beyhaqi, *Istoriia Masuda (1030–1041)*; see the summary of these other writers' works in Clifford Edmund Bosworth's fine analysis, *The Ghaznavids: Their Empire in Eastern Afghanistan and Eastern India, 994–1040*, London, 1963, and reprinted, New Delhi, 2015, pp. 10 ff.

3. The most authoritative account of Mahmud's army is that of Bosworth, *The Ghaznavid*, pp. 98–128.

4. This oft-cited figure is disputed by Achena and Masse, who claim the total was twenty: *Le Livre de Science 1*, Paris, 1986, p. 262. Cited in Goodman, *Avicenna*, p. 46, n. 23.

5. Abu'l-Fazl Beyhaqi, *Translation of the Tarikh-I-Sultan Mahmud-I-Ghaznavi or, the History of Sultan Mahmud of Ghazni*, G. Roos-Keppel and Qazi Abdul Ghani Khan, transl., Lahore, 1908, p.22.

6. Bosworth, *The Ghaznavids*, p. 95.

7. Nazim, *The Life and Times of Sultan Mahmud of Ghazna*, p. 144, fn. 6.

8. On Mahmud's crusades against Mutazilies and Qarmatians (Karajites), see Nazim, *The Life and Times of Sultan Mahmud of Ghazna*, pp. 171 ff.

9. Ibid., p. 159.

10. On Caliph Mansur's support for Mahmud's crusades, see Hakim Mohammed Said and Ansar Zaid Khan, *Al-Biruni: His Times, Life, and Works*, Karachi, 1981, pp. 43, 58–59.

11. Nazim, *The Life and Times of Sultan Mahmud of Ghazna*, pp. 53–54.

12. Bosworth, *The Ghaznavids*, pp. 62–69.

13. Nazim, *The Life and Times of Sultan Mahmud of Ghazna*, p. 153.

14. Variously known as Ayaz. Nizami-i-Arudi, *Chahar Maqala*, Edward G. Browne, transl., Cambridge, 1921, pp. 37–38.

15. Bosworth, *The Ghaznavids*, p. 157, fn. 4.

16. Daniel Schlumberger, "Le Palais ghaznévide de Lashkari Bazar," *Syria*, vol. 29, 1952, nos. 3–4.

17. For Mahmud's personal characteristics, see Beyhaqi, *Istoriia Masuda (1030–1041)*, pp. 620 ff.

18. On Farrukhi, see J. T. P. De Bruijn, "Farrokī Sīstānī, Abu'l-Ḥasan ʿAlī," *Encyclopædia Iranica*, http://www.iranicaonline.org/articles/farroki-sistani.

19. On Ferdowsi's relations with Mahmud, see "Ferdowsi, Abu'l-Qasem," *Encyclopaedia Iranica*, https://iranicaonline.org/articles/ferdowsi-index.

20. The poet was Abul Qasim Hasan Unsuri from Balkh, Afghanistan (d. ca. 1039/1040).

21. Nizami-i-Arudi, *Chahar Maqala*, p. 58.

Chapter 9

1. Gutas affirms that Jusjani reported this: *Avicenna and the Aristotelian Tradition*, pp. 60, 101.

2. On Shirazi, see Gutas, *Avicenna and the Aristotelian Tradition*, p. 46, and Gohlman, *The Life of Ibn Sina*, p. 126.

3. This is David E. Reisman's rendering of the title. Gutas translates it as *On the Provenance and Destination*, *Avicenna and the Aristotelian Tradition*, p. 554.

4. Gutas, *Avicenna and the Aristotelian Tradition*, pp. 21–22.

5. Ibid., p. 21.

6. Gunter Luling, "Ein anderer Avicenna: Kritik seiner Autobiographie und ihrer bisherigen Behandlung," *Zeitschrift der Deutschen Morgenländischen Gesellschaft*, vol. 3, no. 1, 1977, pp. 496–509.

7. Gutas, *Avicenna and the Aristotelian Tradition*, p. 223.

8. For a careful assessment of this text, see the extensive notes to Gohlman's *The Life of Ibn Sina*.

9. Epilogue of the *Lesser Destination*, in Gutas, *Avicenna and the Aristotelian Tradition*, p. 23.

10. For the debate over medicine as a "science" (*ilm*), see Leigh M. Chipman, "Is Medicine an *'ilm*? A Preliminary Note on Qutb al-Din al-Shirazi's *al-Tuhfa al-sa'diyya*," in *Avicenna and His Legacy: A Golden Age of Science and Philosophy*, in Y. Tzvi Langermann, ed., Turnhout, Belgium, 2009, pp. 289–300.

11. James E. McClellan III and Harold Dorn, *Science and Technology in World History: An Introduction*, Baltimore, 2006, p. 92.

Chapter 10

1. This theme comes from Yakut (Yaqut), *Irshad*, vol. 4, pp. 311–312, as noted, among others, by Belenitskii, *Ocherk zhizni i trudov Biruni*, Moscow, 1963, p. 279.

2. Biruni, *The Determination of the Coordinates of . . . Cities*, p. 188. Also Syed Hasan Barani, "Muslim Researches in Geodesy," in *Al-Biruni Commemorative Volume*, Calcutta, 1956, p. 35.

3. Abu'l-Fazl Beyhaqi, *Translation of the Tarikh-I-Sultan Mahmud-I-Ghaznavi or, the History of Sultan Mahmud of Ghazni*, G. Roos-Keppel and Qazi Abdul Ghani Khan, transl., Lahore, 1908, p. 25, 41.

4. Ibid., p., 86; Said and Khan, *Al-Biruni: His Times, Life, and Work*, p. 76.

5. Biruni, *The Determination of the Coordinates of . . . Cities*, p. 86.

6. Ibid., p. 188.

7. V. Minorsky, "On Some of Biruni's Informants," in *Al-Biruni Commemoration Volume*, Victor Courtois, M. Ishaque, eds., Calcutta, 1956, p. 235.

8. Abu Raikhan Beruni (sic., Biruni), *Sobranie svedenii poznaniia dragotsennostei (Minerologiia)*, A. M. Belenitskii, transl., intro., Moscow, 1963, pp. 28–29.

9. Bulgakov, *Zhizn i trudy Beruni*, p. 141.

10. Abu Raikhan Berini (sic., Biruni), *Geodeziia*, P. G. Bulgakov, transl. and ed., Tashkent, 1966, pp. 28–29.

11. Biruni, *The Determination of the Coordinates of . . . Cities*, p. 1.

12. Ibid., p. 3.

13. Biruni, *The Determination of the Coordinates of . . . Cities*, p. 6; Berini, *Geodeziia*, p. 85.

14. Biruni, *The Determination of the Coordinates of . . . Cities*, pp. 14–16.

15. On the basis of a surviving document in Cairo, Bulgakov discussed these in detail in *Zhizn i trudy Beruni*, pp. 145 ff.

16. These are meticulously detailed in E. S. Kennedy's brilliant *A Commentary upon Biruni's Kitab Tahdid al-Amakin*, Beirut, 1973. See also Imanullah Jan, "Comments

on Tahdid Nikayah al-Amakin li Tasheh Masafah al Masakin," in *Al-Biruni Commemorative Volume*, H. M. Saud, ed., Karachi, 1974, pp. 522, ff.

17. For a comprehensive discussion of the problem of longitude, see Dava Sobel, *Longitude*, New York, 1995.

18. Barani, "Muslim Researches in Geodesy," p. 35; Saiyid Samad Husain Rizvi, "A Newly Discovered Book of Al-Biruni 'Gjhurrat-uz-Zijat' and Al-Biruni's Measurement of Earth's Dimensions," Hakim Mohammed Said, ed., *Al-Biruni Commemorative Volume*, Islamabad, 1974, pp. 605 ff.; and Alberto Gomez Gomez, "Biruni's Measurement of the Earth," 2015, https://www.academia.edu/8166456/Birunis_m easurement_of_the_Earth?email_work_card=view-paper.

19. Rizvi, "A Newly Discovered Book of Al-Biruni 'Ghurrat-Uz-Zijat,'" p. 619.

20. A thorough review of Biruni's argument is Syed Hasan Barani, "Muslim Research on Geodesy," in *Al-Biruni Commemoration Volume*, pp. 19–44.

21. These figures are based on the slightly reworked calculations that Biruni included in his *Canon (Al-Kanun-ul-masudi)* rather than those in the Determination of the Coordinates of . . . Cities. See also Said and Khan, *Al-Biruni: His Times, Life, and Work*, p. 170.

22. This book is available only in an unedited Arabic edition, Hydarabad, 1948; Bulgakov, *Zhizn i trudy Beruni*, pp. 155–158.

23. For a discussion of his experimental means of studying shadows, see B. A. Rozenfeld, M. M. Rozhanskaia, and E. K. Sokolovskaia, *Abu-r-Raykhan al-Biruni, 973–1048*, Moscow, 2013, ch. 4.

24. Ibid., "Astronomy," pp. 85–126.

25. *Alberuni's India*, p. 637.

Chapter 11

1. For Aruzi's account, see Edward Browne, ed., *A Revised Translation of the Chahár maqála ("Four Discourses") of Nizámí-i' Arúdí of Samarqand, Followed by an Abridged Translation of Mírzá Muhammad's Notes to the Persian Text*, London/Cambridge, 1921, pp. 90–93.

2. Jon McGinnis, *Avicenna*, Oxford, 2010, p. 23. Dimitri Gutas titles this work "Cardiac Remedies," in *Avicenna and the Aristotelian Tradition*, 2nd ed., Leiden, 2014, p. 514.

3. Titled by Gutas "The Lesser Destination," in *Avicenna and the Aristotelian Tradition*, 2nd ed., Leiden, 2014, pp. 102–103.

4. For the controversy over the identity and dating of this work, see Gutas, "The Lesser Destination," pp. 102–103, 472–476.

5. Gutas, *Avicenna and the Aristotelian Tradition*, p. 102.

6. Lenn E. Goodman, *Avicenna*, Ithaca, 2006, p. 26.

7. Abul-Hasan Bahmanyar ibn Marzban Sarali Ajami Azarbayijani, d. 1067.

8. Goodman, *Avicenna*, p. 27. The story of The Lady's rebuke to Mahmud and of Mahmud's demand for Ibn Sina is reported by Abu 'l-'Fazl Bayhaki (Beyhaqi), *Istoriia Masuda (1030–1041)*, A.K. Arends, transl., Moscow, 1969, pp. 684, ff and mentioned by Soheil M. Afnan, *Avicenna: His Life and Works*, London, 1958, p. 66.

9. William F. Gohlman, *The Life of Ibn Sina*, Albany, 1974, p. 51 and n. 67, where Golhman convincingly hypothesizes that the "wealthy lady" was in fact "The Lady," Shirin.

10. Gutas, *Avicenna and the Aristotelian Tradition*, p. 31.

11. Gohlman, *The Life of Ibn Sina*, p. 107, n. 62.

12. Ibid., p. 55.

13. Adam Mez, *The Renaissance of Islam*, New Delhi, 1995, pp. 202, 204. Jon McGinnis raised this point in his fine *Avicenna*, Oxford, 2010, pp. 22–23.

14. Gohlman, *The Life of Ibn Sina*, p. 87.

15. Alaei Moghadam J., and Mousavi Haji, "A Research on Newly Discovered Architectural Remains of Fardaghan in Farahan (A Sassanian Fire Temple or an Islamic Castle)," *International Journal of Humanities*, no. 24, 2017, pp. 81–102; see also Egyptian novelist Yousef Zaidan's *Fardaqan*, available only in Arabic and in a 2019 Italian translation, *Nel Castello di Fardaqan*.

16. Adapted from Afnan, *Avicenna: His Life and Works*, p. 70.

17. C. E. Bosworth, "'Ala'-al-Dawla Mohammad," *Encyclopædia Iranica*, I/7, pp. 773–774; online version is http://www.iranicaonline.org/articles/ala-al-dawla-abu-jafar-mohammad-b (accessed on May 15, 2014).

18. For an overview of regional developments in the era of Ala ad-Dawla, see C. E. Bosworth, "The Political and Dynastic History of the Iranian World (AD 1000–1217)," *Cambridge History of Iran*, Cambridge, vol. 5, 1968, pp. 1–203.

19. Afnan, *Avicenna: His Life and Works*, p. 70.

Chapter 12

1. Beyhaqi, *Translation of the Tarikh-I-Sultan Mahmud-I-Ghaznavi... or, the History of Sultan Mahmud of Ghazni*, p. 41.

2. S. P. Tolstov, in his *Po sledam drevnekhorezmiiskoi tsivilizatsi* (Moscow-Leningrad, 1948), draws on both written and archaeological evidence to affirm that Khwarazm had always been closely linked with India.

3. Abu Raikhan Biruni (Alberuni, Beruni), *Chronology of Ancient Nations*, Edward C. Sachau, transl, London, 1879, chs. 32–35; Bulgakov, *Zhizn i trudy Beruni*, p. 193.

4. See his *The Determination of the Coordinates of . . . Cities (Kitab Tahdid Nihayat al-Amakin Litashih al-Masakin)*, Jamil Ali, ed., Beirut, 1967, pp. 195, 260.

5. *Alberuni's India*, vol. 1, p. 154.

6. On Biruni's travels in India, see Abolhasan Dehkan, "Geographical Places Visited by Al-Biruni," in *Al-Biruni Commemorative Volume*, Calcutta, 1956, pp. 454–457.

7. Noemie Verden, "Bīrūnī as a Source for the Study of Indian Culture and History," https://www.academia.edu/3324348/B%C4%ABr%C5%ABn%C4%AB_as_a_source_for_the_study_of_Indian_culture_and_history?email_work_card=thumbnail.

8. On Biruni's command of Sanskrit, see Sunita Kumar Chatterji, "Al-Biruni and Sanskrit," in *Al-Biruni Commemoration Volume*, pp. 83–100.

9. On Biruni's use of oral sources generally, see V. Minorsky, "On Some of Biruni's Informants," *Albiruni Commemoration Volume*, Calcutta, 1956 pp. 231–239.

10. These writers are ably discussed by Hilman Latief, *Comparative Religion in Medieval Muslim Literature*, Jakarta, 2012.

11. *Alberuni's India*, vol. 1, p. 1.

12. Ibid., vol. 1, p. 19. For a recent Indian view on this work, see Avinash Singh, "Al Biruni's India," https://www.academia.edu/33759626/Al_Birunis_India?email_work_card=title.

13. *Alberuni's India*, vol. 1, p. 180.

14. Ibid., vol. 1, pp. 17 ff.

15. Ibid., vol. 1, p. 7.

16. Ibid.

17. Ibid., vol. 1, p. 23.

18. Suniti Kumar Chatterji, "Biruni and Sanskrit," in *Al-Biruni Commemoration Volume*, Calcutta, 1951, pp. 83–100.

19. John J. O'Connor and Edmund F. Robertson, "Varāhamihira," MacTutor History of Mathematics Archive, University of St. Andrews, 1999.

20. On this issue and on Biruni's competence as a translator, see Bulgakov, *Zhizn i trudy Beruni*, p. 202.

21. *Alberuni's India*, vol. 1, p. 244.

22. Ibid., vol. 1, pp. 276–277.

23. Ibid., vol. 1, p. 376.

24. Ibid., vol. 1, p. 227, where he quotes Brahmagupta calling Aryabhata a termite.

25. Ibid., vol. 1, ch. 20.

26. *Alberuni's India*, vol. 1, p. 236.

27. Ibid., vol. 2, ch. 59.

28. Ibid., vol. 2, ch, 59, pp. 110–111.

29. Ibid., vol. 1, p. 174.

30. Ibid., vol. 1, pp. 135 ff.

31. Ibid., vol. 1, ch. 15.

32. Ibid., vol. 1, p. 272.

33. Ibid., vol. 1, chs. 18, 25.

34. Biruni, *The Determination of the Coordinates of . . . Cities*, pp. 14–16; also Barani, *Al-Biruni and His Magnum Opus Al-Qanun u'l -Masudi*, p. lxviii.

35. *Alberuni's India*, pp. 400–401.

36. Ibid., ch. 22.

37. Ibid., ch. 31.

38. Ibid., vol. 2, pp. 104–106.

39. Ibid., vol. 1, pp. 312 ff.

40. Ibid., vol. 1, p. 304.

41. *Alberuni's India*, ch. 23.

42. Ibid., vol. 1, p. 7.

43. Ibid., vol. 1, pp. 319 ff.

44. Ibid., vol. 1, p. 320.

45. Ibid., vol. 1, pp. 131 ff.

46. "Al-Biruni's Arabic Version of Patanjali's Yoga Sutras," Shlomo Pines and Tuvia Gelblum, transl., *Bulletin of the School of Oriental and African Studies*, University of London, vols. 29/2, 1966, 40/3, 1977, and 46/2, 1983; and the more recent translation, *The Yoga Sutras of Patañjali*, Mario Kozah, transl. and ed., New York, 2020. The above insights on this work are drawn from Mario Kozah, *The Birth of Indology as an Islamic Science: Al-Bīrūnī's Treatise on Yoga Psychology*, Leiden, 2015.

47. *Alberuni's India*, vol. 1, pp. 38–39.

48. Ibid., vol. 1, pp. 311–333.

49. Ibid., vol. 1, p. 45.

50. Ibid., vol. 1. p. 87.

51. Ibid., vol. 1, p. 69.

52. Ibid., vol. 1, p. 96

53. Ibid., vol. 1, p. 74.

54. Ibid., vol. 1, pp. 14–15.

55. Ibid., vol. 1, p. 50.

56. Ibid., vol. 1, p. 124.

57. Ibid., vol. 1, p. 111.

58. Ibid., vol. 1, pp. 116, 121.

59. Ibid., vol. 1, pp. 18 ff.

60. Ibid.

61. Ibid., vol. 1, p. 251.

62. Ibid., vol. 1, pp. 22–23.

63. Ibid., vol. 1. pp. 4–5.

64. Ibid., Translator's Introduction, vol. 1, p. xxiii.

Chapter 13

1. Avicenna, *Canon of Medicine*, Leah Bakhtiar, ed., Chicago, 2009, vol. I, p. 9.

2. Ibid., vol. I, p. 11.

3. Ibid., vol. I, p. 39.

4. Ibid., vol. I, p. 49.

5. Ibid., vol. I, p. 146.

6. Ibid., vol. I, p. 163. On Ibn Sina's distinction among psychology, metaphysics, and logic, see Jari Kaukua, "Avicenna on Negative Judgments," April 20, 2016, https://www.academia.edu/16395165/Avicenna_on_Negative_Judgment?email_work_card=thumbnail.

7. Ibn Sina's *Najat*, cited by Seyyed Hossein Nasr, *An Introduction to Islamic Cosmological Doctrines*, Albany, 1993, p. 260.

8. Heinrich von Staden, *Herophilus: The Art of Medicine in Early Alexandria*, Cambridge, 1989.

9. Avicenna, *Canon of Medicine*, vol. I, pp. l, li.

10. Ibid., vol. I, p. l.

11. Peter E. Pormann, "Avicenna on Medical Practice, Epistemology, and the Physiology of the Inner Senses," in *Interpreting Avicenna*, Peter Adamson, ed., Cambridge, 2013, pp. 96–98.

12. Cristina Alvarez-Millan, "The Case History in Medieval Islamic Medical Literature: Tajarib and Mujarrabat as Sources," *Medical History*, 2010, no. 54, pp. 194–215; also Pormann, "Avicenna on Medical Practice, Epistemology, and the Physiology of the Inner Senses," pp. 96–97.

13. Afnan, *Avicenna: His Life and Works*, p. 206.

14. Avicenna, *Canon of Medicine*, vol. I, p. lxxi.

15. Abū Bakr Muhammad ibn Zakariyyā al-Rāzī, *Doubts on Galen: An English Translation of Rhazes' Forgotten Kitab al-Shukuk ala Jalinus*, Mohammadali M. Shoja, transl., Amsterdam, 2018.

16. Cyril Elgood, *A Medical History of Persia and the Eastern Caliphate*, Cambridge, 2010, pp. 202–203.

17. For an insightful discussion of this issue, see McGinnis, *Avicenna*, pp. 238–240.

18. Ibid., vol. 1, pp. 239–241.

19. Avicenna, *Canon of Medicine*, vol. I, p. 349.

20. Ibid., vol. I, p. 435.

21. Ibid., vol. I, pp. 445–446.

22. Ibid., vol. I, pp. 359–360.

23. Ibid., vol. I, p. 399.

24. Also, see Gutas's discussion, *Avicenna and the Aristotelian Tradition*, pp. 209–213.

25. Avicenna, *Canon of Medicine*, vol. I, p. 289.

26. Ibid., vol. I, p. 468.

27. Pormann and Savage-Smith, *Medieval Islamic Medicine*, ch. 4.

28. Zakaria Virk, "Outstanding Surgeons of Medieval Islam," https://mail.google.com/mail/u/0/#inbox/WhctKJVzfPxGJJnqTnlGkDsBpgmSdhgzmhlcnkMwskbxRbJpDtbQXCqgpgxJxkBFKzJRLGq.

29. See M. Steinschneider, "Wissenschaft und Charlatanerie unter den Arabern in neunten Jahrhundert," in *Beitraege zur Geschichte der arabisch-islamischen Medizin*, 3 vols., Frankfurt, 1987, 1, pp. 39–61.

30. Avicenna, *Poem on Medicine*, Laleh Bakhtiar, adapter, Chicago, 2013, p. 19.

31. Avicenna, "Natural Pharmaceuticals," in *The Canon of Medicine*, Laleh Bakhtiar, compiler, vol. II, Chicago, 2012.

32. Mona Nasser, Alda Tibi, and Emilie Savage-Smith, "Ibn Sina's *Canon of Medicine*: 11th Century Rules for Assessing the Effects of Drugs," *Journal of the Royal Society of Medicine*, vol. 102, no. 2, 2008, pp. 78–80; Mohammad M. Sajadi, Davood Mansouri, and Mohamad-Reza M. Sajadi, "Ibn Sina and the Clinical Trial," *Annals of Internal Medicine*, vol. 150, 2009, pp. 640–643.

33. Avicenna, *Canon of Medicine*, vol. III, pp. 835 ff.

34. Ibid., vol. III, p. 849.

35. Nasr, *An Introduction to Islamic Cosmological Doctrines*, p. 231; Gutas, *Avicenna and the Aristotelian Tradition*, p. 430.

36. Peter E. Pormann, "Medical Practice, Epistemology, and Physiology," *Interpreting Avicenna: Critical Essays*, Peter Adamson, ed., Cambridge, 2013, p. 93.

37. Avicenna, *Canon of Medicine*, vol. I, p. 2.

38. Adapted from the translation by Roger Arnaldez, "The Theory and Practice of Science According to Ibn Sina and al-Biruni," in *Al-Biruni Commemorative Volume*, H. M. Saud, ed., Karachi, 1974, p. 429.

39. Ibid., vol. 1, p. 472.

Chapter 14

1. Syed Hasan Barani, *Al-Biruni and His Magnum Opus "Al- Qanun u'l-Masudi,"* Hyderabad, 1956, p. lxxi.

2. These and the lost works mentioned in the next paragraph are cogently assessed by Bulgakov, *Zhizn i trudy Beruni*, pp. 232–235, and by Barani, *Al-Biruni and His Magnum Opus*, p. 71.

3. Said and Khan, *Al-Biruni: His Times, Life and Works*, p. 91.

4. Ibid., p. 134.

5. Nizami-i-Arudi, *Chahar Maqala*, Edward G. Browne, transl., London, 1921, p. 66.

6. P. G. Bulgakov, "Globus Biruni," *Obshchestvennye nauki v Uzbekistane*, 1965, no. 1.

7. Syed Hasan Barani, *Al-Biruni and His Magnum Opus "Al-Qanun u'l-Masudi,"* Hyderabad, 1956, p. xv.

8. Said and Hakim, *Al-Biruni: His Times, Life and Works*, pp. 81–82; Barani, *The Life and Times of Sultan Mahmud of Ghazni*, pp. 135–137.

9. Beyhaqi, *Translation of the Tarikh-I-Sultan Mahmud-I-Ghaznavi or, the History of Sultan Mahmud of Ghazni*, p. 62.

10. The account of Hasanak's grizzly demise is in Abu'l-Fazl Beyhaqi, *The History of Beyhaqi: The History of Sultan Mas'ud of Ghazna, 1030–1041*, C. E. Bosworth, transl., 3 vols., Cambridge (USA), 2011, vol. 1, pp. 270 ff.

11. Said and Khan, *Al-Biruni: His Times, Life and Works*, p. 74.

12. H. J. J. Winter, "The Place of the Qanun-i-Masudi in the History of Science," *Al Qanunu-l-Masudi (Canon Masudicus)*, vol. 3, Hyderabad, 1956, p. 1.

13. Said and Khan, *Al-Biruni: His Times, Life and Works*, p. 83.

14. See also Clifford Edmund Bosworth, *The Ghaznavids: Their Empire in Eastern Afghanistan and Eastern India, 994–1040*, New Delhi, 2015, p. 234.

15. H. J. J. Winter, "The Place of the *Al-Qanunu'l-Mas'udi (Canon Masudicus)* in the History of Science," in *Al-Qanunu'l-Masudi (Canon Masudicus)*, 3 vols., Hyderabad, 1954, vol. 1, p. 3; see also C. Schoy, "Original Studien aus al-Birunis al-Qanun al Mas'udi," *Isis*, 1923, vol. 5, pp. 5–12. See also Raymond Mercier, "Al-Biruni and the Astronomy of *al-Qanun al-Mas'udi*," *Al-Biruni and His World*, Department of Hebrew and Jewish Studies, University College London, workshop, February 15, 2016, www.ucl.ac.uk/heb rew-jewish/research/accordion/erc-workshops/al-biruni-and-his-world.

16. For Biruni's estimation of the size of the sun and its distance from the earth, see Al-Biruni, *Al-Qanunu'l-Masudi*, Hyderabad, 1954, vol. 1, pp. lvi ff.

17. *Biruni, Al Qanunu'l-Masudi (Canon Masudicus)*, III, Hyderabad, 1956, ch. 9, part 5; Syed Hasan Barani, *Al-Biruni and His Magnum Opus "Al-Qanun'l Masudi,"* Hyderabad, 1956, p. lvii.

18. Bulgakov, *Zhizn i trudy Beruni*, pp. 209–210.
19. This takes up four chapters (45–48) of *India* and the entire section seven of part six of the *Canon*. Bulgakov, *Zhizn i trudy Beruni*, p. 210.
20. Barani, *Al Biruni and His Magnum Opus "Al-Qanun u'l-Masudi,"* p. lxii.
21. Ibid., p. lv; Bulgakov, *Zhizn i trudy Beruni*, p. 212.
22. Biruni, *Al Qanunu -l-Masudi (Canon Masudicus)*, book 5, ch. 8, p. 307.
23. Ibid., pp. xxxiv–xxxv; Bulgakov, *Zhizn i trudy Beruni*, pp. 207–208.
24. A. L. Berger, "Obliquity and Precession for the Last 5,000,000 Years," *Astronomy and Astrophysics*, vol. 51, no. 1, 1976, pp. 127–135.
25. S. Frederick Starr, "So Who Did Discover America?" *History Today*, vol. 63, no. 12, 2013, pp. 1–11.
26. S. Frederick Starr, *Al-Kanun al-Masudi*, book 5, ch. 7.
27. Biruni, *Determination of the Coordinates of . . . Cities*, pp. 25–26; Masudi's *Canon*, translation by Barani, *Al Biruni and His Magnum Opus "Al-Qanun u'l-Masudi,"* pp. xxix–xxx.
28. Biruni, *Determination of the Coordinates of . . . Cities*, pp. 25–26; Masudi's Canon, translation by Barani, *Al Biruni and His Magnum Opus "Al-Qanun u'l-Masudi,"* pp. xxix–xxx.
29. *Alberuni's India*, ch. 26.
30. Beruni, *Al-kanun al-Masudi*, pp. 48–49. On this issue see B. G. Kuznetsov, *Evoliutsiia kartiny mira*, Moscow, 1961, p. 80; see also Said and Khan's brief account, *Al-Biruni: His Times, Life and Works*, pp. 118–119.
31. Yvonne Dold-Samplonius, "Al-Sijzī Abū Saʿīd Ahmad Ibn Muhammad Ibn ʿAbd Al-Jalīl," *Dictionary of Scientific Biography*, vol. 12, pp. 431–432; John J. O'Connor and Edmund F. Robertson, "Abu Said Ahmad ibn Muhammad Al-Sijzi," MacTutor History of Mathematics archive, University of St. Andrews.
32. Museum des Institutes für Geschichte der Arabisch-Islamischen Wissenschaften, *Modell des Sonnensystems und der Erdbewegung ("Planetarium") nach as-Sigzî*, Frankfurt am Main, 2010.
33. There is as yet no evidence that Sijzi or anyone else in the Muslim East knew of Aristarchus of Samos (c. 310–c. 230 BC), who had proposed a similar conception of the solar system.
34. From *Masudi's Canon*, the translation by Barani has been slightly revised by the author. Syed Hasan Barani, *Al Biruni and His Magnum Opus "Al-Qanun u'l-Masudi,"* pp. xvii–xix.
35. For a concise but authoritative summary of this centuries-long polemic, see Nick Huggett and Carl Hoefer, "Absolute and Relational Theories of Space and Motion," *Stanford Encyclopedia of Philosophy*, plato.stanford.edu/entries/spacetime-theories/.
36. Biruni's treatment of his issue has been explored in numerous works by Indian, Russian, and German astronomers, starting with Barani, *Al Biruni and His Magnum Opus "Al-Qanun u'l-Masudi,"* pp. xxii ff.
37. The fullest treatment of Biruni's trigonometry is that of C. Schoy, *Die trigonometrischen Lehren des persischen Atronomen Abu'l Rayhan Muhammad ibn Ahmad al-Biruni*, Hannover, 1927.

38. Bulgakov, *Zhizn i trudy Beruni*, p. 204.
39. For a brilliant exposition of Biruni's astronomical inventions, see B. A. Rozenfeld, M. M. Rozhanskaia, and E. K. Sokolovskaia, "Astronomiecheskie instrument," in *Abu-r-Raykhan al-Biruni, 973–1048*, Moscow, 2013, pp. 127–172.
40. M. A. Kazim, "Al-Biruni and Trigonometry," *Al-Biruni Commemoration Volume*, Calcutta, 1956, p. 163.
41. *Canon Masudi,* book 6, pt. 3.
42. Kazim, "Al-Biruni and Trigonometry," p. 164.
43. Yaqut al-Hamawī (hereafter Yaqut), *Irshad al-arib ila marifar al-adib (Dictionary of Learned Men)*, D. S. Margol, ed., 7 vols., London, 1907/1927, vol. 6, p. 311.

Chapter 15

1. Peter Heath, *Allegory and Philosophy in Ibn Sina*, p. 22.
2. The two versions of Juzjani's account are to be found in Gohlman, *The Life of Ibn Sina*, p. 33, and Gutas, *Avicenna and the Aristotelian Tradition*, pp. 103–104, reprinted here with slight editing.
3. A rigorous analysis of Ibn Sina's metaphysics as a turning point in Muslim thinking is Robert Wisnovsky, *Avicenna's Metaphysics in Context*, London, 2003.
4. "An Epistle on Colitis," *World Digital Library*, www.wdl.org.
5. For translation by W. Trask, see Seyyed Hossein Nasr and Mehdi Aminrazavi, *An Anthology of Philosophy in Persia*, New York, 1999, vol. 1, pp. 260–268. On allegory in general, on *The Book of the Prophet Mohammad's Ascent to Heaven*, and a defense of that work as Ibn Sina's, see Peter Heath, *Allegory and Philosophy in Avicenna*, Philadelphia, 1992, pp. 108 ff.
6. For three excellent expositions of this matter, see Lenn E. Goodman, *Avicenna*, Ithaca, 2006, pp. 149, 155–158, and Jon McGinnis, *Avicenna*, Oxford, 2010, pp. 145–147; and Peter Adamson and Fedor Benevich, "The Thought Experimental Method: Avicenna's Flying Man Argument," *Journal of the American Philosophical Association*, vol. 4, no. 2, 2018, pp. 147–164. See also Ahmed Alwishah, "Ibn Sina's Floating Man Arguments," *Journal of Islamic Philosophy*, vol. 9, 2013, September, pp. 32–53.
7. For a comparison between Ibn Sina and Descartes on another issue, see H. Yaldir, "Ibn Sina (Avicenna) and Descartes on the Faculty of Imagination," *British Journal for the History of Philosophy*, vol. 17, no. 7, 2009, pp. 247–278; and Brandon Zimmerman, "Thomas, Avicenna and the Philosophical Idea of Creation," American Catholic Philosophical Association, November 3, 2012, https://www.academia.edu/2172880/.
8. Hulya Yaldir, "Ibn Sīnā and Descartes on the Origins and Structure of the Universe: Cosmology and Cosmogony," *Journal of Islamic Philosophy*, vol. 5, 2009, p. 52.
9. As noted by Nasr, *An Introduction to Islamic Cosmological Doctrines*, p. 34.
10. Gutas, *Avicenna and the Aristotelian Tradition*, p. 82.
11. For a study of both phases of the Ismaili missionary movement, see S. M. Stern, "The Early Ismaili Missionaries in North-West Persia and in Khurasan and Transoxonia," *Bulletin of the School of Oriental and African Studies*, vol. 23, 1960, pp. 56–90.

12. On Sijistani, see Paul E. Walker, *Early Philosophical Shiism: The Isma'ili Neoplatonism of Abu Ya'qub al-Sijistani*, Cambridge, 2008; Salomon Pines, *La longue recension de la théologie d'Aristote dans ses rapports avec la doctrine ismaélienne*, Morocco, 1955; and R. Strothmann, *Gnosis-Teautobiographische der Ismailiten*, Göttingen, 1943.

13. For the background to this distinction, see A. M. Goichon, *La distinction de l'essence et de l'existence d'apres Ibn Sina (Avicenne)*, Paris, 1937, and D. B. Burrell, "Essence and Existence: Avicenna and Greek Philosophy," *Institut Dominicain d'Etudes Orientales du Caire (MIDEO)*, 1986, vol. 17, pp. 53–66; and for the suggestion that Ibn Sina derived this mainly from Muslim practitioners of *kalam* rather than from the Greeks, see Robert Wisnovsky, "Notes on Avicenna's Concept of Thingness (šay'iyya)," *Arabic Sciences and Philosophy*, vol. 10, 2000, pp. 181–221. For the brave of heart, far the most thorough analysis of this core issue is Wisnowksy's *Avicenna's Metaphysics in Context*, London, 2003, pt. 2.

14. On this point, see Rahim Acar, *Talking About God and Talking About Creation: Avicenna's and Thomas Aquinas' Positions*, Leiden, 2005.

15. For discussions of this that are both detailed and competent, see Goodman, *Avicenna*, pp. 63–83; Afnan, *Avicenna: His Life and Works*, pp. 124–130; and McGinnis, *Avicenna*, pp. 157–158, 182–183, 196 ff.

16. McGinnis, *Avicenna*, pp. 89 ff.

17. Afnan, *Avicenna: His Life and Works*, p. 134.

18. Nasr, *Three Muslim Stages*, p. 52. Thanks to Tajik scholars, we now have translated editions of Ibn Sina's books on plants and animals as well as on minerals. See M. Makhmadjonova and P. G. Sadykov, eds., *Abu Ali Ibn Sina (Avitsenna), Sochineniia*, vol. 9, Dushanbe, 2020–2021.

19. As quoted by Goodman, *Avicenna*, p. 155.

20. Afnan, *Avicenna: His Life and Works*, pp. 162–165.

21. Goodman, *Avicenna*, pp. 39–40, 123 ff.

22. Avicenna, "The Soul," Edward G. Browne, transl., *Literary History of Persia*, vol. 2, pp. 110–111.

23. Biruni, *Chronology of Ancient Nations*, quoted by V. Iu. Zakhidov, "Biruni kak myslitel," in Tolstov, ed., *Biruni: Sbornik statei*, p. 38.

24. Goodman, *Avicenna*, p. 185. The following discussion on Ashari is an abbreviated and greatly simplified version of Goodman's careful exposition, pp. 188–195.

25. On Ibn Sina's logic, see McGinnis, *Avicenna*, pp. 28–52; Afnan, *Avicenna: His Life and Works*, pp. 83–105; Strohmaier, *Avicenna*, pp. 96–97; Tony Street, "Avicenna on the Syllogism," in *Interpreting Avicenna*, Peter Adamson, ed., Cambridge, 2013, pp. 48–70; Goodman, *Avicenna*, pp. 188–211.

26. Street, "Avicenna on the Syllogism," p. 49.

27. Goodman, *Avicenna*, p. 209.

28. Kayhan Özaykal, "Deconstruction of Ibn Sīnā's Essence-Existence Distinction and the Essence of the Necessary Existent," *Darulfunun ilahiyat*, 2018, vol. 29, no. 1, pp. 25–48, http://dx.doi.org/10.26650/di.2018.29.1.0104.

29. For sections 1–5 of *The Cure*, see Avicenna, "La metaphysique *shifa.*" G. C. Anawati, transl., *Etudes musulmanes*, vols. 21, 27, Paris, 1978, 1985; for section 6 see F. Rahman,

ed., *Avicenna's De Anima, Being the Psychological Part of Kitab al-Shifa'*, London, 1959; also Avicenna, *the Metaphysics of the Healing*, Michael E. Marmura, ed., transl., Provo, 2005.

30. Amos Bertolacci, "How Many Recensions of Avicena's *Kitab al Sifa?*," *Oriens*, vol. 40, no. 2, pp. 275–303.

31. Vladimir Lasica, "Avicenna's Proof for God's Existence: The Proof from Ontological Considerations," *Revista Española de Filosofía Medieval*, vol. 26, no. 2, 2019, pp. 25–47.

32. H. Corbin, *Avicenne et le recit visionnaire*, 3 vols., Paris-Tehran, 1952–1954. Partial translation as *Avicenna and the Visionary Recital*, Princeton, 2014; also Nasr's summary: "The Visionary Recitals." *An Introduction to Islamic Cosmological Doctrines*, Albany, 1993, ch. 15, and p. 234.

33. Afnan, *Avicenna: His Life and His Works*, p. 233.

34. Ibid., p. 270.

35. Ibid., p. 261.

36. This general thesis is elaborated fully by H. Corbin, *Avicenne et le recit visionnaire*, 3 vols., Paris-Tehran, 1952–1954.

37. McGinnis, *Avicenna*, pp. 48–49; Strohmaier, *Avicenna*, pp. 97–100.

38. Jon McGinnis, personal communication with the author.

39. Among the most impressive of these is Andreas Lammer, *The Elements of Avicenna's Physics: Greek Sources and Arabic Innovations*, Berlin, 2018.

40. For an authoritative review of Ibn Sina's physics that balances his treatment of authority and innovation, see Andreas Lammer, *The Elements of Avicenna's Physics: Greek Sources and Arabic Innovations*, Berlin, 2018.

41. Nasr, *An Introduction to Islamic Cosmologies*, pp. 242–243.

42. M. Sate al Hosri, "Les Idees d'Avicenne sur la geologie," *Millinaire d'Avicenne: Congres de Bagdad*, Baghdad, 1952, pp. 454–463. On the origin of sedimentary rocks, see E. J. Holmyard's interesting *Avicennae de congelatione et conglutinatione lapidum*, Paris, 1927. On paleontology, see M. J. S. Rudwick, *The Meaning of Fossils: Episodes in the History of Paleontology*, Chicago, 1985, p. 24.

43. Afnan, *Avicenna: His Life and Works*, pp. 220–224.

44. Holmyard, "Avicenne de congelatione . . . ," pp. 22 ff.

45. Afnan, *Avicenna: His Life and Works*, pp. 227–228.

46. Abu Nasr al-Farabi, *Grand Traité de la Musique*, Rudolphe d'Erlanger, trans. and ed., *La musique arabe: Al-Fârâbî, Grand Traité de la Musique*, vols. 1–2, Paris, 2001.

47. See R. Rashed's study, "Mathématiques et philosophie chez Avicenne," presented at the Millenniary Colloquium of Avicenna in New Delhi, New Delhi, 1981.

48. Gutas, *Avicenna and the Aristotelian Tradition*, p. 82.

49. Ibid., pp. 337 ff.

50. Heath, *Allegory and Philosophy in Avicenna (Ibn Sina)*, pp. 147–151.

Chapter 16

1. Bosworth, *The Ghaznavids*, pp. 227-231.
2. Beyhaqi (Russian ed.), p. 611; Nazim, *The Life and Times of Sultan Mahmud of Ghazna*, p. 186.
3. W. Barthold, *Turkestan Down to the Mongol Invasion*, London, 1928, p. 293.
4. Sachau's introduction to *India*, Abu Raikhan Biruni, *Alberuni's India*, Edward C. Sachau, transl., London, 1910, vol. 1, pp. xvi ff.
5. Said and Khan, *Al-Biruni: His Times, Life, and Works*, p. 95.
6. Ibid., p. 93. This was an ode to Abu al-Fath of Bost.
7. Bulgakov, *Zhizn i trudy Beruni*, vol. 2, p. 312, reports that a fragment of this lost work was published by the Soviet scholar A. K. Arends under the title "Vvedenie k perevodu istoriia Masuda," but provides no bibliographic information.
8. Bulgakov, *Zhizn i trudy Beruni*, p. 165.
9. Yāqūt Shihāb al-Dīn ibn-'Abdullāh al-Rūmī al-Hamawī (1179-1229), Bulgakov, *Zhizn i trudy Beruni*, p. 304.
10. Richard Walzer, *Greek into Arabic: Essays on Islamic Philosophy*, Oxford, 1962, p. 17.
11. Bulgakov, *Zhizn i trudy Biruni*, pp. 287-288.
12. Not to mention a donor or patron was rare, but not unheard of. Yet it is hard not to agree with the Russian scholar Bulgakov, who proposed that this was a ruse by Biruni to hide his own initiative.
13. Bulgakov, *Zhizn I trudy Beruni*, p. 289.
14. On Biruni's early astrological writings from Gorgon, see Bulgakov, *Zhizni i trudy Biruni*, pp. 86-91.
15. Biruni, *The Book of Instruction in the Elements of the Art of Astrology by Abu-l-Rayhan Muhammad ibn Ahmad al-Biruni*, R. Ramsay Wright and M. A. Edin, trans., London, 1934; M. A. Kazim, "Al-Biruni and Trigonometry," in *Al-Biruni Commemorative Volume*, Karachi, 1974, pp. 160-66.
16. This was Biruni's tactic in his book on transits: Biruni, *Al-Biruni on Transits*, Mohammad Saffouri and Adnan Ifram, transl., *Oriental Series*, No. 32, Beirut, 1959.
17. S. Pines, "The Semantic Distinction Between the Terms *Astronomy* and *Astrology* According to Al-Biruni," *Isis*, vol. 55, no. 3, September, 1964, pp. 343-349.
18. Barani, *Al Biruni and His Magnum Opus "Al-Qanun u'l-Masudi,"* pp. lxv-lxviii.
19. E. S. Kennedy, with Fuad I. Haddad and David Pingree, "Al-Biruni's Treatise on Astrological Lots," in *Astronomy and Astrology in the Medieval Islamic World*, Edward S. Kennedy, ed., Aldershot, 1998, pp. 1-45. Also, Bulgakov, *Zhizn i trudy Biruni*, pp. 6, 91.
20. Nasr, *An Introduction to Islamic Cosmological Doctrines*, p. 163. Nasr's defense of Biruni as astrologer is to be found at pp. 163-165; also K. B. Nasim, "Al-Biruni as an Astrologer," in *Al-Biruni Commemorative Volume*, Karachi, 1974, pp. 578-581.
21. Biruni, *Geodeziia, Izbrannye proizvedendiia*, P.G. Bulgakov, ed., Tashkent, 1973, p. 260. For Biruni's careful review of astrological principles and indebtedness to the astrologers for their astronomical knowledge see Biruni, *The Book of Instruction in the Elements of the Art of Astrology*, R. Ramsay Wright, transl., London, 1934, p. 332.

22. Ibid.

23. Iu. Zakhidov, "Biruni kak myslitel," in *Biruni: Sbornik statei*, S. P. Tolstov, ed., Moscow, 1950, p. 41.

24. Barani, *Al-Biruni and His Magnum Opus "Al-Qanun u'l-Masudi,"* p. lxv.

25. Quoted from Biruni, *Al-Qanunu'l-Masudi (Canon Masiducus)*, 3 vols., Hyderabad, 1954–1956, vol. 1, p. lxvi.

26. A. M. Belenetskii, *Ocherk zhizni I trudov Biruni*, Moscow, 1963, p. 286.

27. Bosworth, *The Ghaznavids*, p. 88.

28. Fragments of this work are preserved in texts by other authors. Bulgakov, *Zhizn Zhizn i Trudy Beruni*, p. 120.

29. Ibid., p. 322.

30. Charles Pellat and D. M. Hawke, transl., *Introduction to the Life and Times of Jahiz*, Berkeley, 1969; William Hutchins, transl., *Nine Essays of al-Jahiz*, London, 1989.

31. The best translation and edition in any language is by A. M. Belenitskii: Biruni, *Sobranie svedenii dlia poznaniia dragotsennostei* (Minerlogiia), Moscow, 1963; see also an essay by G. G. Lemmlein, "Minerologicheskie svedeniia Biruni," in S. P. Tolstov, *Biruni: Sbornik statei*, Moscow-Leningrad, 1950, pp. 88–127.

    On specific gravity, see the collection *Iz istorii fiziko-matematicheskikh nauk na srednevekovom vostoke*, vol. VI, Moscow, 1983, pp. 141–174.

32. Belenitskii, *Sobranie svedenii . . .* , p. 409.

33. Biruni, *Sobranie svedenii . . .* , p. 87. The author was Utarid Ibn Muhammad.

34. S. Mahdihasan, "Interpreting Al-Biruni's Observations on Indian Alchemy," in *Al-Biruni Commemorative Volume*, H. M. Said, ed., Islamabad, 1974, pp. 524–529. While Bulgakov upholds Biruni's staunch opposition to alchemy, *Zhizn i trudy Beruni*, p. 187, Nasr offers a more nuanced assessment, *An Introduction to Islamic Cosmological Doctrines*, pp. 147–149.

35. B. A. Rozenfeld, M. M. Rozanskaia, and Z. K. Sokolovskaia, *Abu-r-Raikhan al-Biruni*, Moscow, 2014, ch. 6.

36. Abu Raikhan Biruni, *Al-Biruni's Book on Pharmacy and Materia Medica: Introduction, Commentary, and Evaluation*, S. K. Hamarneh and H. M. Said, eds. and transls., Karachi, 1973.

37. Kamal Muhammad Habib, "*The Kitab al Saydanah*: Structure and Approach," in *Al-Biruni Commemorative Volume*, Islamabad, 1974, pp. 458–473.

38. Bulgakov, *Zhizn i trudy Biruni*, p. 340.

39. Habib, "The *Kitab al -Saydanah*," p. 459.

40. Quoted by S. P. Tolstov, "Biruni I ego vremia," in *Biruni: Sbornik statei*, S. P. Tolstov, ed., Moscow-Leningrad, 1950, p. 15.

41. Ibid., p. 337.

42. A. Abdurazakov, "Alchemy and Chemistry in Early Islamic Central Asia," in *History of Civilizations of Central Asia*, vol. 4, part 2, p. 236.

43. This section is based on Biruni's introduction to his study of minerology, Biruni, *Sobranie svedenii poznaniia dragotsennostei (Minerologiia)*, A. M. Belenitskii, transl., intro., Moscow, 1963, pp. 27–28. See also Syed H. H. Nadvi, "Al-Biruni and His *Kitab al Jahamir Fi-Ma Rifah al Jawahir*: Ethical Reflections and Moral Philosophy," H. M. Said, ed., Karachi, 1974, pp. 530–544.

44. Biruni, *The Determination of the Coordinates of . . . Cities*, p. 4.

45. Ibid., p. 5.

46. See Syed H. H. Nadvi, "Biruni and His *Kitab Al-Jamahirr: Fi-Ma'Rifah al-Jamahirs*: Ethical Reflections and Moral Philosophy," in *Al-Biruni Commemorative Volume*, pp. 530 ff.

47. Evidence for Biruni's visits to Bost is his paper on determining the direction of the Qibla from that locale.

48. Yaqut, *Irshad* (Russian edition), vol. 6, p. 309, Also, Belenitskii, *Ocherk zhizni I trudov Biruni*, p. 290.

49. Bosworth, in his biographical sketch of Biruni, attributes this date to the Tajik scholar Karimov, "Biruni, Abu Rayhan, a Life," *Encyclopædia Iranica*, vol. 4, no. 3, 1990, p. 276.

Chapter 17

1. Afnan, *Avicenna: His Life and Works*, p. 70.

2. Gutas, *Avicenna and the Aristotelian Tradition*, p. 467.

3. Ahmed H. al-Rahim, "Avicenna's Immediate Disciples: Their Lives and Works," *Avicenna and His Legacy*, Langermann, ed., p. 9.

4. Entitled *Najat* or *The Salvation*, see Gutas, *Avicenna and the Aristotelian Tradition*, pp. 115 ff. Many analysts have explored the differing nuances between this work and the relevant sections of *The Cure*. Gutas, *Avicenna and the Aristotelian Tradition*, p. 225.

5. Gohlman, *The Life of Ibn Sina*, pp. 81–82.

6. Rahim, "Avicenna's Immediate Disciples," pp. 1–26.

7. Gutas, *Avicenna and the Aristotelian Tradition*, p. 503 fn.

8. David C. Reisman, "The Life and Times of Avicenna," in *Interpreting Avicenna: Critical Essays*, Peter Adamson, ed., Cambridge, 2013, pp. 15–19.

9. Ibid., p. 19.

10. Gutas, *Avicenna and the Aristotelian Tradition*, p. 330.

11. Ibid., p. 158.

12. Ibid., p. 223.

13. Afnan, *Avicenna: His Life and Works*, p. 77.

14. Ibid., p. 78.

15. David C. Reisman, "The Life and Times of Avicenna: Patronage and Learning in Medieval Islam," *Interpreting Avicenna: Critical Essays*, Peter Adamson, ed., Cambridge, 2013, p. 24.

16. Ibid.

17. Gutas, *Avicenna and the Aristotelian Tradition*, pp. 121–122, 255.

18. Louis Gardet, "Avicenne et le probleme de sa 'philosophie orientale,' " *La Revue de Caire*, vol. 27, no. 21, 1951.

19. Gutas, *Avicenna and the Aristotelian Tradition*, p. 255.

20. Several recent studies of these issues are to be found in Shahin Rahman, Tony Street, and Hassan Tahiri, eds., *The Unity of Science in the Arabic Tradition: Science Logic, and Epistemology and Their Interaction*, Dordrecht, 2008.

21. Ibid., p. 68, with grammar slightly edited.

22. Ibid., 324.

23. Seyyed Hossein Nasr, *Three Musim Sages: Avicenna Suhrawardi, Ibn Arab*, Lahore, 1988, p. 43.

24. L. Gardet, "L'Experience mystique selon Avicenne," *La Revue Caire*, 1951, no. 27, p. 64; also, J. Houben, "Avicenna and Mysticism," *Indo-Iranica*, 1953, no. 6, p. 15; Nasr, *An Introduction to Islamic Cosmological Doctrines*, pp. 182–183.

25. Goodman, *Avicenna*, p. 39.

26. A thorough discussion of Ibn Sina and alchemy is J. Ruska, "Die Alchemie des Avicenna," *Isis*, 1934, vol. 21, pp. 14–51.

27. Nazim, *Sultan Mahmud of Ghazna*, pp. 159–160.

28. For a meticulous reconstruction of the chronology of these events and insightful analysis of existing fragments of *Fair Judgment*, see Gutas, *Avicenna and the Aristotelian Tradition*, pp. 147–159.

29. "Letter to Kiya," Gutas, *Avicenna and the Aristotelian Tradition*, p. 58.

30. Afnan, *Avicenna, His Life and Works*, p. 77.

31. Gohlman, *The Life of Ibn Sina*, p. 89.

32. Ibid., pp. 85–87.

33. This assumes the earlier date for Ibn Sina's birth discussed above, p. 15.

Chapter 18

1. Gohlman, *The Life of Ibn Sina*, pp. 135–136; Gutas, *Avicenna and the Aristotelian Tradition*, pp. 149–151. Gutas, *Avicenna and the Aristotelian Tradition*, pp. 122, 436.

2. C. E. Bosworth, *The Later Ghaznavids*, New York, 1977, ch. 4.

3. Gutas, *Avicenna and the Aristotelian Tradition*, p. 436.

4. His only known student was Abu l Fadla as-Serakhsi, who left a note in the margin of a manuscript by Biruni. P. G. Bulgakov, *Zhizn i trudy Beruni*, Tashkent, 1972, p. 364.

5. Yakut (Yaqut), *Irshad*, vol. 6, p. 312.

6. An appreciative study on Ibn Zuhr is by Henry Azar, *The Sage of Seville: Ibn Zuhr, His Time, and His Medical Legacy*, Cairo, 2008.

7. Peter E. Pormann and Emilie Savage-Smith, *Medieval Islamic Medicine*, Washington, 2007, p. 79, fn. 59.

8. Jamal Moosavi, "The Place of Avicenna in the History of Medicine," *Journal of Medical Biotechnology*, 2008, April–June, pp. 3–8.

9. Hakim Syed Zillur Rahman, "Unani Medicine in India: Its Origin and Fundamental Concepts," *History of Science, Philosophy and Culture in Indian Civilization*, vol. 4, part 2, New Delhi, 2001, pp. 298–325. Also, n.a., *Unani System of Medicine*, Department of Ayush, Ministry of Health and Family Welfare, New Delhi, 2013.

10. For biographical information, see Frank Griffel, *Al-Ghazali's Philosophical Theology*, Oxford, 2009.

11. The full text is translated and edited by Michael F. Marmura: A. Ghazali, *The Incoherence of the Philosophers*, Provo, 2000.

12. Ibid., p. 226.
13. Ibid.
14. Ibid., pp. 208–225.
15. A thorough discussion of this issue is to be found in Griffel, *Al-Ghazali's Philosophical Theology*, chs. 6–7.
16. Ibid., p. 2.
17. Ibid., p. 1.
18. Ibid., p. 6.
19. Ibid., pp. 226–227. Frank Griffel refines Ghazali's views on apostasy at different points in his career but without challenging the severity of his charge against Ibn Sina, in Griffel, "Toleration and Exclusion: al-Shafi-i and al-Ghazali on the Treatment of Apostates," *Bulletin of the School of Oriental and African Studies*, vol. 64, no. 3, 2001, pp. 329–354.
20. Robert Wisnovsky, "Avicenna's Islamic Reception," in *Interpreting Avicenna*, Peter Adamson, ed., Cambridge, 2013, p. 206.
21. Unfortunately, the author did not have access to Andreas Lammer's book in progress, *The Heirs of Avicenna: Philosophy in the Islamic East from the 12th to the 13th Century*, forthcoming.
22. See Frank Griffel, "On Fahr al-Din al-Razi's Life and the Patronage He Received," *Journal of Islamic Studies*, vol. 18, no. 3, 2007, pp. 313–344, and Griffel, *Al-Ghazali's Philosophical Theology*, chs. 4 ff.
23. Ayman Shihadeh, "Avicenna's Theodicy and al-Razi's Anti-Theodicy," in *Intellectual History of the Islamic World*, vol. 7, 2019, pp. 61–84.
24. G .C. Anawati, "Fahr al-Din al-Razi," in *Encyclopedia of Islam*, 2nd ed., Leiden, 1960–2002, vol. 2, pp. 751–755.
25. Amos, "'Averroes ubique Avicennam persequitur': Albert the Great's Approach to the Physics of the Sifä' in the Light of Averroes' Criticisms," in *The Arabic, Hebrew and Latin Reception of Avicenna's Physics and Cosmology*, ed. D. N. Hasse and A. Bertolacci, Berlin, 2018, p. 397.
26. See Wisnovsky's analysis, "On the Emergence of Maragha Avicennism," *Oriens*, vol. 46, 2018, pp. 263–331. While acknowledging Wisnovsky's argument that Ibn Sina himself drew on the practitioners of *kalam*, Jon McGinnis argues the case for Ibn Sina's drawings from the Graeco-Arabic Aristotelian tradition and especially Farabi's treatment of the deity as the First Cause of the cosmos: "Old Complexes and New Possibilities: Ibn Sīnā's Modal Metaphysics in Context," *Journal of Islamic Philosophy*, vol. 7, 2011, pp. 3–34. On appropriation, see Sajjad H. Rizvi, "An Avicennian Engagement with and Appropriation of Mullā Ṣadrā Šīrāzī (d. 1045/1636)," *Oriens*, vol. 48, 2020, pp. 219–249.
27. On *kalam*, see W. L. Craig, *The Kalam Cosmological Argument*, London, 1979; and H. A. Wolfson, *The Philosophy of the Kalam*, Cambridge, 1976. See also Peter Adamson, *Philosophy in the Islamic World*, New York, 2016, p. 181.
28. Amos Bertolacci, "Avicenna's Kitāb al-Šifä' (Book of the Cure/Healing): The Manuscripts Preserved in Turkey and Their Significance," *The Reception of the Classical Arabic Philosophy in the Ottoman Empire*, J. Jabbour, ed., Mélanges de l'Université Saint-Joseph, vol. 67, 2017–2018, pp. 265–304 ff.

29. For an overview of Judaism and Ibn Sina, see Gad Freudenthal and Mauro Zonta, "The Reception of Avicenna in Jewish Cultures, East and West," *Interpreting Avicenna*, Peter Adamson, ed., Cambridge, 2013, pp. 214–242; and for a fine-grained study of Muslim-Jewish intellectual interaction, see Lenn E. Goodman, *Jewish and Islamic Philosophy*, New Brunswick, 1999, esp. chs. 1, 4.

30. Goodman, *Jewish and Islamic Philosophy*, p. 8.

31. Ibid., p. 13.

32. L. V. Berman, "Maimonides, the Disciple of Alfarabi," *Israel Oriental Studies*, no. 4, 1974, pp. 54–78.

33. Alfred L. Ivrey, "The *Guide* and Maimonides' Philosophical Sources," Kenneth Seeskin, ed., *The Cambridge Companion to Maimonides*, Cambridge, 2005, pp. 68–72.

34. Sajjad H. Rizvi, "An Avicennian Engagement with and Appropriation of Mullā Ṣadrā Šīrāzī (d. 1045/1636)," *Oriens*, vol. 48, 2020, pp. 219–249.

35. Bulgakov, *Zhizn i trudy Beruni*, p. 365. One might also note the thirteenth-century collector of Biruni's works, Ibrahmim ibn Muhammad al-Gadanfor at-Tabrizi, the Syrian geographer Abu-l-Fida, and the Egyptian encyclopedist al-Kalkashandi, all of whom at least mention Biruni.

36. Nasr, *An Introduction to Islamic Cosmologies*, p. 112.

37. A thorough compilation of extant copies of Biruni's *Canon* is being prepared by Eleonora Bacchi, "The Manuscript Tradition of al-Biruni's *Canon Masudicus*," conference on "Al-Biruni and His World," University College, London, Department of Hebrew and Jewish Studies, Workshop 7 February, 2016: https://www.researchgate.net/publicat ion/294722686_The_Manuscript_Tradition_of_al-Biruni's_Canon_Masudicus.

38. Nur ad-Din al-Bitruji (d. ca. 1204) was a judge and astronomer from Andalusia who, like Biruni, sought to push beyond Ptolemy's model of the solar system. See Julio Samsó, "Al-Bitruji Al-Ishbili, Abu Ishaq," *Dictionary of Scientific Biography*, vol. 15, New York, 1976, pp. 33–36.

39. U. I. Krachkovskii, "*Arabskaia geograficheskaia literatura*," *Izbrannye sochineniia*, Moscow-Leningrad, 1957, vol. 4, p. 529; and A. M. Belenitskii's essay on the place of Biruni's mineralogical study in the history of eastern minerology, in his translation of Biruni's, *Sobranie svedenii dlia poznaniia dragotsennostei (Minerologiia)*, A.M. Belenitskii, trans. and ed., Moscow, 1963, p. 418.

40. B. Akhmedov, "Makhmud ibn Vali i ego entsiklopedicheskii trud," *Obshchestvennye nauki v Uzbekistane*, 1969, no. 1, pp. 63–64.

41. Juan Cole, trans., *The Rubaiyat of Omar Khayyam*, London, 2020, pp. 3–16.

42. For a concise overview of Khayyam and his relationship to Biruni, see A. Youschkevitch and B. Rosenfeld, 1973, "al-Khayyāmī," in *Dictionary of Scientific Biography*, New York, 1973, vol. vii, pp. 323–334.

43. On Khazini's development of Biruni's minerology, see Belenitskii, "Mesto mineralogicheskogo traktata Biruni, v istorii vostochnoi mineralogii," in Biruni, *Sobranie svedenii dlia poznaniia dragotsennostei*, pp. 414–416. D. R. Hill, "Physics and Mechanics," in *History of Civilization of Central Asia*, vol. 4, pt. 2, Paris, 2000, pp. 254–259.

44. For a major surviving work by Tusi, see Jamil Raceb, ed. and transl., *Nasir al-Din Tusi's Memoir on Astronomy (al-Tadhkira fi ʿilm al-hay')*, 2 vols., in *Sources in the History of Mathematics and Physical Sciences*, New York, 1993.

45. Wisnovsky, "On the Emergence of Maragha Avicennism," pp. 263 ff.

46. These issues are carefully analyzed by Robert Wisnowsky, "Towards a Genealogy of Avicennism," *Oriens*, vol. 42, 2014, pp. 323–363; and in "On the Emergence of Maragha Avicennism."

47. M. A. Kazim, "Al-Biruni and Trigonometry," *Al-Biruni Commemorative Volume*, Islamabad, 1974, p. 162.

48. Jamil Raqer, transl. and ed., *Nasir al-Din Tusi's Memoir on Astronomy*, 2 vols., *Sources in the History of Mathematics and Physical Sciences*, New York, 1993. Also "Al-Tusi, Nasir biography," www-history.mcs.st-andrews.ac.uk.; and "Nasir al-Din al-Tusi (1201–1274)," www-history.mcs.st-andrews.ac.uk.

49. Nizam al-a'Raj, Mu'yed al-Din al-Arad-Najmedin Cathy, Najmd al-Din Qazvini, Allame Qutbuddin Shirazi, Fahruddin Maraghi, Muhyi al-Din al-Maghribi (d. 1283), Mu'ayyid al-Din al-'Urdi (1200–1266), who helped design the observatory at Maragha.

50. Stephen P. Blake, "The Observatory in Maragha," *Astronomy and Astrology in the Islamic World*, Edinburgh, 2016, p. 65. For an early study, see E. Wiedemann and T. W. Juynboll, "Avicennas Schrift über ein von ihmersonnenes Beobachtungsinstrument," *Acta Orientalia*, vol. 11, 1926, pp. 81–167. More comprehensive is S. M. Mozaffari and S. M. G. Zotti, "Ghāzān Khān's Astronomical Innovations at Marāgha Observatory," *Journal of the American Oriental Society*, vol. 132, 2012, pp. 395–425. Extended version at 280208-text de l'article-284090-1-10-20140908.pdf.

51. D. Y. Yusupova, *Piasma Giyas ad-Dina Kashi k svoemu otsu iz Samarkanda v Kashan*, Tashkent, 1979, pp. 53–57; T. N. Kori-Nieziy, *Ulugbek va uning ilmiy merosi*, Tashkent, 1971, pp. 95 ff.; also K. Krisciunas, "The Legacy of Ulugh Beg," *AACR Bulletin*, vol. 5, no. 1, 1992.

52. In his argument against "philosophy," Qushji followed the world of Ibn Al-Shatir (1304–1375). As of this writing, Qushchi's work is not available in any Western language. See, however, Kaynak Yayınları, *Ali Kuşçu, Çağını Aşan Bilim İnsanı*, Istanbul, 2010, and George Saliba, "Al-Qushji's Reform of the Ptolemaic Model for Mercury," *Arabic Sciences and Philosophy*, vol. 3, 1993, pp. 161–203.

53. See George Saliba's fascinating, "Revisiting the Astronomical Contacts Between the World of Islam and Renaissance Europe: The Byzantine Connection," in *The Occult Sciences in Byzantium*, Paul Magdalino and Maria Mavroudi, eds., Geneva, 2006, pp. 361–374.

54. C. Burnett, "Arabic into Latin: The Reception of Arabic Philosophy into Western Europe," in *The Cambridge Companion of Arabic Philosophy*, Cambridge, 2005, pp. 370–404.

55. Amos Bertolacci, "The Reception of Avicenna in Latin Medieval Culture," *Interpreting Avicenna*, pp. 259–264.

56. Amos Bertolacci, "The Latin Translation and the Original Version of the Ilāhiyyāt (Science of Divine Things) of Avicenna's Kitāb al-Šifā,'" *Documenti e Studi sulla Tradizione Filosofica Medievale*, vol. 28, 2017, pp. 481–514.

57. Bertolacci, "The Reception of Avicenna in Latin Medieval Culture," pp. 245–248, and "A Community of Translators: The Latin Medieval Versions of Avicenna's *Kitab al-Shifa (Book of the Cure)*," in *Communities of Learning: Networks and the Shaping of Intellectual Identity in Europe, 1100–1450*, John N. Crossley and Constant J. Mews, eds., Turnhout, 2011, pp. 37–54. Amos Bertolacci, "Albert the Great and the Preface

of Avicenna's Kitāb al-Šifā," in *Avicenna and His Heritage. Acts of the International Colloquium*, J. Janssens and D. De Smet, eds., Leuven, 2002, pp. 131–152, and "On the Latin Reception of Avicenna's Metaphysics before Albertus Magnus: An Attempt at Periodization," in *The Arabic, Hebrew and Latin Reception of Avicenna's Metaphysics*, D. N. Hasse and A. Bertolacci, eds., Berlin, 2012, pp. 197–223.

58. On Arabic-Latin influences overall, see Charles S. F. Burnett, *The Translators and Their Intellectual and Social Context: Arabic into Latin in the Middle Ages*, Farnham, UK, 2009, p. 267; D. N. Hasse, *Success and Suppression: Arabic Sciences and Philosophy in the Renaissance*, Cambridge, 2016; also G. Quadri, *La philosophie arabe dans l'Europe medievale*, Paris, 1947.

59. See A. M. Goichon's classic study, *La Philosophie d'Avicenne et son influence en Europe medievale*, 2nd ed., Paris, 1951; also Dag Nikolaus Hasse, "The Influence of Arabic and Islamic Philosophy on the Latin West," *Stanford Encyclopedia of Philosophy*, revised, Stanford, 2020, https://plato.stanford.edu/entries/arabic-islamic-influence/. For Ibn Sina and a fourth-century Roman thinker on this point, see Michael Chase, "Essence and Existence in Marius Victorinus and in Avicenna," *Revue de Philosophie Ancienne*, vol. 37, no. 1, 2019, pp. 101–151.

60. McGinnis, *Avicenna*, pp. 172–177.

61. Louis de Raeymaeker, *Vergelijkende studie over de betekenis van het "zijn" in de metafysiek van Avicenna en die van Thomas van Aquino*, Brussels, 1955, pp. 11 ff.

62. An authoritative evaluation of the impact of Avicenna's metaphysics is Dag Nikolaus Hasse, ed., *The Arabic, Hebrew and Latin Reception of Avicenna's Metaphysics*, Berlin, 2011. On Ibn Sina and Aquinas, see Pasquale Porro, "Immateriality and Separation in Avicenna and Thomas Aquinas," *The Arabic, Hebrew, and Latin Reception of Avacenna's Metaphysics*, Dag Nikolaus Hasse, Amos Berolacci, eds. Boston, 2011, pp. 275–308; Kara Richardson, "Avicenna and Aquinas on Form and Generation," loc. cit., pp. 251–274; and Robert Wisnovsky, *Avicenna's Metaphysics in Context*, London, 2003, pp. 145–180.

63. Brandon Zimmerman summarizes the several views on this issue in "Thomas, Avicenna and the Philosophical Idea of Creation," American Catholic Philosophical Association, November 3, 2012, https://www.academia.edu/2172880/.

64. On this point, see Rahim Acar, *Talking About God and Talking About Creation: Avicenna's and Thomas Aquinas' Positions*, Leiden, 2005.

65. St. Thomas Aquinas, *On the Unity of Intellect*, Milwaukee, 1968; and *On the Eternity of the World*, Milwaukee, 1964.

66. Goodman, *Avicenna*, intro., p. xiii.

67. On him, see "John Duns Scotus," *Stanford Encyclopedia of Philosophy*, https://plato.stanford.edu/entries/duns-scotus/.

68. Amos Bertolacci, "On the Latin Reception of Avicenna's Metaphysics before Albertus Magnus: An Attempt at Periodization," *The Arabic, Hebrew, and Latin Reception of Avicenna's Metaphysics*, A. Bertolacci and D. N. Hasse, eds., Berlin, 2012, pp. 197–223.

69. Also known as Gerard of Cremona, but not to be confused with the earlier Gerard of Cremona, who worked as a translator at the newly reconquered capital of Toledo in Castille.

70. For an incomplete but valuable listing, see Said Naficy, *Bibliographie des principaux travaux europeens sur Avicenne*, Tehran, 1953.

71. M.N. Abrams, *Norton Anthology of English Literature*, 7th ed., vol. 1. *Canterbury Tales*, lines 413–423.

72. S. H. N. "Avicenna," *Encyclopaedia Britannica*, 1993 ed., vol. 1, pp. 739–740.

73. For a meticulously researched overview of these and related developments, see Nancy G. Siraisi, *Avicenna in Renaissance Italy: The Canon and Medical Teaching in Italian Universities after 1500*, Princeton, 1987, pp. 194–201. The following discussion is based on her research.

    John Aubrey, *Brief Lives*, Oxford, 1898, p. 300, as cited by Siraisi, *Avicenna in Renaissance Italy*, p. 353.

74. Ibid., pp. 143, 151.

75. For an interesting study of the rejection of Galen's and Ibn Sinia's medicine, see Walter Pagel, *Paracelsus: An Introduction to Philosophical Medicine in the Era of the Renaissance*, Basel, 1958.

76. John Aubrey, *Brief Lives*, Oxford, 1898, p. 300, as cited by Siraisi, *Avicenna in Renaissance Italy*, p. 353.

77. On Biruni and other Muslim thinkers in Sicily, see Hubert Houben, *Roger II of Sicily: Ruler Between East and West*, Cambridge, 2002.

78. Gunther Mensching, "Roger Bacon and Islamic Physics and Metaphysics," *Thomas d'Aquin et ses sources arabes/Aquinas and the Arabs*, Paris, 2014, https://www.acade mia.edu/10752599/Thomas_d_Aquin_et_ses_sources_arabes_Aquinas_and_the_ Arabs_Bulletin_de_Philosophie_Médiévale_2013.

79. M. S. Khan, "Tabaqat al-Umam of Qadi Sa'id al-Anfalusi (1029–1070 A.D.)," *Indian Journal of the History of Science*, vol. 30, 1995, nos. 2–4.

80. Nasr, *An Introduction to Islamic Cosmological Doctrines*, p. 112.

81. For a clear analysis of Tusi's astronomy and a judicious overview of the likely impact of the Tusi Couple on Copernicus, see George Saliba, *Islamic Science and the Making of the European Renaissance*, Cambridge, 2007, pp. 155 ff. and ch. 6.

82. Cited as a possible transmitter is Ibn al-Shatir (1304–1375), a Syrian astronomer whose *The Final Quest Concerning the Rectification of Principles* employed the Tusi Couple to do away with the traditional account of the speed change of planets in the course of their orbits. See also the detailed accounts in N. M. Swerdlow and O. Neugebauer, *Mathematical Astronomy in Copernicus's "De Revolutionibus,"* New York, 1984; F. Jamil Ragep, "Copernicus and His Islamic Predecessors: Some Historical Remarks," *Filozofski vestnik*, Ljubljana, vol. 25, 2004, no. 2, pp. 125–142; and Emilie Savage-Smith (November 2008), "Islamic Influence on Copernicus," *Journal for the History of Astronomy*, vol. 39, no. 1, 2008, pp. 538–541.

83. Summarized in Saliba, *Islamic Science and the Making of the European Renaissance*, pp. 199–214.

84. H. J. J. Winter, "The Place of *Al-Qanun 'l-Masudi (Canon Masudicus)* in the History of Science," *Al Qanun 'l-Masudi (Canon Masudicus)*, Hyderabad, 1956, vol. 1, p. 7; see N. Khanykov, *Memoire sur la partie meridionale de l'Asie centrale*, Paris, 1861.

85. Karl Popper, *Logik der Forschung*, Vienna, 1935. transl. as *The Logic of Scientific Discovery*, Abingdon-on-Thames, 1959.

86. George Sarton, *Introduction to the History of Science*, 3 vols., Baltimore, 1927–1948.

Chapter 19

1. Biruni, *Geodeziia*, p. 106.

2. J. Lameer, "Avicenna's Concupiscence," *Islamic Sciences and Philosophy*, vol. 23, no. 1, 2013, pp. 277–289.

3. This refers to his use of his teacher Abdhallah al-Natali's research on Dioscorides in his *Canon*. While there has been debate over whether this was the same Naftali who appeared in Gurganj, Ibn Sina himself confirms that it was. Gohlman, *The Life of Ibn Sina*, p. 25.

4. Gutas, *Avicenna and the Aristotelian Tradition*, p. 16.

5. Ibid., p. 197.

6. Biruni, *The Chronology of Ancient Nations*, p. 84.

7. Quoted by Paul Feyerabend, *Against Method*, London, New York, 1975, p. 49.

8. Ibid., p. 7.

9. Biruni, *Sobranie svedenii poznaniia dragotsennostei (Mineralogiia)*, A. M. Belenitskii, transl. and intro., Moscow, 1963, p. 4; also A. M. Belenitskii, "O minerologii Biruni," S. P. Tolstov, *Biruni: Sbornik statei*, Moscow-Leningrad, 1950, p. 38.

10. Alberuni, *Chronology of Ancient Nations*, pp. 294–295.

11. Bulgakov, *Zhizn i trudy Beruni*, p. 150.

12. Biruni, *Chronology of Ancient Nations*, p. 4; also A. M. Belenitskii, "Mesto minerologichskogo traktata Biruni v istorii vostochnoi mineralogii," in Biruni, "*Sobranie svedenii dlia poznaniia dragotsennostei (Mineralogiia)*, Moscow, 1963, p. 38.

13. *Alberuni's India*, vol. 1, p. 160.

14. *Alberuni's India*, vol. 1, p. 776; also Barani, *Al-Biruni and His Magnum Opus "An-Qanun u'l-Masudi,"* p. lviii, liv.

15. In his *The Determination of the Coordinates of . . . Cities, India*, and *Masud's Canon*.

16. *Alberuni's India*, vol. 1, Islamabad, 1974, p. 637.

17. R. Arnaldez, "The Theory and Practice of Science According to Ibn Sina and al-Biruni," *Al-Biruni Commemorative Volume*, H. N. Said, ed., Karachi, 1974, p. 432.

18. Saleh K. Hamarneh, "Notes on Al-Biruni's Views of Al-Razi's Works," in *Al-Biruni Commemorative Volume*, p. 477.

19. For Biruni, see, among others, *Sobranie svedenii poznaniia dragotsennostei (Mineralogiia)*, A. M. Belenitskii, transl., and intro., Moscow, 1963, pp. 11–34. For Ibn Sina, see especially the last six chapters of his *Metaphysics*. Contrast these passages to Erwin Rosenthal's claim that practically every page of Ibn Sina's writing contained

thoughts on politics; *Political Thought in Medieval Islam: An Introductory Outline*, Westport, 1985, 147.

20. This section draws on Jon McGinnis's excellent chapter on "Value Theory" in his *Avicenna*, pp. 209–226.

21. Ibid., p. 219.

22. James W. Morris, "The Philosopher-Prophet in Avicenna's Political Philosophy," in *The Political Aspects of Islamic Philosophy*, Charles E. Butterworth, ed., Cambridge, MA, 1992, pp. 152–198.

23. Biruni, *India*, vol. I, p. 320.

24. For full citations in support of Biruni's supposed materialism see Bulgakov, *Zhizn i trudy Beruni*, pp. 210 ff.

25. Ibid.

26. Ibid.

27. Jamil Ragep, "Freeing Astronomy from Philosophy: An Aspect of Islamic Influence on Science," *Osiris*, 2001, no. 16, pp. 49 ff.

28. Biruni, *Sobranie svedenii dlia posnaniia dragotsennostei (mineralogiia)*, A. M. Belenetskii, transl., G. G. Lemmlein, ed., Tashkent, 1963

29. Paul E. Walker, *Abu Yaqub al-Sijistani*, London, 1996, p. 32.

30. Joep Lameer, "Towards a New Edition of Avicenna's *Kitab al-Isharat wa-l-tanbihat*," *Journal of Islamic Manuscripts*, vol. 4, no. 2, 2013, pp. 199–248.

31. Mohd. Badruddin Alavi, "Some Aspects of the Literary and Poetical Activities of Avicenna," in *Avicenna Commemoration Volume*, V. Courteois, ed., Calcutta, 1956, pp. 179–186.

32. Alberuni, *Chronology of Ancient Nations*, I, p. 115.

33. Ibid., p. 114.

34. Nasr, *An Introduction to Islamic Cosmological Doctrines*, p. 113. For a Muslim defense of Biruni's religious affirmations, see pp. 166–176.

35. Cited from *Minerology* by S. H. Barani, Ibn Sina, and Al-Biruni, *Avicenna Commemoration Volume*, Calcutta, 1956, p. 13.

36. *Alberuni's India*, vol. I, pp. 400–401.

37. Ibid., p. 433.

38. Ibid., vol. I, pp. 400–401.

39. Nasr, *An Introduction to Islamic Cosmology*, p. 115.

40. Quoted by Arnaldez, "The Theory and Practice of Science According to Ibn Sina and al-Biruni," p. 433.

41. Biruni, *The Determination of the Coordinates of . . . Cities*, p. 3.

42. Resianne Fontaine, " 'Happy Is He Whose Children Are Boys': Abu Ibn Dauda and Avicenna on Evil," Dag Nikolaus Hasse and A. Bertolacci, eds., *The Arabic, Hebrew, and Latin Reception of Avicenna's Metaphysics*, Berlin/Boston, 2012, pp. 161 ff.

43. Thomas S. Kuhn, *The Structure of Scientific Revolutions*, Chicago, 1962, esp. ch. 6, 7.

44. Virgil, *Georgics*, Books I–II, "Felix qui potuit rerum cognoscere causas."

Bibliography

Abdurazakov, "Alchemy and Chemistry in Early Islamic Central Asia," in *History of Civilizations of Central Asia*, vol. 4, part 2, p. 236.

Rahim Acar, "The Possibility of Equation Between Reason and Revelation: Was Ibn Sina a Deist?" *International Journal of Religion and Philosophical Research*, vol. 1, no. 1, 2018, pp. 6–18.

Rahim Acar, *Talking About God and Talking About Creation: Avicenna's and Thomas Aquinas' Positions*, Leiden, 2005.

Peter Adamson, *Classical Philosophy, Oxford, 2016.*

Peter Adamson, ed., *Interpreting Avicenna: Critical Essays*, Cambridge, 2013.

Peter Adamson, *Philosophy in the Islamic World*, New York, 2016.

Peter Adamson, with Fedor Benevich, "The Thought Experimental Method: Avicenna's Flying Man Argument," *Journal of the American Philosophical Association*, vol. 4, no. 2, 2018, pp. 147–164.

Soheil M. Afnan, *Avicenna, His Life and Works*, London 1958.

I. I. Ahmad, "Al-Biruni's Astronomical Works," *Bulletin of Cairo University*, Cairo, no. 48, 1959, and no. 57, 1962.

I. I. Ahmad, "The Works of Al-Bayrouni," *Bulletin of Cairo University*, Cairo, no. 50, 1959.

B. Akhmedov, "Makhmud ibn Vali i ego entsiklopedicheskii trud," *Obshchestvennye nauki v Uzbekistane*, 1969, no. 1, pp. 63–64.

Ahmed H. al-Rahim, "Avicenna's Immediate Disciples: Their Lives and Works," *Avicenna and His Legacy*, Langermann, ed., p. 9.

Roger Arnaldez, "The Theory and Practice of Science According to Ibn Sina and al-Biruni," in *Al-Biruni Commemorative Volume*, Hakim Said, ed., Islamabad, 1979, pp. 428–435.

Cristina Alvarez-Millan, "The Case History in Medieval Islamic Medical Literature: Tajarib and Mujarrabat as Sources," *Medical History*, no. 54, 2010, pp. 194–215.

Al-Biruni, *Al-Qanunu'l-Masudi*, Hyderabad, 1954, vol. 1, pp. lvi, ff.

"Al-Biruni and His World," Department of Hebrew and Jewish Studies University College London, workshop of February 15, 2016, https://blogs.ucl.ac.uk/calendars-ancient-medieval-project/2016/10/03/al-biruni.

Ahmed Alwishah, "Ibn Sina's Floating Man Arguments," *Journal of Islamic Philosophy*, vol. 9, 2013, September, pp. 32–53.

Georges C. Anawati, "Biruni, Abu Rayhan, Pharmacology and Mineralogy," www.iranicaonline.org, 1989.

G. C. Anawati, transl., *Etudes musulmanes*, vols. 21, 27, Paris, 1978, 1985.

G. C. Anawati, "Fakhr al-Din al-Razi," *Encyclopedia of Islam*, 2nd ed., Leiden, 1960–2002. vol. 2, pp. 751–755.

K. A. Arends, *Biruni: Sbornik statei k 1000- letiiu so dnia ego rozhdeniia*,Tashkent, 1975.

Aristotle, *Prior Analytics,* A. J. Jenkinson, transl., Middletown, DE, 2016.

Aristotle, *The Complete Works of Aristotle: The Revised Oxford Translation*, Jonathan Barnes, ed., Oxford, 1984.

Nizami-i-Arudi, (Abu'l Fadl Beyhaqi), A Revised Translation of the Chahár maqála ("Four discourses") of Nizámí-i'Arúdí of Samarqand), Edward G. Browne, transl. London, 1921.

M. S. Asimov and C. E. Bosworth, eds., *History of Civilizations of Central Asia*, vol. 4, pt. 1, 2, Paris, 1998.

Kemal Ataman, "Understanding Other Religions: Al-Biruni and Gadamar's 'Fusion of Horizons,'" *Cultural Heritages and Contemporary Change*, Series II-A, *Islam*, vol. 19, Washington, 2008.

Avicenna (Ibn Sina), *Sochineniia*, 9 vols., Dushanbe, 1979–2021.

Avicenna (Ibn Sina), *Canon of Medicine*, Laleh Bakhtiar, comp., 5 vols., Chicago, 2012.

Avicenna (Ibn Sina), *Avicenna's Deliverance: Logic*, Asad Q. Ahmed, transl. and ed., Oxford, 2014.

Avicenna (Ibn Sina), *Avicenna's Psychology*, F. Rahman, transl., London, 1959.

Avicenna (Ibn Sina), *Avicenna's Psychology*, Laleh Bakhtiar, transl., Chicago, 2013.

Avicenna (Ibn Sina), "al-As'ilah wa'lajwibah (Questions and Answers) Including the Further Answers of al-Biruni and al-Ma'sumi's Defense of Ibn Sina" (in Farsi), S. H. Nasr and M. Mohaghegh, transl. and ed., High Council of Culture and Art, Tehran, 1973, pp. 74–85. English translation: "Ibn-Sina-Al-Biruni Correspondence," Rafiq Berjak, Muzaffar Iqbal, transls., *Islam and Science*, vols. 1–5, 2003–2007.

Avicenna (Ibn Sina), *Refutation de l'astrologie*, Yahya Jean Michot, transl., Beirut-Paris, 2006.

Avicenna (Ibn Sina), "An Epistle on Colitis," World Digital Library, www.wdl.org.

Avicenna (Ibn Sina), *Poem on Medicine (Urjusa fi'l tibb)*, Laleh Bakhtiar, comp., Chicago, 2013.

Avicenna (Ibn Sina), *Remarks and Admonitions: Logic*, part 1, S. C. Inati, transl., Toronto, 1984.

Avicenna (Ibn Sina), *The Metaphysics of the Healing*, Michael E. Marmura, transl., Provo, 2005.

Avicenna (Ibn Sina), "The Soul," Edward G. Browne, transl., *Literary History of Persia*, vol. 2, pp. 110–111.

Avicenna (Ibn Sina), *Avicenna's Psychology. An English Translation of Kit'b al-Naj't, Book II, Chapter VI, with Historico-Philosophical Notes and Textual Improvements on the Cairo Edition*, Fazlur Rahman, transl., London, 1952.

Avicenna (Ibn Sina), Jon McGinnis, transl., ed., *The Physics of the Healing: A Parallel English-Arabic Text*, 2 vols., Provo, 2009.

Avicenna (Ibn Sina), *Avicenna on Theology*, Arthur J. Arberry, transl., Westport, 1951.

Avicenna (Ibn Sina), *Avicenna's Treatise on Logic*, F. Zabeeh, transl., The Hague, 1971.

Avicenna (Ibn Sina), *The Life of Ibn Sina*, William F. Gohlman, transl., Albany, 1974.

Department of Ayush, Ministry of Health and Family Welfare, New Delhi, *Unami System of Medicine*, New Delhi, 2013.

Henry Azar, *The Sage of Seville: Ibn Zuhr, His Time, and His Medical Legacy*, Cairo, 2008.

Eleonora Bacchi, "The Manuscript Tradition of al-Biruni's *Canon Masudicus*," conference on "Al-Biruni and His World," University College, London, Department of Hebrew and Jewish Studies, Workshop 7, February 2016, https://www.researchgate.net/publicat ion/294722686_The_Manuscript_Tradition_of_al-Biruni's_Canon_Masudicus.

Syed Hasan Barani, *Al Biruni and His Magnum Opus "Al-Qanun u'l-Masudi,"* Hyderabad, 1956.

W. Barthold, *Turkestan Down to the Mongol Invasion*, London, 1928.

Abu l'Fazl Bayhaqi, *Istoriia Masuda (1030–1041)*, A. K. Arends, transl., Moscow, 1969.

A. M. Belenitskii, "Kartina mira po Biruni," *Uchenye zapiski LGU*, vol. 1, Leningrad, 1949.

A. M. Belenitskii, *Ocherk zhizni i trudov Biruni*, Moscow, 1963.

A. M. Belenitskii, "Mesto minerologichskogo traktata Biruni v istorii vostochnoi minerologii," in Biruni, *Sobranie svedenii dlia poznaniia dragotsennostei (Minerologiia)*, Moscow, 1963.

Fedor Benevich, "The Thought Experimental Method: Avicenna's Flying Man Argument," *Journal of the American Philosophical Association*, vol.4, no.2, 2018, pp. 147–164.

B. Ben-Yahia, "Avicenne medicin. Sa vie, son oeuvre," *La Revue d'Histoire des Sciences*, vol. 5, 1952, pp. 350 ff.

L. Berger, "Obliquity and Precession for the Last 5,000,000 Years," *Astronomy and Astrophysics*, vol. 51, no. 1, 1976, pp. 127–135.

L. V. Berman, "Maimonides, the Disciple of Alfarabi," *Israel Oriental Studies*, no. 4, 1974, pp. 54–78.

Amos Bertolacci, "Avicenna's Kitāb al-Šifā' (Book of the Cure/Healing): The Manuscripts Preserved in Turkey and Their Significance," in *The Reception of the Classical Arabic Philosophy in the Ottoman Empire*, J. Jabbour, ed., Mélanges de l'Université Saint-Joseph, vol. 67, 2017–2018, pp. 265–304 ff.

Amos Bertolacci, "The Distinction of Essence and Existence in Avicenna's Metaphysics: The Text and Its Context," in *Islamic Philosophy, Science, Culture, and Religion: Studies in Honor of Dimitri Gutas*, F. Opwis and D. C. Reisman, eds., Leiden, 2012, pp. 257–288.

Amos Bertolacci, "How Many Recensions of Avicenna's *Kitab al Sifa*?" *Oriens*, vol. 4, no. 2, 2012, pp. 275–303.

Amos Bertolacci, "The Latin Translation and the Original Version of the Ilāhiyyāt (Science of Divine Things) of Avicenna's Kitāb al-Šifā,'" *Documenti e Studi sulla Tradizione Filosofica Medievale*, vol. 28, 2017, pp. 481–514.

Amos Bertolacci, "Averroes ubique Avicennam 'persequitur': Albert the Great's Approach to the Physics of the Sifā' in the Light of Averroes' Criticisms," *The Arabic, Hebrew and Latin Reception of Avicenna's Physics and Cosmology*, ed. D. N. Hasse and A. Bertolacci, Berlin, 2018, pp. 397–431.

Abu'l-Fazl Bayhaki (Beyhaqi), *Istoriia Masuda (1030-1041)*, A.K. Arends, transl., Moscow, 1969.

Abu'l-Fazl Beyhaqi, *The History of Beyhaqi: The History of Sultan Mas'ud of Ghazna, 1030–1041*, C.E. Bosworth, transl., 3 vols., Cambridge (USA), 2011.

Abu'l-Fazl Bayhaqi, *Translation of the Tarikh-I-Sultan Mahmud-I-Ghaznavi or, the History of Sultan Mahmud of Ghazni*, G. Roos-Keppel and Qazi Abdul Ghani Khan, transl., Lahore, 1908.

Abu Musa Mohammad Arif Billah, ed., *Book of Abstracts: First Biruni (Al-Biruni) International Conference*, Dhaka, 2014.

E. E. Birtels, ed. and transl., *Kabus-name, perevod, statia, i primechaniia*, Moscow, 1953.

Abu Raikhan Biruni (Alberuni, Beruni), *The Chronology of Ancient Nations*, Edward C. Sachau, transl., London, 1879.

Abu Raikhan Biruni, *Alberuni's India*, Edward C. Sachau, transl., London, 1910.

Abu Raikhan Biruni, *Al-Kanun-ul-Masudi (Canon Masudicus)*, M. Farooq, transl. and ed., Aligarh, 1929.

Abu Raikhan Biruni, *Al Qanunu 'l-Masudi (Canon Masudicus)*, 3 vols., Hyderabad, 1954–1956.

Abu Raikhan Biruni, *The Yoga Sutras of Patañjali*, Mario Kozah, transl. and ed., New York, 2020.

Abu Raikhan Biruni, *Al-Biruni's Arabic Version of Patanjali's Yoga Sutras*, Shlomo Pines and Tuvia Gelblum, transl., *Bulletin of the School of Oriental and African Studies*, University of London, vols. 29/2, 1966, 40/3, 1977, and 46/2, 1983.

Abu Raikhan Biruni, *Izbrannye proizvedeniia*, various editors, 6 vols., Tashkent, 1957–1975.

Abu Raikhan Biruni, *Geodesiia, Izbrannye proizvedeniia*, P. G. Bulgakov, ed., Tashkent, 1973.

Abu Raikhan Biruni, *The Exhaustive Treatise on Shadows*, E. S. Kennedy, transl., 2 vols., Aleppo, 1976.

Abu Raikhan Biruni, P. Kraus, *Epitre de Beruni, contenant le repertoire des oeuvres de Muhammad ibn Zakariya ar-Razi*, P. Kraus, transl. and ed., Paris, 1936.

Abu Raikhan Biruni, *Al-Kanun al-Masudi, Izbrannye proizvedenii*, vol. 3, Tashkent, 1973.

Abu Raikhan Biruni, *Kitab Tahdid Nihayat al-Amakin Litashih al-Masakin*, transl. as "The Determination of the Coordinates of Positions for the Correction of Distances between Cities," Jamil Ali, ed., Beirut, 1967.

Abu Raikhan Biruni, *Sobranie svedenii poznaniia dragotsennostei (Minerologiia)*, A. M. Belenitskii, transl., intro., Moscow, 1963.

Abu Raikhan Biruni, *The Exhaustive Treatise on Shadows by Abu al-Rayhan Muhammad b. Ahmad. Al-Biruni*, E. S. Kennedy, transl. and ed., 2 vols., Aleppo, 1976.

Abu Raikhan Biruni, *The Book of Most Comprehensive on Knowledge of Precious Stones: Al-Biruni's Book on Minerology*, H. M. Said, transl. and ed., Islamabad, 1989.

Abu Raikhan Biruni, *The Book of Instruction in the Elements of the Art of Astrology*, R. Ramsay Wright and M.A. Edin, transl., London, 1934.

Abu Raikhan Biruni, *Kniga vrazumleniia nachatkam nauki o zvezdakh*, B. A. Rozenfeld and A. Akhmedov, eds., Tashkent, 1975.

Abu Raikhan Biruni, *Al-Biruni on Transits*, Mohammad Saffouri and Adnan Ifram, transl., Oriental Series No. 32, Beirut, 1959.

Abu Raikhan Biruni, *Al-Biruni's Book on Pharmacy and Materia Medica: Introduction, Commentary, and Evaluation*, S. K. Hamarneh and H. M. Said, eds. and transls., Karachi, 1973.

Abu Raijhan Biruni, *Risalah al-Biruni on al-Razi's Life and Contribution*, Nurdent Deuraseh, ed., Kuala Lumpur, 2016.

Amos Bertolacci, "Albert the Great and the Preface of Avicenna's Kitāb al-Šifā'," in *Avicenna and His Heritage. Acts of the International Colloquium*, J. Janssens and D. De Smet, eds., Leuven 2002, pp. 131–152.

Amos Bertolacci, "A Community of Translators: The Latin Medieval Versions of Avicenna's Book of the Cure," in *Communities of Learning: Networks and the Shaping of Intellectual Identity in Europe 1100–1500*, C. J. Mews and J. N. Crossley, eds., Turnhout 2011, pp. 37–54.

Amos Bertolacci, "How Many Recensions of Avicenna's Kitab al Sifa?," *Oriens*, vol. 40, no. 2., 2012, pp. 275–303.

Amos Bertolacci, "The Latin Translation and the Original Version of the Ilāhiyyāt (Science of Divine Things) of Avicenna's Kitāb al-Šifā,'" *Documenti e Studi sulla Tradizione Filosofica Medievale*, vol. 28, 2017, pp. 481–514.

Amos Bertolacci, "On the Latin Reception of Avicenna's Metaphysics before Albertus Magnus: An Attempt at Periodization," *The Arabic, Hebrew and Latin Reception of Avicenna's Metaphysics*, A. Bertolacci, and D. N. Hasse, eds., Berlin 2012.

Amos Bertolacci, *The Reception of Aristotle's Metaphysics in Avicenna's Kitab al Sifa*, Leiden, 2006.

Amos Bertolacci, "The Reception of Avicenna in Latin Medieval Culture," *Interpreting Avicenna*, pp. 259–264.

Stephen P. Blake, "The Observatory in Maragha," *Astronomy and Astrology in the Islamic World*, Edinburgh, 2016.

D. J. Boilot, "L'Oeuvre d'al-Berumi: Essai bibliographique," Institut Dominicain d'etudes orientales du Caire, *Melanges*, vol. 2, Cairo, 1955.

Clifford Edmund Bosworth, "'Ala'-al-Dawla Mohammad," *Encyclopædia Iranica*, I/7, pp. 773–774.

Clifford Edmund Bosworth, "Biruni, Abu Rayhan, a Life," *Encyclopædia Iranica*, vol. 4, pp. 274–276, http://www.iranicaonline.org/articles/biruni-abu-rayhan-i-life.

Clifford Edmund Bosworth, *The Ghaznavids: Their Empire in Eastern Afghanistan and Eastern India, 994–1040*, New Delhi, 2015.

Clifford Edmund Bosworth, "The Political and Dynastic History of the Iranian World (AD 1000–1217)," *Cambridge History of Iran*, Cambridge, vol. 5, 1968, pp. 1–203.

Edward Browne, ed., *A Revised Translation of the Chahár maqála ("Four Discourses") of Nizámí-i' Arúdí of Samarqand, Followed by an Abridged Translation of Mírzá Muhammad's Notes to the Persian Text*, London/Cambridge, 1921, pp. 90–93.

D. B. Burrell, "Essence and Existence: Avicenna and Greek Philosophy," *Institut Dominicain d'Etudes Orientales du Caire* (MIDEO), vol. 17, 1986, pp. 53–66.

P. G. Bulgakov, *Zhizn i trudy Beruni*, Tashkent, 1972.

P. G. Bulgakov, "Globus Biruni," *Obshchestvennye nauki v Uzbekistane*, no. 1, 1965.

B. Burnett, "Arabic into Latin: The Reception of Arabic Philosophy into Western Europe," in *The Cambridge Companion of Arabic Philosophy*, Cambridge, 2005, pp. 370–404.

Charles S. F. Burnett, *The Translators and Their Intellectual and Social Context: Arabic into Latin in the Middle Ages*, Farnham, UK, 2009.

Michael Chase, "Essence and Existence in Marius Victorinus and in Avicenna," *Revue de Philosophie Ancienne*, vol. 37, no.1, 2019, pp. 101–151.

Suniti Kumar Chatterji, "Biruni and Sanskrit," in *Al- Biruni Commemoration Volume*, Calcutta, 1951, pp. 83–100.

P. Chelkowski, ed., *The Scholar and the Saint: Studies in Commemoration of Abul Rayhan al Biruni and Jalal al-Din al-Rumi*, New York, 1975.

Juan Cole, trans., *The Rubaiyat of Omar Khayyam*, London, 2020.

M. L. Colish, "Avicenna's Theory of Efficient Causation and Its Influence on St. Thomas Aquinas," *Tommaso d'Aquino nel suo Settimo Centenario*, Rome, 1976, pp. 296–306.

H. Corbin, *Avicenne et le recit visionnaire*, 3 vols., Paris-Tehran, 1952–1954. Partial translation as *Avicenna and the Visionary Recital*, Princeton, 2014.

Victor Courtois and M. Ishaque, eds., *Avicenna Commemoration Volume*, Calcutta, 1956.

Yvonne Dold-Samplonius, "Al-Sijzī Abū Saʿīd Aḥmad Ibn Muḥammad Ibn ʿAbd Al-Jalīl," *Dictionary of Scientific Biography*, vol. 12, pp. 431–432.

W. L. Craig, *The Kalam Cosmological Argument*, London, 1979.

Francois Clement de Blois, "'Al-Bayrouni, the Twelve Apostles and the Twelve Months of the Juian Year,' Winds of Jingjiao. Studies on Syriac Christianity in China and Central Asia," Li Tang and Dietmar W. Winkler, eds., *Orientalia Patristica Oecumenica*, vol. 9, Salzburg, 2016, pp. 155–160.

Francois Clement de Blois, "Biruni, Abu Rayhan: History of Religion," www.iranicaonline.org., 2010.

Daniel de Haan, "Where Does Avicenna Demonstrate the Existence of God?," *Arabic Sciences and Philosophy*, vol. 26, 2016, pp. 97–128.

Louis de Raeymaeker, *Vergelijkende studie over de betekenis van het "zijn" in de metafysiek van Avicenna en die van Thomas van Aquino*, Brussels, 1955.

A. Vibert Douglas, "Al-Biruni, Persian Scholar, 973–1048," *Journal of the Royal Astronomical Society of Canada*, vol. 67, 1973, pp. 209–211.

G. D. Dzhalalov, "Biruni i astronomicheskaia nauka," *Biruni: velikii uchenyi srednevekovia*, Tashkent, 1950.

G. D. Dzhalalov, "Biruni I kartografiia," *Izvestiia AN-UzSSR*, no. 1, 1950.

Heidrun Eichner, "Essence and Existence: Thirteenth-Century Perspectives in Arabic-Islamic Philosophy and Theology," in Dag Nikolaus Hasse and Amos Bertolacci, eds., *The Arabic, Hebrew and Latin Reception of Avicenna's Metaphysics*, loc. cit., Berlin, pp. 123–152.

Cyril Elgood, *A Medical History of Persia and the Eastern Caliphate*, Cambridge, 2010.

Osman Ergin, "Ibn Sina Bibliogafyasi," *Oriens*, vol. 11, no. 1–2, 1958.

Abu Nasr al-Farabi, *La musique arabe: Al-Fârâbî, Grand Traité de la Musique*, Rudolphe d'Erlanger, transl. and ed., vols. 1–2, Paris, 2001.

Mohammad Farooq, *Al-Kanun-ul-Masudi*, Aligarh, 1929.

Paul Feyeabend, *Against Method*, London, New York, 1975.

Resianne Fontaine, "'Happy Is He Whose Children Are Boys': Abu Ibn Dauda and Avicenna on Evil," *The Arabic, Hebrew, and Latin Reception of Avicenna's Metaphysics*, Dag Nikolaus Hasse and A. Bertolacci, eds., Berlin/Boston, 2012.

Gad Freudenthal and Mauro Zonta, "The Reception of Avicenna in Jewish Cultures, East and West," *Interpreting Avicenna*, Peter Adamson, ed., Cambridge, 2013, pp. 214–242.

Louis Gardet, *La Pensee religieuse d' Avicenne*, Paris, 1951.

Louis Gardet, "Avicenne et le probleme de sa 'philosophie orientale," *La Revue de Caire*, vol. 27, no. 21, 1951.

Louis Gardet, "l'Experience mystique selon Avicenne," *La Revue du Caire*, vol. 27, pp. 56–67, 1951.

A. M. Goichon, *Introduction d'Avicenne*, Paris, 1933.

A. M. Goichon, *La distinction de l'essence et de l'existence d'apres Ibn Sina*, Paris, 1937.

A. M. Goichon, *La Philosophie d'Avicenne et son influence en Europe medievale*, 2nd ed., Paris, 1951. transl., with M.S. Khan, *The Philosophy of Avicenna and Its Influence on Medieval Europe*, New Delhi, 1969.

Alberto Gomez Gomez, "Biruni's Measurement of the Earth," 2015, https://www.academia.edu/8166456/Birunis_measurement_of_the_Earth?email_work_card=view-paper.

Lenn E. Goodman, *Avicenna*, Ithaca, 2006.

Lenn E. Goodman, *Jewish and Islamic Philosophy*, New Brunswick, 1999.

Frank Griffel, *Al Ghazali's Philosophical Theology*, Oxford, 2009.

Frank Griffel, "Al-Ġazālī's Concept of Prophecy: The Introduction of Avicennan Psychology into Aš'arite Theology," *Arabic Science and Philosophy*, vol. 14, 2004, pp. 101–144.

Frank Griffel, "Toleration and Exclusion: al-Shafi-I and al-Ghazali on the Treatment of Apostates," *Bulletin of the School of Oriental and African Studies*, vol. 64, no. 3, 2001, pp. 329–354.

Frank Griffel, "On Fakhr al-Din al-Razi's Life and the Patronage He Received," *Journal of Islamic Studies,* vol. 18, no. 3, 2007, pp. 313–344.

Frank Griffel, "The Introduction of Avicennian Psychology into the Muslim Theological Discourse: The Case of al Ghazali (d. 1111)," *Arabic Sciences and Philosophy*, vol. 14, 2004, pp. 101–144.

Dimitri Gutas, *Avicenna and the Aristotelian Tradition*, 2nd ed., Leiden, 2014.

Dimitri Gutas, "The Heritage of Avicenna: The Golden Age of Arabic Sciences and Philosophy. c. 1000–1315," J. Janssens and D. De Smet, eds., *Avicenna and His Heritage*, Acts of the International Colloquium, Leuven, September 8, 1999. Leuven, 2002.

Dimitri Gutas, "Avicenna's Madhab, with an Appendix on the Question of His Date of Birth," *Quaderni di Studi Arabi* (Atti del XIII Congresso dell'Union Europienne d'Arabisants et d'Islamisants), Venice, 1987–1988, vol. 5/6, pp. 323–336.

Jules Hanssens, "Ibn Sina and His Heritage in the Islamic World and in the Latin West," *Ibn Sina and His Influence on the Arabic and Latin World*, Aldershot, 2006.

W. Hartner and M. Schramm, "AlBiruni and His Theory of the Solar Apogee," in *Scientific Change*, A. C. Crombie, ed., New York, 1963, pp. 206–221.

Dag Nikolaus Hasse, ed., *The Arabic, Hebrew and Latin Reception of Avicenna's Metaphysics*, Berlin, 2011.

Dag Nikolaus Hasse, *Avicenna's "De Anima" in the Latin West: The Formation of a Peripatetic Philosophy of the Soul, 1160–1300*, Warburg Institute Studies and Texts, vol. 1, London, 2000.

Dag Nikolaus Hasse, *Success and Suppression: Arabic Sciences and Philosophy in the Renaissance*. Cambridge, 2016.

Dag Nikolaus Hasse, with A. Bertolacci, ed., "The Arabic, Hebrew and Latin Reception of Avicenna's Physic and Cosmology," *Scienta Graeco-Arabica*, vol. 7, Berlin, 2012.

Dag Nikolaus Hasse, "Influence of Arabic and Islamic Philosophy on the Latin West," *Stanford Encyclopedia of Philosophy*, Standford, 2020. https://plato.stanford.edu/entries/arabic-islamic-influence/.

Peter Heath, *Allegory and Philosophy in Avicenna (Ibn Sina)*, Philadelphia, 1992.

Mahmoud El Hefny, *Ibn Sina's Musiklehre hauptsachlich an seinan "Najat" erlautert*, Berlin, 1934.

M. Cruz Hernández, "La teoría musical de Ibn Sīnā en el Kitāb al-šifā'," *Milenario de Avicenna II*, Madrid, 1981, vol. 2, pp. 27–36.

D. R. Hill, "Physics and Mechanics," in *History of Civilization of Central Asia*, vol. 4, pt. 2, Paris, 2000, pp. 254–259.

D. R. Hill, "Al Biruni's Mechanical Calendar," *Annals of Science*, vol. 42, Abingdon-on-Thamas, 1985, pp. 139–163.

Hubert Houben, *Roger II of Sicily: Ruler Between East and West*, Cambridge, 2002.

E. J. Holmyard, *Avicennae de congelatione et conglutinatione lapidum*, Paris, 1927.

M. Sate al-Hosri, "Les Idees d'Avicenne sur la geologie," *Millinaire d'Avicenne: Congres de Bagdad*, Baghdad, 1952.

J. Houben, "Avicenna and Mysticism," *Indo-Iranica*, no. 6, 1953, pp. 1–18.

Nick Huggett and Carl Hoefer, "Absolute and Relational Theories of Space and Motion," *Stanford Encyclopedia of Philosophy*, plato.stanford.edu/entries/spacetime-theories/.

H. Husmann, *Grundlagen der antiken und orientalischen Musikkultur*, Berlin, 1961.

William Hutchins, transl., *Nine Essays of al-Jahiz*, London, 1989.

M. O. Iushkevich, ed., *Mukhammad ibn Musa al-Khorezmi*, Moscow, 1983.

Alfred L. Ivrey, "The Rizvi and Maimonides' Philosophical Sources," Kenneth Seeskin, ed., *The Cambridge Companion to Maimonides*, Cambridge, 2005, pp. 58–81.

A. Jeffery, "Alberuni's Contribution to Comparative Religion," *Albiruni Commemoration Volume*, Wahshet Khan, Bahadur Reza Ali, eds., Calcutta, 1956, pp. 129–159.

Wahshat Khan, Biahadur Reza Ali, eds., *Al-Biruni Commemoration Volume*, London, 1951.

A. S. Khan, *A Bibliography of the Works of Abu'l-Raihan al-Biruni*, New Delhi, 1982.

M. A. Khan and M. A. Saleem, *Al-Biruni's Discovery of India: An Interpretative Study*, Amsterdam, 2011.

M. S. Khan, "Tabaqat al-Umam of Qadi Sa'id al-Anfalusi (1029–1070 A.D.), *Indian Journal of the History of Science*, vol. 30, 1995.

Jari Kaukua, "Avicenna on Negative Judgments," April 20, 2016, https://www.academia.edu/16395165/Avicenna_on_Negative_Judgment?email_work_card=thumbnail.

M. Kaur, "Avicenna: His Life, Works, and Impact," *Studies in the History of Medicine*, vol. 7, 1983, pp. 216–235.

B. M. Kedrov and B. A. Rozenfeld, *Abu Rayhan Biruni*, Moscow, 1973.

Edward S. Kennedy, "Biruni," *Dictionary of Scientific Biography*, New York, 1970, pp. 147–158.

Edward S. Kennedy, *A Commentary upon Biruni's Kitab Tahdid al-Amakin*, Beirut, 1973.

Edward S. Kennedy, "A Fifteenth-Century Planetary Computer: al-Kashi's 'Tabaq al-Maneteq' II: Longitudes, Distances, and Equations of the Planets," *Isis*, vol. 43, no. 1, 1952, pp. 42–50.

Edward S. Kennedy and A. Muruwwa, "Biruni on the Solar Equation," *Journal of Near Eastern Studies*, vol. 17, 1958, pp. 112–121.

Edward S. Kennedy, with Fuad I. Haddad and David Pingree, "Al-Biruni's Treatise on Astrological Lots," *Astronomy and Astrology in the Medieval Islamic World*, Edward S. Kennedy, ed., Aldershot, 1987.

N. Khanykov, *Memoire sur la partie meridionale de l'Asie centrale*, Paris, 1861.

Judith Klinginder, "Bid'a or Sunna: The Taylasan as a Contested Garment in the Mamluk Period," in *Al-Suyuti: a Polymath of the Mamluk Period*, Leiden, 2017.

T. N. Kori-Nieziy, *Ulugbek va uning ilmiy merosi*, Tashkent, 1971.

Mario Kozah, *The Birth of Indology as an Islamic Science: Al-Bīrūnī's Treatise on Yoga Psychology*, Leiden, 2015.

U. I. Krachkovskii, "*Arabskaia geograficheskaia literatura*," *Izbrannye sochineniia*, Moscow-Leningrad, 1957.

K. Krisciunas, "The Legacy of Ulugh Beg," *AACR Bulletin*, vol. 5, no. 1, 1992.

Thomas S. Kuhn, *The Copernican Revolution: Planetary Astronomy in the Development of Western Thought*, Cambridge, 1957.

Thomas S. Kuhn, *The Structure of Scientific Revolutions*, Chicago, 2012.

B. G. Kuznetsov, *Evoliutsiia kartiny mira*, Moscow, 1961.

Joep Lameer, "Avicenna's Concupiscence," *Islamic Sciences and Philosophy*, vol. 23, no. 1, 2013, pp. 277–289.

Joep Lameer, "Towards a New Edition of Avicenna's *Kitab al-Isharat wa-l-tambihat*," *Journal of Islamic Manuscripts*, vol. 4, no. 2, 2013, pp. 99–248.

Andreas Lammer, *The Elements of Avicenna's Physics: Greek Sources and Arabic Innovations*, Berlin, 2018.

Andreas Lammer, "Avicenna," *Wiley-Blackwell Encyclopedia of Philosophy of Religion*, 2020, https://www.academia.edu/34359503/Avicenna_Wiley_Blackwell_Encyclopedia_of_Philosophy_of_Religion_accepted_forthcoming_2020_?auto=download.

Andreas Lammer, "The Heirs of Avicenna: Philosophy in the Islamic East from the 12th to the 13th Century," forthcoming.

Y. T. Langermann, ed., *Avicenna and His Legacy*, Turnhout, 2009.

M. Laniar, *A Bio-Bibliography for Biruni*, Lanham, 2006.

Vladimir Lasica, "Avicenna's Proof for God's Existence: The Proof from Ontological Considerations," *Revista Española de Filosofía Medieval*, vol. 26, no. 2, 2019, pp. 25–47.

Hilman Latief, *Comparative Religion in Medieval Muslim Literature*, Jakarta, 2012.

V. A. Lavrov, *Gradostroitelnaia kultura Srednei Azii*, Moscow, 1950.

Bruce B. Lawrence, "Biruni, Abu Rayhan:. Indology," www.iranicaonline.org, 1989.

P. Luckey, *Die Rechenkunst bei Ǧamšīd b. Mas'ūd al-Kāšī*, Wiesbaden, 1951.

Guenter Luling, "Ein anderer Avicenna: Kritik seiner Autobiographie und ihrer bisherigen Behandlung," *Zeitschrift der Deutschen Morgenländischen Gesellschaft*, vol. 3, 1977, pp. 496–509.

Guenter Luling, "Old Complexes and New Possibilities: Ibn Sīnā's Modal Metaphysics in Context," *Journal of Islamic Philosophy*, vol. 7, 2011, pp. 3–34.

M. Makhmadjonova and P. G. Sadykov, eds., *Abu Ali Ibn Sina (Avitsenna), Sochineniia*, vol. 9, Dushanbe, 2020–2021.

George Malagaris, *Biruni*, New York, 2020.

Michael F. Marmura: A; Ghazali, *The Incoherence of the Philosophers*, Provo, 2000.

G. P. Matvievskaia, "Iz istorii fiziko-matematicheskikh nauk na srednevekovom vostoke," Nauchnoe nasledsatvo, vol. vi, Moscow, 1983.

Jon McGinnis, *Avicenna*, Oxford, 2010.

Jon McGinnis, "New Light on Avicenna: Optics and Its Role in Avicennan Theories of Vision, Cognition and Emanation," in *Philosophical Psychology in Arabic Thought and the Latin Aristotelianism of the 13th Century*, Luis López-Farjeat and Jörg Tellkamp, eds. Paris, 2013, pp. 41–57.

Jon McGinnis, "Old Complexities and New Possibilities: Ibn Sīnā's Modal Metaphysics in Context," *Journal of Islamic Philosophy*, vol. 7, 2011, pp. 3–34.

Jon McGinnis, "The Ultimate Why Question: Avicenna on Why God Is Absolutely Necessary," *The Ultimate Why Question: Why Is There Anything at All Rather Than Nothing Whatsoever?*, John Wippel, ed., Washington, 2011, pp. 65–83.

Gunther Mensching, "Roger Bacon and Islamic Physics and Metaphysics," *Thomas d'Aquin et ses sources arabes/Aquinas and the Arabs*, Paris, 2014, https://www.academia.edu/10752599/Thomas_d_Aquin_et_ses_sources_arabes_Aquinas_and_the_Arabs_Bulletin_de_Philosophie_Médiévale_2013.

Raymond Mercier, "Al-Biruni and the Astronomy of *al-Qanun al-Mas'udi*," *Al-Biruni and His World,* Department of Hebrew and Jewish Studies University College London, workshop, February 15, 2016, www.ucl.ac.uk/hebrew-jewish/research/accordion/erc-workshops/al-biruni-and-his-world.

Adam Mez, *The Renaissance of Islam*, New Delhi, 1995.

Millenary of Abu Raihan Muhammad ibn Ahmad al Biruni: Papers Presented on the Occasion of al-Biruni International Congress, no editor, Karachi, 1974.

Vladimir Minorsky, "Medieval Iran and Its Neighbors," *Collected Studies*, series 166, vol. III, London, 1978.

M. Mirza, "Biruni's Thought and Legacy," *Wiley's Religion Compass*, vol. 5, no. 10, October, 2011, pp. 609–623.

J. Alaei Moghadam and S. R. Mousavi Haji, "A Research on Newly Discovered Architectural Remains of Fardaghan in Farahan (A Sassanian Fire Temple or an Islamic Castle)," *International Journal of Humanities*, no. 24, no. 3, 2017, pp. 81–102.

Jamal Moosavi, "The Place of Avicenna in the History of Medicine," *Journal of Medical Biotechnology*, 2008, April–June, pp. 3–8.

David Morgan, *Medieval Persia, 1040–1797*, Harlow, 1998.

James W. Morris, "The Philosopher-Prophet in Avicenna's Political Philosophy," *The Political Aspects of Islamic Philosophy*, Charles E. Butterworth, ed., Cambridge, MA, 1992, pp. 152–198.

S. M. Mozaffari and G. Zotti, "Ghāzān Khān's Astronomical Innovations at Marāgha Observatory," *Journal of the American Oriental Society*, vol. 132, no. 3, 2012, pp. 395–425. Extended version at 280208-text de l'article-284090-1-10-20140908.pdf.

B. N. Mukherjee, *India in Early Central Asia*, New Delhi, 1996.

Museum des Institutes für Geschichte der Arabisch-Islamischen Wissenschaften, *Modell des Sonnensystems und der Erdbewegung ("Planetarium") nach as-Siğzî*, Frankfurt am Main, 2010.

Syed H. H. Nadvi, "Al-Biruni and His *Kitab al Jahamir Fi-Ma Rifah al Jawahir*: Ethical Reflections and Moral Philosophy," H. M. Said, ed., Karachi, 1974, pp. 530–544.

Said Naficy, *Bibliographie des principaux travaux europeens sur Avicenne*, Tehran, 1953.

Mona Nasser, Alda Tibi, and Emilie Savage-Smith, "Ibn Sina's *Canon of Medicine*: 11th Century Rules for Assessing the Effects of Drugs," *Journal of the Royal Society of Medicine*, vol. 102, no. 2, 2008, pp. 78–80.

Seyyed Hossein Nasr, *An Introduction to Islamic Cosmological Doctrines*, Albany, 1993.

Seyyed Hossein Nasr, *Al-Biruni: An Annotated Bibliography*, Tehran, 1973.

Seyyed Hossein Nasr, *Abu Rayhan Biruni: Scientist and Scholar Extraordinary*, Tehran, 1973.

Seyyed Hossein Nasr, *Islamic Philosophy from Its Origin to the Present*, Albany, 2006.

Seyyed Hossein Nasr, *Three Muslim Sages*, New York, 1976.

Seyyed Hossein Nasr and Mehdi Aminrazavi, *An Anthology of Philosophy in Persia*, New York, 1999.

Muhammad Nazim, *The Life and Times of Sultan Mahmud of Ghazna*, Cambridge, 1931.

John J. O'Connor and Edmund F. Robertson, "Abu Ja'far Muhammad ibn Musa Al-Khwarizmi," MacTutor History of Mathematics Archive, University of St. Andrews,

John J. O'Connor and Edmund F. Robertson, "Abu Said Ahmad ibn Muhammad Al-Sijzi," MacTutor History of Mathematics Archive, University of St. Andrews, 1999.

John J. O'Connor and Edmund F. Robertson, "Varāhamihira," MacTutor History of Mathematics archive, University of St. Andrews, 1999.

Kayhan Özaykal, "Deconstruction of Ibn Sina's Essence-Existence Distinction and the Essence of the Necessary Existent," *Darufunun ilayiyat*, vol. 29, no. 2, 2018, pp. 25–48. http://dx.doi.org/10.26650/di.2018.29.1.0104.

Walter Pagel, *Paracelsus; an Introduction to Philosophical Medicine in the Era of the Renaissance*, Basel, 1958.

Charles Pellat and D. M. Hawke, transl., *Introduction to the Life and Times of Jahiz*, Berkeley, 1969.

S. Pines, "The Semantic Distinction between Astronomy and Astrology According to Al-Biruni," *Isis*, vol. 55, no. 2, 1964.

Shlomo Pines, Tuvia Gelblum, translators, "Al-Biruni's Arabic Version of Patanjali's Yoga Sutras," *Bulletin of the School of Oriental and African Studies*, University of London, vols. 29/2, 1966, 40/3, 1977, and 46/2, 1983.

David Pingree, "Biruni, Abu Rayhan: Bibliography," www.iranicaonline.org., February 1, 2010.

David Pingree, "Biruni, Abu Rayhan: Geography," www.iranicaonline.org, 2010.

David Pingree, "Biruni, Abu Rayhan: History and Chronology," www.iranicaonline.org, 2010.

Karl R. Popper, *The Logic of Scientific Discovery*, Abingdon-on-Thames, 1959.

Peter. E. Pormann, "Avicenna on Medical Practice, Epistemology, and the Physiology of the Inner Senses," in *Interpreting Avicenna*, Peter Adamson, ed., Cambridge, 2013, pp. 96–98.

Peter E. Pormann, "Medical Practice, Epistemology, and Physiology," *Interpreting Avicenna: Critical Essays*, Peter Adamson, ed., Cambridge, 2013, p. 93.

Peter E. Pormann and Emilie Savage-Smith, *Medieval Islamic Medicine*, Washington, DC, 2007.

G. Quadri, *La philosophie arabe dans l'Europe medievale*, Paris, 1947.

W. V. Quine, *Pursuit of Truth*, Cambridge, 1990.

Jamil Raceb, ed. and transl., *Nasir al-Din Tusi's Memoir on Astronomy (al-Tadhkira fi `ilm al-hay')*, 2 vols., in *Sources in the History of Mathematics and Physical Sciences*, New York, 1993.

Jamil Raqer, transl. and ed., *Nasir al-Din Tusi's Memoir on Astronomy, 2 vols., Sources in the History of Mathematics and Physical Sciences*, New York, 1993.

F. Jamil Ragep, "Copernicus and His Islamic Predecessors: Some Historical Remarks," Filozofski vestnik, Ljubljana, vol. XXV, 2004, no. 2, pp. 125–142.

F. Rahman, ed., *Avicenna's De Anima, Being the Psychological Part of Kitab al-Shifa'*, London, 1959.

Hakim Syed Zillur Rahman, "Unani Medicine in India: Its Origin and Fundamental Concepts," *History of Science, Philosophy and Culture in Indian Civilization*, vol. 4, part 2, New Delhi, 2001, pp. 298–325.

Hakim Syed Zillur Rahman, "Commentators and Translators of Ibn Sina's Canon of Medicine," Zakaria Virk, transl., https://www.academia.edu/6527080/Canon_of_Medicine_of_Ibn_Sena_its_translators_and_commentators.

Shahin Rahman, Tony Street, and Hassan Tahiri, eds., *The Unity of Science in the Arabic Tradition: Science, Logic, and Epistemology and Their Interaction*, Dordrecht, 2008.

Roshdi Rashed, "Mathematiques et Philosophie chez Avicenne," in *Études sur Avicenne*, J. Jolivet and R. Rashed, eds., Paris, 1984, pp. 29–39.

Roshdi Rashed, "Mathématiques et philosophie chez Avicenne," presented at the *Millenniary Colloquium of Avicenna in New Delhi*, New Delhi, 1981.

Abū Bakr Muhammad ibn Zakariyyā al-Rāzī, *Doubts on Galen: An English Translation of Rhazes' Forgotten Kitab al-Shukuk ala Jalinus*, Mohammadali M. Shoja, transl., London, 2018.

Abū Bakr Muhammad ibn Zakariyyā al-Rāzī, *Razi's Traditional Psychology*, A. J. Arberry, transl., Damascus, n.d.

Rashed M. Reinaud, "Introduction Generale a la Geographie des Orientaux," *Géographie d'Abuféda*, Paris, 1923, vol. 1.

David C. Reisman, ed., *Before and After Avicenna: Proceedings of the First Conference of the Avicenna Study Group*, Leiden, 2003.

Sajjad H. Rizvi, "An Avicennian Engagement with and Appropriation of Mullā Ṣadrā Šīrāzī (d. 1045/1636)," *Oriens*, vol. 48, 2020, pp. 219–249.

Erwin Rosenthal, *Political Thought in Medieval Islam: An Introductory Outline*, Westport, CT, 1985.

B. A. Rozenfeld, S. A. Krasnova, and M. M. Rozhanskaia, "O matematicheskikh rabotah Abu-r Raikhana al- Biruni," *Iz istorii nauki i tekhniki v stranakh Vostoka*, vol. 3, Moscow, 1963.

B. A. Rozenfeld, M. M. Rozhanskaia, and E. K. Sokolovskaia, *Abu-r-Raykhan al-Biruni: velikii uzhenyi-entsiplopedist*, Moscow, 2013.

B. A. Rozenfeld, M. M. Rozanskaia, and Z. K. Sokolovskaia, *Abu-r-Raikhan al-Biruni*, Moscow, 2014.

B. A. Rozenfeld, M. M. Rozhanskaia, and E. K. Sokolovskaia, "Astronomiecheskie instrument," in *Abu-r-Raykhan al-Biruni, 973–1048, Moscow, 2013*," pp. 127–172.

M. J. S. Rudwick, *The Meaning of Fossils: Episodes in the History of Paleontology*, Chicago, 1985, p. 24.

J. Ruska, "Die Alchemie des Avicenna," *Isis*, vol. 21, 1934, pp. 14–51.

Hakim Mohammed Said, ed., *Al-Biruni Commemorative Volume*, Islamabad, 1979.

Hakim Mohammed Said and Ansar Zahid Khan, *Al-Biruni: His Times, Life, and Works*, Karachi, 1981.

George Saliba, *Islamic Science and the Making of the European Renaissance*, Cambridge (Mass.) and London, 2007

Mohammad M. Sajadi, Davood Mansouri, and Mohamad-Reza M. Sajadi, "Ibn Sina and the Clinical Trial," *Annals of Internal Medicine*, vol. 150, 2009, pp. 640–643.

George Saliba, "Biruni, Abu Rayhan: Mathematics and Astronomy," www.iranicaonline .org, 2010.

George Saliba, *A History of Arabic Astronomy: Planetary Theories During the Golden Age of Islam*, New York, 1994.

Mohammad M. Sajadi, Davood Mansouri, and Mohamad-Reza M. Sajadi, "Ibn Sina and the Clinical Trial," *Annals of Internal Medicine*, vol. 150, 2009, pp. 640–643.

George Saliba, "Al-Qushji's Reform of the Ptolemaic Model for Mercury," *Arabic Sciences and Philosophy*, vol. 3, 1993, pp. 161–203.

George Saliba, "Revisiting the Astronomical Contacts Between the World of Islam and Renaissance Europe: The Byzantine Connection," in *The Occult Sciences in Byzantium*, Paul Magdalino and Maria Mavroudi, eds., Geneva, 2006, pp. 361–374.

L. Samian, "Reason and Spirit in Al-Biruni's Philosophy of Mathematics," *Reason, Spirit and the Sacral in the New Enlightenment, Islamic Philosophy and Occidental Phenomenology in Dialogue*, A. T. Tymieniecka, ed., Netherlands, 2011, pp. 137–146.

Julio Samsó, "Al-Bitruji Al-Ishbili, Abu Ishaq," *Dictionary of Scientific Biography*, vol. 15, Charles Coulston Gillispie, ed., New York, 1976, pp. 33–36.

Julio Samso, "Biruni- al-Andalus," *From Baghdad to Barcelona: Studies in the Islamic Exact Sciences in Honour of Prof. Juan Vernet, Anuari de Filologia*, vol. 19, 1996.

George Sarton, *Introduction to the History of Science*, 3 vols., Baltimore, 1927–1948.

Emilie Savage-Smith (November 2008), "Islamic Influence on Copernicus," *Journal for the History of Astronomy*, vol. 39, no.1, 2008, pp. 538–541.

Bill Scheppler, *Al-Biruni, Master Astronomer and Muslim Scholar of the Eleventh Century*, New York, 2014.

Carl Schoy, "Aus der astronomischen Geographie der Araber," *Isis*, vol. 5, no. 1, 1923, pp. 51–74.

Carl Schoy, "Beitrage zur arabischen Trigonometrie," *Isis*, vol. 5, no. 2, 1923, pp. 364–399.

Carl Schoy, "Original Studien aus al-Biruni's al-Qanun al Mas'udi," *Isis*, vol. 5, no. 3, 1923, pp. 5–12.

Carl Schoy, *Die trigonometrischen Lehren des persischen Atronomen Abu'l Rayhan Muhammad ibn Ahmad al-Biruni*, Hannover, 1927.

Rudolf Sellheim, review of Ergin's *Ibn Sina Bibliografyasi, Oriens*, vol. 2, 1958, pp. 231–239.

Arvind Sharma, *Studies in Alberuni's India*, Wiesbaden, 1983.

Ayman Shihadeh, "Avicenna's Theodicy and al-Razi's Anti-Theodicy," *Intellectual History of the Islamic World*, vol. 7, 2019, pp. 61–84.

Akhtar Husain Siddiqi, "Biruni," *Geographers: Biobibliographic Studies*, Geoffrey J. Martin, ed., London, 1991, vol. 13, pp. 1–10.

Avinash Singh, "Al Biruni's India," https://www.academia.edu/33759626/Al_Birunis_ India?email_work_card=title.

Nancy G. Siraisi, *Avicenna in Renaissance Italy: The Canon and Medical Teaching in Italian Universities after 1500*, Princeton, 1987.

S. Kh. Sirazhdinov, ed., *Iz istorii vostochnoi matematiki i astronomii*, Tashkent, 1984.

C. P. Snow, *The Two Cultures*, Cambridge, 1998.

Dava Sobel, *Longitude*, New York, 1995.

Amelia Carolina Sparavigna, "The Science of al-Biruni," *International Journal of Sciences*, vol. 2, no. 12, December 2013, pp. 52–60.

Kevin M. Staley, "Avicenna, Aquinas and the Real Distinction: In Defense of Mere Possibilities or Why Existence Matters," https://www.anselm.edu/sites/default/files/Documents/Institut.

S. Frederick Starr, *Lost Enlightenment, Central Asia's Golden Age*, Princeton, 2012.

S. Frederick Starr, "The Invention of World History," *History Today*, vol. 67. no. 7, 2017, pp. 36–47.

S. Frederick Starr, "So Who Did Discover America?" *History Today*, vol. 63, no. 12, 2013, pp. 34–39.

M. Steinschneider, "Wissenschaft und Charlatanerie unter den Arabern in neunten Jahrhundert," *Beitraege zur Geschichte der arabisch-islamischen Medizin*, 3 vols., Frankfurt, 1987, vol. 1, pp. 39–61.

J. Stephenson, "The Classification of the Sciences According to Nasiruddin Tusi," *Isis*, no. 2, 1923, pp. 329–338.

S. M. Stern, "The Early Ismaili Missionaries in North-West Persia and in Khurasan and Transoxonia," *Bulletin of the School of Oriental and African Studies*, vol. 23, 1960, pp. 56–90.

Tony Street, "Avicenna on the Syllogism," in *Interpreting Avicenna*, Peter Adamson, ed., Cambridge, 2013, pp. 48–70.

Gotthard Strohmaier, *Avicenna*, Munich, 1999.

Gotthard Strohmaier, "Avicenna und al-Biruni im Dialog uber aristotelische Naturphilosophie," *Naturwissenschaft und ihre Rezeption*, K. Doering and G. Woehrle, eds., Bamberg, 1992.

R. Strothmann, *Gnosis-Teautobiographische der Ismailiten*, Göttingen, 1943.

N. M. Swerdlow and O. Neugebauer, *Mathematical Astronomy in Copernicus's "De Revolutionibus,"* New York, 1984.

Gail Marlowe Taylor, *The Alchemy of al-Razi*, North Charleston, 2014.

S. P. Tolstov, *Biruni: Sbornik statei*, Moscow-Leningrad, 1950.

S. P. Tolstov, *Po sledam drevnekhorezemskoi tsivilizatsii*, Moscow-Leningrad, 1948.

Unani System of Medicine, Department of Ayush, Ministry of Health and Family Welfare, New Delhi, 2013.

M. Ullman, *Die Medicin in Islam*, Leiden, 1972.

Hasan Zeki Validi, "Der Islam und die geographisches Wissenschaft," *Geographische Zeitschrift*, 1934, pp. 361–372.

Noemie Verden, "Bīrūnī as a Source for the Study of Indian Culture and History," https://www.academia.edu/3324348/B%C4%ABr%C5%ABn%C4%AB_as_a_source_for_the_study_of_Indian_culture_and_history?email_work_card=thumbnail.

Virgil, *Georgics*, Books I–II, "Felix qui potuit rerum cognoscere causas."

Zakaria Virk, *Muslim Contributions to Science*, Berlin, 2019.

Zakaria Virk, "Outstanding Surgeons of Medieval Islam," https://mail.google.com/mail/u/0/#inbox/WhctKJVzfPxGJJnqTnlGkDsBpgmSdhgzmhlcnkMwskbxRbJpDtbQXCqgpgxJxkBFKzJRLGq.

Heinrich von Staden, *Herophilus: The Art of Medicine in Early Alexandria,* Cambridge, 1989.

Paul E. Walker, *Early Philosophical Shiism: The Isma'ili Neoplatonism of Abu Ya'qub al-Sijistani,* Cambridge, 2008.

Richard Walzer, *Greek into Arabic: Essays on Islamic Philosophy,* Oxford, 1962.

G. M. Wickens, ed., *Avicenna: Scientist and Philosopher: A Millenary Symposium,* London, 1952.

E. Wiedemann and T. W. Juynboll, "Avicennas Schrift über ein von ihmersonnenes Beobachtungsinstrument." *Acta Orientalia,* vol. 11, 1926, pp. 81–167.

H. J. J. Winter, "The Place of the Qanun-i-Masudi in the History of Science," *Al Qanunu-l-Masudi (Canon Masudicus),* 3, Hyderabad, 1956, pp. 1–13.

Robert Wisnovsky, *Avicenna's Metaphysics in Context,* Ithaca, 2003.

Robert Wisnovsky, "Avicenna's Islamic Reception," *Interpreting Avicenna: Critical Essays,* Peter Adamson, ed., Cambridge, 2013, pp. 190–213.

Robert Wisnovsky, "Avicennism, an Exegetical Practice in the Early Commentaries on the Isharat," *Oriens,* vol. 46, 2013, pp. 349–378.

Robert Wisnovsky, "Essence and Existence in the Eleventh and Twelfth Century Islamic East (Masriq): A Sketch," in *The Arabic, Hebrew and Latin Reception of Avicenna's Metaphysics,* Adamson, ed., pp. 27–50.

Robert Wisnovsky, "Final and Efficient Causality in Avicenna's Cosmology and Theology," *Quaestio: The Yearbook of the History of Metaphysics,* Turnhout, 2002, pp. 97–123.

Robert Wisnovsky, "Notes on Avicenna's Concept of Thingness (šay'iyya)," *Arabic Sciences and Philosophy,* 2000, pp. 181–221.

Robert Wisnovsky, "On the Emergence of Maragha Avicennism," *Oriens,* vol. 46, 2018, pp. 263–331.

Robert Wisnovsky, "Towards a Genealogy of Avicennism," *Oriens,* vol. 42, 2014, pp. 323–363.

H. A. Wolfson, *The Philosophy of the Kalam,* Cambridge, 1976.

Yaqut al-Hamawī, *Irshad al-arib ila marifar al-adib (Dictionary of Learned Men),* D. S. Margol, ed., 7 vols., London, 1907–1927.

Hulya Yaldir, "Ibn Sina (Avicenna) and Descartes on the Faculty of Imagination," *British Journal for the History of Philosophy,* vol. 17, no. 7, 2009, pp. 247–278.

Hulya Yaldir, "Ibn Sīnā and Descartes on the Origins and Structure of the Universe: Cosmology and Cosmogony," *Journal of Islamic Philosophy,* vol. 5, 2009, pp. 3–58.

Michio Yano, "Bīrūnī: Abū al-Rayḥān Muḥammad ibn Aḥmad al-Bīrūnī," Thomas Hockey et al., eds., *The Biographical Encyclopedia of Astronomers,* New York, 2007, pp. 131–133.

Ehsan Yarshater, "Biruni," *Encyclopedia Iranica,* New York, 1990, vol. 4, pp. 274–287.

Ehsan Yarshater and Dale Bishop, eds., *Selected Papers, Presented at Biruni Symposia,* New York, 1976.

Kaynak Yayınları, *Ali Kuşçu, Çagını Aşan Bilim İnsanı,* Istanbul, 2010.

A. Youschkevitch and B. Rosenfeld, 1973, "al-Khayyāmī," in *Dictionary of Scientific Biography,* New York, 1973, vol. VII, pp. 323–334.

D. Y. Yusupova, *Piasma Giyas ad-Dina Kashi k svoemu otsu iz Samarkanda v Kashan,* Tashkent, 1979.

Yousef Zaiden. *Fardikan.* Alexandria, 2016. Sole translation is to Italian, *Nel Castello di Fardiqan.* Kindle, 2020.

Iu. Zakhidov, "Biruni kak myslitel," in *Biruni: Sbornik statei,* S. P. Tolstov, ed., Moscow, 1950, p. 41.

Iu. N. Zavodovskii, *Abu Ali Ibn Sina: zhizn i tvorchstvo,* Dushanbe, 1980.

Brandon Zimmerman, "Thomas, Avicenna and the Philosophical Idea of Creation," *American Catholic Philosophical Association,* November 3, 2012. https://www.academia.edu/2172880/.

Index

For the benefit of digital users, indexed terms that span two pages (e.g., 52–53) may, on occasion, appear on only one of those pages.

Page numbers followed by n. indicate endnotes.

Cain, 176
Cairo, Egypt, 17–18, 190
calculus of finite differences, 2–3, 146
calendars
  Biruni's calendar clock, 133
  Biruni's *Chronology of Ancient Nations*, 52–59
  leap year (intercalation), 57–58, 228
Canon of Medicine (Ibn Sina), 3–4, 62, 81–82, 95–96, 98–99, 116–31, 132, 149–50, 152, 162, 185–86, 188–91, 219–20
  criticism of, 189–90, 222
  inspiration for, 11
  Latin translations, 208–9
  page count, 4, 81–82, 178
  printed editions, 210
  title, 81
  versified synopsis, 188
  Volume I, 116, 122–23, 128–29
  Volume II, 116, 126–27, 152
  Volume III, 116, 128–29
  Volume IV, 116, 128–29
  Volume V, 116, 127, 134, 148
  Western reception, 208, 209–10
Canterbury Tales (Chaucer), 208–9
caravans, 63, 148–49, 189
cartography, 90, 138
categorization, 124
Cathedral of Santa Sabina, 205–6
celebrity status, 149
celery seeds, 185–86
Center for Avicenna Studies (Dushanbe), 4
Central Asia, 1–2, 4, 8
Chaldeans, 57
Chaucer, Geoffrey, 7–8, 208–9
chemistry, 3, 163, 174
chess, four-player, 113
China, 54–55
Choresm or Choresmia. *see* Khwarazm
Christianity, 25, 54, 56, 149, 184, 207
  Gnostic, 163
  Greek, 10–11
  Nestorian, 54, 57
  Syrian, 10–11, 36, 54, 57
The Chronology of Ancient Nations (Biruni), 52–59, 83, 104, 136, 170–71, 197–98, 217, 218, 226
  translations, 212

Cicero, 53
Clement of Alexandria, 166
clinical trials, 3–4
clocks, 133
colic, 97–98, 99, 185–86
colitis, 152, 178
A Collection of Information on the Recognition of Jewels (Biruni), 173–74
Columbus, 27, 141
commissions, 77
comparative studies, 111, 112
A Compendium of the Soul (Ibn Sina), 29–30
The Compilation (Ibn Sina), 30
concubines, enslaved, 216
Constantine Africanus, 208
Copernicus (Mikolaj Kopernik), 7–8, 60–61, 201, 212
copyists, 7
Corrections to the "Elements" by al-Farghani, 92
cosine (term), 107–8
cosmology, 96–100, 119, 153–54, 191
cultural studies
  anthropology, 3, 55
  India (Biruni), 102–15
cupidity, 168
The Cure (al-Shifa) (Ibn Sina), 151–67, 178, 181, 195, 201, 206, 219–20
  Latin versions, 204
Cures of the Heart (Ibn Sina), 94–95

Da Monte, Gianbattista, 209–10
Dandanaqan, Turkmenistan, 172–73
Dante, 7–8, 208–9
al-Dawla, Ala, 99–100, 101, 148, 149–50, 168–69, 178, 183, 184–86
  correspondence with Ibn Sina, 180
al-Dawla, Fahr, 36, 50, 94
al-Dawla, Majd, 94–95, 96–97, 101, 183–84
al-Dawla, Sama', 99–100, 101
al-Dawla, Shams, 96–98, 99–100, 101
Daylamites, 99–100
de Khanekov, Nicolas, 212
decimal system, 103–4
Delhi, India, 190
Descartes, 2–3, 144, 153–54